THREE ESSAYS

John Stuart Mill

THREE ESSAYS

ON LIBERTY

REPRESENTATIVE GOVERNMENT

THE SUBJECTION OF WOMEN

OXFORD   NEW YORK

OXFORD UNIVERSITY PRESS

Oxford University Press, Walton Street, Oxford OX2 6DP
London Glasgow New York Toronto
Delhi Bombay Calcutta Madras Karachi
Kuala Lumpur Singapore Hong Kong Tokyo
Nairobi Dar es Salaam Cape Town
Melbourne Auckland
and associate companies in
Beirut Berlin Ibadan Mexico City Nicosia

Oxford is a trade mark of Oxford University Press

On Liberty *was first published in 1859;* Representative
Government *in 1861; and* The Subjection of Women *in
1869. This edition was first published in The World's Classics
in one volume in 1912, and reprinted in 1924, 1927, 1933,
1940, 1942, 1946, 1952, 1954, 1960, 1963, 1966, 1969,
1971, and 1974
First issued as an Oxford University Press paperback 1975
Reprinted 1978, 1981, 1983*

*Printed in Great Britain by
The Guernsey Press Co. Ltd.,
Guernsey, Channel Islands.*

CONTENTS

PAGE

Introduction vii

ON LIBERTY

CHAP.
I. INTRODUCTORY 5
II. OF THE LIBERTY OF THOUGHT AND DISCUSSION 22
III. OF INDIVIDUALITY, AS ONE OF THE ELEMENTS
OF WELL-BEING 69
IV. OF THE LIMITS TO THE AUTHORITY OF SOCIETY
OVER THE INDIVIDUAL . . . 92
V. APPLICATIONS 115

CONSIDERATIONS ON REPRESENTATIVE GOVERNMENT

CHAP.
I. TO WHAT EXTENT FORMS OF GOVERNMENT ARE
A MATTER OF CHOICE 145
II. THE CRITERION OF A GOOD FORM OF GOVERN-
MENT 157
III. THAT THE IDEALLY BEST FORM OF GOVERN-
MENT IS REPRESENTATIVE GOVERNMENT . 179
IV. UNDER WHAT SOCIAL CONDITIONS REPRESENTA-
TIVE GOVERNMENT IS INAPPLICABLE . 199
V. OF THE PROPER FUNCTIONS OF REPRESENTA-
TIVE BODIES 211
VI. OF THE INFIRMITIES AND DANGERS TO WHICH
REPRESENTATIVE GOVERNMENT IS LIABLE 229
VII. OF TRUE AND FALSE DEMOCRACY; REPRE-
SENTATION OF ALL, AND REPRESENTATION
OF THE MAJORITY ONLY . . . 247

CHAP.   PAGE

VIII. OF THE EXTENSION OF THE SUFFRAGE . . 272

IX. SHOULD THERE BE TWO STAGES OF ELECTION? 294

X. OF THE MODE OF VOTING 301

XI. OF THE DURATION OF PARLIAMENTS . . 320

XII. OUGHT PLEDGES TO BE REQUIRED FROM MEMBERS OF PARLIAMENT? . . . 323

XIII. OF A SECOND CHAMBER 335

XIV. OF THE EXECUTIVE IN A REPRESENTATIVE GOVERNMENT 344

XV. OF LOCAL REPRESENTATIVE BODIES . . 363

XVI. OF NATIONALITY, AS CONNECTED WITH REPRESENTATIVE GOVERNMENT . . . 380

XVII. OF FEDERAL REPRESENTATIVE GOVERNMENTS . 389

XVIII. OF THE GOVERNMENT OF DEPENDENCIES BY A FREE STATE 401

THE SUBJECTION OF WOMEN

CHAPTER I 427

CHAPTER II 460

CHAPTER III 484

CHAPTER IV 521

Bibliography 549

INTRODUCTION

THE three essays collected in this volume were published within ten years of one another. *On Liberty* appeared in 1859, *Representative Government* in 1861, and *The Subjection of Women* in 1869. Naturally the degree of attention that they received differed, *On Liberty* soon finding itself, where it has remained, at the centre of a lively and far-ranging controversy. But all three essays were soon accepted into the canon of European political and social thought, and nothing that has occurred in the intervening years has seriously affected their standing as classics of the subject. Their claim upon our attention and interest rests on at least two separate counts.

In the first place, these essays can be seen as the distillation of the thinking of one highly intelligent, highly sensitive man who spent the greater part of his life occupied with the theory and the practice of society. Brought up inside one of the most austere and ambitious ideologies to take root in England—classical Utilitarianism—John Stuart Mill as a young man felt himself compelled to try to enrich or to supplement the arid intellectual diet of his youth by what he could import from a number of different sources. Utilitarianism as Mill learnt it was fundamentally a product of the eighteenth century. It preserved many of the intellectual principles—and, it must be said, not a few of the intellectual prejudices—of the European Enlightenment. It would be no great distortion of Mill's career to say that what he did was to graft on to an eighteenth-century stock of ideas some of the new concerns that came into cultivation in the nineteenth century: the sense of history, reverence for nature, the high value placed upon self-knowledge and expression, a feeling for the complexity of society, an ardent concern for human liberty, a new and secularized awareness of the failings of human nature. In breaking out of the narrow confines of the Enlightenment Mill invoked the values of Romanticism. All three essays in this volume, but particularly *On Liberty*, can be seen as documents in the history of his emancipation and also as records of the intellectual balance or synthesis that he achieved. Read in this way, they find their natural background in Mill's *Autobiography*, a powerful and fascinating work, in which it becomes easy to sense the tremendous emotional import that the process of intellectual self-enlargement had for Mill. For this reason, if no other, these works are bound to retain a biographical interest: though they also transcend it.

For, secondly, they remain unsurpassed as expressions of a certain political philosophy. Clarity, reasonableness, eloquence make them the finest statements of one of the two great traditions of social thought that have competed for the support of progressive men and women in the last two hundred years. And here again it is Mill himself who provides the best background for the understanding of his thinking. For, with the possible exception of Alexander Herzen, there was no one in the whole of the nineteenth century who had a sharper sense of the conflict that existed within liberal thought than Mill, and in the Introductory Chapter of *On Liberty*, where his aim is merely to set out the questions that he will raise in the course of the essay and to explain why they had fallen out of favour in recent years, he allows us to see precisely what this conflict was over.

The central concern of the essay, he tells us, is to be that of the proper sphere of state action. When is the state justified in restricting the liberty of the citizen? When is the citizen entitled to claim that his freedom has been unduly or unfairly curtailed? Those who maintained that these questions, which were agreed on all sides to have been the initial inspiration of liberalism, were no longer of relevance, did so because of an assumption on which the questions seemed to them to rest—the assumption that, in any society, the rulers are of necessity distinct, in aim and interest, from the ruled, so that the ruled always stand in need of protection from the rulers. However, to the new liberals, this assumption was no longer so obviously correct. By the end of the eighteenth century a state of society could be envisaged in which the rulers were the same as the ruled, and in such a society the traditional premises of liberalism would fail of application. Indeed, once the state passed into popular control, attempts to place restrictions upon its freedom of action would be worse than irrelevant: they would be injurious to the better interests of the ruled. Accordingly, the task for liberalism was to put these questions to one side, and to concentrate on the issue, at once theoretical and practical, how the institution of popular control in this sense could be achieved. As Mill paraphrased it,

> What was now wanted was that the rulers should be identified with the people: that their interest and will should be the interest and will of the nation. The nation did not need to be protected against its own will. There was no fear of its tyrannising over itself.

This conception of society, according to which in certain favoured circumstances the traditional dichotomies of government could be altogether transcended, had come to be fairly widely accepted by Mill's day as a premise of advanced political thinking. Mill goes on, ' Those who admit any limit to what a government may do, except in the case of such governments as they think ought not to exist, stand out as brilliant exceptions among the political thinkers of the Continent '. And if the situation in England was appreciably different, this was so, he thought, only because of a happy alteration of circumstances. Mill's estimate of the relative strength of the forces engaged may have been exaggerated, but his analysis of the issues on which they confronted one another is surely right.

In talking of ' the brilliant exceptions ' to the new liberal ideology, Mill would doubtless have had in mind men like Benjamin Constant, Alexis de Tocqueville, Wilhelm von Humboldt, and Thomas Carlyle; very diverse thinkers but from all of whom Mill carried away something. And as for the new ideology itself, it is evident that he is here thinking of the teaching of Jean-Jacques Rousseau who in the *Contrat Social* had so radically reinterpreted the issues of political legitimacy. If one of the two great traditions of advanced political thought finds its best expression in the work of Mill, the other can be identified with Rousseau; that which Mill expresses may be called ' libertarian ' and that which Rousseau typifies may be called ' collectivist '—though, of course, in each thinker statements may be found which make these ready-made labels seem inappropriate.

Mill's opposition to Rousseau-ite thinking, and his reversion to an earlier form of liberalism, derives from two fundamental convictions, one relating primarily to Man, the other relating primarily to Society. The conviction relating to Man is this: that any compulsion that is brought to bear upon the individual—compulsion, that is, as opposed to the pressures of argument or persuasion or even moral disapprobation—is more likely than not to be against his true interests. This is so because either the external authority will miscalculate those interests, or, if it doesn't, just in virtue of its authority being external, it will, in enforcing those interests, most probably distance or alienate the individual from them. The conviction relating to Society is this: that, no matter what form of government obtains, the state, in seeking to get itself obeyed, is bound to bring compulsion to bear upon the individual.

These two convictions put together are clearly incompatible with the Rousseau-ite conception of liberalism: for precisely what they dispute is that there could be such an identity of ruler and ruled as to render irrelevant questions about the proper limits of state action or the sphere of inviolable individual liberty. However, what they are compatible with, at any rate as things now stand, is the total rejection of civil authority; indeed, some earlier thinkers, such as William Godwin, had argued for anarchism from not dissimilar premises. If Mill resisted the anarchist conclusion, he did so by invoking an assumption which might at first seem quite independent: that is, that though the individual has something to fear from the state, he has also something to fear from the encroachment of other individuals, if they are unconstrained.

However, we take a step significantly further into the understanding of Mill's thought when we appreciate that this seemingly independent assumption fits together with the two convictions about Man and Society to form part of an overall conception of human nature, and that this conception—or, perhaps better, this conception and the many different applications that Mill finds for it—is the most interesting and innovatory aspect of his philosophy. For Mill is one of those rare thinkers, like Hobbes or Rousseau or (in certain guises) Marx, who at all points rested his moral and social theory on a conception of what human nature is: whereas others have either done without one or concocted one that would justify pre-existent theory. With Mill one feels that a theory of man was, and remained, his prime inspiration.

Mill's conception of human nature may be considered under two broad headings: negative and positive.

On the negative side Mill denied the uniformity of human nature. In doing so he rejected a belief that, explicitly or implicitly, had been central to the thought of the European Enlightenment and thus, by descent, to classical Utilitarianism. At a blow he undercut both benevolent despotism of the kind largely favoured by the *philosophes* and any facile version of anarchism. For to maintain either that individuals could safely be left entirely to their own devices or that they could be centrally regulated down to any significant degree of detail by a well-informed public-spirited bureaucracy would seem to presuppose that, at any rate in their aims and interests, men were reasonably interchangeable.

On the positive side Mill asserted the diversity of human nature in a way that needs to be carefully identified. To begin with, the diversity with which Mill was concerned was not a diversity based on physical or biological differences, at any rate of a gross kind. The essay on *The Subjection of Women* is highly relevant at this point, for there we can see Mill reserving some of his most acid criticism for arguments in favour of sexual discrimination based on just such considerations. The diversity that Mill asserted was irreducibly psychological in its ground—which is not, of course, to say that it could not have physiological concomitants or conditions. The starting-point for Mill—as indeed for his Utilitarian predecessors—is that man like any other species is pleasure-seeking. What, however, is peculiar to man, and what gives human nature its distinctive character, is how he seeks it. For human beings obtain pleasure not simply in pleasurable sensations—which they do—but also in the realization of certain projects. The different projects of each individual will have a tendency to cohere, and in favoured circumstances they will come together to form an overall project or a ' plan of life '.

That happiness for the human individual consists essentially in the realization of his own plan of life—where there is no guarantee that what is one man's plan will be another's—is sufficient to establish the diversity of human nature. But in order to understand the particular way in which Mill asserted this thesis we need to grasp two further respects in which he thought a plan of life to be personal to the individual whose it is. It is personal in that each individual should form it for himself, rather than accept it from others. And it is personal in that—at least where this is feasible—the individual should realize it for himself, rather than depend on having it realized for him. In other words, central to Mill's conception of man as a pleasure-seeking creature is the attribute frequently referred to in the writings of two distinguished philosophers of our own day, both firmly in the ' libertarian ' tradition—Bertrand Russell and Noam Chomsky—as ' creativity '.

This last point is extremely important if we are to avoid a widespread error in the interpretation of Mill. Mill himself claimed on a variety of occasions that all his moral and social thought derived from the principle of utility: that is, that in the determination of all personal or public decisions the only consideration to which weight should be attached is the resultant balance of pleasure and pain. Of recent years it has become conventional to set aside these professions and to regard Mill's moral and social thought as partially grounded in values that are quite independent of and at times inconsistent with utility: values such as liberty or self-development. The argument of, for instance, *On Liberty* must, it is argued, be based on such a commitment. But this line of reasoning is cogent only if we leave out of account Mill's actual views about human nature and if we insist that Utilitarianism is necessarily conjoined—as indeed it was in the case of its founders—with a highly simplistic psychology: with, in other words, a belief in the uniformity of human nature and the equation of pleasure with discrete pleasurable sensations. Once it is appreciated that Utilitarianism can be conjoined with a more complex psychology, then the temptation to attribute to Mill subscription to non-utilitarian values loses all force. For, if one thinks that man is such that he can achieve real pleasure or happiness only through the formation and actualization of a plan of life suited to his own particular nature, then, one will, in according to utility ultimate value, recognize that liberty and self-development have instrumental value. Liberty and self-development may seem independent of utility on some crude interpretation of utility, but take what Mill calls ' utility in the largest sense, grounded in the permanent interests of man as a progressive being ' and they become necessary. Free and open discussion, the consideration and pursuit of experience and opinion in all their variety, are prerequisites if the individual is to decide how his own unique nature is to be fulfilled. The same point is made more vividly when Mill claims that it is essential for the development of mankind that men should be permitted, indeed encouraged, to conduct ' experiments of living '.

Nevertheless Mill also saw that, once the principle of utility was reinterpreted so as to bring it into line with the new psychology, or with what is actually involved in man's pursuit of happiness, then its application brings in train problems that did not exist for his predecessors with their simpler interpretation of the principle. Of course, some of these problems are purely practical, but a theoretical problem of some complexity arises from the fact that, though man is essentially creative, not all men are equally creative, and indeed in some creativity is no more than a potentiality. In some men, through force of circumstances the capacity to devise an adequate plan of life is underdeveloped, and in others it can be said not to be developed at all.

Here then we have the first part of the problem. For, in so far as the capacity to devise plans of life is not developed, there is a *prima facie* case for thinking that the reinterpreted principle of utility, with its emphasis on liberty and self-development, does not apply. And Mill says as much. He says that the principles developed in *On Liberty* apply only to human beings in the maturity of their faculties, and for whole peoples whose faculties are immature he thought that their best hope lay in ' an Akbar or a Charlemagne '. But the question then arises, where is the line of demarcation to be drawn? How mature must a human being be to be mature? But at this point a second part of the problem comes into motion, and overtakes the first. For, if the principle of utility in its reinterpreted form applies only to those who have a conception of their own happiness, is there not, all the same, some kind of obligation, residual or derivative from the principle, to encourage the capacity to form such a conception in those who have not attained it—as well as, for that matter, to protect or reinforce it in those who have? And the answer, as Mill saw it, was that there certainly is. If we now ask how this is to be achieved, it would seem to have been Mill's opinion that the conditions which a man's conception of happiness requires for its formation and realization are precisely those which are also required for either the development or the reinforcement (as the case may be) of the capacity to originate such a conception: supremely, that is, a state of free and open inquiry and discussion.

Another way of looking at the matter is to see that for Mill unlike his predecessors Utilitarianism is a two-tiered morality. The upper tier consists in the direct application of the principle of utility: that is to say, the advocacy of measures which offer a favourable balance of pleasure over pain, where pleasure and pain can be calculated only in the light of the various conceptions of happiness, the different plans of life that the individuals affected have formed. But the principle of utility thus understood presupposes that individuals have formed their own conceptions of happiness or plans of life. In some cases, however, they will not have done so: and, if they have not done so, this will most likely be because their capacity to do so has been insufficiently developed. This leads to the lower tier of Utilitarianism—what might be called the indirect or oblique application of the principle of utility—which is precisely concerned with the fostering of this capacity, in so far as this is possible, and with the safeguarding of it once it has developed. In other words, on the lower tier the preconditions of the upper tier are secured.

It is only by appreciating this aspect of Mill's thinking, which has been overlooked by his commentators, that its structure as a whole can be grasped. For instance, hostile critics of Mill have, from Fitzjames Stephen onwards, made much of certain seeming inconsistencies in *On Liberty*, but these inconsistencies correspond to the tension between the two different applications, direct and indirect, of the principle of utility, and, once we have sorted this out, they correspondingly fall into place. So in the Introductory Chapter and in Chapters IV and V Mill is principally concerned with the direct application of the principle of utility. In distinguishing between actions that concern only their agents and actions that concern others as well, and in insisting that in the case of the former society has no right ever to intervene whereas in the case of the latter it might in certain circumstances have such a right, he was simply trying to ensure, in concrete terms, that society should not act where its action was bound to lead to an overall balance of pain over pleasure. (A common argument against Mill at this stage is to suggest that the protection he seeks for the individual through this principle is purely notional in that there are not and could not be actions which concerned only the agent: such actions form an empty class. But, as I have tried to show elsewhere, this is a misunderstanding of Mill, since by self-regarding actions he meant not simply those actions which affect the agent alone, but those actions which affect either the agent alone or others but only in so far as they think these actions wrong—which is by no means an empty class—and that he had good utilitarian grounds for understanding them thus.) In Chapters II and III Mill is principally concerned with the indirect application of the principle of utility. In advocating that people should cultivate individuality and enjoy a very wide-ranging liberty of opinion, he was in large part concerned that people should be able to form, and to go on being able to form, plans of life so that they should be fully fit to have the principle of utility directly applied to them.

The two-tiered nature of Mill's Utilitarianism is also evident in the essay *Representative Government*. For Mill, while arguing that representative democracy is the best form of government for a population mature in its faculties in that it is most likely to advance its interests, also thought that an ancillary case for representative democracy rests on its capacity to encourage and sustain maturity of faculty. Democratic government is calculated to favour the active or self-helping type of character.

However, the central interest of this essay must lie in Mill's attempt to justify representative democracy on the basis of the reinterpreted principle of utility: that is to say, to show that it is the required form of government, given both Utilitarianism and an adequate or sufficiently complex psychology.

The preliminary step in this argument we have already had occasion to consider. From the diversity of human nature, which is central to the new psychology, Mill concludes that direct democracy is impossible. And if, he goes on, in the face of this fact we persist in believing that direct democracy is desirable, then what will result is a form of government which is not democracy at all but is often confused with it: the rule of the Many, or the government of the whole people by a mere majority of the people. At this point two questions arise. The first is: if the diversity of human nature makes direct democracy impossible, how can representative democracy hope to satisfy the heterogeneous and conflicting interests to which this diversity gives rise? And the second is: how can democracy ever be anything but the rule of the Many, for how is it possible that there should be rule of the whole people by the whole people?

The two questions are, of course, related, and it is Mill's strategy to answer the first through the second. In other words, he tried to show that representative democracy meets the requirements of a sophisticated utilitarianism through exhibiting what representative democracy really is and, more significantly, what it certainly isn't. And he thought that before we can recognize representative democracy as providing ' the ideally best polity ', we must make two adjustments in the way in which we normally think of it: each adjustment relating to one of the two constituents into which the term ' democracy ' can be etymologically resolved—demo-cracy, or rule of the people.

The first adjustment is in the notion of ruling or governing. If democracy is the form of government in which the people rule or govern, then greater attention must be paid than is usual to what activity it is that is thereby ascribed to the people. They are not, Mill maintained, supposed to *do* the business of government: rather, they are supposed to *control* the business of government. This interpretation, and the corresponding distinction between doing and controlling, was first put forward by Mill in 1835 in a review of the first volume of Tocqueville's *Democracy in America*, and even then it was not an altogether new idea. It had, for instance, been advanced by Benjamin Constant in his brilliant but neglected essay, *On the Liberty of the Ancients compared with that of the Moderns*, but what is peculiar to Mill is the tenacity, the seriousness with which he pursued the implications of this idea over twenty-five years and more of reflection.

In his earlier writings on representative democracy Mill thought that the principal implication of thus understanding what it is for the people to rule was that the representative should be under no obligation to commit himself in advance on any specific political programme to those whom he represented. The people were, of course, entitled to be informed about the personal character, the ability, and the general political opinions and sentiments of the man for whom they were asked to vote: but, once they had satisfied themselves on this score, and had made their choice, then, Mill maintained, they must take the man on trust until the moment came when they could pass a retrospective judgement on the legislative decisions in which he had participated. To many contemporaries of Mill it seemed that, if the people were entitled to judge legislation after it had been passed, it could only be to the general good if the representatives had advance knowledge of how this judgement was likely to go so that they could anticipate it. In practical politics this expressed

itself as a drift towards the idea of ' the mandate '. To
Mill, however, this was anathema, for it meant, as he saw
it, a way in which the function of controlling government,
which did indeed belong to the people, surreptitiously
converted itself into the function of doing the business of
government, which, as we have seen, belonged to the
people only on an erroneous view of democracy. Mill
resorted to the language of Burke to express his disapproval: ' The substitution of delegation for representation,' he wrote, is ' the one and only danger of
democracy '. However, by the time Mill wrote *Representative Government*, his views had hardened. If it was
wrong that the people should as a whole try to do the
business of government, then it was also wrong—he had
now come to feel—that their representatives should undertake to do it for them, and he put forward the proposal,
perhaps not fully absorbed into the body of the essay,
that legislation should always be initiated by a more
specialized body, or ' Commission of Legislation ', over
which the people's representatives would exercise a form
of control analogous to that which the people exercised
over them.

However, if in one respect *Representative Government*
records a contraction in what it is that the people are
supposed to do when in a democracy they rule, in another
respect what it records is an enlargement. The notion of
controlling government may have lost some ground to that
of doing the business of government: but the ground that
it retains proves richer than was recognized. For it is,
Mill now appreciated, only on a very narrow view of what
control of government amounts to that it amounts to
no more than saying yes or no to a given piece of legislation. In many cases, for instance, might not a more
reasonable reaction on the part of the people's representatives be to suggest ways in which the piece of
legislation might be emended, or supplemented, or
pruned of irrelevance, or rendered more flexible to changes
in circumstance? (And here we have an echo of the

famous argument that Mill deploys in *On Liberty* when he points out that for any opinion the possibilities are more numerous than that it should be totally true or that it should be totally false: there are many many other possibilities according to the degree to which the opinion might be true or false.) Accordingly for Mill a simple vote upon a proposed measure resulting either in acceptance or in rejection is no more than the minimum that could be expected of a representative assembly in exercising control over legislation. What might also, and very reasonably, be expected of it is that it should discuss the topics dealt with by the legislation and deliberate upon the proposals themselves. And as the view taken of what it is to control the business enlarges so this part of the assembly's work will move to the fore.

But, if the representative assembly is to take the task of debating legislation as seriously as that of voting upon it, then it must be adequately equipped to do so. And what this effectively means is that its constitution must be determined with this in mind. It must contain within itself as wide a spectrum of opinion as is to be found amongst the people outside. And it is to this end that one of Mill's proposals to which he himself attached the greatest significance but which nevertheless has been widely misunderstood is directed: I refer to Mill's advocacy of Proportional Representation in the selection of the representative assembly.

Critics insensitive to the general direction of Mill's argument about democracy have seized upon this proposal and used it to attach to him the label ' conservative '. Mill supported Proportional Representation so as—it is said—to ' limit ' democracy. But the issue cannot be settled so speedily. For, Proportional Representation in its various forms being ultimately a way of relating the distribution of opinion within the assembly to the distribution of opinion without, its advocacy can be judged only by taking into account the function that the assembly is expected to discharge. It is only against the background of this function that any one method of bringing the two distributions into relation will seem superior to any other.

Now, as we have seen, Mill thought that, if the people in a democracy are to do what they are supposed to do—that is to say, to rule through controlling the business of government—then the assembly must discharge more functions than one. It must, of course, be a ' legislative assembly ': but it is no less, indeed rather more, important that it should be ' a deliberative assembly '. It must accept or reject specific legislative proposals put to it, but it must also debate the issues that these proposals are designed to meet. And to each of these functions there corresponds a constraint upon the method by which the assembly is constituted—or, to put it another way, the representatives are selected. In so far as the assembly is to be a legislative body it is necessary, but also sufficient, that the majority opinion among the people is the majority opinion in the assembly. In so far as the assembly is to be a deliberative body, it is necessary that each and every minority opinion of any seriousness should find some voice in the assembly to express it: and any move in the direction of giving it a bigger voice—below, that is, the ceiling imposed by the legislative function—is desirable. And since such a move is just what Proportional Representation secures, Proportional Representation is desirable. And desirable, it must be insisted on, from the point of view of democracy. To regard Proportional Representation as a limitation upon democracy is, Mill would argue, to take a quite inadequate view of democracy.

A more cogent, if obscurer, charge is that Mill's advocacy of Proportional Representation and other related measures has to do with elitism. Now Mill was certainly prepared to distinguish between, say, a broader and a narrower outlook, between opinion that was educated and opinion that was uneducated, between excellence and mediocrity: and he also thought that these distinctions were politically relevant. A political system, indeed a democratic system, could and should take account of them. But for Mill these distinctions, as well as the more fundamental distinction adumbrated in his essay *Utilitarianism* between higher and lower pleasures, were grounded in human nature itself and in the special character of man's quest for happiness. Breadth of outlook, education, excellence were not mere rationalizations of existing social divisions; they were, rather, the tried and proved means of self-fulfilment, and it was Mill's belief that, in favourable circumstances, they, and along with them the pursuit of happiness itself in its specifically human mode, would become very widely, if not universally, diffused. Nevertheless it remains a fact that some of the proposals for the constitution of the assembly, or the modes of election, that Mill thought in the interim to be appropriate would nowadays be found by those with precisely his concern for democracy quite unacceptable. Yet in each instance Mill argued clearly and with distinction, and his case for Proportional Representation as an essential ingredient of representative democracy remains unanswered. There is certainly no substance to the charge that Mill favoured the rule of experts: one of the nineteenth-century ideals of governments that he explicitly rejected was the kind of technocracy extolled by Auguste Comte.

Before leaving this, the first, adjustment that Mill wished us to make in the way in which we normally think of democracy—namely that the sense in which the people rule or govern in a democracy is that they control the business of government—it would be useful to see it in relation to Mill's conception of human nature. At its lowest the relation, as we have seen, is simply this: that it is because of Mill's conception of human nature, more specifically because of its negative side, that this adjustment is necessary. It is because human nature is not uniform that the people should control, rather than do, the business of government. But there is more to the relation than this. For, if the negative side of Mill's conception of human nature makes this adjustment necessary, the positive side of that conception gives the adjustment a value that it would not otherwise have. Because human nature is not just diverse, but diverse in the particular way in which it is, popular control of the business of government can, at any rate in favoured circumstances, amount to rule of the whole people by the whole people. And this is because human diversity is essentially correlated with diversity of opinion, and conflicting opinion, unlike, say, conflicting interest, does not have to remain in a permanent posture of confrontation. When two or more opinions diverge, there is always the possibility of reconciliation or synthesis. Representative democracy, with a deliberative assembly as its core, offers the possibility of government of the whole people by the whole people in so far as it conduces to a form of government to which the opinions of all have made a significant and appropriate contribution.

To see what is further required if this possibility is to be realized, we turn to the second adjustment that Mill thought was necessary in the way in which we normally think about democracy: and this is an adjustment in the notion of the people, where it is the people that rule. Now, as we have just seen, democracy, according to Mill, is attained when, though in the final resort the opinion of the many prevails over the opinion of the few, all have contributed, or have had the opportunity to contribute, to the formation of this opinion. But that all can contribute to the opinion of the many presupposes that the many is simply the numerical majority. Its identity lies in, and solely in, its superiority in numbers. The many is not, in other words, a class or social unit, knit together by ties of common advantage, with interests persisting over time—which also happens to be numerous. For, when the many is thus constituted, its opinion is really the expression of its interest, it is not susceptible to argument or persuasion, it has nothing to learn from debate, and in consequence when it prevails, democracy is not attained.

Here then we have the second adjustment that Mill

would have us make in our normal thinking about what democracy is. And that is that we should give up the equation of the rule of the people with the rule of the labouring classes or the poor: or, for that matter—as Mill might have wanted to add had he come to know a type of ' advanced ' society of our day, with its reversal of the traditional distribution of wealth—with the rule of the middle classes or the affluent, should they be the most numerous single socio-economic group in the society.

At this point Mill might profitably be seen as placing Aristotle on his head. For to Aristotle it was a super-ficial characterization of democracy, prevalent amongst his contemporaries but fundamentally misleading, to think of democracy as the rule of the many. It might be that in effect, but it was not that essentially. It was essentially the rule of the poor and, if democracy was in effect the rule of the many, this was only because of the contingent fact that in any city the poor formed the bulk of the population. Now Mill did not deny that there were many societies concerning which Aristotle's observation would count as a profound insight. There were forms of government in which those who ruled did so because they were poor not because they were numerous. But the conclusion to be drawn was not that which Aristotle drew. A form of government which is truly characterized as the rule of the poor is falsely called ' democracy '. The demos, where this is by definition what rules in a democracy, is not a social class.

The matter, however, cannot rest there. For, given a society in which one social class does indeed constitute a numerical majority, what is to be done? More specific-ally, what are the prospects in such a society for democ-racy? And here, once again, we come to a problem in the interpretation of Mill. For those who wish to think of Mill as a conservative conclude that, being against working-class rule, he must therefore have been in favour of an attenuated democracy, whatever he might profess. But there is another possible view to take. And that is that Mill, being in favour of ' true ' democracy, was therefore against any form of class society. In other words, Mill recognized that the permanent division of society into different interest groups, or the existence within society of a standing majority, was incompatible with democracy: and in consequence he thought that any such system should be abolished in the cause of democracy. There is at least as much evidence in Mill's writings to bear out this second interpretation as there is to support the first.

The Subjection of Women represents the application to a particular issue—and one on which Mill had all his intellectual life held very strong views—of the principle adumbrated in *On Liberty* that happiness requires freedom. Central to the essay, as I have already observed, is the thesis that the distinction between male and female corresponds to no significant difference in psychology. One of the essay's earlier translators, Sigmund Freud, criticized the essay precisely on this score. Mill, Freud wrote in a letter to his fiancée in 1885, had overlooked the fact that ' human beings consist of men and women and that this distinction is the most significant one that exists '. But the criticism, even if sound in its premise, does not reach its target. For, though the thesis that men and women do not differ psychologically may be central to the essay, it is not central to the argument of the essay. On the contrary: it is Mill's point throughout that psychological differences between people, so far from justifying unequal treatment, necessitate equality of treatment: for it is only in an atmosphere of equal freedom that people can work out different plans of life that will then correspond to the differences between them.

RICHARD WOLLHEIM

December, 1974

ON LIBERTY

The grand, leading principle, towards which every argument unfolded in these pages directly converges, is the absolute and essential importance of human development in its richest diversity.—WILHELM VON HUMBOLDT: *Sphere and Duties of Government.*

To the beloved and deplored memory of her who was the inspirer, and in part the author, of all that is best in my writings—the friend and wife whose exalted sense of truth and right was my strongest incitement, and whose approbation was my chief reward—I dedicate this volume. Like all that I have written for many years, it belongs as much to her as to me ; but the work as it stands has had, in a very insufficient degree, the inestimable advantage of her revision ; some of the most important portions having been reserved for a more careful re-examination, which they are now never destined to receive. Were I but capable of interpreting to the world one half the great thoughts and noble feelings which are buried in her grave, I should be the medium of a greater benefit to it, than is ever likely to arise from anything that I can write, unprompted and unassisted by her all but unrivalled wisdom.

ON LIBERTY

CHAPTER I

INTRODUCTORY

THE subject of this Essay is not the so-called Liberty of the Will, so unfortunately opposed to the misnamed doctrine of Philosophical Necessity; but Civil, or Social Liberty: the nature and limits of the power which can be legitimately exercised by society over the individual. A question seldom stated, and hardly ever discussed, in general terms, but which profoundly influences the practical controversies of the age by its latent presence, and is likely soon to make itself recognized as the vital question of the future. It is so far from being new, that, in a certain sense, it has divided mankind, almost from the remotest ages; but in the stage of progress into which the more civilized portions of the species have now entered, it presents itself under new conditions, and requires a different and more fundamental treatment.

The struggle between Liberty and Authority is the most conspicuous feature in the portions of history with which we are earliest familiar, particularly in that of Greece, Rome, and England. But in old times this contest was between subjects, or some classes of subjects, and the Government. By liberty, was meant protection against the tyranny of the political rulers. The rulers were conceived (except in some of the popular governments of Greece) as in a necessarily antagonistic position to the people whom they ruled. They consisted of a governing One, or a governing tribe or caste, who derived their authority from inheritance or conquest, who, at all events, did not hold it at the pleasure of the governed, and whose supremacy

men did not venture, perhaps did not desire, to contest, whatever precautions might be taken against its
oppressive exercise. Their power was regarded as
necessary, but also as highly dangerous; as a weapon
which they would attempt to use against their subjects, no less than against external enemies. To prevent
the weaker members of the community from being
preyed upon by innumerable vultures, it was needful
that there should be an animal of prey stronger than
the rest, commissioned to keep them down. But as
the king of the vultures would be no less bent upon
preying on the flock than any of the minor harpies,
it was indispensable to be in a perpetual attitude of
defence against his beak and claws. The aim, therefore, of patriots was to set limits to the power which
the ruler should be suffered to exercise over the community; and this limitation was what they meant
by liberty. It was attempted in two ways. First,
by obtaining a recognition of certain immunities, called
political liberties or rights, which it was to be regarded
as a breach of duty in the ruler to infringe, and which,
if he did infringe, specific resistance, or general rebellion, was held to be justifiable. A second, and generally
a later expedient, was the establishment of constitutional checks, by which the consent of the community,
or of a body of some sort, supposed to represent its
interests, was made a necessary condition to some of
the more important acts of the governing power. To
the first of these modes of limitation, the ruling power,
in most European countries, was compelled, more or
less, to submit. It was not so with the second; and,
to attain this, or when already in some degree possessed, to attain it more completely, became everywhere the principal object of the lovers of liberty.
And so long as mankind were content to combat one
enemy by another, and to be ruled by a master, on
condition of being guaranteed more or less efficaciously
against his tyranny, they did not carry their aspirations
beyond this point.

A time, however, came, in the progress of human

affairs, when men ceased to think it a necessity of nature that their governors should be an independent power, opposed in interest to themselves. It appeared to them much better that the various magistrates of the State should be their tenants or delegates, revocable at their pleasure. In that way alone, it seemed, could they have complete security that the powers of government would never be abused to their disadvantage. By degrees this new demand for elective and temporary rulers became the prominent object of the exertions of the popular party, wherever any such party existed; and superseded, to a considerable extent, the previous efforts to limit the power of rulers. As the struggle proceeded for making the ruling power emanate from the periodical choice of the ruled, some persons began to think that too much importance had been attached to the limitation of the power itself. *That* (it might seem) was a resource against rulers whose interests were habitually opposed to those of the people. What was now wanted was, that the rulers should be identified with the people; that their interest and will should be the interest and will of the nation. The nation did not need to be protected against its own will. There was no fear of its tyrannizing over itself. Let the rulers be effectually responsible to it, promptly removable by it, and it could afford to trust them with power of which it could itself dictate the use to be made. Their power was but the nation's own power, concentrated, and in a form convenient for exercise. This mode of thought, or rather perhaps of feeling, was common among the last generation of European liberalism, in the Continental section of which it still apparently predominates. Those who admit any limit to what a government may do, except in the case of such governments as they think ought not to exist, stand out as brilliant exceptions among the political thinkers of the Continent. A similar tone of sentiment might by this time have been prevalent in our own country, if the circumstances which for a time encouraged it, had continued unaltered.

But, in political and philosophical theories, as well
as in persons, success discloses faults and infirmities
which failure might have concealed from observation.
The notion, that the people have no need to limit their
power over themselves, might seem axiomatic, when
popular government was a thing only dreamed about,
or read of as having existed at some distant period of
the past. Neither was that notion necessarily disturbed
by such temporary aberrations as those of the French
Revolution, the worst of which were the work of an
usurping few, and which, in any case, belonged, not
to the permanent working of popular institutions, but
to a sudden and convulsive outbreak against monarchical and aristocratic despotism. In time, however, a
democratic republic came to occupy a large portion of
the earth's surface, and made itself felt as one of the
most powerful members of the community of nations ;
and elective and responsible government became subject to the observations and criticisms which wait upon
a great existing fact. It was now perceived that such
phrases as ' self-government ', and ' the power of the
people over themselves ', do not express the true state
of the case. The ' people ' who exercise the power are
not always the same people with those over whom it
is exercised ; and the ' self-government ' spoken of is
not the government of each by himself, but of each
by all the rest. The will of the people, moreover,
practically means the will of the most numerous or
the most active *part* of the people ; the majority, or
those who succeed in making themselves accepted
as the majority ; the people, consequently, *may*
desire to oppress a part of their number ; and precautions are as much needed against this as against
any other abuse of power. The limitation, therefore,
of the power of government over individuals loses none
of its importance when the holders of power are regularly accountable to the community, that is, to the
strongest party therein. This view of things, recommending itself equally to the intelligence of thinkers
and to the inclination of those important classes in

European society to whose real or supposed interests democracy is adverse, has had no difficulty in establishing itself ; and in political speculations ' the tyranny of the majority ' is now generally included among the evils against which society requires to be on its guard.

Like other tyrannies, the tyranny of the majority was at first, and is still vulgarly, held in dread, chiefly as operating through the acts of the public authorities. But reflecting persons perceived that when society is itself the tyrant—society collectively, over the separate individuals who compose it—its means of tyrannizing are not restricted to the acts which it may do by the hands of its political functionaries. Society can and does execute its own mandates : and if it issues wrong mandates instead of right, or any mandates at all in things with which it ought not to meddle, it practises a social tyranny more formidable than many kinds of political oppression, since, though not usually upheld by such extreme penalties, it leaves fewer means of escape, penetrating much more deeply into the details of life, and enslaving the soul itself. Protection, therefore, against the tyranny of the magistrate is not enough : there needs protection also against the tyranny of the prevailing opinion and feeling ; against the tendency of society to impose, by other means than civil penalties, its own ideas and practices as rules of conduct on those who dissent from them ; to fetter the development, and, if possible, prevent the formation, of any individuality not in harmony with its ways, and compel all characters to fashion themselves upon the model of its own. There is a limit to the legitimate interference of collective opinion with individual independence : and to find that limit, and maintain it against encroachment, is as indispensable to a good condition of human affairs, as protection against political despotism.

But though this proposition is not likely to be contested in general terms, the practical question, where to place the limit—how to make the fitting adjustment

between individual independence and social control—
is a subject on which nearly everything remains to be
done. All that makes existence valuable to any one,
depends on the enforcement of restraints upon the
actions of other people. Some rules of conduct, therefore, must be imposed, by law in the first place, and
by opinion on many things which are not fit subjects
for the operation of law. What these rules should be,
is the principal question in human affairs ; but if we
except a few of the most obvious cases, it is one of
those which least progress has been made in resolving.
No two ages, and scarcely any two countries, have
decided it alike ; and the decision of one age or country
is a wonder to another. Yet the people of any given
age and country no more suspect any difficulty in it,
than if it were a subject on which mankind had always
been agreed. The rules which obtain among themselves
appear to them self-evident and self-justifying. This
all but universal illusion is one of the examples of the
magical influence of custom, which is not only, as the
proverb says, a second nature, but is continually mistaken for the first. The effect of custom, in preventing
any misgiving respecting the rules of conduct which
mankind impose on one another, is all the more complete because the subject is one on which it is not
generally considered necessary that reasons should be
given, either by one person to others, or by each to
himself. People are accustomed to believe, and have
been encouraged in the belief by some who aspire to
the character of philosophers, that their feelings, on
subjects of this nature, are better than reasons, and
render reasons unnecessary. The practical principle
which guides them to their opinions on the regulation
of human conduct, is the feeling in each person's mind
that everybody should be required to act as he, and
those with whom he sympathizes, would like them to
act. No one, indeed, acknowledges to himself that his
standard of judgement is his own liking ; but an
opinion on a point of conduct, not supported by reasons,
can only count as one person's preference ; and if the

reasons, when given, are a mere appeal to a similar preference felt by other people, it is still only many people's liking instead of one. To an ordinary man, however, his own preference, thus supported, is not only a perfectly satisfactory reason, but the only one he generally has for any of his notions of morality, taste, or propriety, which are not expressly written in his religious creed; and his chief guide in the interpretation even of that. Men's opinions, accordingly, on what is laudable or blameable, are affected by all the multifarious causes which influence their wishes in regard to the conduct of others, and which are as numerous as those which determine their wishes on any other subject. Sometimes their reason—at other times their prejudices or superstitions: often their social affections, not seldom their antisocial ones, their envy or jealousy, their arrogance or contemptuousness: but most commonly, their desires or fears for themselves—their legitimate or illegitimate self-interest. Wherever there is an ascendant class, a large portion of the morality of the country emanates from its class interests, and its feelings of class superiority. The morality between Spartans and Helots, between planters and negroes, between princes and subjects, between nobles and roturiers, between men and women, has been for the most part the creation of these class interests and feelings: and the sentiments thus generated, react in turn upon the moral feelings of the members of the ascendant class, in their relations among themselves. Where, on the other hand, a class, formerly ascendant, has lost its ascendancy, or where its ascendancy is unpopular, the prevailing moral sentiments frequently bear the impress of an impatient dislike of superiority. Another grand determining principle of the rules of conduct, both in act and forbearance, which have been enforced by law or opinion, has been the servility of mankind towards the supposed preferences or aversions of their temporal masters, or of their gods. This servility, though essentially selfish, is not hypocrisy; it gives rise to perfectly genuine

sentiments of abhorrence ; it made men burn magicians
and heretics. Among so many baser influences, the
general and obvious interests of society have of course
had a share, and a large one, in the direction of the
moral sentiments : less, however, as a matter of reason,
and on their own account, than as a consequence of
the sympathies and antipathies which grew out of
them : and sympathies and antipathies which had
little or nothing to do with the interests of society,
have made themselves felt in the establishment of
moralities with quite as great force.

The likings and dislikings of society, or of some
powerful portion of it, are thus the main thing which
has practically determined the rules laid down for
general observance, under the penalties of law or
opinion. And in general, those who have been in
advance of society in thought and feeling, have left
this condition of things unassailed in principle, however
they may have come into conflict with it in some of
its details. They have occupied themselves rather in
inquiring what things society ought to like or dislike,
than in questioning whether its likings or dislikings
should be a law to individuals. They preferred endeavouring to alter the feelings of mankind on the
particular points on which they were themselves heretical, rather than make common cause in defence of
freedom, with heretics generally. The only case in
which the higher ground has been taken on principle
and maintained with consistency, by any but an individual here and there, is that of religious belief :
a case instructive in many ways, and not least so as
forming a most striking instance of the fallibility of
what is called the moral sense : for the *odium theo-
logicum,* in a sincere bigot, is one of the most unequi-
vocal cases of moral feeling. Those who first broke
the yoke of what called itself the Universal Church,
were in general as little willing to permit difference of
religious opinion as that church itself. But when the
heat of the conflict was over, without giving a complete victory to any party, and each church or sect

was reduced to limit its hopes to retaining possession of the ground it already occupied ; minorities, seeing that they had no chance of becoming majorities, were under the necessity of pleading to those whom they could not convert, for permission to differ. It is accordingly on this battle-field, almost solely, that the rights of the individual against society have been asserted on broad grounds of principle, and the claim of society to exercise authority over dissentients, openly controverted. The great writers to whom the world owes what religious liberty it possesses, have mostly asserted freedom of conscience as an indefeasible right, and denied absolutely that a human being is accountable to others for his religious belief. Yet so natural to mankind is intolerance in whatever they really care about, that religious freedom has hardly anywhere been practically realized, except where religious indifference, which dislikes to have its peace disturbed by theological quarrels, has added its weight to the scale. In the minds of almost all religious persons, even in the most tolerant countries, the duty of toleration is admitted with tacit reserves. One person will bear with dissent in matters of church government, but not of dogma ; another can tolerate everybody, short of a Papist or a Unitarian ; another, every one who believes in revealed religion ; a few extend their charity a little further, but stop at the belief in a God and in a future state. Wherever the sentiment of the majority is still genuine and intense, it is found to have abated little of its claim to be obeyed.

In England, from the peculiar circumstances of our political history, though the yoke of opinion is perhaps heavier, that of law is lighter, than in most other countries of Europe ; and there is considerable jealousy of direct interference, by the legislative or the executive power, with private conduct ; not so much from any just regard for the independence of the individual, as from the still subsisting habit of looking on the government as representing an opposite interest to the public. The majority have not yet learnt to feel the power of the government their power, or its opinions their opinions. When they do so, individual liberty will probably be as much exposed to invasion from the government, as it already is from public opinion. But, as yet, there is a considerable amount of feeling ready to be called forth against any attempt of the law to control individuals in things in which they have not hitherto been accustomed to be controlled by it; and this with very little discrimination as to whether the matter is, or is not, within the legitimate sphere of legal control; insomuch that the feeling, highly salutary on the whole, is perhaps quite as often misplaced as well grounded in the particular instances of its application. There is, in fact, no recognized principle by which the propriety or impropriety of government interference is customarily tested. People decide according to their personal preferences. Some, whenever they see any good to be done, or evil to be remedied, would willingly instigate the government to undertake the business; while others prefer to bear almost any amount of social evil, rather than add one to the departments of human interests amenable to governmental control. And men range themselves on one or the other side in any particular case, according to this general direction of their sentiments; or according to the degree of interest which they feel in the particular thing which it is proposed that the government should do, or according to the belief they entertain that the government would, or would not, do it in the manner they prefer; but very rarely on account of any opinion to which they consistently adhere, as to what things are fit to be done by a government. And it seems to me that in consequence of this absence of rule or principle, one side is at present as often wrong as the other; the interference of government is, with about equal frequency, improperly invoked and improperly condemned.

The object of this Essay is to assert one very simple principle, as entitled to govern absolutely the dealings of society with the individual in the way of compulsion and control, whether the means used be physical force in the form of legal penalties, or the moral coercion of public opinion. That principle is, that the sole end for which mankind are warranted, individually or collectively, in interfering with the liberty of action of any of their number, is self-protection. That the only purpose for which power can be rightfully exercised over any member of a civilized community, against his will, is to prevent harm to others. His own good, either physical or moral, is not a sufficient warrant. He cannot rightfully be compelled to do or forbear because it will be better for him to do so, because it will make him happier, because, in the opinions of others, to do so would be wise, or even right. These are good reasons for remonstrating with him, or reasoning with him, or persuading him, or entreating him, but not for compelling him, or visiting him with any evil in case he do otherwise. To justify that, the conduct from which it is desired to deter him, must be calculated to produce evil to some one else. The only part of the conduct of any one, for which he is amenable to society, is that which concerns others. In the part which merely concerns himself, his independence is, of right, absolute. Over himself, over his own body and mind, the individual is sovereign.

It is, perhaps, hardly necessary to say that this doctrine is meant to apply only to human beings in the maturity of their faculties. We are not speaking of children, or of young persons below the age which the law may fix as that of manhood or womanhood. Those who are still in a state to require being taken care of by others, must be protected against their own actions as well as against external injury. For the same reason, we may leave out of consideration those backward states of society in which the race itself may be considered as in its nonage. The early difficulties in the way of spontaneous progress are so great, that there is seldom any choice of means for overcoming them; and a ruler full of the spirit of improvement is warranted in the use of any expedients that will attain an end, perhaps otherwise unattainable. Despotism is a legitimate mode of government in dealing with barbarians, provided the end be their improvement, and the means justified by actually effecting that end. Liberty, as a principle, has no application to any state of things anterior to the time when mankind have become capable of being improved by free and equal discussion. Until then, there is nothing for them but implicit obedience to an Akbar or a Charlemagne, if they are so fortunate as to find one. But as soon as mankind have attained the capacity of being guided to their own improvement by conviction or persuasion (a period long since reached in all nations with whom we need here concern ourselves), compulsion, either in the direct form or in that of pains and penalties for non-compliance, is no longer admissible as a means to their own good, and justifiable only for the security of others.

It is proper to state that I forgo any advantage which could be derived to my argument from the idea of abstract right, as a thing independent of utility. I regard utility as the ultimate appeal on all ethical questions; but it must be utility in the largest sense, grounded on the permanent interests of man as a progressive being. Those interests, I contend, authorize the subjection of individual spontaneity to external control, only in respect to those actions of each, which concern the interest of other people. If any one does an act hurtful to others, there is a prima facie case for punishing him, by law, or, where legal penalties are not safely applicable, by general disapprobation. There are also many positive acts for the benefit of others, which he may rightfully be compelled to perform; such as, to give evidence in a court of justice; to bear his fair share in the common defence, or in any other joint work necessary to the interest of the society of which he enjoys the protection; and to perform certain acts of individual beneficence, such as saving a fellow creature's life, or interposing to protect the defenceless against ill-usage, things which whenever it is obviously a man's duty to do, he may rightfully be made responsible to society for not doing. A person may cause evil to others not only by his actions but by his inaction, and in either case he is justly accountable to them for the injury. The latter case, it is true, requires a much more cautious exercise of compulsion than the former. To make any one answerable for doing evil to others, is the rule ; to make him answerable for not preventing evil, is, comparatively speaking, the exception. Yet there are many cases clear enough and grave enough to justify that exception. In all things which regard the external relations of the individual, he is *de jure* amenable to those whose interests are concerned, and if need be, to society as their protector. There are often good reasons for not holding him to the responsibility ; but these reasons must arise from the special expediencies of the case : either because it is a kind of case in which he is on the whole likely to act better, when left to his own discretion, than when controlled in any way in which society have it in their power to control him ; or because the attempt to exercise control would produce other evils, greater than those which it would prevent. When such reasons as these preclude the enforcement of responsibility, the conscience of the agent himself should step into the vacant judgement-seat, and protect those interests of others which have no external protection ; judging himself all the more rigidly, because the case does not admit of his being made accountable to the judgement of his fellow creatures.

But there is a sphere of action in which society, as distinguished from the individual, has, if any, only an indirect interest ; comprehending all that portion of a person's life and conduct which affects only himself, or if it also affects others, only with their free, voluntary, and undeceived consent and participation. When I say only himself, I mean directly, and in the first instance : for whatever affects himself, may affect others through himself ; and the objection which may be grounded on this contingency will receive consideration in the sequel. This, then, is the appropriate region of human liberty. It comprises, first, the inward domain of consciousness; demanding liberty of conscience, in the most comprehensive sense; liberty of thought and feeling; absolute freedom of opinion and sentiment on all subjects, practical or speculative, scientific, moral, or theological. The liberty of expressing and publishing opinions may seem to fall under a different principle, since it belongs to that part of the conduct of an individual which concerns other people; but, being almost of as much importance as the liberty of thought itself, and resting in great part on the same reasons, is practically inseparable from it. Secondly, the principle requires liberty of tastes and pursuits; of framing the plan of our life to suit our own character; of doing as we like, subject to such consequences as may follow: without impediment from our fellow creatures, so long as what we do does not harm them, even though they should think our conduct foolish, perverse, or wrong. Thirdly, from this liberty of each individual, follows the liberty, within the same limits, of combination among individuals; freedom to unite, for any purpose not involving harm to others: the persons combining being supposed to be of full age, and not forced or deceived.

No society in which these liberties are not, on the whole, respected, is free, whatever may be its form of government; and none is completely free in which they do not exist absolute and unqualified. The only freedom which deserves the name, is that of pursuing our own good in our own way, so long as we do not attempt to deprive others of theirs, or impede their efforts to obtain it. Each is the proper guardian of his own health, whether bodily, or mental and spiritual. Mankind are greater gainers by suffering each other to live as seems good to themselves, than by compelling each to live as seems good to the rest.

Though this doctrine is anything but new, and, to some persons, may have the air of a truism, there is no doctrine which stands more directly opposed to the general tendency of existing opinion and practice. Society has expended fully as much effort in the attempt (according to its lights) to compel people to conform to its notions of personal, as of social excellence. The ancient commonwealths thought themselves entitled to practise, and the ancient philosophers countenanced, the regulation of every part of private conduct by public authority, on the ground that the State had a deep interest in the whole bodily and mental discipline of every one of its citizens ; a mode of thinking which may have been admissible in small republics surrounded by powerful enemies, in constant peril of being subverted by foreign attack or internal commotion, and to which even a short interval of relaxed energy and self-command might so easily be fatal, that they could not afford to wait for the salutary permanent effects of freedom. In the modern world, the greater size of political communities, and, above all, the separation between spiritual and temporal authority (which placed the direction of men's consciences in other hands than those which controlled their worldly affairs), prevented so great an interference by law in the details of private life ; but the engines of moral repression have been wielded more strenuously against divergence from the reigning opinion in self-regarding, than even in social matters ; religion, the most powerful of the elements which have entered into the formation of moral feeling, having almost always been governed either by the ambition of a hierarchy, seeking control over every department of human conduct, or by the spirit of Puritanism. And some of those modern reformers who have placed themselves in strongest opposition to the religions of the past, have been no way behind either churches or sects in their assertion of the right of spiritual domination : M. Comte, in particular, whose social system, as unfolded in his *Système de Politique Positive*, aims at establishing (though by moral more than by legal appliances) a despotism of society over the individual, surpassing anything contemplated in the political ideal of the most rigid disciplinarian among the ancient philosophers.

Apart from the peculiar tenets of individual thinkers, there is also in the world at large an increasing inclination to stretch unduly the powers of society over the individual, both by the force of opinion and even by that of legislation : and as the tendency of all the changes taking place in the world is to strengthen society, and diminish the power of the individual, this encroachment is not one of the evils which tend spontaneously to disappear, but, on the contrary, to grow more and more formidable. The disposition of mankind, whether as rulers or as fellow citizens, to impose their own opinions and inclinations as a rule of conduct on others, is so energetically supported by some of the best and by some of the worst feelings incident to human nature, that it is hardly ever kept under restraint by anything but want of power ; and as the power is not declining, but growing, unless a strong barrier of moral conviction can be raised against the mischief, we must expect, in the present circumstances of the world, to see it increase.

It will be convenient for the argument, if, instead of at once entering upon the general thesis, we confine ourselves in the first instance to a single branch of it, on which the principle here stated is, if not fully, yet to a certain point, recognized by the current opinions. This one branch is the Liberty of Thought : from which it is impossible to separate the cognate liberty of speaking and of writing. Although these liberties, to some considerable amount, form part of the political morality of all countries which profess religious toleration and free institutions, the grounds, both philosophical and practical, on which they rest, are perhaps not so familiar to the general mind, nor so thoroughly appreciated by many even of the leaders of opinion, as might have been expected. Those grounds, when rightly understood, are of much wider application than to only one division of the subject, and a thorough consideration of this part of the question will be found the best introduction to the remainder. Those to whom nothing which I am about to say will be new, may therefore, I hope, excuse me, if on a subject which for now three centuries has been so often discussed, I venture on one discussion more.

CHAPTER II

OF THE LIBERTY OF THOUGHT AND DISCUSSION

THE time, it is to be hoped, is gone by, when any defence would be necessary of the ' liberty of the press ' as one of the securities against corrupt or tyrannical government. No argument, we may suppose, can now be needed, against permitting a legislature or an executive, not identified in interest with the people, to prescribe opinions to them, and determine what doctrines or what arguments they shall be allowed to hear. This aspect of the question, besides, has been so often and so triumphantly enforced by preceding writers, that it needs not be specially insisted on in this place. Though the law of England, on the subject of the press, is as servile to this day as it was in the time of the Tudors, there is little danger of its being actually put in force against political discussion, except during some temporary panic, when fear of insurrection drives ministers and judges from their propriety;[1] and,

[1] These words had scarcely been written, when, as if to give them an emphatic contradiction, occurred the Government Press Prosecutions of 1858. That ill-judged interference with the liberty of public discussion has not, however, induced me to alter a single word in the text, nor has it at all weakened my conviction that, moments of panic excepted, the era of pains and penalties for political discussion has, in our own country, passed away. For, in the first place, the prosecutions were not persisted in ; and, in the second, they were never, properly speaking, political prosecutions. The offence charged was not that of criticizing institutions, or the acts or persons of rulers, but of circulating what was deemed an immoral doctrine, the lawfulness of Tyrannicide.

If the arguments of the present chapter are of any validity, there ought to exist the fullest liberty of professing and discussing, as a matter of ethical conviction, any doctrine, however immoral it may be considered. It

speaking generally, it is not, in constitutional countries, to be apprehended, that the government, whether completely responsible to the people or not, will often attempt to control the expression of opinion, except when in doing so it makes itself the organ of the general intolerance of the public. Let us suppose, therefore, that the government is entirely at one with the people, and never thinks of exerting any power of coercion unless in agreement with what it conceives to be their voice. But I deny the right of the people to exercise such coercion, either by themselves or by their government. The power itself is illegitimate. The best government has no more title to it than the worst. It is as noxious, or more noxious, when exerted in accordance with public opinion, than when in opposition to it. If all mankind minus one, were of one opinion, and only one person were of the contrary opinion, mankind would be no more justified in silencing that one person, than he, if he had the power, would be justified in silencing mankind. Were an opinion a personal possession of no value except to the owner; if to be obstructed in the enjoyment of it were simply a private injury, it would make some

would, therefore, be irrelevant and out of place to examine here, whether the doctrine of Tyrannicide deserves that title. I shall content myself with saying that the subject has been at all times one of the open questions of morals; that the act of a private citizen in striking down a criminal, who, by raising himself above the law, has placed himself beyond the reach of legal punishment or control, has been accounted by whole nations, and by some of the best and wisest of men, not a crime, but an act of exalted virtue; and that, right or wrong, it is not of the nature of assassination, but of civil war. As such, I hold that the instigation to it, in a specific case, may be a proper subject of punishment, but only if an overt act has followed, and at least a probable connexion can be established between the act and the instigation. Even then, it is not a foreign government, but the very government assailed, which alone, in the exercise of self-defence, can legitimately punish attacks directed against its own existence.

difference whether the injury was inflicted only on a few persons or on many. But the peculiar evil of silencing the expression of an opinion is, that it is robbing the human race ; posterity as well as the existing generation ; those who dissent from the opinion, still more than those who hold it. If the opinion is right, they are deprived of the opportunity of exchanging error for truth : if wrong, they lose, what is almost as great a benefit, the clearer perception and livelier impression of truth, produced by its collision with error.

It is necessary to consider separately these two hypotheses, each of which has a distinct branch of the argument corresponding to it. We can never be sure that the opinion we are endeavouring to stifle is a false opinion ; and if we were sure, stifling it would be an evil still.

First : the opinion which it is attempted to suppress by authority may possibly be true. Those who desire to suppress it, of course deny its truth ; but they are not infallible. They have no authority to decide the question for all mankind, and exclude every other person from the means of judging. To refuse a hearing to an opinion, because they are sure that it is false, is to assume that *their* certainty is the same thing as *absolute* certainty. All silencing of discussion is an assumption of infallibility. Its condemnation may be allowed to rest on this common argument, not the worse for being common.

Unfortunately for the good sense of mankind, the fact of their fallibility is far from carrying the weight in their practical judgement, which is always allowed to it in theory ; for while every one well knows himself to be fallible, few think it necessary to take any precautions against their own fallibility, or admit the supposition that any opinion, of which they feel very certain, may be one of the examples of the error to which they acknowledge themselves to be liable. Absolute princes, or others who are accustomed to unlimited deference, usually feel this complete confidence in their own opinions on nearly all subjects. People more happily situated, who sometimes hear their opinions disputed, and are not wholly unused to be set right when they are wrong, place the same unbounded reliance only on such of their opinions as are shared by all who surround them, or to whom they habitually defer: for in proportion to a man's want of confidence in his own solitary judgement, does he usually repose, with implicit trust, on the infallibility of ' the world ' in general. And the world, to each individual, means the part of it with which he comes in contact; his party, his sect, his church, his class of society: the man may be called, by comparison, almost liberal and large-minded to whom it means anything so comprehensive as his own country or his own age. Nor is his faith in this collective authority at all shaken by his being aware that other ages, countries, sects, churches, classes, and parties have thought, and even now think, the exact reverse. He devolves upon his own world the responsibility of being in the right against the dissentient worlds of other people ; and it never troubles him that mere accident has decided which of these numerous worlds is the object of his reliance, and that the same causes which make him a Churchman in London, would have made him a Buddhist or a Confucian in Pekin. Yet it is as evident in itself, as any amount of argument can make it, that ages are no more infallible than individuals ; every age having held many opinions which subsequent ages have deemed not only false but absurd ; and it is as certain that many opinions, now general, will be rejected by future ages, as it is that many, once general, are rejected by the present.

The objection likely to be made to this argument would probably take some such form as the following. There is no greater assumption of infallibility in forbidding the propagation of error, than in any other thing which is done by public authority on its own judgement and responsibility. Judgement is given to men that they may use it. Because it may be used erroneously, are men to be told that they ought not to use it at all ? To prohibit what they think pernicious, is not claiming exemption from error, but fulfilling the duty incumbent on them, although fallible, of acting on their conscientious conviction. If we were never to act on our opinions, because those opinions may be wrong, we should leave all our interests uncared for, and all our duties unperformed. An objection which applies to all conduct, can be no valid objection to any conduct in particular. It is the duty of governments, and of individuals, to form the truest opinions they can ; to form them carefully, and never impose them upon others unless they are quite sure of being right. But when they are sure (such reasoners may say), it is not conscientiousness but cowardice to shrink from acting on their opinions, and allow doctrines which they honestly think dangerous to the welfare of mankind, either in this life or in another, to be scattered abroad without restraint, because other people, in less enlightened times, have persecuted opinions now believed to be true. Let us take care, it may be said, not to make the same mistake : but governments and nations have made mistakes in other things, which are not denied to be fit subjects for the exercise of authority : they have laid on bad taxes, made unjust wars. Ought we therefore to lay on no taxes, and, under whatever provocation, make no wars ? Men, and governments, must act to the best of their ability. There is no such thing as absolute certainty, but there is assurance sufficient for the purposes of human life. We may, and must, assume our opinion to be true for the guidance of our own conduct : and it is assuming no more when we forbid bad men to pervert society by the propagation of opinions which we regard as false and pernicious.

I answer, that it is assuming very much more. There is the greatest difference between presuming an opinion to be true, because, with every opportunity for contesting it, it has not been refuted, and assuming its truth for the purpose of not permitting its refutation. Complete liberty of contradicting and disproving our opinion, is the very condition which justifies us in assuming its truth for purposes of action ; and on no other terms can a being with human faculties have any rational assurance of being right.

When we consider either the history of opinion, or the ordinary conduct of human life, to what is it to be ascribed that the one and the other are no worse than they are ?   Not certainly to the inherent force of the human understanding ; for, on any matter not self-evident, there are ninety-nine persons totally incapable of judging of it, for one who is capable ; and the capacity of the hundredth person is only comparative ; for the majority of the eminent men of every past generation held many opinions now known to be erroneous, and did or approved numerous things which no one will now justify. Why is it, then, that there is on the whole a preponderance among mankind of rational opinions and rational conduct ? If there really is this preponderance—which there must be unless human affairs are, and have always been, in an almost desperate state—it is owing to a quality of the human mind, the source of everything respectable in man either as an intellectual or as a moral being, namely, that his errors are corrigible. He is capable of rectifying his mistakes, by discussion and experience. Not by experience alone. There must be discussion, to show how experience is to be interpreted. Wrong opinions and practices gradually yield to fact and argument : but facts and arguments, to produce any effect on the mind, must be brought before it. Very few facts are able to tell their own story, without comments to bring out their meaning. The whole strength and value, then, of human judgement, depending on the one property, that it can be set right when it is wrong, reliance can be placed on it only when the means of setting it right are kept constantly at hand. In the case of any person whose judgement is really deserving of confidence, how has it become

so ? Because he has kept his mind open to criticism
of his opinions and conduct. Because it has been his
practice to listen to all that could be said against him ;
to profit by as much of it as was just, and expound
to himself, and upon occasion to others, the fallacy of
what was fallacious. Because he has felt, that the
only way in which a human being can make some
approach to knowing the whole of a subject, is by
hearing what can be said about it by persons of every
variety of opinion, and studying all modes in which
it can be looked at by every character of mind. No
wise man ever acquired his wisdom in any mode but
this ; nor is it in the nature of human intellect to
become wise in any other manner. The steady habit
of correcting and completing his own opinion by col-
lating it with those of others, so far from causing doubt
and hesitation in carrying it into practice, is the only
stable foundation for a just reliance on it : for, being
cognisant of all that can, at least obviously, be said
against him, and having taken up his position against
all gainsayers—knowing that he has sought for objections and difficulties, instead of avoiding them, and
has shut out no light which can be thrown upon the
subject from any quarter—he has a right to think his
judgement better than that of any person, or any
multitude, who have not gone through a similar process.
It is not too much to require that what the wisest
of mankind, those who are best entitled to trust their
own judgement, find necessary to warrant their relying
on it, should be submitted to by that miscellaneous
collection of a few wise and many foolish individuals,
called the public. The most intolerant of churches,
the Roman Catholic Church, even at the canonization
of a saint, admits, and listens patiently to, a ' devil's
advocate '. The holiest of men, it appears, cannot be
admitted to posthumous honours, until all that the
devil could say against him is known and weighed.
If even the Newtonian philosophy were not permitted
to be questioned, mankind could not feel as complete
assurance of its truth as they now do. The beliefs

which we have most warrant for, have no safeguard to rest on, but a standing invitation to the whole world to prove them unfounded. If the challenge is not accepted, or is accepted and the attempt fails, we are far enough from certainty still; but we have done the best that the existing state of human reason admits of; we have neglected nothing that could give the truth a chance of reaching us: if the lists are kept open, we may hope that if there be a better truth, it will be found when the human mind is capable of receiving it; and in the meantime we may rely on having attained such approach to truth, as is possible in our own day. This is the amount of certainty attainable by a fallible being, and this the sole way of attaining it.

Strange it is, that men should admit the validity of the arguments for free discussion, but object to their being ' pushed to an extreme '; not seeing that unless the reasons are good for an extreme case, they are not good for any case. Strange that they should imagine that they are not assuming infallibility, when they acknowledge that there should be free discussion on all subjects which can possibly be *doubtful*, but think that some particular principle or doctrine should be forbidden to be questioned because it is so *certain*, that is, because *they are certain* that it is certain. To call any proposition certain, while there is any one who would deny its certainty if permitted, but who is not permitted, is to assume that we ourselves, and those who agree with us, are the judges of certainty, and judges without hearing the other side.

In the present age—which has been described as ' destitute of faith, but terrified at scepticism '—in which people feel sure, not so much that their opinions are true, as that they should not know what to do without them—the claims of an opinion to be protected from public attack are rested not so much on its truth, as on its importance to society. There are, it is alleged, certain beliefs, so useful, not to say indispensable to well-being, that it is as much the duty of governments to uphold those beliefs, as to protect any other of the interests of society. In a case of such necessity, and so directly in the line of their duty, something less than infallibility may, it is maintained, warrant, and even bind, governments, to act on their own opinion, confirmed by the general opinion of mankind. It is also often argued, and still oftener thought, that none but bad men would desire to weaken these salutary beliefs ; and there can be nothing wrong, it is thought, in restraining bad men, and prohibiting what only such men would wish to practise. This mode of thinking makes the justification of restraints on discussion not a question of the truth of doctrines, but of their usefulness ; and flatters itself by that means to escape the responsibility of claiming to be an infallible judge of opinions. But those who thus satisfy themselves, do not perceive that the assumption of infallibility is merely shifted from one point to another. The usefulness of an opinion is itself matter of opinion : as disputable, as open to discussion, and requiring discussion as much, as the opinion itself. There is the same need of an infallible judge of opinions to decide an opinion to be noxious, as to decide it to be false, unless the opinion condemned has full opportunity of defending itself. And it will not do to say that the heretic may be allowed to maintain the utility or harmlessness of his opinion, though forbidden to maintain its truth. The truth of an opinion is part of its utility. If we would know whether or not it is desirable that a proposition should be believed, is it possible to exclude the consideration of whether or not it is true ? In the opinion, not of bad men, but of the best men, no belief which is contrary to truth can be really useful : and can you prevent such men from urging that plea, when they are charged with culpability for denying some doctrine which they are told is useful, but which they believe to be false ? Those who are on the side of received opinions, never fail to take all possible advantage of this plea ; you do not find *them* handling the question of utility as if it could be completely abstracted from that of truth : on the contrary, it is, above all, because their doctrine is the ' truth ', that the knowledge or the belief of it is held to be so indispensable.   There can be no fair discussion of the question of usefulness, when an argument so vital may be employed on one side, but not on the other.   And in point of fact, when law or public feeling do not permit the truth of an opinion to be disputed, they are just as little tolerant of a denial of its usefulness.   The utmost they allow is an extenuation of its absolute necessity, or of the positive guilt of rejecting it.

In order more fully to illustrate the mischief of denying a hearing to opinions because we, in our own judgement, have condemned them, it will be desirable to fix down the discussion to a concrete case ; and I choose, by preference, the cases which are least favourable to me—in which the argument against freedom of opinion, both on the score of truth and on that of utility, is considered the strongest. Let the opinions impugned be the belief in a God and in a future state, or any of the commonly received doctrines of morality. To fight the battle on such ground, gives a great advantage to an unfair antagonist ; since he will be sure to say (and many who have no desire to be unfair will say it internally), Are these the doctrines which you do not deem sufficiently certain to be taken under the protection of law ? Is the belief in a God one of the opinions, to feel sure of which, you hold to be assuming infallibility ? But I must be permitted to observe, that it is not the feeling sure of a doctrine (be it what it may) which I call an assumption of infallibility. It is the undertaking to decide that question *for others*, without allowing them to hear what can be said on the contrary side. And I denounce and reprobate this pretension not the less, if put forth on the side of my most solemn convictions. However positive any one's persuasion may be, not only of the falsity but of the pernicious consequences—not only of the pernicious consequences, but (to adopt expressions which I altogether condemn) the immorality and impiety of an opinion; yet if, in pursuance of that private judgement, though backed by the public judgement of his country or his cotemporaries, he prevents the opinion from being heard in its defence, he assumes infallibility. And so far from the assumption being less objectionable or less dangerous because the opinion is called immoral or impious, this is the case of all others in which it is most fatal. These are exactly the occasions on which the men of one generation commit those dreadful mistakes, which excite the astonishment and horror of posterity. It is among such that we find the instances memorable in history, when the arm of the law has been employed to root out the best men and the noblest doctrines; with deplorable success as to the men, though some of the doctrines have survived to be (as if in mockery) invoked, in defence of similar conduct towards those who dissent from *them*, or from their received interpretation.

Mankind can hardly be too often reminded, that there was once a man named Socrates, between whom and the legal authorities and public opinion of his time, there took place a memorable collision. Born in an age and country abounding in individual greatness, this man has been handed down to us by those who best knew both him and the age, as the most virtuous man in it; while *we* know him as the head and prototype of all subsequent teachers of virtue, the source equally of the lofty inspiration of Plato and the judicious utilitarianism of Aristotle, ' *i maëstri di color che sanno*,' the two headsprings of ethical as of all other philosophy. This acknowledged master of all the eminent thinkers who have since lived—whose fame, still growing after more than two thousand years, all but outweighs the whole remainder of the names which make his native city illustrious—was put to death by his countrymen, after a judicial conviction, for impiety and immorality. Impiety, in denying the gods recognized by the State; indeed his accuser asserted (see the *Apologia*) that he believed in no gods at all. Immorality, in being, by his doctrines

and instructions, a ' corruptor of youth '. Of these
charges the tribunal, there is every ground for believing,
honestly found him guilty, and condemned the man
who probably of all then born had deserved best of
mankind, to be put to death as a criminal.

To pass from this to the only other instance of
judicial iniquity, the mention of which, after the condemnation of Socrates, would not be an anti-climax :
the event which took place on Calvary rather more
than eighteen hundred years ago. The man who left
on the memory of those who witnessed his life and
conversation, such an impression of his moral grandeur,
that eighteen subsequent centuries have done homage
to him as the Almighty in person, was ignominiously
put to death, as what ? As a blasphemer. Men did
not merely mistake their benefactor ; they mistook
him for the exact contrary of what he was, and treated
him as that prodigy of impiety, which they themselves
are now held to be, for their treatment of him. The
feelings with which mankind now regard these lament-
able transactions, especially the later of the two, render
them extremely unjust in their judgement of the unhappy actors. These were, to all appearance, not bad
men—not worse than men commonly are, but rather
the contrary ; men who possessed in a full, or somewhat more than a full measure, the religious, moral,
and patriotic feelings of their time and people : the
very kind of men who, in all times, our own included,
have every chance of passing through life blameless
and respected. The high-priest who rent his garments
when the words were pronounced, which, according to
all the ideas of his country, constituted the blackest
guilt, was in all probability quite as sincere in his
horror and indignation, as the generality of respectable
and pious men now are in the religious and moral
sentiments they profess ; and most of those who now
shudder at his conduct, if they had lived in his time,
and been born Jews, would have acted precisely as
he did. Orthodox Christians who are tempted to think
that those who stoned to death the first martyrs must

have been worse men than they themselves are, ought to remember that one of those persecutors was Saint Paul.

Let us add one more example, the most striking of all, if the impressiveness of an error is measured by the wisdom and virtue of him who falls into it. If ever any one, possessed of power, had grounds for thinking himself the best and most enlightened among his cotemporaries, it was the Emperor Marcus Aurelius. Absolute monarch of the whole civilized world, he preserved through life not only the most unblemished justice, but what was less to be expected from his Stoical breeding, the tenderest heart. The few failings which are attributed to him, were all on the side of indulgence : while his writings, the highest ethical product of the ancient mind, differ scarcely perceptibly, if they differ at all, from the most characteristic teachings of Christ. This man, a better Christian in all but the dogmatic sense of the word, than almost any of the ostensibly Christian sovereigns who have since reigned, persecuted Christianity. Placed at the summit of all the previous attainments of humanity, with an open, unfettered intellect, and a character which led him of himself to embody in his moral writings the Christian ideal, he yet failed to see that Christianity was to be a good and not an evil to the world, with his duties to which he was so deeply penetrated. Existing society he knew to be in a deplorable state. But such as it was, he saw, or thought he saw, that it was held together, and prevented from being worse, by belief and reverence of the received divinities. As a ruler of mankind, he deemed it his duty not to suffer society to fall in pieces ; and saw not how, if its existing ties were removed, any others could be formed which could again knit it together. The new religion openly aimed at dissolving these ties : unless, therefore, it was his duty to adopt that religion, it seemed to be his duty to put it down. Inasmuch then as the theology of Christianity did not appear to him true or of divine origin ; inasmuch as this strange history of a crucified

God was not credible to him, and a system which purported to rest entirely upon a foundation to him so wholly unbelievable, could not be foreseen by him to be that renovating agency which, after all abatements, it has in fact proved to be; the gentlest and most amiable of philosophers and rulers, under a solemn sense of duty, authorized the persecution of Christianity. To my mind this is one of the most tragical facts in all history. It is a bitter thought, how different a thing the Christianity of the world might have been, if the Christian faith had been adopted as the religion of the empire under the auspices of Marcus Aurelius instead of those of Constantine. But it would be equally unjust to him and false to truth, to deny, that no one plea which can be urged for punishing anti-Christian teaching, was wanting to Marcus Aurelius for punishing, as he did, the propagation of Christianity. No Christian more firmly believes that Atheism is false, and tends to the dissolution of society, than Marcus Aurelius believed the same things of Christianity; he who, of all men then living, might have been thought the most capable of appreciating it. Unless any one who approves of punishment for the promulgation of opinions, flatters himself that he is a wiser and better man than Marcus Aurelius—more deeply versed in the wisdom of his time, more elevated in his intellect above it—more earnest in his search for truth, or more single-minded in his devotion to it when found;—let him abstain from that assumption of the joint infallibility of himself and the multitude, which the great Antoninus made with so unfortunate a result.

Aware of the impossibility of defending the use of punishment for restraining irreligious opinions, by any argument which will not justify Marcus Antoninus, the enemies of religious freedom, when hard pressed, occasionally accept this consequence, and say, with Dr. Johnson, that the persecutors of Christianity were in the right; that persecution is an ordeal through which truth ought to pass, and always passes successfully, legal penalties being, in the end, powerless against truth, though sometimes beneficially effective against mischievous errors.   This is a form of the argument for religious intolerance, sufficiently remarkable not to be passed without notice.

A theory which maintains that truth may justifiably be persecuted because persecution cannot possibly do it any harm, cannot be charged with being intentionally hostile to the reception of new truths ; but we cannot commend the generosity of its dealing with the persons to whom mankind are indebted for them.   To discover to the world something which deeply concerns it, and of which it was previously ignorant ; to prove to it that it had been mistaken on some vital point of temporal or spiritual interest, is as important a service as a human being can render to his fellow creatures, and in certain cases, as in those of the early Christians and of the Reformers, those who think with Dr. Johnson believe it to have been the most precious gift which could be bestowed on mankind.   That the authors of such splendid benefits should be requited by martyrdom ; that their reward should be to be dealt with as the vilest of criminals, is not, upon this theory, a deplorable error and misfortune, for which humanity should mourn in sackcloth and ashes, but the normal and justifiable state of things.   The propounder of a new truth, according to this doctrine, should stand, as stood, in the legislation of the Locrians, the proposer of a new law, with a halter round his neck, to be instantly tightened if the public assembly did not, on hearing his reasons, then and there adopt his proposition.   People who defend this mode of treating benefactors, cannot be supposed to set much value on the benefit ; and I believe this view of the subject is mostly confined to the sort of persons who think that new truths may have been desirable once, but that we have had enough of them now.

But, indeed, the dictum that truth always triumphs over persecution, is one of those pleasant falsehoods which men repeat after one another till they pass into commonplaces, but which all experience refutes.

History teems with instances of truth put down by persecution. If not suppressed for ever, it may be thrown back for centuries. To speak only of religious opinions : the Reformation broke out at least twenty times before Luther, and was put down. Arnold of Brescia was put down. Fra Dolcino was put down. Savonarola was put down. The Albigeois were put down. The Vaudois were put down. The Lollards were put down. The Hussites were put down. Even after the era of Luther, wherever persecution was persisted in, it was successful. In Spain, Italy, Flanders, the Austrian empire, Protestantism was rooted out; and, most likely, would have been so in England, had Queen Mary lived, or Queen Elizabeth died. Persecution has always succeeded, save where the heretics were too strong a party to be effectually. persecuted. No reasonable person can doubt that Christianity might have been extirpated in the Roman Empire. It spread, and became predominant, because the persecutions were only occasional, lasting but a short time, and separated by long intervals of almost undisturbed propagandism. It is a piece of idle sentimentality that truth, merely as truth, has any inherent power denied to error, of prevailing against the dungeon and the stake. Men are not more zealous for truth than they often are for error, and a sufficient application of legal or even of social penalties will generally succeed in stopping the propagation of either. The real advantage which truth has, consists in this, that when an opinion is true, it may be extinguished once, twice, or many times, but in the course of ages there will generally be found persons to rediscover it, until some one of its reappearances falls on a time when from favourable circumstances it escapes persecution until it has made such head as to withstand all subsequent attempts to suppress it.

It will be said, that we do not now put to death the introducers of new opinions : we are not like our fathers who slew the prophets, we even build sepulchres to them. It is true we no longer put heretics to death ;

and the amount of penal infliction which modern feeling would probably tolerate, even against the most obnoxious opinions, is not sufficient to extirpate them. But let us not flatter ourselves that we are yet free from the stain even of legal persecution. Penalties for opinion, or at least for its expression, still exist by law ; and their enforcement is not, even in these times, so unexampled as to make it at all incredible that they may some day be revived in full force. In the year 1857, at the summer assizes of the county of Cornwall, an unfortunate man,[1] said to be of unexceptionable conduct in all relations of life, was sentenced to twenty-one months' imprisonment, for uttering, and writing on a gate, some offensive words concerning Christianity. Within a month of the same time, at the Old Bailey, two persons, on two separate occasions,[2] were rejected as jurymen, and one of them grossly insulted by the judge and by one of the counsel, because they honestly declared that they had no theological belief ; and a third, a foreigner,[3] for the same reason, was denied justice against a thief. This refusal of redress took place in virtue of the legal doctrine, that no person can be allowed to give evidence in a court of justice, who does not profess belief in a God (any god is sufficient) and in a future state ; which is equivalent to declaring such persons to be outlaws, excluded from the protection of the tribunals ; who may not only be robbed or assaulted with impunity, if no one but themselves, or persons of similar opinions, be present, but any one else may be robbed or assaulted with impunity, if the proof of the fact depends on their evidence. The assumption on which this is grounded is that the oath is worthless, of a person who does not

[1] Thomas Pooley, Bodmin Assizes, July 31, 1857. In December following, he received a free pardon from the Crown.

[2] George Jacob Holyoake, August 17, 1857 ; Edward Truelove, July, 1857.

[3] Baron de Gleichen, Marlborough-street Police Court, August 4, 1857.

believe in a future state ; a proposition which betokens much ignorance of history in those who assent to it (since it is historically true that a large proportion of infidels in all ages have been persons of distinguished integrity and honour) ; and would be maintained by no one who had the smallest conception how many of the persons in greatest repute with the world, both for virtues and for attainments, are well known, at least to their intimates, to be unbelievers. The rule, besides, is suicidal, and cuts away its own foundation. Under pretence that atheists must be liars, it admits the testimony of all atheists who are willing to lie, and rejects only those who brave the obloquy of publicly confessing a detested creed rather than affirm a falsehood. A rule thus self-convicted of absurdity so far as regards its professed purpose, can be kept in force only as a badge of hatred, a relic of persecution ; a persecution, too, having the peculiarity, that the qualification for undergoing it, is the being clearly proved not to deserve it. The rule, and the theory it implies, are hardly less insulting to believers than to infidels. For if he who does not believe in a future state, necessarily lies, it follows that they who do believe are only prevented from lying, if prevented they are, by the fear of hell. We will not do the authors and abettors of the rule the injury of supposing, that the conception which they have formed of Christian virtue is drawn from their own consciousness.

These, indeed, are but rags and remnants of persecution, and may be thought to be not so much an indication of the wish to persecute, as an example of that very frequent infirmity of English minds, which makes them take a preposterous pleasure in the assertion of a bad principle, when they are no longer bad enough to desire to carry it really into practice. But unhappily there is no security in the state of the public mind, that the suspension of worse forms of legal persecution, which has lasted for about the space of a generation, will continue. In this age the quiet surface of routine is as often ruffled by attempts to resuscitate past evils, as to introduce new benefits. What is boasted of at the present time as the revival of religion, is always, in narrow and uncultivated minds, at least as much the revival of bigotry; and where there is the strong permanent leaven of intolerance in the feelings of a people, which at all times abides in the middle classes of this country, it needs but little to provoke them into actively persecuting those whom they have never ceased to think proper objects of persecution.[1] For it is this—it is the opinions men

---

[1] Ample warning may be drawn from the large infusion of the passions of a persecutor, which mingled with the general display of the worst parts of our national character on the occasion of the Sepoy insurrection. The ravings of fanatics or charlatans from the pulpit may be unworthy of notice; but the heads of the Evangelical party have announced as their principle for the government of Hindoos and Mohammedans, that no schools be supported by public money in which the Bible is not taught, and by necessary consequence that no public employment be given to any but real or pretended Christians. An under-Secretary of State, in a speech delivered to his constituents on November 12, 1857, is reported to have said: ' Toleration of their faith ' (the faith of a hundred millions of British subjects), ' the superstition which they called religion, by the British Government, had had the effect of retarding the ascendancy of the British name, and preventing the salutary growth of Christianity. . . . Toleration was the great corner-stone of the religious liberties of this country ; but do not let them abuse that precious word toleration. As he understood it, it meant the complete liberty to all, freedom of worship, *among Christians, who worshipped upon the same foundation.* It meant toleration of all sects and denominations of *Christians who believed in the one mediation.*' I desire to call attention to the fact, that a man who has been deemed fit to fill a high office in the government of this country, under a liberal Ministry, maintains the doctrine that all who do not believe in the divinity of Christ are beyond the pale of toleration. Who, after this imbecile display, can indulge the illusion that religious persecution has passed away, never to return ?

entertain, and the feelings they cherish, respecting those who disown the beliefs they deem important, which makes this country not a place of mental freedom. For a long time past, the chief mischief of the legal penalties is that they strengthen the social stigma. It is that stigma which is really effective, and so effective is it, that the profession of opinions which are under the ban of society is much less common in England, than is, in many other countries, the avowal of those which incur risk of judicial punishment. In respect to all persons but those whose pecuniary circumstances make them independent of the goodwill of other people, opinion, on this subject, is as efficacious as law; men might as well be imprisoned, as excluded from the means of earning their bread. Those whose bread is already secured, and who desire no favours from men in power, or from bodies of men, or from the public, have nothing to fear from the open avowal of any opinions, but to be ill-thought of and ill-spoken of, and this it ought not to require a very heroic mould to enable them to bear. There is no room for any appeal *ad misericordiam* in behalf of such persons. But though we do not now inflict so much evil on those who think differently from us, as it was formerly our custom to do, it may be that we do ourselves as much evil as ever by our treatment of them. Socrates was put to death, but the Socratic philosophy rose like the sun in heaven, and spread its illumination over the whole intellectual firmament. Christians were cast to the lions, but the Christian church grew up a stately and spreading tree, overtopping the older and less vigorous growths, and stifling them by its shade. Our merely social intolerance kills no one, roots out no opinions, but induces men to disguise them, or to abstain from any active effort for their diffusion. With us, heretical opinions do not perceptibly gain, or even lose, ground in each decade or generation; they never blaze out far and wide, but continue to smoulder in the narrow circles of thinking and studious persons among whom they originate, without ever lighting up

the general affairs of mankind with either a true or
a deceptive light. And thus is kept up a state of
things very satisfactory to some minds, because, without the unpleasant process of fining or imprisoning
anybody, it maintains all prevailing opinions outwardly
undisturbed, while it does not absolutely interdict the
exercise of reason by dissentients afflicted with the
malady of thought. A convenient plan for having
peace in the intellectual world, and keeping all things
going on therein very much as they do already. But
the price paid for this sort of intellectual pacification,
is the sacrifice of the entire moral courage of the human
mind. A state of things in which a large portion of
the most active and inquiring intellects find it advisable
to keep the general principles and grounds of their
convictions within their own breasts, and attempt, in
what they address to the public, to fit as much as
they can of their own conclusions to premisses which
they have internally renounced, cannot send forth the
open, fearless characters, and logical, consistent intellects who once adorned the thinking world. The sort
of men who can be looked for under it, are either mere
conformers to commonplace, or time-servers for truth,
whose arguments on all great subjects are meant for
their hearers, and are not those which have convinced
themselves. Those who avoid this alternative, do so
by narrowing their thoughts and interest to things
which can be spoken of without venturing within the
region of principles, that is, to small practical matters,
which would come right of themselves, if but the minds
of mankind were strengthened and enlarged, and which
will never be made effectually right until then : while
that which would strengthen and enlarge men's minds,
free and daring speculation on the highest subjects, is
abandoned.

Those in whose eyes this reticence on the part of
heretics is no evil, should consider in the first place,
that in consequence of it there is never any fair and
thorough discussion of heretical opinions ; and that
such of them as could not stand such a discussion,

though they may be prevented from spreading, do not disappear. But it is not the minds of heretics that are deteriorated most, by the ban placed on all inquiry which does not end in the orthodox conclusions. The greatest harm done is to those who are not heretics, and whose whole mental development is cramped, and their reason cowed, by the fear of heresy. Who can compute what the world loses in the multitude of promising intellects combined with timid characters, who dare not follow out any bold, vigorous, independent train of thought, lest it should land them in something which would admit of being considered irreligious or immoral ? Among them we may occasionally see some man of deep conscientiousness, and subtle and refined understanding, who spends a life in sophisticating with an intellect which he cannot silence, and exhausts the resources of ingenuity in attempting to reconcile the promptings of his conscience and reason with orthodoxy, which yet he does not, perhaps, to the end succeed in doing. No one can be a great thinker who does not recognize, that as a thinker it is his first duty to follow his intellect to whatever conclusions it may lead. Truth gains more even by the errors of one who, with due study and preparation, thinks for himself, than by the true opinions of those who only hold them because they do not suffer themselves to think. Not that it is solely, or chiefly, to form great thinkers, that freedom of thinking is required. On the contrary, it is as much and even more indispensable, to enable average human beings to attain the mental stature which they are capable of. There have been, and may again be, great individual thinkers, in a general atmosphere of mental slavery. But there never has been, nor ever will be, in that atmosphere, an intellectually active people. When any people has made a temporary approach to such a character, it has been because the dread of heterodox speculation was for a time suspended. Where there is a tacit convention that principles are not to be disputed ; where the discussion of the greatest questions which can occupy humanity is considered to be closed, we cannot hope to find that generally high scale of mental activity which has made some periods of history so remarkable. Never when controversy avoided the subjects which are large and important enough to kindle enthusiasm, was the mind of a people stirred up from its foundations, and the impulse given which raised even persons of the most ordinary intellect to something of the dignity of thinking beings. Of such we have had an example in the condition of Europe during the times immediately following the Reformation; another, though limited to the Continent and to a more cultivated class, in the speculative movement of the latter half of the eighteenth century; and a third, of still briefer duration, in the intellectual fermentation of Germany during the Goethian and Fichtean period. These periods differed widely in the particular opinions which they developed; but were alike in this, that during all three the yoke of authority was broken. In each, an old mental despotism had been thrown off, and no new one had yet taken its place. The impulse given at these three periods has made Europe what it now is. Every single improvement which has taken place either in the human mind or in institutions, may be traced distinctly to one or other of them. Appearances have for some time indicated that all three impulses are wellnigh spent; and we can expect no fresh start, until we again assert our mental freedom.

Let us now pass to the second division of the argument, and dismissing the supposition that any of the received opinions may be false, let us assume them to be true, and examine into the worth of the manner in which they are likely to be held, when their truth is not freely and openly canvassed. However unwillingly a person who has a strong opinion may admit the possibility that his opinion may be false, he ought to be moved by the consideration that however true it may be, if it is not fully, frequently, and fearlessly discussed, it will be held as a dead dogma, not a living truth.

There is a class of persons (happily not quite so numerous as formerly) who think it enough if a person assents undoubtingly to what they think true, though he has no knowledge whatever of the grounds of the opinion, and could not make a tenable defence of it against the most superficial objections. Such persons, if they can once get their creed taught from authority, naturally think that no good, and some harm, comes of its being allowed to be questioned. Where their influence prevails, they make it nearly impossible for the received opinion to be rejected wisely and considerately, though it may still be rejected rashly and ignorantly ; for to shut out discussion entirely is seldom possible, and when it once gets in, beliefs not grounded on conviction are apt to give way before the slightest semblance of an argument. Waiving, however, this possibility—assuming that the true opinion abides in the mind, but abides as a prejudice, a belief independent of, and proof against, argument—this is not the way in which truth ought to be held by a rational being. This is not knowing the truth. Truth, thus held, is but one superstition the more, accidentally clinging to the words which enunciate a truth.

If the intellect and judgement of mankind ought to be cultivated, a thing which Protestants at least do not deny, on what can these faculties be more appropriately exercised by any one, than on the things which concern him so much that it is considered necessary for him to hold opinions on them ? If the cultivation of the understanding consists in one thing more than in another, it is surely in learning the grounds of one's own opinions. Whatever people believe, on subjects on which it is of the first importance to believe rightly, they ought to be able to defend against at least the common objections. But, some one may say, ' Let them be *taught* the grounds of their opinions. It does not follow that opinions must be merely parroted because they are never heard controverted. Persons who learn geometry do not simply commit the theorems to memory, but understand and learn likewise the demonstrations; and it would be absurd to say that they remain ignorant of the grounds of geometrical truths, because they never hear any one deny, and attempt to disprove them.' Undoubtedly: and such teaching suffices on a subject like mathematics, where there is nothing at all to be said on the wrong side of the question. The peculiarity of the evidence of mathematical truths is, that all the argument is on one side. There are no objections, and no answers to objections. But on every subject on which difference of opinion is possible, the truth depends on a balance to be struck between two sets of conflicting reasons. Even in natural philosophy, there is always some other explanation possible of the same facts; some geocentric theory instead of heliocentric, some phlogiston instead of oxygen; and it has to be shown why that other theory cannot be the true one: and until this is shown, and until we know how it is shown, we do not understand the grounds of our opinion. But when we turn to subjects infinitely more complicated, to morals, religion, politics, social relations, and the business of life, three-fourths of the arguments for every disputed opinion consist in dispelling the appearances which favour some opinion different from it. The greatest orator, save one, of antiquity, has left it on record that he always studied his adversary's case with as great, if not with still greater, intensity than even his own. What Cicero practised as the means of forensic success, requires to be imitated by all who study any subject in order to arrive at the truth. He who knows only his own side of the case, knows little of that. His reasons may be good, and no one may have been able to refute them. But if he is equally unable to refute the reasons on the opposite side; if he does not so much as know what they are, he has no ground for preferring either opinion. The rational position for him would be suspension of judgement, and unless he contents himself with that, he is either led by authority, or adopts, like the generality of the world, the side to which he feels most inclination. Nor is it enough that he should hear the arguments of adversaries from his own teachers, presented as they state them, and accompanied by what they offer as refutations. That is not the way to do justice to the arguments, or bring them into real contact with his own mind. He must be able to hear them from persons who actually believe them ; who defend them in earnest, and do their very utmost for them. He must know them in their most plausible and persuasive form ; he must feel the whole force of the difficulty which the true view of the subject has to encounter and dispose of ; else he will never really possess himself of the portion of truth which meets and removes that difficulty. Ninety-nine in a hundred of what are called educated men are in this condition ; even of those who can argue fluently for their opinions. Their conclusion may be true, but it might be false for anything they know : they have never thrown themselves into the mental position of those who think differently from them, and considered what such persons may have to say ; and consequently they do not, in any proper sense of the word, know the doctrine which they themselves profess. They do not know those parts of it which explain and justify the remainder ; the considerations which show that a fact which seemingly conflicts with another is reconcilable with it, or that, of two apparently strong reasons, one and not the other ought to be preferred. All that part of the truth which turns the scale, and decides the judgement of a completely informed mind, they are strangers to ; nor is it ever really known, but to those who have attended equally and impartially to both sides, and endeavoured to see the reasons of both in the strongest light. So essential is this discipline to a real understanding of moral and human subjects, that if opponents of all important truths do not exist, it is indispensable to imagine them, and supply them with the strongest arguments which the most skilful devil's advocate can conjure up.

To abate the force of these considerations, an enemy

of free discussion may be supposed to say, that there is no necessity for mankind in general to know and understand all that can be said against or for their opinions by philosophers and theologians. That it is not needful for common men to be able to expose all the misstatements or fallacies of an ingenious opponent. That it is enough if there is always somebody capable of answering them, so that nothing likely to mislead uninstructed persons remains unrefuted. That simple minds, having been taught the obvious grounds of the truths inculcated on them, may trust to authority for the rest, and being aware that they have neither knowledge nor talent to resolve every difficulty which can be raised, may repose in the assurance that all those which have been raised have been or can be answered, by those who are specially trained to the task.

Conceding to this view of the subject the utmost that can be claimed for it by those most easily satisfied with the amount of understanding of truth which ought to accompany the belief of it; even so, the argument for free discussion is no way weakened. For even this doctrine acknowledges that mankind ought to have a rational assurance that all objections have been satisfactorily answered; and how are they to be answered if that which requires to be answered is not spoken? or how can the answer be known to be satisfactory, if the objectors have no opportunity of showing that it is unsatisfactory? If not the public, at least the philosophers and theologians who are to resolve the difficulties, must make themselves familiar with those difficulties in their most puzzling form; and this cannot be accomplished unless they are freely stated, and placed in the most advantageous light which they admit of. The Catholic Church has its own way of dealing with this embarrassing problem. It makes a broad separation between those who can be permitted to receive its doctrines on conviction, and those who must accept them on trust. Neither, indeed, are allowed any choice as to what they will accept; but the clergy, such at least as can be fully confided in, may admissibly and meritoriously make themselves acquainted with the arguments of opponents, in order to answer them, and may, therefore, read heretical books ; the laity, not unless by special permission, hard to be obtained. This discipline recognizes a knowledge of the enemy's case as beneficial to the teachers, but finds means, consistent with this, of denying it to the rest of the world : thus giving to the *élite* more mental culture, though not more mental freedom, than it allows to the mass. By this device it succeeds in obtaining the kind of mental superiority which its purposes require ; for though culture without freedom never made a large and liberal mind, it can make a clever *nisi prius* advocate of a cause. But in countries professing Protestantism, this resource is denied ; since Protestants hold, at least in theory, that the responsibility for the choice of a religion must be borne by each for himself, and cannot be thrown off upon teachers. Besides, in the present state of the world, it is practically impossible that writings which are read by the instructed can be kept from the uninstructed. If the teachers of mankind are to be cognizant of all that they ought to know, everything must be free to be written and published without restraint.

If, however, the mischievous operation of the absence of free discussion, when the received opinions are true, were confined to leaving men ignorant of the grounds of those opinions, it might be thought that this, if an intellectual, is no moral evil, and does not affect the worth of the opinions, regarded in their influence on the character. The fact, however, is, that not only the grounds of the opinion are forgotten in the absence of discussion, but too often the meaning of the opinion itself. The words which convey it, cease to suggest ideas, or suggest only a small portion of those they were originally employed to communicate. Instead of a vivid conception and a living belief, there remain only a few phrases retained by rote ; or, if any part, the shell and husk only of the meaning is retained, the finer essence being lost. The great chapter in human history which this fact occupies and fills, cannot be too earnestly studied and meditated on.

It is illustrated in the experience of almost all ethical doctrines and religious creeds. They are all full of meaning and vitality to those who originate them, and to the direct disciples of the originators. Their meaning continues to be felt in undiminished strength, and is perhaps brought out into even fuller consciousness, so long as the struggle lasts to give the doctrine or creed an ascendancy over other creeds. At last it either prevails, and becomes the general opinion, or its progress stops; it keeps possession of the ground it has gained, but ceases to spread further. When either of these results has become apparent, controversy on the subject flags, and gradually dies away. The doctrine has taken its place, if not as a received opinion, as one of the admitted sects or divisions of opinion : those who hold it have generally inherited, not adopted it ; and conversion from one of these doctrines to another, being now an exceptional fact, occupies little place in the thoughts of their professors. Instead of being, as at first, constantly on the alert either to defend themselves against the world, or to bring the world over to them, they have subsided into acquiescence, and neither listen, when they can help it, to arguments against their creed, nor trouble dissentients (if there be such) with arguments in its favour. From this time may usually be dated the decline in the living power of the doctrine. We often hear the teachers of all creeds lamenting the difficulty of keeping up in the minds of believers a lively apprehension of the truth which they nominally recognize, so that it may penetrate the feelings, and acquire a real mastery over the conduct. No such difficulty is complained of while the creed is still fighting for its existence : even the weaker combatants then know and feel what they are fighting for, and the difference between it and other doctrines ; and in that period of every creed's existence, not a few persons may be found, who have realized its fundamental principles in all the forms of thought, have weighed and considered them in all their important bearings, and have experienced the full effect on the character, which belief in that creed ought to produce in a mind thoroughly imbued with it. But when it has come to be an hereditary creed, and to be received passively, not actively—when the mind is no longer compelled, in the same degree as at first, to exercise its vital powers on the questions which its belief presents to it, there is a progressive tendency to forget all of the belief except the formularies, or to give it a dull and torpid assent, as if accepting it on trust dispensed with the necessity of realizing it in consciousness, or testing it by personal experience ; until it almost ceases to connect itself at all with the inner life of the human being. Then are seen the cases, so frequent in this age of the world as almost to form the majority, in which the creed remains as it were outside the mind, encrusting and petrifying it against all other influences addressed to the higher parts of our nature ; manifesting its power by not suffering any fresh and living conviction to get in, but itself doing nothing for the mind or heart, except standing sentinel over them to keep them vacant.

To what an extent doctrines intrinsically fitted to make the deepest impression upon the mind may remain in it as dead beliefs, without being ever realized in the imagination, the feelings, or the understanding, is exemplified by the manner in which the majority of believers hold the doctrines of Christianity. By Christianity I here mean what is accounted such by all churches and sects—the maxims and precepts contained in the New Testament. These are considered sacred, and accepted as laws, by all professing Christians. Yet it is scarcely too much to say that not one Christian in a thousand guides or tests his individual conduct by reference to those laws. The standard to which he does refer it, is the custom of his nation, his class, or his religious profession. He has thus, on the one hand, a collection of ethical maxims, which he

believes to have been vouchsafed to him by infallible
wisdom as rules for his government ; and on the other,
a set of everyday judgements and practices, which
go a certain length with some of those maxims, not
so great a length with others, stand in direct opposition to some, and are, on the whole, a compromise
between the Christian creed and the interests and suggestions of worldly life. To the first of these standards
he gives his homage ; to the other his real allegiance.
All Christians believe that the blessed are the poor
and humble, and those who are ill-used by the world ;
that it is easier for a camel to pass through the eye
of a needle than for a rich man to enter the kingdom
of heaven ; that they should judge not, lest they be
judged ; that they should swear not at all ; that they
should love their neighbour as themselves ; that if one
take their cloak, they should give him their coat also ;
that they should take no thought for the morrow ;
that if they would be perfect, they should sell all that
they have and give it to the poor. They are not
insincere when they say that they believe these things.
They do believe them, as people believe what they
have always heard lauded and never discussed. But
in the sense of that living belief which regulates conduct, they believe these doctrines just up to the point
to which it is usual to act upon them. The doctrines
in their integrity are serviceable to pelt adversaries
with ; and it is understood that they are to be put
forward (when possible) as the reasons for whatever
people do that they think laudable. But any one who
reminded them that the maxims require an infinity of
things which they never even think of doing, would
gain nothing but to be classed among those very unpopular characters who affect to be better than other
people. The doctrines have no hold on ordinary believers—are not a power in their minds. They have
an habitual respect for the sound of them, but no
feeling which spreads from the words to the things
signified, and forces the mind to take *them* in, and
make them conform to the formula. Whenever con-

duct is concerned, they look round for Mr. A and B
to direct them how far to go in obeying Christ.

Now we may be well assured that the case was not
thus, but far otherwise, with the early Christians. Had
it been thus, Christianity never would have expanded
from an obscure sect of the despised Hebrews into the
religion of the Roman empire. When their enemies
said, ' See how these Christians love one another ' (a
remark not likely to be made by anybody now), they
assuredly had a much livelier feeling of the meaning
of their creed than they have ever had since. And
to this cause, probably, it is chiefly owing that Christianity now makes so little progress in extending its
domain, and after eighteen centuries, is still nearly
confined to Europeans and the descendants of Europeans. Even with the strictly religious, who are much
in earnest about their doctrines, and attach a greater
amount of meaning to many of them than people in
general, it commonly happens that the part which is
thus comparatively active in their minds is that which
was made by Calvin, or Knox, or some such person
much nearer in character to themselves. The sayings
of Christ co-exist passively in their minds, producing
hardly any effect beyond what is caused by mere
listening to words so amiable and bland. There are
many reasons, doubtless, why doctrines which are the
badge of a sect retain more of their vitality than those
common to all recognized sects, and why more pains
are taken by teachers to keep their meaning alive ;
but one reason certainly is, that the peculiar doctrines
are more questioned, and have to be oftener defended
against open gainsayers. Both teachers and learners
go to sleep at their post, as soon as there is no enemy
in the field.

The same thing holds true, generally speaking, of all
traditional doctrines—those of prudence and knowledge
of life, as well as of morals or religion. All languages
and literatures are full of general observations on life,
both as to what it is, and how to conduct oneself in
it ; observations which everybody knows, which every-

body repeats, or hears with acquiescence, which are received as truisms, yet of which most people first truly learn the meaning, when experience, generally of a painful kind, has made it a reality to them. How often, when smarting under some unforeseen misfortune or disappointment, does a person call to mind some proverb or common saying, familiar to him all his life, the meaning of which, if he had ever before felt it as he does now, would have saved him from the calamity. There are indeed reasons for this, other than the absence of discussion : there are many truths of which the full meaning *cannot* be realized, until personal experience has brought it home. But much more of the meaning even of these would have been understood, and what was understood would have been far more deeply impressed on the mind, if the man had been accustomed to hear it argued *pro* and *con* by people who did understand it. The fatal tendency of mankind to leave off thinking about a thing when it is no longer doubtful, is the cause of half their errors. A cotemporary author has well spoken of ' the deep slumber of a decided opinion '.

But what ! (it may be asked) Is the absence of unanimity an indispensable condition of true knowledge ? Is it necessary that some part of mankind should persist in error, to enable any to realize the truth ? Does a belief cease to be real and vital as soon as it is generally received—and is a proposition never thoroughly understood and felt unless some doubt of it remains ? As soon as mankind have unanimously accepted a truth, does the truth perish within them ? The highest aim and best result of improved intelligence, it has hitherto been thought, is to unite mankind more and more in the acknowledgement of all important truths : and does the intelligence only last as long as it has not achieved its object ? Do the fruits of conquest perish by the very completeness of the victory ?

I affirm no such thing. As mankind improve, the number of doctrines which are no longer disputed or doubted will be constantly on the increase : and the well-being of mankind may almost be measured by the number and gravity of the truths which have reached the point of being uncontested. The cessation, on one question after another, of serious controversy, is one of the necessary incidents of the consolidation of opinion ; a consolidation as salutary in the case of true opinions, as it is dangerous and noxious when the opinions are erroneous. But though this gradual narrowing of the bounds of diversity of opinion is necessary in both senses of the term, being at once inevitable and indispensable, we are not therefore obliged to conclude that all its consequences must be beneficial. The loss of so important an aid to the intelligent and living apprehension of a truth, as is afforded by the necessity of explaining it to, or defending it against, opponents, though not sufficient to outweigh, is no trifling drawback from, the benefit of its universal recognition. Where this advantage can no longer be had, I confess I should like to see the teachers of mankind endeavouring to provide a substitute for it ; some contrivance for making the difficulties of the question as present to the learner's consciousness, as if they were pressed upon him by a dissentient champion, eager for his conversion.

But instead of seeking contrivances for this purpose, they have lost those they formerly had. The Socratic dialectics, so magnificently exemplified in the dialogues of Plato, were a contrivance of this description. They were essentially a negative discussion of the great questions of philosophy and life, directed with consummate skill to the purpose of convincing any one who had merely adopted the commonplaces of received opinion, that he did not understand the subject—that he as yet attached no definite meaning to the doctrines he professed ; in order that, becoming aware of his ignorance, he might be put in the way to attain a stable belief, resting on a clear apprehension both of the meaning of doctrines and of their evidence. The school disputations of the middle ages had a somewhat similar object. They were intended to make sure that the pupil understood his own opinion, and (by necessary correlation) the opinion opposed to it, and could enforce the grounds of the one and confute those of the other. These last-mentioned contests had indeed the incurable defect, that the premisses appealed to were taken from authority, not from reason; and, as a discipline to the mind, they were in every respect inferior to the powerful dialectics which formed the intellects of the ' Socratici viri ' : but the modern mind owes far more to both than it is generally willing to admit, and the present modes of education contain nothing which in the smallest degree supplies the place either of the one or of the other. A person who derives all his instruction from teachers or books, even if he escape the besetting temptation of contenting himself with cram, is under no compulsion to hear both sides; accordingly it is far from a frequent accomplishment, even among thinkers, to know both sides; and the weakest part of what everybody says in defence of his opinion, is what he intends as a reply to antagonists. It is the fashion of the present time to disparage negative logic—that which points out weaknesses in theory or errors in practice, without establishing positive truths. Such negative criticism would indeed be poor enough as an ultimate result; but as a means to attaining any positive knowledge or conviction worthy the name, it cannot be valued too highly; and until people are again systematically trained to it, there will be few great thinkers, and a low general average of intellect, in any but the mathematical and physical departments of speculation. On any other subject no one's opinions deserve the name of knowledge, except so far as he has either had forced upon him by others, or gone through of himself, the same mental process which would have been required of him in carrying on an active controversy with opponents. That, therefore, which when absent, it is so indispensable, but so difficult, to create, how worse than absurd it is to forgo, when spontaneously offering itself! If there are any persons who contest a received opinion, or

who will do so if law or opinion will let them, let us
thank them for it, open our minds to listen to them,
and rejoice that there is some one to do for us what
we otherwise ought, if we have any regard for either
the certainty or the vitality of our convictions, to do
with much greater labour for ourselves.

It still remains to speak of one of the principal causes
which make diversity of opinion advantageous, and
will continue to do so until mankind shall have entered
a stage of intellectual advancement which at present
seems at an incalculable distance. We have hitherto
considered only two possibilities: that the received
opinion may be false, and some other opinion, consequently, true; or that, the received opinion being true,
a conflict with the opposite error is essential to a clear
apprehension and deep feeling of its truth. But there
is a commoner case than either of these; when the
conflicting doctrines, instead of being one true and the
other false, share the truth between them; and the
nonconforming opinion is needed to supply the remainder of the truth, of which the received doctrine
embodies only a part. Popular opinions, on subjects
not palpable to sense, are often true, but seldom or
never the whole truth. They are a part of the truth;
sometimes a greater, sometimes a smaller part, but
exaggerated, distorted, and disjoined from the truths
by which they ought to be accompanied and limited.
Heretical opinions, on the other hand, are generally
some of these suppressed and neglected truths, bursting
the bonds which kept them down, and either seeking
reconciliation with the truth contained in the common
opinion, or fronting it as enemies, and setting themselves up, with similar exclusiveness, as the whole
truth. The latter case is hitherto the most frequent,
as, in the human mind, one-sidedness has always been
the rule, and many-sidedness the exception. Hence,
even in revolutions of opinion, one part of the truth
usually sets while another rises. Even progress, which
ought to superadd, for the most part only substitutes,

one partial and incomplete truth for another ; improvement consisting chiefly in this, that the new fragment of truth is more wanted, more adapted to the needs of the time, than that which it displaces. Such being the partial character of prevailing opinions, even when resting on a true foundation, every opinion which embodies somewhat of the portion of truth which the common opinion omits, ought to be considered precious, with whatever amount of error and confusion that truth may be blended. No sober judge of human affairs will feel bound to be indignant because those who force on our notice truths which we should otherwise have overlooked, overlook some of those which we see. Rather, he will think that so long as popular truth is one-sided, it is more desirable than otherwise that unpopular truth should have one-sided asserters too ; such being usually the most energetic, and the most likely to compel reluctant attention to the fragment of wisdom which they proclaim as if it were the whole.

Thus, in the eighteenth century, when nearly all the instructed, and all those of the uninstructed who were led by them, were lost in admiration of what is called civilization, and of the marvels of modern science, literature, and philosophy, and while greatly overrating the amount of unlikeness between the men of modern and those of ancient times, indulged the belief that the whole of the difference was in their own favour ; with what a salutary shock did the paradoxes of Rousseau explode like bombshells in the midst, dislocating the compact mass of one-sided opinion, and forcing its elements to recombine in a better form and with additional ingredients. Not that the current opinions were on the whole farther from the truth than Rousseau's were ; on the contrary, they were nearer to it ; they contained more of positive truth, and very much less of error. Nevertheless there lay in Rousseau's doctrine, and has floated down the stream of opinion along with it, a considerable amount of exactly those truths which the popular opinion wanted ; and these are the deposit which was left behind when the flood subsided. The superior worth of simplicity of life, the enervating and demoralizing effect of the trammels and hypocrisies of artificial society, are ideas which have never been entirely absent from cultivated minds since Rousseau wrote ; and they will in time produce their due effect, though at present needing to be asserted as much as ever, and to be asserted by deeds, for words, on this subject, have nearly exhausted their power.

In politics, again, it is almost a commonplace, that a party of order or stability, and a party of progress or reform, are both necessary elements of a healthy state of political life ; until the one or the other shall have so enlarged its mental grasp as to be a party equally of order and of progress, knowing and distinguishing what is fit to be preserved from what ought to be swept away. Each of these modes of thinking derives its utility from the deficiencies of the other ; but it is in a great measure the opposition of the other that keeps each within the limits of reason and sanity. Unless opinions favourable to democracy and to aristocracy, to property and to equality, to co-operation and to competition, to luxury and to abstinence, to sociality and individuality, to liberty and discipline, and all the other standing antagonisms of practical life, are expressed with equal freedom, and enforced and defended with equal talent and energy, there is no chance of both elements obtaining their due ; one scale is sure to go up, and the other down. Truth, in the great practical concerns of life, is so much a question of the reconciling and combining of opposites, that very few have minds sufficiently capacious and impartial to make the adjustment with an approach to correctness, and it has to be made by the rough process of a struggle between combatants fighting under hostile banners. On any of the great open questions just enumerated, if either of the two opinions has a better claim than the other, not merely to be tolerated, but to be encouraged and countenanced, it is the one which happens at the particular time and place to be in a minority.

That is the opinion which, for the time being, represents the neglected interests, the side of human wellbeing which is in danger of obtaining less than its share.   I am aware that there is not, in this country, any intolerance of differences of opinion on most of these topics.   They are adduced to show, by admitted and multiplied examples, the universality of the fact, that only through diversity of opinion is there, in the existing state of human intellect, a chance of fair play to all sides of the truth.   When there are persons to be found, who form an exception to the apparent unanimity of the world on any subject, even if the world is in the right, it is always probable that dissentients have something worth hearing to say for themselves, and that truth would lose something by their silence.

It may be objected, ' But *some* received principles, especially on the highest and most vital subjects, are more than half-truths.   The Christian morality, for instance, is the whole truth on that subject, and if any one teaches a morality which varies from it, he is wholly in error.'   As this is of all cases the most important in practice, none can be fitter to test the general maxim.   But before pronouncing what Christian morality is or is not, it would be desirable to decide what is meant by Christian morality.   If it means the morality of the New Testament, I wonder that any one who derives his knowledge of this from the book itself, can suppose that it was announced, or intended, as a complete doctrine of morals.   The Gospel always refers to a pre-existing morality, and confines its precepts to the particulars in which that morality was to be corrected, or superseded by a wider and higher ; expressing itself, moreover, in terms most general, often impossible to be interpreted literally, and possessing rather the impressiveness of poetry or eloquence than the precision of legislation.   To extract from it a body of ethical doctrine, has never been possible without eking it out from the Old Testament, that is, from a system elaborate indeed, but in many respects barbarous, and intended only for a barbarous people. St. Paul, a declared enemy to this Judaical mode of interpreting the doctrine and filling up the scheme of his Master, equally assumes a pre-existing morality, namely that of the Greeks and Romans; and his advice to Christians is in a great measure a system of accommodation to that; even to the extent of giving an apparent sanction to slavery. What is called Christian, but should rather be termed theological, morality, was not the work of Christ or the Apostles, but is of much later origin, having been gradually built up by the Catholic church of the first five centuries, and though not implicitly adopted by moderns and Protestants, has been much less modified by them than might have been expected. For the most part, indeed, they have contented themselves with cutting off the additions which had been made to it in the middle ages, each sect supplying the place by fresh additions, adapted to its own character and tendencies. That mankind owe a great debt to this morality, and to its early teachers, I should be the last person to deny; but I do not scruple to say of it, that it is, in many important points, incomplete and one-sided, and that unless ideas and feelings, not sanctioned by it, had contributed to the formation of European life and character, human affairs would have been in a worse condition than they now are. Christian morality (so called) has all the characters of a reaction; it is, in great part, a protest against Paganism. Its ideal is negative rather than positive; passive rather than active; Innocence rather than Nobleness; Abstinence from Evil, rather than energetic Pursuit of Good: in its precepts (as has been well said) ' thou shalt not ' predominates unduly over ' thou shalt '. In its horror of sensuality, it made an idol of asceticism, which has been gradually compromised away into one of legality. It holds out the hope of heaven and the threat of hell, as the appointed and appropriate motives to a virtuous life: in this falling far below the best of the ancients, and doing what lies in it to give to human morality an essentially selfish character, by disconnecting each man's feelings of duty from the interests of his fellow-creatures, except so far as a self-interested inducement is offered to him for consulting them. It is essentially a doctrine of passive obedience ; it inculcates submission to all authorities found established ; who indeed are not to be actively obeyed when they command what religion forbids, but who are not to be resisted, far less rebelled against, for any amount of wrong to ourselves. And while, in the morality of the best Pagan nations, duty to the State holds even a disproportionate place, infringing on the just liberty of the individual ; in purely Christian ethics, that grand department of duty is scarcely noticed or acknowledged. It is in the Koran, not the New Testament, that we read the maxim—' A ruler who appoints any man to an office, when there is in his dominions another man better qualified for it, sins against God and against the State.' What little recognition the idea of obligation to the public obtains in modern morality, is derived from Greek and Roman sources, not from Christian ; as, even in the morality of private life, whatever exists of magnanimity, high-mindedness, personal dignity, even the sense of honour, is derived from the purely human, not the religious part of our education, and never could have grown out of a standard of ethics in which the only worth, professedly recognized, is that of obedience.

I am as far as any one from pretending that these defects are necessarily inherent in the Christian ethics, in every manner in which it can be conceived, or that the many requisites of a complete moral doctrine which it does not contain, do not admit of being reconciled with it. Far less would I insinuate this of the doctrines and precepts of Christ himself. I believe that the sayings of Christ are all, that I can see any evidence of their having been intended to be ; that they are irreconcilable with nothing which a comprehensive morality requires ; that everything which is excellent in ethics may be brought within them, with no greater violence to their language than has been done to it by all who have attempted to deduce from them any practical system of conduct whatever. But it is quite consistent with this, to believe that they contain, and were meant to contain, only a part of the truth ; that many essential elements of the highest morality are among the things which are not provided for, nor intended to be provided for, in the recorded deliverances of the Founder of Christianity, and which have been entirely thrown aside in the system of ethics erected on the basis of those deliverances by the Christian Church. And this being so, I think it a great error to persist in attempting to find in the Christian doctrine that complete rule for our guidance, which its author intended it to sanction and enforce, but only partially to provide. I believe, too, that this narrow theory is becoming a grave practical evil, detracting greatly from the value of the moral training and instruction, which so many well-meaning persons are now at length exerting themselves to promote. I much fear that by attempting to form the mind and feelings on an exclusively religious type, and discarding those secular standards (as for want of a better name they may be called) which heretofore co-existed with and supplemented the Christian ethics, receiving some of its spirit, and infusing into it some of theirs, there will result, and is even now resulting, a low, abject, servile type of character, which, submit itself as it may to what it deems the Supreme Will, is incapable of rising to or sympathizing in the conception of Supreme Goodness. I believe that other ethics than any which can be evolved from exclusively Christian sources, must exist side by side with Christian ethics to produce the moral regeneration of mankind ; and that the Christian system is no exception to the rule, that in an imperfect state of the human mind, the interests of truth require a diversity of opinions. It is not necessary that in ceasing to ignore the moral truths not contained in Christianity, men should ignore any of those which it does contain. Such prejudice, or oversight, when it occurs, is altogether an evil ; but it is one from which

we cannot hope to be always exempt, and must be
regarded as the price paid for an inestimable good.
The exclusive pretension made by a part of the truth
to be the whole, must and ought to be protested
against; and if a reactionary impulse should make
the protestors unjust in their turn, this one-sidedness,
like the other, may be lamented, but must be tolerated.
If Christians would teach infidels to be just to Christianity, they should themselves be just to infidelity.
It can do truth no service to blink the fact, known
to all who have the most ordinary acquaintance with
literary history, that a large portion of the noblest and
most valuable moral teaching has been the work, not
only of men who did not know, but of men who knew
and rejected, the Christian faith.

I do not pretend that the most unlimited use of the
freedom of enunciating all possible opinions would put
an end to the evils of religious or philosophical sec-
tarianism. Every truth which men of narrow capacity
are in earnest about, is sure to be asserted, inculcated,
and in many ways even acted on, as if no other truth
existed in the world, or at all events none that could
limit or qualify the first. I acknowledge that the
tendency of all opinions to become sectarian is not
cured by the freest discussion, but is often heightened
and exacerbated thereby; the truth which ought to
have been, but was not, seen, being rejected all the
more violently because proclaimed by persons regarded
as opponents. But it is not on the impassioned partisan, it is on the calmer and more disinterested by-
stander, that this collision of opinions works its salutary
effect. Not the violent conflict between parts of the
truth, but the quiet suppression of half of it, is the
formidable evil; there is always hope when people are
forced to listen to both sides; it is when they attend
only to one that errors harden into prejudices, and
truth itself ceases to have the effect of truth, by being
exaggerated into falsehood. And since there are few
mental attributes more rare than that judicial faculty
which can sit in intelligent judgement between two

sides of a question, of which only one is represented by an advocate before it, truth has no chance but in proportion as every side of it, every opinion which embodies any fraction of the truth, not only finds advocates, but is so advocated as to be listened to.

We have now recognized the necessity to the mental well-being of mankind (on which all their other well-being depends) of freedom of opinion, and freedom of the expression of opinion, on four distinct grounds; which we will now briefly recapitulate.

First, if any opinion is compelled to silence, that opinion may, for aught we can certainly know, be true. To deny this is to assume our own infallibility.

Secondly, though the silenced opinion be an error, it may, and very commonly does, contain a portion of truth; and since the general or prevailing opinion on any subject is rarely or never the whole truth, it is only by the collision of adverse opinions that the remainder of the truth has any chance of being supplied.

Thirdly, even if the received opinion be not only true, but the whole truth; unless it is suffered to be, and actually is, vigorously and earnestly contested, it will, by most of those who receive it, be held in the manner of a prejudice, with little comprehension or feeling of its rational grounds. And not only this, but, fourthly, the meaning of the doctrine itself will be in danger of being lost, or enfeebled, and deprived of its vital effect on the character and conduct: the dogma becoming a mere formal profession, inefficacious for good, but cumbering the ground, and preventing the growth of any real and heartfelt conviction, from reason or personal experience.

Before quitting the subject of freedom of opinion, it is fit to take some notice of those who say, that the free expression of all opinions should be permitted, on condition that the manner be temperate, and do not pass the bounds of fair discussion. Much might be

said on the impossibility of fixing where these supposed
bounds are to be placed ; for if the test be offence to
those whose opinion is attacked, I think experience
testifies that this offence is given whenever the attack
is telling and powerful, and that every opponent who
pushes them hard, and whom they find it difficult to
answer, appears to them, if he shows any strong feeling
on the subject, an intemperate opponent. But this,
though an important consideration in a practical point
of view, merges in a more fundamental objection. Undoubtedly the manner of asserting an opinion, even
though it be a true one, may be very objectionable,
and may justly incur severe censure. But the principal
offences of the kind are such as it is mostly impossible,
unless by accidental self-betrayal, to bring home to
conviction. The gravest of them is, to argue sophistic-
ally, to suppress facts or arguments, to misstate the
elements of the case, or misrepresent the opposite
opinion. But all this, even to the most aggravated
degree, is so continually done in perfect good faith,
by persons who are not considered, and in many other
respects may not deserve to be considered, ignorant
or incompetent, that it is rarely possible on adequate
grounds conscientiously to stamp the misrepresentation
as morally culpable ; and still less could law presume
to interfere with this kind of controversial misconduct.
With regard to what is commonly meant by intemperate discussion, namely invective, sarcasm, personality, and the like, the denunciation of these weapons
would deserve more sympathy if it were ever proposed
to interdict them equally to both sides ; but it is only
desired to restrain the employment of them against
the prevailing opinion : against the unprevailing they
may not only be used without general disapproval, but
will be likely to obtain for him who uses them the
praise of honest zeal and righteous indignation. Yet
whatever mischief arises from their use, is greatest
when they are employed against the comparatively
defenceless ; and whatever unfair advantage can be
derived by any opinion from this mode of asserting

it, accrues almost exclusively to received opinions.
The worst offence of this kind which can be committed
by a polemic, is to stigmatize those who hold the contrary opinion as bad and immoral men. To calumny
of this sort, those who hold any unpopular opinion
are peculiarly exposed, because they are in general few
and uninfluential, and nobody but themselves feels
much interested in seeing justice done them ; but this
weapon is, from the nature of the case, denied to those
who attack a prevailing opinion : they can neither use
it with safety to themselves, nor, if they could, would
it do anything but recoil on their own cause. In
general, opinions contrary to those commonly received
can only obtain a hearing by studied moderation of
language, and the most cautious avoidance of unnecessary offence, from which they hardly ever deviate even
in a slight degree without losing ground : while un-
measured vituperation employed on the side of the
prevailing opinion, really does deter people from professing contrary opinions, and from listening to those
who profess them. For the interest, therefore, of truth
and justice, it is far more important to restrain this
employment of vituperative language than the other ;
and, for example, if it were necessary to choose, there
would be much more need to discourage offensive
attacks on infidelity, than on religion. It is, however,
obvious that law and authority have no business with
restraining either, while opinion ought, in every instance, to determine its verdict by the circumstances
of the individual case ; condemning every one, on
whichever side of the argument he places himself, in
whose mode of advocacy either want of candour, or
malignity, bigotry, or intolerance of feeling manifest
themselves ; but not inferring these vices from the
side which a person takes, though it be the contrary
side of the question to our own : and giving merited
honour to every one, whatever opinion he may hold,
who has calmness to see and honesty to state what
his opponents and their opinions really are, exag-
gerating nothing to their discredit, keeping nothing

back which tells, or can be supposed to tell, in their favour. This is the real morality of public discussion: and if often violated, I am happy to think that there are many controversialists who to a great extent observe it, and a still greater number who conscientiously strive towards it.

CHAPTER III

OF INDIVIDUALITY, AS ONE OF THE ELEMENTS OF WELL-BEING

SUCH being the reasons which make it imperative that human beings should be free to form opinions, and to express their opinions without reserve ; and such the baneful consequences to the intellectual, and through that to the moral nature of man, unless this liberty is either conceded, or asserted in spite of prohibition ; let us next examine whether the same reasons do not require that men should be free to act upon their opinions—to carry these out in their lives, without hindrance, either physical or moral, from their fellow men, so long as it is at their own risk and peril. This last proviso is of course indispensable. No one pretends that actions should be as free as opinions. On the contrary, even opinions lose their immunity, when the circumstances in which they are expressed are such as to constitute their expression a positive instigation to some mischievous act. An opinion that corn-dealers are starvers of the poor, or that private property is robbery, ought to be unmolested when simply circulated through the press, but may justly incur punishment when delivered orally to an excited mob assembled before the house of a corn-dealer, or when handed about among the same mob in the form of a placard. Acts, of whatever kind, which, without justifiable cause, do harm to others, may be, and in the more important cases absolutely require to be, controlled by the unfavourable sentiments, and, when needful, by the active interference of mankind. The liberty of the individual must be thus far limited ; he must not make himself a nuisance to other people. But if he refrains from molesting others in what concerns them, and merely acts according to his own inclination and judgement in things which concern himself, the same reasons which show that opinion should be free, prove also that he should be allowed, without molestation, to carry his opinions into practice at his own cost. That mankind are not infallible; that their truths, for the most part, are only half-truths; that unity of opinion, unless resulting from the fullest and freest comparison of opposite opinions, is not desirable, and diversity not an evil, but a good, until mankind are much more capable than at present of recognizing all sides of the truth, are principles applicable to men's modes of action, not less than to their opinions. As it is useful that while mankind are imperfect there should be different opinions, so is it that there should be different experiments of living; that free scope should be given to varieties of character, short of injury to others; and that the worth of different modes of life should be proved practically, when any one thinks fit to try them. It is desirable, in short, that in things which do not primarily concern others, individuality should assert itself. Where, not the person's own character, but the traditions or customs of other people are the rule of conduct, there is wanting one of the principal ingredients of human happiness, and quite the chief ingredient of individual and social progress.

In maintaining this principle, the greatest difficulty to be encountered does not lie in the appreciation of means towards an acknowledged end, but in the indifference of persons in general to the end itself. If it were felt that the free development of individuality is one of the leading essentials of well-being; that it is not only a co-ordinate element with all that is designated by the terms civilization, instruction, education, culture, but is itself a necessary part and condition of all those things; there would be no danger that liberty should be undervalued, and the adjustment of the boundaries between it and social control would present no extraordinary difficulty. But the evil is, that individual spontaneity is hardly recognized by the common modes of thinking, as having any intrinsic worth, or deserving any regard on its own account. The majority, being satisfied with the ways of mankind as they now are (for it is they who make them what they are), cannot comprehend why those ways should not be good enough for everybody; and what is more, spontaneity forms no part of the ideal of the majority of moral and social reformers, but is rather looked on with jealousy, as a troublesome and perhaps rebellious obstruction to the general acceptance of what these reformers, in their own judgement, think would be best for mankind. Few persons, out of Germany, even comprehend the meaning of the doctrine which Wilhelm von Humboldt, so eminent both as a savant and as a politician, made the text of a treatise—that 'the end of man, or that which is prescribed by the eternal or immutable dictates of reason, and not suggested by vague and transient desires, is the highest and most harmonious development of his powers to a complete and consistent whole'; that, therefore, the object 'towards which every human being must ceaselessly direct his efforts, and on which especially those who design to influence their fellow men must ever keep their eyes, is the individuality of power and development'; that for this there are two requisites, 'freedom, and variety of situations'; and that from the union of these arise 'individual vigour and manifold diversity', which combine themselves in 'originality'.[1]

Little, however, as people are accustomed to a doctrine like that of Von Humboldt, and surprising as it may be to them to find so high a value attached to individuality, the question, one must nevertheless think, can only be one of degree. No one's idea of excellence in conduct is that people should do absolutely nothing but copy one another. No one would assert that people ought not to put into their mode of life, and into the conduct of their concerns, any impress whatever of their own judgement, or of their

---

[1] *The Sphere and Duties of Government*, from the German of Baron Wilhelm von Humboldt, pp. 11–13.

own individual character. On the other hand, it would be absurd to pretend that people ought to live as if nothing whatever had been known in the world before they came into it; as if experience had as yet done nothing towards showing that one mode of existence, or of conduct, is preferable to another. Nobody denies that people should be so taught and trained in youth, as to know and benefit by the ascertained results of human experience. But it is the privilege and proper condition of a human being, arrived at the maturity of his faculties, to use and interpret experience in his own way. It is for him to find out what part of recorded experience is properly applicable to his own circumstances and character. The traditions and customs of other people are, to a certain extent, evidence of what their experience has taught *them*; presumptive evidence, and as such, have a claim to his deference : but, in the first place, their experience may be too narrow; or they may not have interpreted it rightly. Secondly, their interpretation of experience may be correct, but unsuitable to him. Customs are made for customary circumstances, and customary characters ; and his circumstances or his character may be uncustomary. Thirdly, though the customs be both good as customs, and suitable to him, yet to conform to custom, merely *as* custom, does not educate or develop in him any of the qualities which are the distinctive endowment of a human being. The human faculties of perception, judgement, discriminative feeling, mental activity, and even moral preference, are exercised only in making a choice. He who does anything because it is the custom, makes no choice. He gains no practice either in discerning or in desiring what is best. The mental and moral, like the muscular powers, are improved only by being used. The faculties are called into no exercise by doing a thing merely because others do it, no more than by believing a thing only because others believe it. If the grounds of an opinion are not conclusive to the person's own reason, his reason cannot be strengthened, but is likely to be weakened, by his adopting it : and if the inducements to an act are not such as are consentaneous to his own feelings and character (where affection, or the rights of others, are not concerned) it is so much done towards rendering his feelings and character inert and torpid, instead of active and energetic.

He who lets the world, or his own portion of it, choose his plan of life for him, has no need of any other faculty than the ape-like one of imitation. He who chooses his plan for himself, employs all his faculties. He must use observation to see, reasoning and judgement to foresee, activity to gather materials for decision, discrimination to decide, and when he has decided, firmness and self-control to hold to his deliberate decision. And these qualities he requires and exercises exactly in proportion as the part of his conduct which he determines according to his own judgement and feelings is a large one. It is possible that he might be guided in some good path, and kept out of harm's way, without any of these things. But what will be his comparative worth as a human being ? It really is of importance, not only what men do, but also what manner of men they are that do it. Among the works of man, which human life is rightly employed in perfecting and beautifying, the first in importance surely is man himself. Supposing it were possible to get houses built, corn grown, battles fought, causes tried, and even churches erected and prayers said, by machinery—by automatons in human form—it would be a considerable loss to exchange for these automatons even the men and women who at present inhabit the more civilized parts of the world, and who assuredly are but starved specimens of what nature can and will produce. Human nature is not a machine to be built after a model, and set to do exactly the work prescribed for it, but a tree, which requires to grow and develop itself on all sides, according to the tendency of the inward forces which make it a living thing.

It will probably be conceded that it is desirable people should exercise their understandings, and that

an intelligent following of custom, or even occasionally
an intelligent deviation from custom, is better than
a blind and simply mechanical adhesion to it. To
a certain extent it is admitted, that our understanding
should be our own: but there is not the same willingness to admit that our desires and impulses should be
our own likewise; or that to possess impulses of our
own, and of any strength, is anything but a peril and
a snare. Yet desires and impulses are as much a part
of a perfect human being, as beliefs and restraints:
and strong impulses are only perilous when not properly
balanced; when one set of aims and inclinations is
developed into strength, while others, which ought to
co-exist with them, remain weak and inactive. It is
not because men's desires are strong that they act ill;
it is because their consciences are weak. There is no
natural connexion between strong impulses and a weak
conscience. The natural connexion is the other way.
To say that one person's desires and feelings are
stronger and more various than those of another, is
merely to say that he has more of the raw material
of human nature, and is therefore capable, perhaps of
more evil, but certainly of more good. Strong impulses
are but another name for energy. Energy may be
turned to bad uses; but more good may always be
made of an energetic nature, than of an indolent and
impassive one. Those who have most natural feeling,
are always those whose cultivated feelings may be made
the strongest. The same strong susceptibilities which
make the personal impulses vivid and powerful, are
also the source from whence are generated the most
passionate love of virtue, and the sternest self-control.
It is through the cultivation of these, that society both
does its duty and protects its interests: not by rejecting the stuff of which heroes are made, because it
knows not how to make them. A person whose desires
and impulses are his own—are the expression of his
own nature, as it has been developed and modified by
his own culture—is said to have a character. One
whose desires and impulses are not his own, has no

character, no more than a steam-engine has a character. If, in addition to being his own, his impulses are strong, and are under the government of a strong will, he has an energetic character. Whoever thinks that individuality of desires and impulses should not be encouraged to unfold itself, must maintain that society has no need of strong natures—is not the better for containing many persons who have much character—and that a high general average of energy is not desirable.

In some early states of society, these forces might be, and were, too much ahead of the power which society then possessed of disciplining and controlling them. There has been a time when the element of spontaneity and individuality was in excess, and the social principle had a hard struggle with it. The difficulty then was, to induce men of strong bodies or minds to pay obedience to any rules which required them to control their impulses. To overcome this difficulty, law and discipline, like the Popes struggling against the Emperors, asserted a power over the whole man, claiming to control all his life in order to control his character—which society had not found any other sufficient means of binding. But society has now fairly got the better of individuality; and the danger which threatens human nature is not the excess, but the deficiency, of personal impulses and preferences. Things are vastly changed, since the passions of those who were strong by station or by personal endowment were in a state of habitual rebellion against laws and ordinances, and required to be rigorously chained up to enable the persons within their reach to enjoy any particle of security. In our times, from the highest class of society down to the lowest, every one lives as under the eye of a hostile and dreaded censorship. Not only in what concerns others, but in what concerns only themselves, the individual or the family do not ask themselves—what do I prefer ? or, what would suit my character and disposition ? or, what would allow the best and highest in me to have fair play,

and enable it to grow and thrive ? They ask themselves, what is suitable to my position ? what is usually
done by persons of my station and pecuniary circumstances ? or (worse still) what is usually done by persons
of a station and circumstances superior to mine ? I do
not mean that they choose what is customary, in preference to what suits their own inclination. It does
not occur to them to have any inclination, except for
what is customary. Thus the mind itself is bowed to
the yoke : even in what people do for pleasure, conformity is the first thing thought of ; they like in
crowds ; they exercise choice only among things commonly done : peculiarity of taste, eccentricity of conduct, are shunned equally with crimes : until by dint
of not following their own nature, they have no nature
to follow : their human capacities are withered and
starved : they become incapable of any strong wishes
or native pleasures, and are generally without either
opinions or feelings of home growth, or properly their
own. Now is this, or is it not, the desirable condition
of human nature ?

It is so, on the Calvinistic theory. According to
that, the one great offence of man is self-will. All
the good of which humanity is capable, is comprised
in obedience. You have no choice ; thus you must
do, and no otherwise : ' whatever is not a duty, is
a sin.' Human nature being radically corrupt, there
is no redemption for any one until human nature is
killed within him. To one holding this theory of life,
crushing out any of the human faculties, capacities,
and susceptibilities, is no evil : man needs no capacity,
but that of surrendering himself to the will of God :
and if he uses any of his faculties for any other purpose but to do that supposed will more effectually,
he is better without them. This is the theory of
Calvinism ; and it is held, in a mitigated form, by
many who do not consider themselves Calvinists ; the
mitigation consisting in giving a less ascetic interpretation to the alleged will of God ; asserting it to be his
will that mankind should gratify some of their inclina-

tions; of course not in the manner they themselves
prefer, but in the way of obedience, that is, in a way
prescribed to them by authority; and, therefore,
by the necessary conditions of the case, the same
for all.

In some such insidious form there is at present a
strong tendency to this narrow theory of life, and to
the pinched and hidebound type of human character
which it patronizes. Many persons, no doubt, sincerely
think that human beings thus cramped and dwarfed,
are as their Maker designed them to be; just as many
have thought that trees are a much finer thing when
clipped into pollards, or cut out into figures of animals,
than as nature made them. But if it be any part of
religion to believe that man was made by a good
Being, it is more consistent with that faith to believe,
that this Being gave all human faculties that they
might be cultivated and unfolded, not rooted out and
consumed, and that he takes delight in every nearer
approach made by his creatures to the ideal conception embodied in them, every increase in any of their
capabilities of comprehension, of action, or of enjoyment. There is a different type of human excellence
from the Calvinistic; a conception of humanity as
having its nature bestowed on it for other purposes
than merely to be abnegated. 'Pagan self-assertion'
is one of the elements of human worth, as well as
'Christian self-denial'.[1] There is a Greek ideal of self-
development, which the Platonic and Christian ideal
of self-government blends with, but does not supersede.
It may be better to be a John Knox than an Alcibiades,
but it is better to be a Pericles than either; nor would
a Pericles, if we had one in these days, be without
anything good which belonged to John Knox.

It is not by wearing down into uniformity all that
is individual in themselves, but by cultivating it and
calling it forth, within the limits imposed by the rights
and interests of others, that human beings become

---

[1] Sterling's *Essays*.

a noble and beautiful object of contemplation; and
as the works partake the character of those who do
them, by the same process human life also becomes
rich, diversified, and animating, furnishing more abundant aliment to high thoughts and elevating feelings,
and strengthening the tie which binds every individual
to the race, by making the race infinitely better worth
belonging to. In proportion to the development of
his individuality, each person becomes more valuable
to himself, and is therefore capable of being more
valuable to others. There is a greater fullness of life
about his own existence, and when there is more life
in the units there is more in the mass which is composed of them. As much compression as is necessary
to prevent the stronger specimens of human nature
from encroaching on the rights of others, cannot be
dispensed with; but for this there is ample compensation even in the point of view of human development.
The means of development which the individual loses
by being prevented from gratifying his inclinations to
the injury of others, are chiefly obtained at the expense
of the development of other people. And even to
himself there is a full equivalent in the better development of the social part of his nature, rendered possible
by the restraint put upon the selfish part. To be held
to rigid rules of justice for the sake of others, develops
the feelings and capacities which have the good of
others for their object. But to be restrained in things
not affecting their good, by their mere displeasure,
develops nothing valuable, except such force of
character as may unfold itself in resisting the restraint.
If acquiesced in, it dulls and blunts the whole nature.
To give any fair play to the nature of each, it is essential that different persons should be allowed to lead
different lives. In proportion as this latitude has been
exercised in any age, has that age been noteworthy
to posterity. Even despotism does not produce its
worst effects, so long as individuality exists under it;
and whatever crushes individuality is despotism, by
whatever name it may be called, and whether it pro-

fesses to be enforcing the will of God or the injunctions of men.

Having said that Individuality is the same thing with development, and that it is only the cultivation of individuality which produces, or can produce, well-developed human beings, I might here close the argument: for what more or better can be said of any condition of human affairs, than that it brings human beings themselves nearer to the best thing they can be ? or what worse can be said of any obstruction to good, than that it prevents this ? Doubtless, however, these considerations will not suffice to convince those who most need convincing ; and it is necessary further to show, that these developed human beings are of some use to the undeveloped—to point out to those who do not desire liberty, and would not avail themselves of it, that they may be in some intelligible manner rewarded for allowing other people to make use of it without hindrance.

In the first place, then, I would suggest that they might possibly learn something from them. It will not be denied by anybody, that originality is a valuable element in human affairs. There is always need of persons not only to discover new truths, and point out when what were once truths are true no longer, but also to commence new practices, and set the example of more enlightened conduct, and better taste and sense in human life. This cannot well be gainsaid by anybody who does not believe that the world has already attained perfection in all its ways and practices. It is true that this benefit is not capable of being rendered by everybody alike : there are but few persons, in comparison with the whole of mankind, whose experiments, if adopted by others, would be likely to be any improvement on established practice. But these few are the salt of the earth ; without them, human life would become a stagnant pool. Not only is it they who introduce good things which did not before exist ; it is they who keep the life in those which already existed. If there were nothing new to be done, would human intellect cease to be necessary ? Would it be a reason why those who do the old things should forget why they are done, and do them like cattle, not like human beings ? There is only too great a tendency in the best beliefs and practices to degenerate into the mechanical ; and unless there were a succession of persons whose ever-recurring originality prevents the grounds of those beliefs and practices from becoming merely traditional, such dead matter would not resist the smallest shock from anything really alive, and there would be no reason why civilization should not die out, as in the Byzantine Empire. Persons of genius, it is true, are, and are always likely to be, a small minority ; but in order to have them, it is necessary to preserve the soil in which they grow. Genius can only breathe freely in an *atmosphere* of freedom. Persons of genius are, *ex vi termini, more* individual than any other people—less capable, consequently, of fitting themselves, without hurtful compression, into any of the small number of moulds which society provides in order to save its members the trouble of forming their own character. If from timidity they consent to be forced into one of these moulds, and to let all that part of themselves which cannot expand under the pressure remain unexpanded, society will be little the better for their genius. If they are of a strong character, and break their fetters, they become a mark for the society which has not succeeded in reducing them to commonplace, to point at with solemn warning as ' wild ', ' erratic,' and the like ; much as if one should complain of the Niagara river for not flowing smoothly between its banks like a Dutch canal.

I insist thus emphatically on the importance of genius, and the necessity of allowing it to unfold itself freely both in thought and in practice, being well aware that no one will deny the position in theory, but knowing also that almost every one, in reality, is totally indifferent to it. People think genius a fine thing if it enables a man to write an exciting poem,

or paint a picture. But in its true sense, that of
originality in thought and action, though no one says
that it is not a thing to be admired, nearly all, at heart,
think that they can do very well without it. Unhappily
this is too natural to be wondered at. Originality is
the one thing which unoriginal minds cannot feel the use
of. They cannot see what it is to do for them : how
should they ? If they could see what it would do for
them, it would not be originality. The first service
which originality has to render them, is that of opening
their eyes : which being once fully done, they would
have a chance of being themselves original. Meanwhile, recollecting that nothing was ever yet done
which some one was not the first to do, and that all
good things which exist are the fruits of originality,
let them be modest enough to believe that there is
something still left for it to accomplish, and assure
themselves that they are more in need of originality,
the less they are conscious of the want.

In sober truth, whatever homage may be professed,
or even paid, to real or supposed mental superiority,
the general tendency of things throughout the world
is to render mediocrity the ascendant power among
mankind. In ancient history, in the middle ages, and
in a diminishing degree through the long transition
from feudality to the present time, the individual was
a power in himself ; and if he had either great talents
or a high social position, he was a considerable power.
At present individuals are lost in the crowd. In politics
it is almost a triviality to say that public opinion now
rules the world. The only power deserving the name
is that of masses, and of governments while they make
themselves the organ of the tendencies and instincts
of masses. This is as true in the moral and social
relations of private life as in public transactions. Those
whose opinions go by the name of public opinion, are
not always the same sort of public : in America they
are the whole white population ; in England, chiefly
the middle class. But they are always a mass, that
is to say, collective mediocrity. And what is a still

greater novelty, the mass do not now take their opinions from dignitaries in Church or State, from ostensible leaders, or from books. Their thinking is done for them by men much like themselves, addressing them or speaking in their name, on the spur of the moment, through the newspapers. I am not complaining of all this. I do not assert that anything better is compatible, as a general rule, with the present low state of the human mind. But that does not hinder the government of mediocrity from being mediocre government. No government by a democracy or a numerous aristocracy, either in its political acts or in the opinions, qualities, and tone of mind which it fosters, ever did or could rise above mediocrity, except in so far as the sovereign Many have let themselves be guided (which in their best times they always have done) by the counsels and influence of a more highly gifted and instructed One or Few. The initiation of all wise or noble things, comes and must come from individuals; generally at first from some one individual. The honour and glory of the average man is that he is capable of following that initiative; that he can respond internally to wise and noble things, and be led to them with his eyes open. I am not countenancing the sort of 'hero-worship' which applauds the strong man of genius for forcibly seizing on the government of the world and making it do his bidding in spite of itself. All he can claim is, freedom to point out the way. The power of compelling others into it, is not only inconsistent with the freedom and development of all the rest, but corrupting to the strong man himself. It does seem, however, that when the opinions of masses of merely average men are everywhere become or becoming the dominant power, the counterpoise and corrective to that tendency would be, the more and more pronounced individuality of those who stand on the higher eminences of thought. It is in these circumstances most especially, that exceptional individuals, instead of being deterred, should be encouraged in acting differently from the mass. In

other times there was no advantage in their doing so,
unless they acted not only differently, but better. In
this age, the mere example of nonconformity, the mere
refusal to bend the knee to custom, is itself a service.
Precisely because the tyranny of opinion is such as to
make eccentricity a reproach, it is desirable, in order
to break through that tyranny, that people should be
eccentric. Eccentricity has always abounded when and
where strength of character has abounded ; and the
amount of eccentricity in a society has generally been
proportional to the amount of genius, mental vigour,
and moral courage which it contained. That so few
now dare to be eccentric, marks the chief danger of
the time.

I have said that it is important to give the freest
scope possible to uncustomary things, in order that it
may in time appear which of these are fit to be converted into customs. But independence of action, and
disregard of custom, are not solely deserving of encouragement for the chance they afford that better
modes of action, and customs more worthy of general
adoption, may be struck out ; nor is it only persons
of decided mental superiority who have a just claim
to carry on their lives in their own way. There is no
reason that all human existence should be constructed
on some one or some small number of patterns. If
a person possesses any tolerable amount of common
sense and experience, his own mode of laying out his
existence is the best, not because it is the best in itself,
but because it is his own mode. Human beings are
not like sheep ; and even sheep are not undistinguish-
ably alike. A man cannot get a coat or a pair of boots
to fit him, unless they are either made to his measure,
or he has a whole warehouseful to choose from : and
is it easier to fit him with a life than with a coat, or
are human beings more like one another in their whole
physical and spiritual conformation than in the shape
of their feet ? If it were only that people have diversities of taste, that is reason enough for not attempting
to shape them all after one model. But different per-

sons also require different conditions for their spiritual development; and can no more exist healthily in the same moral, than all the variety of plants can in the same physical, atmosphere and climate. The same things which are helps to one person towards the cultivation of his higher nature, are hindrances to another. The same mode of life is a healthy excitement to one, keeping all his faculties of action and enjoyment in their best order, while to another it is a distracting burthen, which suspends or crushes all internal life. Such are the differences among human beings in their sources of pleasure, their susceptibilities of pain, and the operation on them of different physical and moral agencies, that unless there is a corresponding diversity in their modes of life, they neither obtain their fair share of happiness, nor grow up to the mental, moral, and aesthetic stature of which their nature is capable. Why then should tolerance, as far as the public sentiment is concerned, extend only to tastes and modes of life which extort acquiescence by the multitude of their adherents? Nowhere (except in some monastic institutions) is diversity of taste entirely unrecognized; a person may, without blame, either like or dislike rowing, or smoking, or music, or athletic exercises, or chess, or cards, or study, because both those who like each of these things, and those who dislike them, are too numerous to be put down. But the man, and still more the woman, who can be accused either of doing ' what nobody does ', or of not doing ' what everybody does ', is the subject of as much depreciatory remark as if he or she had committed some grave moral delinquency. Persons require to possess a title, or some other badge of rank, or of the consideration of people of rank, to be able to indulge somewhat in the luxury of doing as they like without detriment to their estimation. To indulge somewhat, I repeat: for whoever allow themselves much of that indulgence, incur the risk of something worse than disparaging speeches—they are in peril of a commission *de lunatico*, and of having their property taken from them and given to their relations.[1]

There is one characteristic of the present direction of public opinion, peculiarly calculated to make it intolerant of any marked demonstration of individuality. The general average of mankind are not only moderate in intellect, but also moderate in inclinations: they have no tastes or wishes strong enough to incline them to do anything unusual, and they consequently do not understand those who have, and class all such with the wild and intemperate whom they are accustomed

[1] There is something both contemptible and frightful in the sort of evidence on which, of late years, any person can be judicially declared unfit for the management of his affairs; and after his death, his disposal of his property can be set aside, if there is enough of it to pay the expenses of litigation—which are charged on the property itself. All the minute details of his daily life are pried into, and whatever is found which, seen through the medium of the perceiving and describing faculties of the lowest of the low, bears an appearance unlike absolute commonplace, is laid before the jury as evidence of insanity, and often with success; the jurors being little, if at all, less vulgar and ignorant than the witnesses; while the judges, with that extraordinary want of knowledge of human nature and life which continually astonishes us in English lawyers, often help to mislead them. These trials speak volumes as to the state of feeling and opinion among the vulgar with regard to human liberty. So far from setting any value on individuality—so far from respecting the right of each individual to act, in things indifferent, as seems good to his own judgement and inclinations, judges and juries cannot even conceive that a person in a state of sanity can desire such freedom. In former days, when it was proposed to burn atheists, charitable people used to suggest putting them in a mad-house instead: it would be nothing surprising nowadays were we to see this done, and the doers applauding themselves, because, instead of persecuting for religion, they had adopted so humane and Christian a mode of treating these unfortunates, not without a silent satisfaction at their having thereby obtained their deserts.

to look down upon. Now, in addition to this fact which is general, we have only to suppose that a strong movement has set in towards the improvement of morals, and it is evident what we have to expect. In these days such a movement has set in ; much has actually been effected in the way of increased regularity of conduct, and discouragement of excesses ; and there is a philanthropic spirit abroad, for the exercise of which there is no more inviting field than the moral and prudential improvement of our fellow creatures. These tendencies of the times cause the public to be more disposed than at most former periods to prescribe general rules of conduct, and endeavour to make every one conform to the approved standard. And that standard, express or tacit, is to desire nothing strongly. Its ideal of character is to be without any marked character ; to maim by compression, like a Chinese lady's foot, every part of human nature which stands out prominently, and tends to make the person markedly dissimilar in outline to commonplace humanity.

As is usually the case with ideals which exclude one-half of what is desirable, the present standard of approbation produces only an inferior imitation of the other half. Instead of great energies guided by vigorous reason, and strong feelings strongly controlled by a conscientious will, its result is weak feelings and weak energies, which therefore can be kept in outward conformity to rule without any strength either of will or of reason. Already energetic characters on any large scale are becoming merely traditional. There is now scarcely any outlet for energy in this country except business. The energy expended in this may still be regarded as considerable. What little is left from that employment, is expended on some hobby ; which may be a useful, even a philanthropic hobby, but is always some one thing, and generally a thing of small dimensions. The greatness of England is now all collective : individually small, we only appear capable of anything great by our habit of combining ; and with this our moral and religious philanthropists are perfectly con-

tented. But it was men of another stamp than this
that made England what it has been; and men of
another stamp will be needed to prevent its decline.

The despotism of custom is everywhere the standing
hindrance to human advancement, being in unceasing
antagonism to that disposition to aim at something
better than customary, which is called, according to
circumstances, the spirit of liberty, or that of progress
or improvement. The spirit of improvement is not
always a spirit of liberty, for it may aim at forcing
improvements on an unwilling people; and the spirit
of liberty, in so far as it resists such attempts, may
ally itself locally and temporarily with the opponents
of improvement; but the only unfailing and permanent
source of improvement is liberty, since by it there are
as many possible independent centres of improvement
as there are individuals. The progressive principle,
however, in either shape, whether as the love of liberty
or of improvement, is antagonistic to the sway of
Custom, involving at least emancipation from that
yoke; and the contest between the two constitutes
the chief interest of the history of mankind. The
greater part of the world has, properly speaking, no
history, because the despotism of Custom is complete.
This is the case over the whole East. Custom is there,
in all things, the final appeal; justice and right mean
conformity to custom; the argument of custom no
one, unless some tyrant intoxicated with power, thinks
of resisting. And we see the result. Those nations
must once have had originality; they did not start
out of the ground populous, lettered, and versed in
many of the arts of life; they made themselves all
this, and were then the greatest and most powerful
nations of the world. What are they now? The
subjects or dependants of tribes whose forefathers
wandered in the forests when theirs had magnificent
palaces and gorgeous temples, but over whom custom
exercised only a divided rule with liberty and progress.
A people, it appears, may be progressive for a certain
length of time, and then stop: when does it stop?

When it ceases to possess individuality. If a similar change should befall the nations of Europe, it will not be in exactly the same shape : the despotism of custom with which these nations are threatened is not precisely stationariness. It proscribes singularity, but it does not preclude change, provided all change together. We have discarded the fixed costumes of our forefathers ; every one must still dress like other people, but the fashion may change once or twice a year. We thus take care that when there is change it shall be for change's sake, and not from any idea of beauty or convenience ; for the same idea of beauty or convenience would not strike all the world at the same moment, and be simultaneously thrown aside by all at another moment. But we are progressive as well as changeable : we continually make new inventions in mechanical things, and keep them until they are again superseded by better ; we are eager for improvement in politics, in education, even in morals, though in this last our idea of improvement chiefly consists in persuading or forcing other people to be as good as ourselves. It is not progress that we object to ; on the contrary, we flatter ourselves that we are the most progressive people who ever lived. It is individuality that we war against : we should think we had done wonders if we had made ourselves all alike ; forgetting that the unlikeness of one person to another is generally the first thing which draws the attention of either to the imperfection of his own type, and the superiority of another, or the possibility, by combining the advantages of both, of producing something better than either. We have a warning example in China—a nation of much talent, and, in some respects, even wisdom, owing to the rare good fortune of having been provided at an early period with a particularly good set of customs, the work, in some measure, of men to whom even the most enlightened European must accord, under certain limitations, the title of sages and philosophers. They are remarkable, too, in the excellence of their apparatus for impressing, as far as possible, the best wisdom they possess upon every mind in the community, and securing that those who have appropriated most of it shall occupy the posts of honour and power. Surely the people who did this have discovered the secret of human progressiveness, and must have kept themselves steadily at the head of the movement of the world. On the contrary, they have become stationary—have remained so for thousands of years; and if they are ever to be farther improved, it must be by foreigners. They have succeeded beyond all hope in what English philanthropists are so industriously working at—in making a people all alike, all governing their thoughts and conduct by the same maxims and rules; and these are the fruits. The modern *régime* of public opinion is, in an unorganized form, what the Chinese educational and political systems are in an organized; and unless individuality shall be able successfully to assert itself against this yoke, Europe, notwithstanding its noble antecedents and its professed Christianity, will tend to become another China.

What is it that has hitherto preserved Europe from this lot? What has made the European family of nations an improving, instead of a stationary portion of mankind? Not any superior excellence in them, which, when it exists, exists as the effect, not as the cause; but their remarkable diversity of character and culture. Individuals, classes, nations, have been extremely unlike one another: they have struck out a great variety of paths, each leading to something valuable; and although at every period those who travelled in different paths have been intolerant of one another, and each would have thought it an excellent thing if all the rest could have been compelled to travel his road, their attempts to thwart each other's development have rarely had any permanent success, and each has in time endured to receive the good which the others have offered. Europe is, in my judgement, wholly indebted to this plurality of paths for its progressive and many-sided development. But it already begins to possess this benefit in a considerably less degree. It is decidedly advancing towards the Chinese ideal of making all people alike. M. de Tocqueville, in his last important work, remarks how much more the Frenchmen of the present day resemble one another, than did those even of the last generation. The same remark might be made of Englishmen in a far greater degree. In a passage already quoted from Wilhelm von Humboldt, he points out two things as necessary conditions of human development, because necessary to render people unlike one another; namely, freedom, and variety of situations. The second of these two conditions is in this country every day diminishing. The circumstances which surround different classes and individuals, and shape their characters, are daily becoming more assimilated. Formerly, different ranks, different neighbourhoods, different trades and professions, lived in what might be called different worlds; at present, to a great degree in the same. Comparatively speaking, they now read the same things, listen to the same things, see the same things, go to the same places, have their hopes and fears directed to the same objects, have the same rights and liberties, and the same means of asserting them. Great as are the differences of position which remain, they are nothing to those which have ceased. And the assimilation is still proceeding. All the political changes of the age promote it, since they all tend to raise the low and to lower the high. Every extension of education promotes it, because education brings people under common influences, and gives them access to the general stock of facts and sentiments. Improvements in the means of communication promote it, by bringing the inhabitants of distant places into personal contact, and keeping up a rapid flow of changes of residence between one place and another. The increase of commerce and manufactures promotes it, by diffusing more widely the advantages of easy circumstances, and opening all objects of ambition, even the highest, to general competition, whereby the desire of rising becomes no longer the character of a particular class, but of all classes. A more powerful agency than even all these, in bringing about a general similarity among mankind, is the complete establishment, in this and other free countries, of the ascendancy of public opinion in the State. As the various social eminences which enabled persons entrenched on them to disregard the opinion of the multitude, gradually become levelled; as the very idea of resisting the will of the public, when it is positively known that they have a will, disappears more and more from the minds of practical politicians; there ceases to be any social support for nonconformity—any substantive power in society, which, itself opposed to the ascendancy of numbers, is interested in taking under its protection opinions and tendencies at variance with those of the public.

The combination of all these causes forms so great a mass of influences hostile to Individuality, that it is not easy to see how it can stand its ground. It will do so with increasing difficulty, unless the intelligent part of the public can be made to feel its value— to see that it is good there should be differences, even though not for the better, even though, as it may appear to them, some should be for the worse. If the claims of Individuality are ever to be asserted, the time is now, while much is still wanting to complete the enforced assimilation. It is only in the earlier stages that any stand can be successfully made against the encroachment. The demand that all other people shall resemble ourselves, grows by what it feeds on. If resistance waits till life is reduced *nearly* to one uniform type, all deviations from that type will come to be considered impious, immoral, even monstrous and contrary to nature. Mankind speedily become unable to conceive diversity, when they have been for some time unaccustomed to see it.

CHAPTER IV

WHAT, then, is the rightful limit to the sovereignty of the individual over himself ? Where does the authority of society begin ? How much of human life should be assigned to individuality, and how much to society ?

Each will receive its proper share, if each has that which more particularly concerns it. To individuality should belong the part of life in which it is chiefly the individual that is interested ; to society, the part which chiefly interests society.

Though society is not founded on a contract, and though no good purpose is answered by inventing a contract in order to deduce social obligations from it, every one who receives the protection of society owes a return for the benefit, and the fact of living in society renders it indispensable that each should be bound to observe a certain line of conduct towards the rest. This conduct consists, first, in not injuring the interests of one another ; or rather certain interests, which, either by express legal provision or by tacit understanding, ought to be considered as rights ; and secondly, in each person's bearing his share (to be fixed on some equitable principle) of the labours and sacrifices incurred for defending the society or its members from injury and molestation. These conditions society is justified in enforcing at all costs to those who endeavour to withhold fulfilment. Nor is this all that society may do. The acts of an individual may be hurtful to others, or wanting in due consideration for their welfare, without going the length of violating any of their constituted rights. The offender may then be justly punished by opinion, though not by law. As soon as any part of a person's conduct affects prejudicially the interests of others, society has jurisdiction over it, and the question whether the general welfare will or will not be promoted by interfering with it, becomes open to discussion. But there is no room for entertaining any such question when a person's conduct affects the interests of no persons besides himself, or needs not affect them unless they like (all the persons concerned being of full age, and the ordinary amount of understanding). In all such cases there should be perfect freedom, legal and social, to do the action and stand the consequences.

It would be a great misunderstanding of this doctrine to suppose that it is one of selfish indifference, which pretends that human beings have no business with each other's conduct in life, and that they should not concern themselves about the well-doing or well-being of one another, unless their own interest is involved. Instead of any diminution, there is need of a great increase of disinterested exertion to promote the good of others. But disinterested benevolence can find other instruments to persuade people to their good, than whips and scourges, either of the literal or the metaphorical sort. I am the last person to undervalue the self-regarding virtues; they are only second in importance, if even second, to the social. It is equally the business of education to cultivate both. But even education works by conviction and persuasion as well as by compulsion, and it is by the former only that, when the period of education is past, the self-regarding virtues should be inculcated. Human beings owe to each other help to distinguish the better from the worse, and encouragement to choose the former and avoid the latter. They should be for ever stimulating each other to increased exercise of their higher faculties, and increased direction of their feelings and aims towards wise instead of foolish, elevating instead of degrading, objects and contemplations. But neither one person, nor any number of persons, is warranted in saying to another human creature of ripe years, that he shall not do with his life for his own benefit what he chooses to do with it. He is the person most interested in his own well-being : the interest which any other person, except in cases of strong personal attachment, can have in it, is trifling, compared with that which he himself has ; the interest which society has in him individually (except as to his conduct to others) is fractional, and altogether indirect : while, with respect to his own feelings and circumstances, the most ordinary man or woman has means of knowledge· immeasurably surpassing those that can be possessed by any one else. The interference of society to overrule his judgement and purposes in what only regards himself, must be grounded on general presumptions ; which may be altogether wrong, and even if right, are as likely as not to be misapplied to individual cases, by persons no better acquainted with the circumstances of such cases than those are who look at them merely from without. In this department, therefore, of human affairs, Individuality has its proper field of action. In the conduct of human beings towards one another, it is necessary that general rules should for the most part be observed, in order that people may know what they have to expect ; but in each person's own concerns, his individual spontaneity is entitled to free exercise. Considerations to aid his judgement, exhortations to strengthen his will, may be offered to him, even obtruded on him, by others ; but he himself is the final judge. All errors which he is likely to commit against advice and warning, are far outweighed by the evil of allowing others to constrain him to what they deem his good.

I do not mean that the feelings with which a person is regarded by others, ought not to be in any way affected by his self-regarding qualities or deficiencies. This is neither possible nor desirable. If he is eminent in any of the qualities which conduce to his own good, he is, so far, a proper object of admiration. He is so much the nearer to the ideal perfection of human nature. If he is grossly deficient in those qualities, a sentiment the opposite of admiration will follow.

There is a degree of folly, and a degree of what may be called (though the phrase is not unobjectionable) lowness or depravation of taste, which, though it cannot justify doing harm to the person who manifests it, renders him necessarily and properly a subject of distaste, or, in extreme cases, even of contempt : a person could not have the opposite qualities in due strength without entertaining these feelings. Though doing no wrong to any one, a person may so act as to compel us to judge him, and feel to him, as a fool, or as a being of an inferior order : and since this judgement and feeling are a fact which he would prefer to avoid, it is doing him a service to warn him of it beforehand, as of any other disagreeable consequence to which he exposes himself. It would be well, indeed, if this good office were much more freely rendered than the common notions of politeness at present permit, and if one person could honestly point out to another that he thinks him in fault, without being considered unmannerly or presuming. We have a right, also, in various ways, to act upon our unfavourable opinion of any one, not to the oppression of his individuality, but in the exercise of ours. We are not bound, for example, to seek his society ; we have a right to avoid it (though not to parade the avoidance), for we have a right to choose the society most acceptable to us. We have a right, and it may be our duty, to caution others against him, if we think his example or conversation likely to have a pernicious effect on those with whom he associates. We may give others a preference over him in optional good offices, except those which tend to his improvement. In these various modes a person may suffer very severe penalties at the hands of others, for faults which directly concern only himself ; but he suffers these penalties only in so far as they are the natural, and, as it were, the spontaneous consequences of the faults themselves, not because they are purposely inflicted on him for the sake of punishment. A person who shows rashness, obstinacy, self-conceit—who cannot live within moderate means—who cannot restrain himself from hurtful indulgences—who pursues animal pleasures at the expense of those of feeling and intellect—must expect to be lowered in the opinion of others, and to have a less share of their favourable sentiments ; but of this he has no right to complain, unless he has merited their favour by special excellence in his social relations, and has thus established a title to their good offices, which is not affected by his demerits towards himself.

What I contend for is, that the inconveniences which are strictly inseparable from the unfavourable judgement of others, are the only ones to which a person should ever be subjected for that portion of his conduct and character which concerns his own good, but which does not affect the interests of others in their relations with him. Acts injurious to others require a totally different treatment. Encroachment on their rights ; infliction on them of any loss or damage not justified by his own rights ; falsehood or duplicity in dealing with them ; unfair or ungenerous use of advantages over them ; even selfish abstinence from defending them against injury—these are fit objects of moral reprobation, and, in grave cases, of moral retribution and punishment. And not only these acts, but the dispositions which lead to them, are properly immoral, and fit subjects of disapprobation which may rise to abhorrence. Cruelty of disposition ; malice and ill nature ; that most anti-social and odious of all passions, envy ; dissimulation and insincerity ; irascibility on insufficient cause, and resentment disproportioned to the provocation ; the love of domineering over others ; the desire to engross more than one's share of advantages (the πλεονεξία of the Greeks) ; the pride which derives gratification from the abasement of others ; the egotism which thinks self and its concerns more important than everything else, and decides all doubtful questions in its own favour ;—these are moral vices, and constitute a bad and odious moral character : unlike the self-regarding faults previously mentioned, which are not properly immoralities, and to whatever pitch they may be carried, do not constitute wickedness. They may be proofs of any amount of folly, or want of personal dignity and self-respect; but they are only a subject of moral reprobation when they involve a breach of duty to others, for whose sake the individual is bound to have care for himself. What are called duties to ourselves are not socially obligatory, unless circumstances render them at the same time duties to others. The term duty to oneself, when it means anything more than prudence, means self-respect or self-development; and for none of these is any one accountable to his fellow creatures, because for none of them is it for the good of mankind that he be held accountable to them.

The distinction between the loss of consideration which a person may rightly incur by defect of prudence or of personal dignity, and the reprobation which is due to him for an offence against the rights of others, is not a merely nominal distinction. It makes a vast difference both in our feelings and in our conduct towards him, whether he displeases us in things in which we think we have a right to control him, or in things in which we know that we have not. If he displeases us, we may express our distaste, and we may stand aloof from a person as well as from a thing that displeases us; but we shall not therefore feel called on to make his life uncomfortable. We shall reflect that he already bears, or will bear, the whole penalty of his error; if he spoils his life by mismanagement, we shall not, for that reason, desire to spoil it still further: instead of wishing to punish him, we shall rather endeavour to alleviate his punishment, by showing him how he may avoid or cure the evils his conduct tends to bring upon him. He may be to us an object of pity, perhaps of dislike, but not of anger or resentment; we shall not treat him like an enemy of society: the worst we shall think ourselves justified in doing is leaving him to himself, if we do not interfere benevolently by showing interest or concern for him. It is far otherwise if he has infringed the rules necessary for the protection of his fellow creatures, individually or collectively. The evil consequences of his acts do not then fall on himself, but on others; and society, as the protector of all its members, must retaliate on him; must inflict pain on him for the express purpose of punishment, and must take care that it be sufficiently severe. In the one case, he is an offender at our bar, and we are called on not only to sit in judgement on him, but, in one shape or another, to execute our own sentence; in the other case, it is not our part to inflict any suffering on him, except what may incidentally follow from our using the same liberty in the regulation of our own affairs, which we allow to him in his.

The distinction here pointed out between the part of a person's life which concerns only himself, and that which concerns others, many persons will refuse to admit. How (it may be asked) can any part of the conduct of a member of society be a matter of indifference to the other members? No person is an entirely isolated being; it is impossible for a person to do anything seriously or permanently hurtful to himself, without mischief reaching at least to his near connexions, and often far beyond them. If he injures his property, he does harm to those who directly or indirectly derived support from it, and usually diminishes, by a greater or less amount, the general resources of the community. If he deteriorates his bodily or mental faculties, he not only brings evil upon all who depended on him for any portion of their happiness, but disqualifies himself for rendering the services which he owes to his fellow creatures generally; perhaps becomes a burthen on their affection or benevolence; and if such conduct were very frequent, hardly any offence that is committed would detract more from the general sum of good. Finally, if by his vices or follies a person does no direct harm to others, he is nevertheless (it may be said) injurious by his example; and ought to be compelled to control

himself, for the sake of those whom the sight or knowledge of his conduct might corrupt or mislead.

And even (it will be added) if the consequences of
misconduct could be confined to the vicious or thought-
less individual, ought society to abandon to their own
guidance those who are manifestly unfit for it ?   If
protection against themselves is confessedly due to
children and persons under age, is not society equally
bound to afford it to persons of mature years who are
equally incapable of self-government ?   If gambling,
or drünkenness, or incontinence, or idleness, or un-
cleanliness, are as injurious to happiness, and as great
a hindrance to improvement, as many or most of the
acts prohibited by law, why (it may be asked) should
not law, so far as is consistent with practicability and
social convenience, endeavour to repress these also ?
And as a supplement to the unavoidable imperfections
of law, ought not opinion at least to organize a powerful
police against these vices, and visit rigidly with social
penalties those who are known to practise them ?
There is no question here (it may be said) about
restricting individuality, or impeding the trial of new
and original experiments in living.   The only things it
is sought to prevent are things which have been tried
and condemned from the beginning of the world until
now ;   things which experience has shown not to be
useful or suitable to any person's individuality.   There
must be some length of time and amount of experience,
after which a moral or prudential truth may be regarded as established :   and it is merely desired to
prevent generation after generation from falling over
the same precipice which has been fatal to their predecessors.

I fully admit that the mischief which a person does
to himself may seriously affect, both through their
sympathies and their interests, those nearly connected
with him, and in a minor degree, society at large.
When, by conduct of this sort, a person is led to
violate a distinct and assignable obligation to any
other person or persons, the case is taken out of the

self-regarding class, and becomes amenable to moral disapprobation in the proper sense of the term. If, for example, a man, through intemperance or extravagance, becomes unable to pay his debts, or, having undertaken the moral responsibility of a family, becomes from the same cause incapable of supporting or educating them, he is deservedly reprobated, and might be justly punished ; but it is for the breach of duty to his family or creditors, not for the extravagance. If the resources which ought to have been devoted to them, had been diverted from them for the most prudent investment, the moral culpability would have been the same. George Barnwell murdered his uncle to get money for his mistress, but if he had done it to set himself up in business, he would equally have been hanged. Again, in the frequent case of a man who causes grief to his family by addiction to bad habits, he deserves reproach for his unkindness or ingratitude ; but so he may for cultivating habits not in themselves vicious, if they are painful to those with whom he passes his life, or who from personal ties are dependent on him for their comfort. Whoever fails in the consideration generally due to the interests and feelings of others, not being compelled by some more imperative duty, or justified by allowable self-preference, is a subject of moral disapprobation for that failure, but not for the cause of it, nor for the errors, merely personal to himself, which may have remotely led to it. In like manner, when a person disables himself, by conduct purely self-regarding, from the performance of some definite duty incumbent on him to the public, he is guilty of a social offence. No person ought to be punished simply for being drunk ; but a soldier or a policeman should be punished for being drunk on duty. Whenever, in short, there is a definite damage, or a definite risk of damage, either to an individual or to the public, the case is taken out of the province of liberty, and placed in that of morality or law.

But with regard to the merely contingent, or, as it

may be called, constructive injury which a person causes to society, by conduct which neither violates any specific duty to the public, nor occasions perceptible hurt to any assignable individual except himself; the inconvenience is one which society can afford to bear, for the sake of the greater good of human freedom. If grown persons are to be punished for not taking proper care of themselves,. I would rather it were for their own sake, than under pretence of preventing them from impairing their capacity of rendering to society benefits which society does not pretend it has a right to exact. But I cannot consent to argue the point as if society had no means of bringing its weaker members up to its ordinary standard of rational conduct, except waiting till they do something irrational, and then punishing them, legally or morally, for it. Society has had absolute power over them during all the early portion of their existence : it has had the whole period of childhood and nonage in which to try whether it could make them capable of rational conduct in life. The existing generation is master both of the training and the entire circumstances of the generation to come ; it cannot indeed make them perfectly wise and good, because it is itself so lamentably deficient in goodness and wisdom ; and its best efforts are not always, in individual cases, its most successful ones ; but it is perfectly well·able to make the rising generation, as a whole, as good as, and a little better than, itself. If society lets any considerable number of its members grow up mere children, incapable of being acted on by rational consideration of distant motives, society has itself to blame for the consequences. Armed not only with all the powers of education, but with the ascendancy which the authority of a received opinion always exercises over the minds who are least fitted to judge for themselves ; and aided by the *natural* penalties which cannot be prevented from falling on those who incur the distaste or the contempt of those who know them ; let not society pretend that it needs, besides all this, the power to

issue commands and enforce obedience in the personal
concerns of individuals, in which, on all principles of
justice and policy, the decision ought to rest with
those who are to abide the consequences.   Nor is there
anything which tends more to discredit and frustrate
the better means of influencing conduct, than a resort
to the worse.   If there be among those whom it is
attempted to coerce into prudence or temperance, any
of the material of which vigorous and independent
characters are made, they will infallibly rebel against
the yoke.   No such person will ever feel that others
have a right to control him in his concerns, such as
they have to prevent him from injuring them in theirs ;
and it easily comes to be considered a mark of spirit
and courage to fly in the face of such usurped authority,
and do with ostentation the exact opposite of what it
enjoins ;   as in the fashion of grossness which succeeded, in the time of Charles II, to the fanatical
moral intolerance of the Puritans.   With respect to
what is said of the necessity of protecting society from
the bad example set to others by the vicious or the
self-indulgent ;   it is true that bad example may have
a pernicious effect, especially the example of doing
wrong to others with impunity to the wrong-doer.   But
we are now speaking of conduct which, while it does
no wrong to others, is supposed to do great harm to
the agent himself : and I do not see how those who
believe this, can think otherwise than that the example,
on the whole, must be more salutary than hurtful,
since, if it displays the misconduct, it displays also
the painful or degrading consequences which, if the
conduct is justly censured, must be supposed to be in
all or most cases attendant on it.

   But. the strongest of all the arguments against the
interference of the public with purely personal conduct, is that when it does interfere, the odds are that
it interferes wrongly, and in the wrong place.   On
questions of social morality, of duty to others, the
opinion of the public, that is, of an overruling majority,
though often wrong, is likely to be still oftener right ;

because on such questions they are only required to
judge of their own interests; of the manner in which
some mode of conduct, if allowed to be practised,
would affect themselves. But the opinion of a similar
majority, imposed as a law on the minority, on questions of self-regarding conduct, is quite as likely to be
wrong as right; for in these cases public opinion
means, at the best, some people's opinion of what is
good or bad for other people; while very often it does
not even mean that; the public, with the most perfect
indifference, passing over the pleasure or convenience
of those whose conduct they censure, and considering
only their own preference. There are many who consider as an injury to themselves any conduct which
they have a distaste for, and resent it as an outrage
to their feelings; as a religious bigot, when charged
with disregarding the religious feelings of others, has
been known to retort that they disregard his feelings,
by persisting in their abominable worship or creed.
But there is no parity between the feeling of a person
for his own opinion, and the feeling of another who
is offended at his holding it; no more than between
the desire of a thief to take a purse, and the desire
of the right owner to keep it. And a person's taste
is as much his own peculiar concern as his opinion or
his purse. It is easy for any one to imagine an ideal
public, which leaves the freedom and choice of individuals in all uncertain matters undisturbed, and only
requires them to abstain from modes of conduct which
universal experience has condemned. But where has
there been seen a public which set any such limit to
its censorship? or when does the public trouble itself
about universal experience? In its interferences with
personal conduct it is seldom thinking of anything but
the enormity of acting or feeling differently from itself;
and this standard of judgement, thinly disguised, is
held up to mankind as the dictate of religion and
philosophy, by nine-tenths of all moralists and speculative writers. These teach that things are right because they are right; because we feel them to be so.

They tell us to search in our own minds and hearts for laws of conduct binding on ourselves and on all others. What can the poor public do but apply these instructions, and make their own personal feelings of good and evil, if they are tolerably unanimous in them, obligatory on all the world?

The evil here pointed out is not one which exists only in theory; and it may perhaps be expected that I should specify the instances in which the public of this age and country improperly invests its own preferences with the character of moral laws. I am not writing an essay on the aberrations of existing moral feeling. That is too weighty a subject to be discussed parenthetically, and by way of illustration. Yet examples are necessary, to show that the principle I maintain is of serious and practical moment, and that I am not endeavouring to erect a barrier against imaginary evils. And it is not difficult to show, by abundant instances, that to extend the bounds of what may be called moral police, until it encroaches on the most unquestionably legitimate liberty of the individual, is one of the most universal of all human propensities.

As a first instance, consider the antipathies which men cherish on no better grounds than that persons whose religious opinions are different from theirs, do not practise their religious observances, especially their religious abstinences. To cite a rather trivial example, nothing in the creed or practice of Christians does more to envenom the hatred of Mohammedans against them, than the fact of their eating pork. There are few acts which Christians and Europeans regard with more unaffected disgust, than Mussulmans regard this particular mode of satisfying hunger. It is, in the first place, an offence against their religion; but this circumstance by no means explains either the degree or the kind of their repugnance; for wine also is forbidden by their religion, and to partake of it is by all Mussulmans accounted wrong, but not disgusting. Their aversion to the flesh of the 'unclean beast' is, on the contrary, of that peculiar character, resembling an instinctive

antipathy, which the idea of uncleanness, when once
it thoroughly sinks into the feelings, seems always to
excite even in those whose personal habits are anything
but scrupulously cleanly, and of which the sentiment
of religious impurity, so intense in the Hindoos, is
a remarkable example. Suppose now that in a people,
of whom the majority were Mussulmans, that majority
should insist upon not permitting pork to be eaten
within the limits of the country. This would be nothing
new in Mohammedan countries.[1] Would it be a legitimate exercise of the moral authority of public opinion ?
and if not, why not ? The practice is really revolting
to such a public. They also sincerely think that it is
forbidden and abhorred by the Deity. Neither could
the prohibition be censured as religious persecution.
It might be religious in its origin, but it would not be
persecution for religion, since nobody's religion makes
it a duty to eat pork. The only tenable ground of
condemnation would be, that with the personal tastes
and self-regarding concerns of individuals the public
has no business to interfere.

To come somewhat nearer home : the majority of
Spaniards consider it a gross impiety, offensive in the
highest degree to the Supreme Being, to worship him
in any other manner than the Roman Catholic ; and
no other public worship is lawful on Spanish soil. The

---

[1] The case of the Bombay Parsees is a curious instance
in point. When this industrious and enterprising tribe,
the descendants of the Persian fire-worshippers, flying
from their native country before the Caliphs, arrived in
Western India, they were admitted to toleration by the
Hindoo sovereigns, on condition of not eating beef. When
those regions afterwards fell under the dominion of Mohammedan conquerors, the Parsees obtained from them a continuance of indulgence, on condition of refraining from
pork. What was at first obedience to authority became
a second nature, and the Parsees to this day abstain both
from beef and pork. Though not required by their religion,
the double abstinence has had time to grow into a custom
of their tribe; and custom, in the East, is a religion.

people of all Southern Europe look upon a married
clergy as not only irreligious, but unchaste, indecent,
gross, disgusting. What do Protestants think of these
perfectly sincere feelings, and of the attempt to enforce
them against non-Catholics ? Yet, if mankind are
justified in interfering with each other's liberty in
things which do not concern the interests of others,
on what principle is it possible consistently to exclude
these cases ? or who can blame people for desiring to
suppress what they regard as a scandal in the sight
of God and man ? No stronger case can be shown
for prohibiting anything which is regarded as a personal
immorality, than is made out for suppressing these
practices in the eyes of those who regard them as
impieties ; and unless we are willing to adopt the logic
of persecutors, and to say that we may persecute others
because we are right, and that they must not persecute
us because they are wrong, we must beware of admitting
a principle of which we should resent as a gross injustice the application to ourselves.

The preceding instances may be objected to, although
unreasonably, as drawn from contingencies impossible
among us : opinion, in this country, not being likely
to enforce abstinence from meats, or to interfere with
people for worshipping, and for either marrying or not
marrying, according to their creed or inclination. The
next example, however, shall be taken from an interference with liberty which we have by no means passed
all danger of. Wherever the Puritans have been sufficiently powerful, as in New England, and in Great
Britain at the time of the Commonwealth, they have
endeavoured, with considerable success, to put down all
public, and nearly all private, amusements : especially
music, dancing, public games, or other assemblages
for purposes of diversion, and the theatre. There are
still in this country large bodies of persons by whose
notions of morality and religion these recreations are
condemned ; and those persons belonging chiefly to
the middle class, who are the ascendant power in the
present social and political condition of the kingdom,

it is by no means impossible that persons of these
sentiments may at some time or other command a
majority in Parliament. How will the remaining portion of the community like to have the amusements
that shall be permitted to them regulated by the
religious and moral sentiments of the stricter Calvinists
and Methodists ? Would they not, with considerable
peremptoriness, desire these intrusively pious members
of society to mind their own business ? This is precisely what should be said to every government and
every public, who have the pretension that no person
shall enjoy any pleasure which they think wrong. But
if the principle of the pretension be admitted, no one
can reasonably object to its being acted on in the
sense of the majority, or other preponderating power
in the country ; and all persons must be ready to
conform to the idea of a Christian commonwealth, as
understood by the early settlers in New England, if
a religious profession similar to theirs should ever succeed in regaining its lost ground, as religions supposed
to be declining have so often been known to do.

To imagine another contingency, perhaps more likely
to be realized than the one last mentioned. There is
confessedly a strong tendency in the modern world
towards a democratic constitution of society, accompanied or not by popular political institutions. It is
affirmed that in the country where this tendency is
most completely realized—where both society and the
government are most democratic—the United States—
the feeling of the majority, to whom any appearance
of a more showy or costly style of living than they
can hope to rival is disagreeable, operates as a tolerably effectual sumptuary law, and that in many parts
of the Union it is really difficult for a person possessing
a very large income, to find any mode of spending it,
which will not incur popular disapprobation. Though
such statements as these are doubtless much exaggerated as a representation of existing facts, the state
of things they describe is not only a conceivable and
possible, but a probable result of democratic feeling,

combined with the notion that the public has a right to a veto on the manner in which individuals shall spend their incomes. We have only further to suppose a considerable diffusion of Socialist opinions, and it may become infamous in the eyes of the majority to possess more property than some very small amount, or any income not earned by manual labour. Opinions similar in principle to these, already prevail widely among the artisan class, and weigh oppressively on those who are amenable to the opinion chiefly of that class, namely, its own members. It is known that the bad workmen who form the majority of the operatives in many branches of industry, are decidedly of opinion that bad workmen ought to receive the same wages as good, and that no one ought to be allowed, through piecework or otherwise, to earn by superior skill or industry more than others can without it. And they employ a moral police, which occasionally becomes a physical one, to deter skilful workmen from receiving, and employers from giving, a larger remuneration for a more useful service. If the public have any juris-diction over private concerns, I cannot see that these people are in fault, or that any individual's particular public can be blamed for asserting the same authority over his individual conduct, which the general public asserts over people in general.

But, without dwelling upon supposititious cases, there are, in our own day, gross usurpations upon the liberty of private life actually practised, and still greater ones threatened with some expectation of suc-cess, and opinions propounded which assert an un-limited right in the public not only to prohibit by law everything which it thinks wrong, but in order to get at what it thinks wrong, to prohibit any number of things which it admits to be innocent.

Under the name of preventing intemperance, the people of one English colony, and of nearly half the United States, have been interdicted by law from making any use whatever of fermented drinks, except for medical purposes: for prohibition of their sale is in fact, as it is intended to be, prohibition of their use. And though the impracticability of executing the law has caused its repeal in several of the States which had adopted it, including the one from which it derives its name, an attempt has notwithstanding been commenced, and is prosecuted with considerable zeal by many of the professed philanthropists, to agitate for a similar law in this country. The association, or ' Alliance ' as it terms itself, which has been formed for this purpose, has acquired some notoriety through the publicity given to a correspondence between its Secretary and one of the very few English public men who hold that a politician's opinions ought to be founded on principles. Lord Stanley's share in this correspondence is calculated to strengthen the hopes already built on him, by those who know how rare such qualities as are manifested in some of his public appearances, unhappily are among those who figure in political life. The organ of the Alliance, who would ' deeply deplore the recognition of any principle which could be wrested to justify bigotry and persecution ', undertakes to point out the ' broad and impassable barrier ' which divides such principles from those of the association. ' All matters relating to thought, opinion, conscience, appear to me,' he says, ' to be without the sphere of legislation ; all pertaining to social act, habit, relation, subject only to a discretionary power vested in the State itself, and not in the individual, to be within it.' No mention is made of a third class, different from either of these, viz. acts and habits which are not social, but individual ; although it is to this class, surely, that the act of drinking fermented liquors belongs. Selling fermented liquors, however, is trading, and trading is a social act. But the infringement complained of is not on the liberty of the seller, but on that of the buyer and consumer ; since the State might just as well forbid him to drink wine, as purposely make it impossible for him to obtain t. The Secretary, however, says, ' I claim, as a citizen, ₁ right to legislate whenever my social rights are invaded by the social act of another.' And now for the definition of these 'social rights'. 'If anything invades my social rights, certainly the traffic in strong drink does. It destroys my primary right of security, by constantly creating and stimulating social disorder. It invades my right of equality, by deriving a profit from the creation of a misery I am taxed to support. It impedes my right to free moral and intellectual development, by surrounding my path with dangers, and by weakening and demoralizing society, from which I have a right to claim mutual aid and intercourse.' A theory of 'social rights', the like of which probably never before found its way into distinct language : being nothing short of this—that it is the absolute social right of every individual, that every other individual shall act in every respect exactly as he ought ; that whosoever fails thereof in the smallest particular, violates my social right, and entitles me to demand from the legislature the removal of the grievance. So monstrous a principle is far more dangerous than any single interference with liberty ; there is no violation of liberty which it would not justify ; it acknowledges no right to any freedom whatever, except perhaps to that of holding opinions in secret, without ever disclosing them : for, the moment an opinion which I consider noxious passes any one's lips, it invades all the 'social rights' attributed to me by the Alliance. The doctrine ascribes to all mankind a vested interest in each other's moral, intellectual, and even physical perfection, to be defined by each claimant according to his own standard.

Another important example of illegitimate interference with the rightful liberty of the individual, not simply threatened, but long since carried into triumphant effect, is Sabbatarian legislation. Without doubt, abstinence on one day in the week, so far as the exigencies of life permit, from the usual daily occupation, though in no respect religiously binding on any except Jews, is a highly beneficial custom. And inasmuch as this custom cannot be observed without a general consent to that effect among the industrious classes, therefore, in so far as some persons by working may impose the same necessity on others, it may be allowable and right that the law should guarantee to each the observance by others of the custom, by suspending the greater operations of industry on a particular day. But this justification, grounded on the direct interest which others have in each individual's observance of the practice, does not apply to the self-chosen occupations in which a person may think fit to employ his leisure ; nor does it hold good, in the smallest degree, for legal restrictions on amusements. It is true that the amusement of some is the day's work of others ; but the pleasure, not to say the useful recreation, of many, is worth the labour of a few, provided the occupation is freely chosen, and can be freely resigned. The operatives are perfectly right in thinking that if all worked on Sunday, seven days' work would have to be given for six days' wages : but so long as the great mass of employments are suspended, the small number who for the enjoyment of others must still work, obtain a proportional increase of earnings ; and they are not obliged to follow those occupations, if they prefer leisure to emolument. If a further remedy is sought, it might be found in the establishment by custom of a holiday on some other day of the week for those particular classes of persons. The only ground, therefore, on which restrictions on Sunday amusements can be defended, must be that they are religiously wrong ; a motive of legislation which never can be too earnestly protested against. 'Deorum injuriae Diis curae.' It remains to be proved that society or any of its officers holds a commission from on high to avenge any supposed offence to Omnipotence, which is not also a wrong to our fellow creatures. The notion that it is one man's duty that another should be religious, was the foundation of all the religious persecutions ever perpetrated, and if admitted, would fully justify them. Though the feeling which breaks out in the repeated attempts to stop railway

travelling on Sunday, in the resistance to the opening
of Museums, and the like, has not the cruelty of the
old persecutors, the state of mind indicated by it is
fundamentally the same. It is a determination not to
tolerate others in doing what is permitted by their
religion, because it is not permitted by the persecutor's
religion. It is a belief that God not only abominates
the act of the misbeliever, but will not hold us guiltless
if we leave him unmolested.

I cannot refrain from adding to these examples of
the little account commonly made of human liberty,
the language of downright persecution which breaks
out from the press of this country, whenever it feels
called on to notice the remarkable phenomenon of
Mormonism. Much might be said on the unexpected
and instructive fact, that an alleged new revelation,
and a religion founded on it, the product of palpable
imposture, not even supported by the *prestige* of extraordinary qualities in its founder, is believed by hundreds
of thousands, and has been made the foundation of
a society, in the age of newspapers, railways, and the
electric telegraph. What here concerns us is, that this
religion, like other and better religions, has its martyrs ;
that its prophet and founder was, for his teaching, put
to death by a mob ; that others of its adherents lost
their lives by the same lawless violence ; that they
were forcibly expelled, in a body, from the country
in which they first grew up ; while, now that they
have been chased into a solitary recess in the midst
of a desert, many in this country openly declare that
it would be right (only that it is not convenient) to
send an expedition against them, and compel them by
force to conform to the opinions of other people. The
article of the Mormonite doctrine which is the chief
provocative to the antipathy which thus breaks through
the ordinary restraints of religious tolerance, is its
sanction of polygamy ; which, though permitted to
Mohammedans, and Hindoos, and Chinese, seems to
excite unquenchable animosity when practised by persons who speak English, and profess to be a kind of

Christians. No one has a deeper disapprobation than I have of this Mormon institution; both for other reasons, and because, far from being in any way countenanced by the principle of liberty, it is a direct infraction of that principle, being a mere riveting of the chains of one-half of the community, and an emancipation of the other from reciprocity of obligation towards them. Still, it must be remembered that this relation is as much voluntary on the part of the women concerned in it, and who may be deemed the sufferers by it, as is the case with any other form of the marriage institution; and however surprising this fact may appear, it has its explanation in the common ideas and customs of the world, which teaching women to think marriage the one thing needful, make it intelligible that many a woman should prefer being one of several wives, to not being a wife at all. Other countries are not asked to recognize such unions, or release any portion of their inhabitants from their own laws on the score of Mormonite opinions. But when the dissentients have conceded to the hostile sentiments of others, far more than could justly be demanded; when they have left the countries to which their doctrines were unacceptable, and established themselves in a remote corner of the earth, which they have been the first to render habitable to human beings; it is difficult to see on what principles but those of tyranny they can be prevented from living there under what laws they please, provided they commit no aggression on other nations, and allow perfect freedom of departure to those who are dissatisfied with their ways. A recent writer, in some respects of considerable merit, proposes (to use his own words) not a crusade, but a *civilizade*, against this polygamous community, to put an end to what seems to him a retrograde step in civilization. It also appears so to me, but I am not aware that any community has a right to force another to be civilized. So long as the sufferers by the bad law do not invoke assistance from other communities, I cannot admit that persons entirely unconnected with them ought to step in and require that a condition of things with which all who are directly interested appear to be satisfied, should be put an end to because it is a scandal to persons some thousands of miles distant, who have no part or concern in it. Let them send missionaries, if they please, to preach against it ; and let them, by any fair means (of which silencing the teachers is not one), oppose the progress of similar doctrines among their own people. If civilization has got the better of barbarism when barbarism had the world to itself, it is too much to profess to be afraid lest barbarism, after having been fairly got under, should revive and conquer civilization. A civilization that can thus succumb to its vanquished enemy, must first have become so degenerate, that neither its appointed priests and teachers, nor anybody else, has the capacity, or will take the trouble, to stand up for it. If this be so, the sooner such a civilization receives notice to quit, the better. It can only go on from bad to worse, until destroyed and regenerated (like the Western Empire) by energetic barbarians.

CHAPTER V

THE principles asserted in these pages must be more generally admitted as the basis for discussion of details, before a consistent application of them to all the various departments of government and morals can be attempted with any prospect of advantage. The few observations I propose to make on questions of detail, are designed to illustrate the principles, rather than to follow them out to their consequences. I offer, not so much applications, as specimens of application ; which may serve to bring into greater clearness the meaning and limits of the two maxims which together form the entire doctrine of this Essay, and to assist the judgement in holding the balance between them, in the cases where it appears doubtful which of them is applicable to the case.

The maxims are, first, that the individual is not accountable to society for his actions, in so far as these concern the interests of no person but himself. Advice, instruction, persuasion, and avoidance by other people if thought necessary by them for their own good, are the only measures by which society can justifiably express its dislike or disapprobation of his conduct. Secondly, that for such actions as are prejudicial to the interests of others, the individual is accountable, and may be subjected either to social or to legal punishment, if society is of opinion that the one or the other is requisite for its protection.

In the first place, it must by no means be supposed, because damage, or probability of damage, to the interests of others, can alone justify the interference of society, that therefore it always does justify such interference. In many cases, an individual, in pursuing a legitimate object, necessarily and therefore legitimately causes pain or loss to others, or intercepts a good which they had a reasonable hope of obtaining. Such oppositions of interest between individuals often arise from bad social institutions, but are unavoidable while those institutions last; and some would be unavoidable under any institutions. Whoever succeeds in an overcrowded profession, or in a competitive examination; whoever is preferred to another in any contest for an object which both desire, reaps benefit from the loss of others, from their wasted exertion and their disappointment. But it is, by common admission, better for the general interest of mankind, that persons should pursue their objects undeterred by this sort of consequences. In other words, society admits no right, either legal or moral, in the disappointed competitors, to immunity from this kind of suffering; and feels called on to interfere, only when means of success have been employed which it is contrary to the general interest to permit—namely, fraud or treachery, and force.

Again, trade is a social act. Whoever undertakes to sell any description of goods to the public, does what affects the interest of other persons, and of society in general; and thus his conduct, in principle, comes within the jurisdiction of society: accordingly, it was once held to be the duty of governments, in all cases which were considered of importance, to fix prices, and regulate the processes of manufacture. But it is now recognized, though not till after a long struggle, that both the cheapness and the good quality of commodities are most effectually provided for by leaving the producers and sellers perfectly free, under the sole check of equal freedom to the buyers for supplying themselves elsewhere. This is the so-called doctrine of Free Trade, which rests on grounds different from, though equally solid with, the principle of individual liberty asserted in this Essay. Restrictions on trade, or on production for purposes of trade, are indeed restraints; and all restraint, *quâ* restraint, is an evil: but the restraints in question affect only that part of conduct which society is competent to restrain, and are wrong solely because they do not really produce the results which it is desired to produce by them. As the principle of individual liberty is not involved in the doctrine of Free Trade, so neither is it in most of the questions which arise respecting the limits of that doctrine; as for example, what amount of public control is admissible for the prevention of fraud by adulteration; how far sanitary precautions, or arrangements to protect workpeople employed in dangerous occupations, should be enforced on employers. Such questions involve considerations of liberty, only in so far as leaving people to themselves is always better, *caeteris paribus*, than controlling them: but that they may be legitimately controlled for these ends, is in principle undeniable. On the other hand, there are questions relating to interference with trade, which are essentially questions of liberty; such as the Maine Law, already touched upon; the prohibition of the importation of opium into China; the restriction of the sale of poisons; all cases, in short, where the object of the interference is to make it impossible or difficult to obtain a particular commodity. These interferences are objectionable, not as infringements on the liberty of the producer or seller, but on that of the buyer.

One of these examples, that of the sale of poisons, opens a new question; the proper limits of what may be called the functions of police; how far liberty may legitimately be invaded for the prevention of crime, or of accident. It is one of the undisputed functions of government to take precautions against crime before it has been committed, as well as to detect and punish it afterwards. The preventive function of government, however, is far more liable to be abused, to the prejudice of liberty, than the punitory function; for there is hardly any part of the legitimate freedom of action of a human being which would not admit of being represented, and fairly too, as increasing the facilities for some form or other of delinquency. Nevertheless, if a public authority, or even a private person, sees any one evidently preparing to commit a crime, they are not bound to look on inactive until the crime is committed, but may interfere to prevent it. If poisons were never bought or used for any purpose except the commission of murder, it would be right to prohibit their manufacture and sale. They may, however, be wanted not only for innocent but for useful purposes, and restrictions cannot be imposed in the one case without operating in the other. Again, it is a proper office of public authority to guard against accidents. If either a public officer or any one else saw a person attempting to cross a bridge which had been ascertained to be unsafe, and there were no time to warn him of his danger, they might seize him and turn him back, without any real infringement of his liberty ; for liberty consists in doing what one desires, and he does not desire to fall into the river. Nevertheless, when there is not a certainty, but only a danger of mischief, no one but the person himself can judge of the sufficiency of the motive which may prompt him to incur the risk : in this case, therefore (unless he is a child, or delirious, or in some state of excitement or absorption incompatible with the full use of the reflecting faculty), he ought, I conceive, to be only warned of the danger ; not forcibly prevented from exposing himself to it. Similar considerations, applied to such a question as the sale of poisons, may enable us to decide which among the possible modes of regulation are or are not contrary to principle. Such a precaution, for example, as that of labelling the drug with some word expressive of its dangerous character, may be enforced without violation of liberty : the buyer cannot wish not to know that the thing he possesses has poisonous qualities. But to require in all cases the certificate of a medical practitioner, would make it sometimes impossible, always expensive, to obtain the article for legitimate uses. The only mode apparent to me, in which difficulties may be thrown in the way of crime committed through this means, without any infringement, worth taking into account, upon the liberty of those who desire the poisonous substance for other purposes, consists in providing what, in the apt language of Bentham, is called 'preappointed evidence'. This provision is familiar to every one in the case of contracts. It is usual and right that the law, when a contract is entered into, should require as the condition of its enforcing performance, that certain formalities should be observed, such as signatures, attestation of witnesses, and the like, in order that in case of subsequent dispute, there may be evidence to prove that the contract was really entered into, and that there was nothing in the circumstances to render it legally invalid: the effect being, to throw great obstacles in the way of fictitious contracts, or contracts made in circumstances which, if known, would destroy their validity. Precautions of a similar nature might be enforced in the sale of articles adapted to be instruments of crime. The seller, for example, might be required to enter in a register the exact time of the transaction, the name and address of the buyer, the precise quality and quantity sold; to ask the purpose for which it was wanted, and record the answer he received. When there was no medical prescription, the presence of some third person might be required, to bring home the fact to the purchaser, in case there should afterwards be reason to believe that the article had been applied to criminal purposes. Such regulations would in general be no material impediment to obtaining the article, but a very considerable one to making an improper use of it without detection.

The right inherent in society, to ward off crimes against itself by antecedent precautions, suggests the obvious limitations to the maxim, that purely self-regarding misconduct cannot properly be meddled with in the way of prevention or punishment. Drunkenness, for example, in ordinary cases, is not a fit subject for legislative interference; but I should deem it perfectly legitimate that a person, who had once been convicted of any act of violence to others under the influence of drink, should be placed under a special legal restriction, personal to himself; that if he were afterwards found drunk, he should be liable to a penalty, and that if when in that state he committed another offence, the punishment to which he would be liable for that other offence should be increased in severity. The making himself drunk, in a person whom drunkenness excites to do harm to others, is a crime against others. So, again, idleness, except in a person receiving support from the public, or except when it constitutes a breach of contract, cannot without tyranny be made a subject of legal punishment; but if, either from idleness or from any other avoidable cause, a man fails to perform his legal duties to others, as for instance to support his children, it is no tyranny to force him to fulfil that obligation, by compulsory labour, if no other means are available.

Again, there are many acts which, being directly injurious only to the agents themselves, ought not to be legally interdicted, but which, if done publicly, are a violation of good manners, and coming thus within the category of offences against others, may rightfully be prohibited. Of this kind are offences against decency; on which it is unnecessary to dwell, the rather as they are only connected indirectly with our subject, the objection to publicity being equally strong in the case of many actions not in themselves condemnable, nor supposed to be so.

There is another question to which an answer must be found, consistent with the principles which have been laid down. In cases of personal conduct supposed to be blameable, but which respect for liberty precludes society from preventing or punishing, because the evil directly resulting falls wholly on the agent; what the agent is free to do, ought other persons to be equally free to counsel or instigate? This question is not free from difficulty. The case of a person who solicits another to do an act, is not strictly a case of self-regarding conduct. To give advice or offer inducements to any one, is a social act, and may, therefore,

like actions in general which affect others, be supposed
amenable to social control.   But a little reflection
corrects the first impression, by showing that if the
case is not strictly within the definition of individual
liberty, yet the reasons on which the principle of individual liberty is grounded, are applicable to it.   If
people must be allowed, in whatever concerns only
themselves, to act as seems best to themselves at their
own peril, they must equally be free to consult with
one another about what is fit to be so done ; to exchange opinions, and give and receive suggestions.
Whatever it is permitted to do, it must be permitted
to advise to do.   The question is doubtful, only when
the instigator derives a personal benefit from his advice ; when he makes it his occupation, for subsistence
or pecuniary gain, to promote what society and the
State consider to be an evil.   Then, indeed, a new
element of complication is introduced ; namely, the
existence of classes of persons with an interest opposed
to what is considered as the public weal, and whose
mode of living is grounded on the counteraction of it.
Ought this to be interfered with, or not ?   Fornica-
tion, for example, must be tolerated, and so must
gambling ; but should a person be free to be a pimp,
or to keep a gambling-house ?   The case is one of
those which lie on the exact boundary line between
two principles, and it is not at once apparent to which
of the two it properly belongs.   There are arguments
on both sides.   On the side of toleration it may be
said, that the fact of following anything as an occupation, and living or profiting by the practice of it, cannot
make that criminal which would otherwise be admissible ; that the act should either be consistently permitted or consistently prohibited ; that if the principles
which we have hitherto defended are true, society has
no business, *as* society, to decide anything to be wrong
which concerns only the individual ; that it cannot go
beyond dissuasion, and that one person should be as
free to persuade, as another to dissuade.   In opposition
to this it may be contended, that although the public,

or the State, are not warranted in authoritatively deciding, for purposes of repression or punishment, that such or such conduct affecting only the interests of the individual is good or bad, they are fully justified in assuming, if they regard it as bad, that its being so or not is at least a disputable question : That, this being supposed, they cannot be acting wrongly in endeavouring to exclude the influence of solicitations which are not disinterested, of instigators who cannot possibly be impartial—who have a direct personal interest on one side, and that side the one which the State believes to be wrong, and who confessedly promote it for personal objects only. There can surely, it may be urged, be nothing lost, no sacrifice of good, by so ordering matters that persons shall make their election, either wisely or foolishly, on their own prompting, as free as possible from the arts of persons who stimulate their inclinations for interested purposes of their own. Thus (it may be said) though the statutes respecting unlawful games are utterly indefensible— though all persons should be free to gamble in their own or each other's houses, or in any place of meeting established by their own subscriptions, and open only to the members and their visitors—yet public gambling-houses should not be permitted. It is true that the prohibition is never effectual, and that, whatever amount of tyrannical power may be given to the police, gambling-houses can always be maintained under other pretences ; but they may be compelled to conduct their operations with a certain degree of secrecy and mystery, so that nobody knows anything about them but those who seek them ; and more than this, society ought not to aim at. There is considerable force in these arguments. I will not venture to decide whether they are sufficient to justify the moral anomaly of punishing the accessary, when the principal is (and must be) allowed to go free ; of fining or imprisoning the procurer, but not the fornicator, the gambling-house keeper, but not the gambler. Still less ought the common operations of buying and selling to be interfered with on analogous grounds. Almost every article which is bought and sold may be used in excess, and the sellers have a pecuniary interest in encouraging that excess ; but no argument can be founded on this, in favour, for instance, of the Maine Law ; because the class of dealers in strong drinks, though interested in their abuse, are indispensably required for the sake of their legitimate use. The interest, however, of these dealers in promoting intemperance is a real evil, and justifies the State in imposing restrictions and requiring guarantees which, but for that justification, would be infringements of legitimate liberty.

A further question is, whether the State, while it permits, should nevertheless indirectly discourage conduct which it deems contrary to the best interests of the agent ; whether, for example, it should take measures to render the means of drunkenness more costly, or add to the difficulty of procuring them by limiting the number of the places of sale. On this as on most other practical questions, many distinctions require to be made. To tax stimulants for the sole purpose of making them more difficult to be obtained, is a measure differing only in degree from their entire prohibition ; and would be justifiable only if that were justifiable. Every increase of cost is a prohibition, to those whose means do not come up to the augmented price ; and to those who do, it is a penalty laid on them for gratifying a particular taste. Their choice of pleasures, and their mode of expending their income, after satisfying their legal and moral obligations to the State and to individuals, are their own concern, and must rest with their own judgement. These considerations may seem at first sight to condemn the selection of stimulants as special subjects of taxation for purposes of revenue. But it must be remembered that taxation for fiscal purposes is absolutely inevitable ; that in most countries it is necessary that a considerable part of that taxation should be indirect ; that the State, therefore, cannot help imposing penalties, which to some persons may be prohibitory, on the use of some articles of consumption. It is hence the duty of the State to consider, in the imposition of taxes, what commodities the consumers can best spare ; and *a fortiori*, to select in preference those of which it deems the use, beyond a very moderate quantity, to be positively injurious. Taxation, therefore, of stimulants, up to the point which produces the largest amount of revenue (supposing that the State needs all the revenue which it yields) is not only admissible, but to be approved of.

The question of making the sale of these commodities a more or less exclusive privilege, must be answered differently, according to the purposes to which the restriction is intended to be subservient. All places of public resort require the restraint of a police, and places of this kind peculiarly, because offences against society are especially apt to originate there. It is, therefore, fit to confine the power of selling these commodities (at least for consumption on the spot) to persons of known or vouched-for respectability of conduct ; to make such regulations respecting hours of opening and closing as may be requisite for public surveillance, and to withdraw the licence if breaches of the peace repeatedly take place through the connivance or incapacity of the keeper of the house, or if it becomes a rendezvous for concocting and preparing offences against the law. Any further restriction I do not conceive to be, in principle, justifiable. The limitation in number, for instance, of beer and spirit houses, for the express purpose of rendering them more difficult of access, and diminishing the occasions of temptation, not only exposes all to an inconvenience because there are some by whom the facility would be abused, but is suited only to a state of society in which the labouring classes are avowedly treated as children or savages, and placed under an education of restraint, to fit them for future admission to the privileges of freedom. This is not the principle on which the labouring classes are professedly governed in any free country ; and no person who sets due value on freedom will give his adhesion to their being so governed, unless after all

efforts have been exhausted to educate them for freedom and govern them as freemen, and it has been
definitively proved that they can only be governed as
children. The bare statement of the alternative shows
the absurdity of supposing that such efforts have been
made in any case which needs be considered here. It
is only because the institutions of this country are
a mass of inconsistencies, that things find admittance
into our practice which belong to the system of despotic,
or what is called paternal, government, while the
general freedom of our institutions precludes the
exercise of the amount of control necessary to render
the restraint of any real efficacy as a moral education.

It was pointed out in an early part of this Essay,
that the liberty of the individual, in things wherein
the individual is alone concerned, implies a corresponding liberty in any number of individuals to regulate by
mutual agreement such things as regard them jointly,
and regard no persons but themselves. This question
presents no difficulty, so long as the will of all the
persons implicated remains unaltered; but since that
will may change, it is often necessary, even in things
in which they alone are concerned, that they should
enter into engagements with one another; and when
they do, it is fit, as a general rule, that those engagements should be kept. Yet, in the laws, probably, of
every country, this general rule has some exceptions.
Not only persons are not held to engagements which
violate the rights of third parties, but it is sometimes
considered a sufficient reason for releasing them from
an engagement, that it is injurious to themselves. In
this and most other civilized countries, for example,
an engagement by which a person should sell himself,
or allow himself to be sold, as a slave, would be null
and void; neither enforced by law nor by opinion.
The ground for thus limiting his power of voluntarily
disposing of his own lot in life, is apparent, and is very
clearly seen in this extreme case. The reason for not
interfering, unless for the sake of others, with a person's
voluntary acts, is consideration for his liberty. His

voluntary choice is evidence that what he so chooses is desirable, or at the least endurable, to him, and his good is on the whole best provided for by allowing him to take his own means of pursuing it.   But by selling himself for a slave, he abdicates his liberty ; he forgoes any future use of it beyond that single act. He therefore defeats, in his own case, the very purpose which is the justification of allowing him to dispose of himself.   He is no longer free ; but is thenceforth in a position which has no longer the presumption in its favour, that would be afforded by his voluntarily remaining in it.   The principle of freedom cannot require that he should be free not to be free.   It is not freedom, to be allowed to alienate his freedom.   These reasons, the force of which is so conspicuous in this peculiar case, are evidently of far wider application ; yet a limit is everywhere set to them by the necessities of life, which continually require, not indeed that we should resign our freedom, but that we should consent to this and the other limitation of it.   The principle, however, which demands uncontrolled freedom of action in all that concerns only the agents themselves, requires that those who have become bound to one another, in things which concern no third party, should be able to release one another from the engagement : and even without such voluntary release, there are perhaps no contracts or engagements, except those that relate to money or money's worth, of which one can venture to say that there ought to be no liberty whatever of retractation.   Baron Wilhelm von Humboldt, in the excellent essay from which I have already quoted, states it as his conviction, that engagements which involve personal relations or services, should never be legally binding beyond a limited duration of time ; and that the most important of these engagements, marriage, having the peculiarity that its objects are frustrated unless the feelings of both the parties are in harmony with it, should require nothing more than the declared will of either party to dissolve it. This subject is too important, and too complicated, to be discussed in a parenthesis, and I touch on it only so far as is necessary for purposes of illustration. If the conciseness and generality of Baron Humboldt's dissertation had not obliged him in this instance to content himself with enunciating his conclusion without discussing the premisses, he would doubtless have recognized that the question cannot be decided on grounds so simple as those to which he confines himself. When a person, either by express promise or by conduct, has encouraged another to rely upon his continuing to act in a certain way—to build expectations and calculations, and stake any part of his plan of life upon that supposition—a new series of moral obligations arises on his part towards that person, which may possibly be overruled, but cannot be ignored. And again, if the relation between two contracting parties has been followed by consequences to others; if it has placed third parties in any peculiar position, or, as in the case of marriage, has even called third parties into existence, obligations arise on the part of both the contracting parties towards those third persons, the fulfilment of which, or at all events the mode of fulfilment, must be greatly affected by the continuance or disruption of the relation between the original parties to the contract. It does not follow, nor can I admit, that these obligations extend to requiring the fulfilment of the contract at all costs to the happiness of the reluctant party; but they are a necessary element in the question; and even if, as Von Humboldt maintains, they ought to make no difference in the *legal* freedom of the parties to release themselves from the engagement (and I also hold that they ought not to make *much* difference), they necessarily make a great difference in the *moral* freedom. A person is bound to take all these circumstances into account, before resolving on a step which may affect such important interests of others; and if he does not allow proper weight to those interests, he is morally responsible for the wrong. I have made these obvious remarks for the better illustration of the general principle of liberty, and not because they are at all needed on the particular question, which, on the contrary, is usually discussed as if the interest of children was everything, and that of grown persons nothing.

I have already observed that, owing to the absence of any recognized general principles, liberty is often granted where it should be withheld, as well as withheld where it should be granted ; and one of the cases in which, in the modern European world, the sentiment of liberty is the strongest, is a case where, in my view, it is altogether misplaced. A person should be free to do as he likes in his own concerns ; but he ought not to be free to do as he likes in acting for another, under the pretext that the affairs of the other are his own affairs. The State, while it respects the liberty of each in what specially regards himself, is bound to maintain a vigilant control over his exercise of any power which it allows him to possess over others. This obligation is almost entirely disregarded in the case of the family relations, a case, in its direct influence on human happiness, more important than all others taken together. The almost despotic power of husbands over wives needs not be enlarged upon here, because nothing more is needed for the complete removal of the evil, than that wives should have the same rights, and should receive the protection of law in the same manner, as all other persons ; and because, on this subject, the defenders of established injustice do not avail themselves of the plea of liberty, but stand forth openly as the champions of power. It is in the case of children, that misapplied notions of liberty are a real obstacle to the fulfilment by the State of its duties. One would almost think that a man's children were supposed to be literally, and not metaphorically, a part of himself, so jealous is opinion of the smallest interference of law with his absolute and exclusive control over them ; more jealous than of almost any interference with his own freedom of action : so much less do the generality of mankind value liberty than power. Consider, for example, the case of education.

Is it not almost a self-evident axiom, that the State should require and compel the education, up to a certain standard, of every human being who is born its citizen? Yet who is there that is not afraid to recognize and assert this truth? Hardly any one indeed will deny that it is one of the most sacred duties of the parents (or, as law and usage now stand, the father), after summoning a human being into the world, to give to that being an education fitting him to perform his part well in life towards others and towards himself. But while this is unanimously declared to be the father's duty, scarcely anybody, in this country, will bear to hear of obliging him to perform it. Instead of his being required to make any exertion or sacrifice for securing education to the child, it is left to his choice to accept it or not when it is provided gratis! It still remains unrecognized, that to bring a child into existence without a fair prospect of being able, not only to provide food for its body, but instruction and training for its mind, is a moral crime, both against the unfortunate offspring and against society; and that if the parent does not fulfil this obligation, the State ought to see it fulfilled, at the charge, as far as possible, of the parent.

Were the duty of enforcing universal education once admitted, there would be an end to the difficulties about what the State should teach, and how it should teach, which now convert the subject into a mere battle-field for sects and parties, causing the time and labour which should have been spent in educating, to be wasted in quarrelling about education. If the government would make up its mind to *require* for every child a good education, it might save itself the trouble of *providing* one. It might leave to parents to obtain the education where and how they pleased, and content itself with helping to pay the school fees of the poorer classes of children, and defraying the entire school expenses of those who have no one else to pay for them. The objections which are urged with reason against State education, do not apply to the enforcement of education by the State, but to the State's taking upon itself to direct that education : which is a totally different thing. That the whole or any large part of the education of the people should be in State hands, I go as far as any one in deprecating. All that has been said of the importance of individuality of character, and diversity in opinions and modes of conduct, involves, as of the same unspeakable importance, diversity of education. A general State education is a mere contrivance for moulding people to be exactly like one another : and as the mould in which it casts them is that which pleases the predominant power in the government, whether this be a monarch, a priesthood, an aristocracy, or the majority of the existing generation in proportion as it is efficient and successful, it establishes a despotism over the mind, leading by natural tendency to one over the body. An education established and controlled by the State should only exist, if it exist at all, as one among many competing experiments, carried on for the purpose of example and stimulus, to keep the others up to a certain standard of excellence. Unless, indeed, when society in general is in so backward a state that it could not or would not provide for itself any proper institutions of education, unless the government undertook the task : then, indeed, the government may, as the less of two great evils, take upon itself the business of schools and universities, as it may that of joint-stock companies, when private enterprise, in a shape fitted for undertaking great works of industry, does not exist in the country. But in general, if the country contains a sufficient number of persons qualified to provide education under government auspices, the same persons would be able and willing to give an equally good education on the voluntary principle, under the assurance of remuneration afforded by a law rendering education compulsory, combined with State aid to those unable to defray the expense.

The instrument for enforcing the law could be no other than public examinations, extending to all

children, and beginning at an early age.   An age might
be fixed at which every child must be examined, to
ascertain if he (or she) is able to read.   If a child proves
unable, the father, unless he has some sufficient ground
of excuse, might be subjected to a moderate fine, to be
worked out, if necessary, by his labour, and the child
might be put to school at his expense.   Once in every
year the examination should be renewed, with a gradually extending range of subjects, so as to make the
universal acquisition, and what is more, retention, of
a certain minimum of general knowledge, virtually
compulsory.   Beyond that minimum, there should be
voluntary examinations on all subjects, at which all
who come up to a certain standard of proficiency might
claim a certificate.   To prevent the State from exercising, through these arrangements, an improper influence
over opinion, the knowledge required for passing an
examination (beyond the merely instrumental parts of
knowledge, such as languages and their use) should,
even in the higher classes of examinations, be confined
to facts and positive science exclusively.   The examinations on religion, politics, or other disputed topics,
should not turn on the truth or falsehood of opinions,
but on the matter of fact that such and such an opinion
is held, on such grounds, by such authors, or schools,
or churches.   Under this system, the rising generation
would be no worse off in regard to all disputed truths,
than they are at present ; they would be brought up
either churchmen or dissenters as they now are, the
State merely taking care that they should be instructed
churchmen, or instructed dissenters.   There would be
nothing to hinder them from being taught religion, if
their parents chose, at the same schools where they
were taught other things.   All attempts by the State to
bias the conclusions of its citizens on disputed subjects,
are evil ; but it may very properly offer to ascertain
and certify that a person possesses the knowledge,
requisite to make his conclusions, on any given subject,
worth attending to.   A student of philosophy would
be the better for being able to stand an examination

both in Locke and in Kant, whichever of the two he takes up with, or even if with neither : and there is no reasonable objection to examining an atheist in the evidences of Christianity, provided he is not required to profess a belief in them. The examinations, however, in the higher branches of knowledge should, I conceive, be entirely voluntary. It would be giving too dangerous a power to governments, were they allowed to exclude any one from professions, even from the profession of teacher, for alleged deficiency of qualifications : and I think, with Wilhelm von Humboldt, that degrees, or other public certificates of scientific or professional acquirements, should be given to all who present themselves for examination, and stand the test ; but that such certificates should confer no advantage over competitors, other than the weight which may be attached to their testimony by public opinion.

It is not in the matter of education only, that misplaced notions of liberty prevent moral obligations on the part of parents from being recognized, and legal obligations from being imposed, where there are the strongest grounds for the former always, and in many cases for the latter also. The fact itself, of causing the existence of a human being, is one of the most responsible actions in the range of human life. To undertake this responsibility—to bestow a life which may be either a curse or a blessing—unless the being on whom it is to be bestowed will have at least the ordinary chances of a desirable existence, is a crime against that being. And in a country either overpeopled, or threatened with being so, to produce children, beyond a very small number, with the effect of reducing the reward of labour by their competition, is a serious offence against all who live by the remuneration of their labour. The laws which, in many countries on the Continent, forbid marriage unless the parties can show that they have the means of supporting a family, do not exceed the legitimate powers of the State : and whether such laws be expedient or not (a question mainly dependent on local circumstances and feelings), they are not objectionable as violations of liberty. Such laws are interferences of the State to prohibit a mischievous act—an act injurious to others, which ought to be a subject of reprobation, and social stigma, even when it is not deemed expedient to superadd legal punishment. Yet the current ideas of liberty, which bend so easily to real infringements of the freedom of the individual in things which concern only himself, would repel the attempt to put any restraint upon his inclinations when the consequence of their indulgence is a life or lives of wretchedness and depravity to the offspring, with manifold evils to those sufficiently within reach to be in any way affected by their actions. When we compare the strange respect of mankind for liberty, with their strange want of respect for it, we might imagine that a man had an indispensable right to do harm to others, and no right at all to please himself without giving pain to any one.

I have reserved for the last place a large class of questions respecting the limits of government interference, which, though closely connected with the subject of this Essay, do not, in strictness, belong to it. These are cases in which the reasons against interference do not turn upon the principle of liberty: the question is not about restraining the actions of individuals, but about helping them : it is asked whether the government should do, or cause to be done, something for their benefit, instead of leaving it to be done by themselves, individually, or in voluntary combination.

The objections to government interference, when it is not such as to involve infringement of liberty, may be of three kinds.

The first is, when the thing to be done is likely to be better done by individuals than by the government. Speaking generally, there is no one so fit to conduct any business, or to determine how or by whom it shall be conducted, as those who are personally interested in it. This principle condemns the interferences, once so common, of the legislature, or the officers of government, with the ordinary processes of industry. But this part of the subject has been sufficiently enlarged upon by political economists, and is not particularly related to the principles of this Essay.

The second objection is more nearly allied to our subject. In many cases, though individuals may not do the particular thing so well, on the average, as the officers of government, it is nevertheless desirable that it should be done by them, rather than by the government, as a means to their own mental education—a mode of strengthening their active faculties, exercising their judgement, and giving them a familiar knowledge of the subjects with which they are thus left to deal. This is a principal, though not the sole, recommendation of jury trial (in cases not political); of free and popular local and municipal institutions; of the conduct of industrial and philanthropic enterprises by voluntary associations. These are not questions of liberty, and are connected with that subject only by remote tendencies; but they are questions of development. It belongs to a different occasion from the present to dwell on these things as parts of national education; as being, in truth, the peculiar training of a citizen, the practical part of the political education of a free people, taking them out of the narrow circle of personal and family selfishness, and accustoming them to the comprehension of joint interests, the management of joint concerns—habituating them to act from public or semi-public motives, and guide their conduct by aims which unite instead of isolating them from one another. Without these habits and powers, a free constitution can neither be worked nor preserved; as is exemplified by the too-often transitory nature of political freedom in countries where it does not rest upon a sufficient basis of local liberties. The management of purely local business by the localities, and of the great enterprises of industry by the union of those who voluntarily supply the pecuniary means, is further recommended by all the advantages which have been set forth in this Essay as belonging to individuality of development, and diversity of modes of action. Government operations tend to be everywhere alike. With individuals and voluntary associations, on the contrary, there are varied experiments, and endless diversity of experience. What the State can usefully do, is to make itself a central depository, and active circulator and diffuser, of the experience resulting from many trials. Its business is to enable each experimentalist to benefit by the experiments of others; instead of tolerating no experiments but its own.

The third, and most cogent reason for restricting the interference of government, is the great evil of adding unnecessarily to its power. Every function superadded to those already exercised by the government, causes its influence over hopes and fears to be more widely diffused, and converts, more and more, the active and ambitious part of the public into hangers-on of the government, or of some party which aims at becoming the government. If the roads, the railways, the banks, the insurance offices, the great joint-stock companies, the universities, and the public charities, were all of them branches of the government; if, in addition, the municipal corporations and local boards, with all that now devolves on them, became departments of the central administration; if the employés of all these different enterprises were appointed and paid by the government, and looked to the government for every rise in life; not all the freedom of the press and popular constitution of the legislature would make this or any other country free otherwise than in name. And the evil would be greater, the more efficiently and scientifically the administrative machinery was constructed—the more skilful the arrangements for obtaining the best qualified hands and heads with which to work it. In England it has of late been proposed that all the members of the civil service of government should be selected by competitive examination, to obtain for those employments the most intelligent and instructed persons procurable; and much has been said and written for and against this proposal. One of the arguments most insisted on by its opponents, is that the occupation of a permanent official servant of the State does not hold out sufficient prospects of emolument and importance to attract the highest talents, which will always be able to find a more inviting career in the professions, or in the service of companies and other public bodies. One would not have been surprised if this argument had been used by the friends of the proposition, as an answer to its principal difficulty. Coming from the opponents it is strange enough. What is urged as an objection is the safety-valve of the proposed system. If indeed all the high talent of the country *could* be drawn into the service of the government, a proposal tending to bring about that result might well inspire uneasiness. If every part of the business of society which required organized concert, or large and comprehensive views, were in the hands of the government, and if government offices were universally filled by the ablest men, all the enlarged culture and practised intelligence in the country, except the purely speculative, would be concentrated in a numerous bureaucracy, to whom alone the rest of the community would look for all things: the multitude for direction and dictation in all they had to do; the able and aspiring for personal advancement. To be admitted into the ranks of this bureaucracy, and when admitted, to rise therein, would be the sole objects of ambition. Under this régime, not only is the outside public ill-qualified, for want of practical experience, to criticize or check the mode of operation of the bureaucracy, but even if the accidents of despotic or the natural working of popular institutions occasionally raise to the summit a ruler or rulers of reforming inclinations, no reform can be effected which is contrary to the interest of the bureaucracy. Such is the melancholy condition of the Russian empire, as shown in the accounts of those who have had sufficient opportunity of observation. The Czar himself is powerless against the bureaucratic body; he can send any one of them to Siberia, but he cannot govern without them, or against their will. On every decree of his they have a tacit veto, by merely refraining from carrying it into effect. In countries of more advanced civilization and of a more insurrectionary spirit, the public, accustomed to expect everything to be done for them by the State, or at least to do nothing for themselves without asking from the State not only leave to do it, but even how it is to be done, naturally hold the State responsible for all evil which befalls them, and when the evil exceeds their amount of patience, they rise against the government and make what is called a revolution; whereupon somebody else, with or without legitimate authority from the nation, vaults into the seat, issues his orders to the bureaucracy, and everything goes on much as it did before; the bureaucracy being unchanged, and nobody else being capable of taking their place.

A very different spectacle is exhibited among a people accustomed to transact their own business. In France, a large part of the people having been engaged in military service, many of whom have held at least the rank of non-commissioned officers, there are in every popular insurrection several persons competent to take the lead, and improvise some tolerable plan of action. What the French are in military affairs, the Americans are in every kind of civil business; let them be left without a government, every body of Americans is able to improvise one, and to carry on that or any other public business with a sufficient amount of intelligence, order, and decision. This is what every free people ought to be: and a people capable of this is certain to be free; it will never let itself be enslaved by any man or body of men because these are able to seize and pull the reins of the central administration. No bureaucracy can hope to make such a people as this do or undergo anything that they do not like. But where everything is done through the bureaucracy, nothing to which the bureaucracy is really adverse can be done at all. The constitution of such countries is an organization of the experience and practical ability of the nation, into a disciplined body for the purpose of governing the rest; and the more perfect that organization is in itself, the more successful in drawing to itself and educating for itself the persons of greatest capacity from all ranks of the community, the more complete is the bondage of all, the members of the bureaucracy included. For the governors are as much the slaves of their organization and discipline, as the governed are of the governors. A Chinese mandarin is as much the tool and creature of a despotism as the humblest cultivator. An individual Jesuit is to the utmost degree of abasement the slave of his order, though the order itself exists for the collective power and importance of its members.

It is not, also, to be forgotten, that the absorption of all the principal ability of the country into the governing body is fatal, sooner or later, to the mental activity and progressiveness of the body itself. Banded together as they are—working a system which, like all systems, necessarily proceeds in a great measure by fixed rules—the official body are under the constant temptation of sinking into indolent routine, or, if they now and then desert that mill-horse round, of rushing into some half-examined crudity which has struck the fancy of some leading member of the corps: and the sole check to these closely allied, though seemingly opposite, tendencies, the only stimulus which can keep the ability of the body itself up to a high standard, is liability to the watchful criticism of equal ability outside the body. It is indispensable, therefore, that the means should exist, independently of the government, of forming such ability, and furnishing it with the opportunities and experience necessary for a correct judgement of great practical affairs. If we would possess permanently a skilful and efficient body of functionaries—above all, a body able to originate and willing to adopt improvements; if we would not have our bureaucracy degenerate into a pedantocracy, this body must not engross all the occupations which form and cultivate the faculties required for the government of mankind.

To determine the point at which evils, so formidable to human freedom and advancement, begin, or rather at which they begin to predominate over the benefits attending the collective application of the force of society, under its recognized chiefs, for the removal of the obstacles which stand in the way of its well-being ; to secure as much of the advantages of centralized power and intelligence, as can be had without turning into governmental channels too great a proportion of the general activity—is one of the most difficult and complicated questions in the art of government. It is, in a great measure, a question of detail, in which many and various considerations must be kept in view, and no absolute rule can be laid down. But I believe that the practical principle in which safety resides, the ideal to be kept in view, the standard by which to test all arrangements intended for overcoming the difficulty, may be conveyed in these words : the greatest dissemination of power consistent with efficiency ; but the greatest possible centralization of information, and diffusion of it from the centre. Thus, in municipal administration, there would be, as in the New England States, a very minute division among separate officers, chosen by the localities, of all business which is not better left to the persons directly interested ; but besides this, there would be, in each department of local affairs, a central superintendence, forming a branch of the general government. The organ of this superintendence would concentrate, as in a focus, the variety of information and experience derived from the conduct of that branch of public business in all the localities, from everything analogous which is done in foreign countries, and from the general principles of political science. This central organ should have a right to know all that is done, and its special duty should be that of making the knowledge acquired in one place available for others. Emancipated from the petty prejudices and narrow views of a locality by its elevated position and comprehensive sphere of observation, its advice would naturally carry much authority ; but its actual power, as a permanent institution, should, I conceive, be limited to compelling the local officers to obey the laws laid down for their guidance. In all things not provided for by general rules, those officers should be left to their own judgement, under responsibility to their constituents. For the violation of rules, they should be responsible to law, and the rules themselves should be laid down by the legislature ; the central administrative authority only watching over their execution, and if they were not properly carried into effect, appealing, according to the nature of the case, to the tribunals to enforce the law, or to the constituencies to dismiss the functionaries who had not executed it according to its spirit. Such, in its general conception, is the central superintendence which the Poor Law Board is intended to exercise over the administrators of the Poor Rate throughout the country. Whatever powers the Board exercises beyond this limit, were right and necessary in that peculiar case, for the cure of rooted habits of maladministration in matters deeply affecting not the localities merely, but the whole community ; since no locality has a moral right to make itself by mismanagement a nest of pauperism, necessarily overflowing into other localities, and impairing the moral and physical condition of the whole labouring community. The powers of administrative coercion and subordinate legislation possessed by the Poor Law Board (but which, owing to the state of opinion on the subject, are very scantily exercised by them), though perfectly justifiable in a case of first-rate national interest, would be wholly out of place in the superintendence of interests purely local. But a central organ of information and instruction for all the localities, would be equally valuable in all departments of administration. A government cannot have too much of the kind of activity which does not impede, but aids and stimulates, individual exertion and development. The mischief begins when, instead of calling forth the activity and powers of individuals and bodies, it substitutes its own activity for theirs ; when, instead of informing, advising, and, upon occasion, denouncing, it makes them work in fetters, or bids them stand aside and does their work instead of them. The worth of a State, in the long run, is the worth of the individuals composing it ; and a State which postpones the interests of *their* mental expansion and elevation, to a little more of administrative skill, or of that semblance of it which practice gives, in the details of business ; a State which dwarfs its men, in order that they may be more docile instruments in its hands even for beneficial purposes—will find that with small men no great thing can really be accomplished ; and that the perfection of machinery to which it has sacrificed everything, will in the end avail it nothing, for want of the vital power which, in order that the machine might work more smoothly, it has preferred to banish.

CONSIDERATIONS

ON

REPRESENTATIVE GOVERNMENT

PREFACE

THOSE who have done me the honour of reading my previous writings, will probably receive no strong impression of novelty from the present volume; for the principles are those to which I have been working up during the greater part of my life, and most of the practical suggestions have been anticipated by others or by myself. There is novelty, however, in the fact of bringing them together, and exhibiting them in their connexion; and also, I believe, in much that is brought forward in their support. Several of the opinions at all events, if not new, are for the present as little likely to meet with general acceptance as if they were.

It seems to me, however, from various indications, and from none more than the recent debates on Reform of Parliament, that both Conservatives and Liberals (if I may continue to call them what they still call themselves) have lost confidence in the political creeds which they nominally profess, while neither side appears to have made any progress in providing itself with a better. Yet such a better doctrine must be possible; not a mere compromise, by splitting the difference between the two, but something wider than either, which, in virtue of its superior comprehensiveness, might be adopted by either Liberal or Conservative without renouncing anything which he really feels to be valuable in his own creed. When so many feel obscurely the want of such a doctrine, and so few even flatter themselves that they have attained it, any one may without presumption offer what his own thoughts, and the best that he knows of those of others, are able to contribute towards its formation.

CHAPTER I

ALL speculations concerning forms of government bear the impress, more or less exclusive, of two conflicting theories respecting political institutions; or, to speak more properly, conflicting conceptions of what political institutions are.

By some minds, government is conceived as strictly a practical art, giving rise to no questions but those of means and an end. Forms of government are assimilated to any other expedients for the attainment of human objects. They are regarded as wholly an affair of invention and contrivance. Being made by man, it is assumed that man has the choice either to make them or not, and how or on what pattern they shall be made. Government, according to this conception, is a problem, to be worked like any other question of business. The first step is to define the purposes which governments are required to promote. The next, is to inquire what form of government is best fitted to fulfil those purposes. Having satisfied ourselves on these two points, and ascertained the form of government which combines the greatest amount of good with the least of evil, what further remains is to obtain the concurrence of our countrymen, or those for whom the institutions are intended, in the opinion which we have privately arrived at. To find the best form of government; to persuade others that it is the best; and having done so, to stir them up to insist on having it, is the order of ideas in the minds of those who adopt this view of political philosophy. They look upon a constitution in the same light (difference of scale being allowed for) as they would upon a steam plough, or a threshing machine.

To these stand opposed another kind of political reasoners, who are so far from assimilating a form of government to a machine, that they regard it as a sort of spontaneous product, and the science of government as a branch (so to speak) of natural history. According to them, forms of government are not a matter of choice. We must take them, in the main, as we find them. Governments cannot be constructed by premeditated design. They ' are not made, but grow '. Our business with them, as with the other facts of the universe, is to acquaint ourselves with their natural properties, and adapt ourselves to them. The fundamental political institutions of a people are considered by this school as a sort of organic growth from the nature and life of that people : a product of their habits, instincts, and unconscious wants and desires, scarcely at all of their deliberate purposes. Their will has had no part in the matter but that of meeting the necessities of the moment by the contrivances of the moment, which contrivances, if in sufficient conformity to the national feelings and character, commonly last, and by successive aggregation constitute a polity, suited to the people who possess it, but which it would be vain to attempt to superinduce upon any people whose nature and circumstances had not spontaneously evolved it.

It is difficult to decide which of these doctrines would be the most absurd, if we could suppose either of them held as an exclusive theory. But the principles which men profess, on any controverted subject, are usually a very incomplete exponent of the opinions they really hold. No one believes that every people is capable of working every sort of institutions. Carry the analogy of mechanical contrivances as far as we will, a man does not choose even an instrument of timber and iron on the sole ground that it is in itself the best. He considers whether he possesses the other requisites which must be combined with it to render its employment advantageous, and in particular whether those by whom it will have to be worked, possess the knowledge and skill necessary for its management. On the other hand, neither are those who speak of institutions as if they were a kind of living organisms, really the political fatalists they give themselves out to be. They do not pretend that mankind have absolutely no range of choice as to the government they will live under, or that a consideration of the consequences which flow from different forms of polity is no element at all in deciding which of them should be preferred. But though each side greatly exaggerates its own theory, out of opposition to the other, and no one holds without modification to either, the two doctrines correspond to a deep-seated difference between two modes of thought; and though it is evident that neither of these is entirely in the right, yet it being equally evident that neither is wholly in the wrong, we must endeavour to get down to what is at the root of each, and avail ourselves of the amount of truth which exists in either.

Let us remember, then, in the first place, that political institutions (however the proposition may be at times ignored) are the work of men; owe their origin and their whole existence to human will. Men did not wake on a summer morning and find them sprung up. Neither do they resemble trees, which, once planted, ' are ay growing ' while men ' are sleeping '. In every stage of their existence they are made what they are by human voluntary agency. Like all things, therefore, which are made by men, they may be either well or ill made ; judgement and skill may have been exercised in their production, or the reverse of these. And again, if a people have omitted, or from outward pressure have not had it in their power, to give themselves a constitution by the tentative process of applying a corrective to each evil as it arose, or as the sufferers gained strength to resist it, this retardation of political progress is no doubt a great disadvantage to them, but it does not prove that what has been found good for others would not have been good also for them, and will not be so still when they think fit to adopt it.

On the other hand, it is also to be borne in mind that political machinery does not act of itself. As it is first made, so it has to be worked, by men, and even by ordinary men. It needs, not their simple acquiescence, but their active participation; and must be adjusted to the capacities and qualities of such men as are available. This implies three conditions. The people for whom the form of government is intended must be willing to accept it; or at least not so unwilling, as to oppose an insurmountable obstacle to its establishment. They must be willing and able to do what is necessary to keep it standing. And they must be willing and able to do what it requires of them to enable it to fulfil its purposes. The word 'do' is to be understood as including forbearances as well as acts. They must be capable of fulfilling the conditions of action, and the conditions of self-restraint, which are necessary either for keeping the established polity in existence, or for enabling it to achieve the ends, its conduciveness to which forms its recommendation.

The failure of any of these conditions renders a form of government, whatever favourable promise it may otherwise hold out, unsuitable to the particular case.

The first obstacle, the repugnance of the people to the particular form of government, needs little illustration, because it never can in theory have been overlooked. The case is of perpetual occurrence. Nothing but foreign force would induce a tribe of North American Indians to submit to the restraints of a regular and civilized government. The same might have been said, though somewhat less absolutely, of the barbarians who overran the Roman Empire. It required centuries of time, and an entire change of circumstances, to discipline them into regular obedience even to their own leaders, when not actually serving under their banner. There are nations who will not voluntarily submit to any government but that of certain families, which have from time immemorial had the privilege of supplying them with chiefs. Some nations could not, except by foreign conquest, be made to endure a monarchy; others are equally averse to a republic. The hindrance often amounts, for the time being, to impracticability.

But there are also cases in which, though not averse to a form of government—possibly even desiring it— a people may be unwilling or unable to fulfil its conditions. They may be incapable of fulfilling such of them as are necessary to keep the government even in nominal existence. Thus a people may prefer a free government, but if, from indolence, or carelessness, or cowardice, or want of public spirit, they are unequal to the exertions necessary for preserving it; if they will not fight for it when it is directly attacked; if they can be deluded by the artifices used to cheat them out of it; if by momentary discouragement, or temporary panic, or a fit of enthusiasm for an individual, they can be induced to lay their liberties at the feet even of a great man, or trust him with powers which enable him to subvert their institutions; in all these cases they are more or less unfit for liberty : and though it may be for their good to have had it even for a short time, they are unlikely long to enjoy it. Again, a people may be unwilling or unable to fulfil the duties which a particular form of government requires of them. A rude people, though in some degree alive to the benefits of civilized society, may be unable to practise the forbearances which it demands : their passions may be too violent, or their personal pride too exacting, to forgo private conflict, and leave to the laws the avenging of their real or supposed wrongs. In such a case, a civilized government, to be really advantageous to them, will require to be in a considerable degree despotic : to be one over which they do not themselves exercise control, and which imposes a great amount of forcible restraint upon their actions. Again, a people must be considered unfit for more than a limited and qualified freedom, who will not co-operate actively with the law and the public authorities, in the repression of evil-doers. A people who are more disposed to shelter a criminal than to apprehend him;

who, like the Hindoos, will perjure themselves to screen
the man who has robbed them, rather than take trouble
or expose themselves to vindictiveness by giving
evidence against him; who, like some nations of
Europe down to a recent date, if a man poniards
another in the public street, pass by on the other side,
because it is the business of the police to look to the
matter, and it is safer not to interfere in what does
not concern them; a people who are revolted by an
execution, but not shocked at an assassination—
require that the public authorities should be armed
with much sterner powers of repression than elsewhere,
since the first indispensable requisites of civilized life
have nothing else to rest on.   These deplorable states
of feeling, in any people who have emerged from
savage life, are, no doubt, usually the consequence of
previous bad government, which has taught them to
regard the law as made for other ends than their good,
and its administrators as worse enemies than those
who openly violate it.   But however little blame may
be due to those in whom these mental habits have
grown up, and however the habits may be ultimately
conquerable by better government, yet while they
exist, a people so disposed cannot be governed with as
little power exercised over them, as a people whose
sympathies are on the side of the law, and who are
willing to give active assistance in its enforcement.
Again, representative institutions are of little value,
and may be a mere instrument of tyranny or intrigue,
when the generality of electors are not sufficiently
interested in their own government to give their vote,
or, if they vote at all, do not bestow their suffrages on
public grounds, but sell them for money, or vote at the
beck of some one who has control over them, or whom
for private reasons they desire to propitiate.   Popular
election thus practised, instead of a security against
misgovernment, is but an additional wheel in its
machinery.   Besides these moral hindrances, mechanical difficulties are often an insuperable impediment to
forms of government.   In the ancient world, though

there might be, and often was, great individual or local independence, there could be nothing like a regulated popular government, beyond the bounds of a single city-community; because there did not exist the physical conditions for the formation and propagation of a public opinion, except among those who could be brought together to discuss public matters in the same agora. This obstacle is generally thought to have ceased by the adoption of the representative system. But to surmount it completely, required the press, and even the newspaper press, the real equivalent, though not in all respects an adequate one, of the Pnyx and the Forum. There have been states of society in which even a monarchy of any great territorial extent could not subsist, but unavoidably broke up into petty principalities, either mutually independent, or held together by a loose tie like the feudal: because the machinery of authority was not perfect enough to carry orders into effect at a great distance from the person of the ruler. He depended mainly upon voluntary fidelity for the obedience even of his army, nor did there exist the means of making the people pay an amount of taxes sufficient for keeping up the force necessary to compel obedience throughout a large territory. In these and all similar cases, it must be understood that the amount of the hindrance may be either greater or less. It may be so great as to make the form of government work very ill, without absolutely precluding its existence, or hindering it from being practically preferable to any other which can be had. This last question mainly depends upon a consideration which we have not yet arrived at—the tendencies of different forms of government to promote Progress.

We have now examined the three fundamental conditions of the adaptation of forms of government to the people who are to be governed by them. If the supporters of what may be termed the naturalistic theory of politics, mean but to insist on the necessity of these three conditions; if they only mean that no government can permanently exist, which does not fulfil the first and second conditions, and, in some considerable measure, the third ; their doctrine, thus limited, is incontestable. Whatever they mean more than this, appears to me untenable. All that we are told about the necessity of an historical basis for institutions, of their being in harmony with the national usages and character, and the like, means either this, or nothing to the purpose. There is a great quantity of mere sentimentality connected with these and similar phrases, over and above the amount of rational meaning contained in them. But, considered practically, these alleged requisites of political institutions are merely so many facilities for realizing the three conditions. When an institution, or a set of institutions, has the way prepared for it by the opinions, tastes, and habits of the people, they are not only more easily induced to accept it, but will more easily learn, and will be, from the beginning, better disposed, to do what is required of them both for the preservation of the institutions, and for bringing them into such action as enables them to produce their best results. It would be a great mistake in any legislator not to shape his measures so as to take advantage of such pre-existing habits and feelings, when available. On the other hand, it is an exaggeration to elevate these mere aids and facilities into necessary conditions. People are more easily induced to do, and do more easily, what they are already used to ; but people also learn to do things new to them. Familiarity is a great help ; but much dwelling on an idea will make it familiar, even when strange at first. There are abundant instances in which a whole people have been eager for untried things. The amount of capacity which a people possess for doing new things, and adapting themselves to new circumstances, is itself one of the elements of the question. It is a quality in which different nations, and different stages of civilization, differ much from one another. The capability of any given people for fulfilling the conditions of a given form of government, cannot be pronounced on by any sweeping rule. Knowledge of the particular people, and general practical judgement and sagacity, must be the guides. There is also another consideration not to be lost sight of. A people may be unprepared for good institutions; but to kindle a desire for them is a necessary part of the preparation. To recommend and advocate a particular institution or form of government, and set its advantages in the strongest light, is one of the modes, often the only mode within reach, of educating the mind of the nation not only for accepting or claiming, but also for working, the institution. What means had Italian patriots, during the last and present generation, of preparing the Italian people for freedom in unity, but by inciting them to demand it? Those, however, who undertake such a task, need to be duly impressed, not solely with the benefits of the institution or polity which they recommend, but also with the capacities, moral, intellectual, and active, required for working it; that they may avoid, if possible, stirring up a desire too much in advance of the capacity.

The result of what has been said is, that, within the limits set by the three conditions so often adverted to, institutions and forms of government are a matter of choice. To inquire into the best form of government in the abstract (as it is called) is not a chimerical, but a highly practical employment of scientific intellect; and to introduce into any country the best institutions which, in the existing state of that country, are capable of, in any tolerable degree, fulfilling the conditions, is one of the most rational objects to which practical effort can address itself. Everything which can be said by way of disparaging the efficacy of human will and purpose in matters of government, might be said of it in every other of its applications. In all things there are very strict limits to human power. It can only act by wielding some one or more of the forces of nature. Forces, therefore, that can be applied to the desired use, must exist; and will only act according to their own laws. We cannot make the river run back-

wards ; but we do not therefore say that watermills
' are not made, but grow '.   In politics as in mechanics,
the power which is to keep the engine going must be
sought for outside the machinery ; and if it is not forth-
coming, or is insufficient to surmount the obstacles
which may reasonably be expected, the contrivance
will fail.   This is no peculiarity of the political art ;
and amounts only to saying that it is subject to the
same limitations and conditions as all other arts.

At this point we are met by another objection, or
the same objection in a different form.   The forces, it
is contended, on which the greater political phenomena
depend, are not amenable to the direction of politicians
or philosophers.   The government of a country, it is
affirmed, is, in all substantial respects, fixed and determined beforehand by the state of the country in regard
to the distribution of the elements of social power.
Whatever is the strongest power in society will obtain
the governing authority ; and a change in the political
constitution cannot be durable unless preceded or
accompanied by an altered distribution of power in
society itself.   A nation, therefore, cannot choose its
form of government.   The mere details, and practical
organization, it may choose ; but the essence of the
whole, the seat of the supreme power, is determined
for it by social circumstances.

That there is a portion of truth in this doctrine, I
at once admit ; but to make it of any use, it must be
reduced to a distinct expression and proper limits.
When it is said that the strongest power in society
will make itself strongest in the government, what is
meant by power ?   Not thews and sinews ; otherwise
pure democracy would be the only form of polity that
could exist.   To mere muscular strength, add two
other elements, property and intelligence, and we are
nearer the truth, but far from having yet reached it.
Not only is a greater number often kept down by a less,
but the greater number may have a preponderance in
property, and individually in intelligence, and may
yet be held in subjection, forcibly or otherwise, by

a minority in both respects inferior to it. To make these various elements of power politically influential, they must be organized ; and the advantage in organization is necessarily with those who are in possession of the government. A much weaker party in all other elements of power, may greatly preponderate when the powers of government are thrown into the scale ; and may long retain its predominance through this alone : though, no doubt, a government so situated is in the condition called in mechanics unstable equilibrium, like a thing balanced on its smaller end, which, if once disturbed, tends more and more to depart from, instead of reverting to, its previous state.

But there are still stronger objections to this theory of government, in the terms in which it is usually stated. The power in society which has any tendency to convert itself into political power, is not power quiescent, power merely passive, but active power ; in other words, power actually exerted ; that is to say, a very small portion of all the power in existence. Politically speaking, a great part of all power consists in will. How is it possible, then, to compute the elements of political power, while we omit from the computation anything which acts on the will ? To think that because those who wield the power in society wield in the end that of government, therefore it is of no use to attempt to influence the constitution of the government by acting on opinion, is to forget that opinion is itself one of the greatest active social forces. One person with a belief, is a social power equal to ninety-nine who have only interests. They who can succeed in creating a general persuasion that a certain form of government, or social fact of any kind, deserves to be preferred, have made nearly the most important step which can possibly be taken towards ranging the powers of society on its side. On the day when the proto-martyr was stoned to death at Jerusalem, while he who was to be the Apostle of the Gentiles stood by ' consenting unto his death ', would any one have supposed that the party of that stoned man were then and there the strongest power in society ? And has not the event proved that they were so ? Because theirs was the most powerful of then existing beliefs. The same element made a monk of Wittenberg, at the meeting of the Diet of Worms, a more powerful social force than the Emperor Charles V, and all the princes there assembled. But these, it may be said, are cases in which religion was concerned, and religious convictions are something peculiar in their strength. Then let us take a case purely political, where religion, so far as concerned at all, was chiefly on the losing side. If any one requires to be convinced that speculative thought is one of the chief elements of social power, let him bethink himself of the age in which there was scarcely a throne in Europe which was not filled by a liberal and reforming king, a liberal and reforming emperor, or, strangest of all, a liberal and reforming pope ; the age of Frederic the Great, of Catherine II, of Joseph II, of Peter Leopold, of Benedict XIV, of Ganganelli, of Pombal, of Aranda ; when the very Bourbons of Naples were liberals and reformers, and all the active minds among the noblesse of France were filled with the ideas which were soon after to cost them so dear. Surely a conclusive example how far mere physical and economic power is from being the whole of social power. It was not by any change in the distribution of material interests, but by the spread of moral convictions, that negro slavery has been put an end to in the British Empire and elsewhere. The serfs in Russia owe their emancipation, if not to a sentiment of duty, at least to the growth of a more enlightened opinion respecting the true interest of the State. It is what men think, that determines how they act ; and though the persuasions and convictions of average men are in a much greater degree determined by their personal position than by reason, no little power is exercised over them by the persuasions and convictions of those whose personal position is different, and by the united authority of the instructed. When, therefore, the instructed in general can be brought to recognize one social arrangement, or political or other institution, as good, and another as bad, one as desirable, another as condemnable, very much has been done towards giving to the one, or withdrawing from the other, that preponderance of social force which enables it to subsist. And the maxim, that the government of a country is what the social forces in existence compel it to be, is true only in the sense in which it favours, instead of discouraging, the attempt to exercise, among all forms of government practicable in the existing condition of society, a rational choice.

CHAPTER II

THE CRITERION OF A GOOD FORM OF GOVERNMENT

THE form of government for any given country being (within certain definite conditions) amenable to choice, it is now to be considered by what test the choice should be directed ; what are the distinctive characteristics of the form of government best fitted to promote the interests of any given society.

Before entering into this inquiry, it may seem necessary to decide what are the proper functions of government ; for, government altogether being only a means, the eligibility of the means must depend on their adaptation to the end. But this mode of stating the problem gives less aid to its investigation than might be supposed, and does not even bring the whole of the question into view. For, in the first place, the proper functions of a government are not a fixed thing, but different in different states of society ; much more extensive in a backward than in an advanced state. And, secondly, the character of a government or set of political institutions cannot be sufficiently estimated while we confine our attention to the legitimate sphere of governmental functions. For though the goodness of a government is necessarily circumscribed within that sphere, its badness unhappily is not.   Every kind and degree of evil of which mankind are susceptible, may be inflicted on them by their government ; and none of the good which social existence is capable of, can be any further realized than as the constitution of the government is compatible with, and allows scope for, its attainment.   Not to speak of indirect effects, the direct meddling of the public authorities has no necessary limits but those of human existence ; and the influence of government on the well-being of society can be considered or estimated in reference to nothing less than the whole of the interests of humanity.

Being thus obliged to place before ourselves, as the test of good and bad government, so complex an object as the aggregate interests of society, we would willingly attempt some kind of classification of those interests, which, bringing them before the mind in definite groups, might give indication of the qualities by which a form of government is fitted to promote those various interests respectively.   It would be a great facility if we could say, the good of society consists of such and such elements ; one of these elements requires such conditions, another such others: the government, then, which unites in the greatest degree all these conditions, must be the best.   The theory of government would thus be built up from the separate theorems of the elements which compose a good state of society.

Unfortunately, to enumerate and classify the constituents of social well-being, so as to admit of the formation of such theorems, is no easy task.   Most of those who, in the last or present generation, have applied themselves to the philosophy of politics in any comprehensive spirit, have felt the importance of such a classification ; but the attempts which have been made towards it are as yet limited, so far as I am aware, to a single step.   The classification begins and ends with a partition of the exigencies of society between the two heads of Order and Progress (in the phraseology of French thinkers) ; Permanence and Progression, in the words of Coleridge.   This division is plausible and seductive, from the apparently clean-cut opposition between its two members, and the remarkable difference between the sentiments to which they appeal. But I apprehend that (however admissible for purposes of popular discourse), the distinction between Order, or Permanence, and Progress, employed to define the qualities necessary in a government, is unscientific and incorrect.

For, first, what are Order and Progress ? Concerning Progress there is no difficulty, or none which is apparent at first sight. When Progress is spoken of as one of the wants of human society, it may be supposed to mean Improvement. That is a tolerably distinct idea. But what is Order ? Sometimes it means more, sometimes less, but hardly ever the whole of what human society needs except improvement.

In its narrowest acceptation, Order means Obedience. A government is said to preserve order, if it succeeds in getting itself obeyed. But there are different degrees of obedience, and it is not every degree that is commendable. Only an unmitigated despotism demands that the individual citizen shall obey unconditionally every mandate of persons in authority. We must at least limit the definition to such mandates as are general, and issued in the deliberate form of laws. Order, thus understood, expresses, doubtless, an indispensable attribute of government. Those who are unable to make their ordinances obeyed, cannot be said to govern. But though a necessary condition, this is not the object of government. That it should make itself obeyed is requisite, in order that it may accomplish some other purpose. We are still to seek what is this other purpose, which government ought to fulfil, abstractedly from the idea of improvement, and which has to be fulfilled in every society, whether stationary or progressive.

In a sense somewhat more enlarged, Order means the preservation of peace, by the cessation of private violence. Order is said to exist, where the people of the country have, as a general rule, ceased to prosecute their quarrels by private force, and acquired the habit of referring the decision of their disputes and the redress of their injuries to the public authorities. But in this larger use of the term, as well as in the former narrow one, Order expresses rather one of the conditions of government, than either its purpose or the criterion of its excellence. For the habit may be well established of submitting to the government, and referring all disputed matters to its authority, and yet the manner in which the government deals with those disputed matters, and with the other things about which it concerns itself, may differ by the whole interval which divides the best from the worst possible.

If we intend to comprise in the idea of Order, all that society requires from its government, which is not included in the idea of Progress, we must define Order as the preservation of all kinds and amounts of good which already exist, and Progress as consisting in the increase of them. This distinction does comprehend in one or the other section everything which a government can be required to promote. But, thus understood, it affords no basis for a philosophy of government. We cannot say that, in constituting a polity, certain provisions ought to be made for Order and certain others for Progress; since the conditions of Order, in the sense now indicated, and those of Progress, are not opposite, but the same. The agencies which tend to preserve the social good which already exists, are the very same which promote the increase of it, and vice versa : the sole difference being, that a greater degree of those agencies is required for the latter purpose than for the former.

What, for example, are the qualities in the citizens individually, which conduce most to keep up the amount of good conduct, of good management, of success and prosperity, which already exist in society ? Everybody will agree that those qualities are, industry, integrity, justice, and prudence. But are not these, of all qualities, the most conducive to improvement ? and is not any growth of these virtues in the community, in itself the greatest of improvements ? If so, whatever qualities in the government are promotive of industry, integrity, justice, and prudence, conduce alike to permanence and to progression ; only there is needed more of those qualities to make the society decidedly progressive, than merely to keep it permanent.

What, again, are the particular attributes in human beings, which seem to have a more especial reference to Progress, and do not so directly suggest the ideas of Order and Preservation ? They are chiefly the qualities of mental activity, enterprise, and courage. But are not all these qualities fully as much required for preserving the good we have, as for adding to it ? If there is anything certain in human affairs, it is that valuable acquisitions are only to be retained by the continuation of the same energies which gained them. Things left to take care of themselves inevitably decay. Those whom success induces to relax their habits of care and thoughtfulness, and their willingness to encounter disagreeables, seldom long retain their good fortune at its height. The mental attribute which seems exclusively dedicated to Progress, and is the culmination of the tendencies to it, is Originality, or Invention. Yet this is no less necessary for Permanence ; since, in the inevitable changes of human affairs, new inconveniences and dangers continually grow up, which must be encountered by new resources and contrivances, in order to keep things going on even only as well as they did before. Whatever qualities, therefore, in a government, tend to encourage activity, energy, courage, originality, are requisites of Permanence as well as of Progress ; only a somewhat less degree of them will on the average suffice for the former purpose than for the latter.

To pass now from the mental to the outward and objective requisites of society ; it is impossible to point out any contrivance in politics, or arrangement of social affairs, which conduces to Order only, or to Progress only ; whatever tends to either promotes both. Take, for instance, the common institution of a police. Order is the object which seems most immediately interested in the efficiency of this part of the social organization. Yet if it is effectual to promote Order, that is, if it represses crime, and enables every one to feel his person and property secure, can any state of things be more conducive to Progress ? The greater security of property is one of the main conditions and causes of greater production, which is Progress in its most familiar and vulgarest aspect. The better repression of crime represses the dispositions which tend to crime, and this is Progress in a somewhat higher sense. The release of the individual from the cares and anxieties of a state of imperfect protection, sets his faculties free to be employed in any new effort for improving his own state and that of others : while the same cause, by attaching him to social existence, and making him no longer see present or prospective enemies in his fellow creatures, fosters all those feelings of kindness and fellowship towards others, and interest in the general well-being of the community, which are such important parts of social improvement.

Take, again, such a familiar case as that of a good system of taxation and finance. This would generally be classed as belonging to the province of Order. Yet what can be more conducive to Progress ? A financial system which promotes the one, conduces, by the very same excellences, to the other. Economy, for example, equally preserves the existing stock of national wealth, and favours the creation of more. A just distribution of burthens, by holding up to every citizen an example of morality and good conscience applied to difficult adjustments, and an evidence of the value which the highest authorities attach to them, tends in an eminent degree to educate the moral sentiments of the community, both in respect of strength and of discrimination. Such a mode of levying the taxes as does not impede the industry, or unnecessarily interfere with the liberty, of the citizen, promotes, not the preservation only, but the increase of the national wealth, and encourages a more active use of the individual faculties. And vice versa, all errors in finance and taxation which obstruct the improvement of the people in wealth and morals, tend also, if of sufficiently serious amount, positively to impoverish and demoralize them. It holds, in short, universally, that when Order and Permanence are taken in their widest sense, for the stability of existing advantages, the requisites of Progress are but the requisites of Order in a greater degree ; those of Permanence merely those of Progress, in a somewhat smaller measure.

In support of the position that Order is intrinsically different from Progress, and that preservation of existing and acquisition of additional good are sufficiently distinct to afford the basis of a fundamental classification, we shall perhaps be reminded that Progress may be at the expense of Order ; that while we are acquiring, or striving to acquire, good of one kind, we may be losing ground in respect to others : thus there may be progress in wealth, while there is deterioration in virtue.   Granting this, what it proves is, not that Progress is generically a different thing from Permanence, but that wealth is a different thing from virtue.   Progress is permanence and something more ; and it is no answer to this, to say that Progress in one thing does not imply Permanence in everything. No more does Progress in one thing imply Progress in everything.   Progress of any kind includes Permanence in that same kind ; whenever Permanence is sacrificed to some particular kind of Progress, other Progress is still more sacrificed to it ; and if it be not worth the sacrifice, not the interest of Permanence alone has been disregarded, but the general interest of Progress has been mistaken.

If these improperly contrasted ideas are to be used at all in the attempt to give a first commencement of scientific precision to the notion of good government, it would be more philosophically correct to leave out of the definition the word Order, and to say that the best government is that which is most conducive to Progress.   For Progress includes Order, but Order does not include Progress.   Progress is a greater degree of

that of which Order is a less. Order, in any other
sense, stands only for a part of the pre-requisites of
good government, not for its idea and essence. Order
would find a more suitable place among the conditions
of Progress; since, if we would increase our sum of
good, nothing is more indispensable than to take due
care of what we already have. If we are endeavouring
after more riches, our very first rule should be, not to
squander uselessly our existing means. Order, thus
considered, is not an additional end to be reconciled
with Progress, but a part and means of Progress itself.
If a gain in one respect is purchased by a more than
equivalent loss in the same or in any other, there is not
Progress. Conduciveness to Progress, thus understood,
includes the whole excellence of a government.

But, though metaphysically defensible, this definition
of the criterion of good government is not appropriate,
because, though it contains the whole of the truth, it
recalls only a part. What is suggested by the term
Progress is the idea of moving onward, whereas the
meaning of it here is quite as much the prevention of
falling back. The very same social causes—the same
beliefs, feelings, institutions, and practices—are as
much required to prevent society from retrograding,
as to produce a further advance. Were there no
improvement to be hoped for, life would not be the less
an unceasing struggle against causes of deterioration;
as it even now is. Politics, as conceived by the
ancients, consisted wholly in this. The natural tendency of men and their works was to degenerate,
which tendency, however, by good institutions vir-
tuously administered, it might be possible for an
indefinite length of time to counteract. Though we no
longer hold this opinion; though most men in the
present age profess the contrary creed, believing that
the tendency of things, on the whole, is towards
improvement; we ought not to forget, that there is an
incessant and ever-flowing current of human affairs
towards the worse, consisting of all the follies, all the
vices, all the negligences, indolences, and supinenesses

of mankind ; which is only controlled, and kept from sweeping all before it, by the exertions which some persons constantly, and others by fits, put forth in the direction of good and worthy objects. It gives a very insufficient idea of the importance of the strivings which take place to improve and elevate human nature and life, to suppose that their chief value consists in the amount of actual improvement realized by their means, and that the consequence of their cessation would merely be that we should remain as we are. A very small diminution of those exertions would not only put a stop to improvement, but would turn the general tendency of things towards deterioration ; which, once begun, would proceed with increasing rapidity, and become more and more difficult to check, until it reached a state often seen in history, and in which many large portions of mankind even now grovel ; when hardly anything short of superhuman power seems sufficient to turn the tide, and give a fresh commencement to the upward movement.

These reasons make the word Progress as unapt as the terms Order and Permanence, to become the basis for a classification of the requisites of a form of government. The fundamental antithesis which these words express does not lie in the things themselves, so much as in the types of human character which answer to them. There are, we know, some minds in which caution, and others in which boldness, predominates : in some, the desire to avoid imperilling what is already possessed is a stronger sentiment than that which prompts to improve the old and acquire new advantages ; while there are others who lean the contrary way, and are more eager for future than careful of present good. The road to the ends of both is the same ; but they are liable to wander from it in opposite directions. This consideration is of importance in composing the personnel of any political body : persons of both types ought to be included in it, that the tendencies of each may be tempered, in so far as they are excessive, by a due proportion of the other. There needs no express provision to ensure this object, provided care is taken to admit nothing inconsistent with it.　The natural and spontaneous admixture of the old and the young, of those whose position and reputation are made, and those who have them still to make, will in general sufficiently answer the purpose, if only this natural balance is not disturbed by artificial regulation.

Since the distinction most commonly adopted for the classification of social exigencies does not possess the properties needful for that use, we have to seek for some other leading distinction better adapted to the purpose.　Such a distinction would seem to be indicated by the considerations to which I now proceed.

If we ask ourselves on what causes and conditions good government in all its senses, from the humblest to the most exalted, depends, we find that the principal of them, the one which transcends all others, is the qualities of the human beings composing the society over which the government is exercised.

We may take, as a first instance, the administration of justice ; with the more propriety, since there is no part of public business in which the mere machinery, the rules and contrivances for conducting the details of the operation, are of such vital consequence.　Yet even these yield in importance to the qualities of the human agents employed.　Of what efficacy are rules of procedure in securing the ends of justice, if the moral condition of the people is such that the witnesses generally lie, and the judges and their subordinates take bribes ?　Again, how can institutions provide a good municipal administration, if there exists such indifference to the subject, that those who would administer honestly and capably cannot be induced to serve, and the duties are left to those who undertake them because they have some private interest to be promoted ?　Of what avail is the most broadly popular representative system, if the electors do not care to choose the best member of parliament, but choose him who will spend

most money to be elected ?   How can a representative
assembly work for good, if its members can be bought, or
if their excitability of temperament, uncorrected by public
discipline or private self-control, makes them incapable
of calm deliberation, and they resort to manual violence
on the floor of the House, or shoot at one another with
rifles ?   How, again, can government, or any joint concern, be carried on in a tolerable manner by people so
envious, that if one among them seems likely to succeed
in anything, those who ought to co-operate with him
form a tacit combination to make him fail ?   Whenever
the general disposition of the people is such, that each
individual regards those only of his interests which are
selfish, and does not dwell on, or concern himself for,
his share of the general interest, in such a state of things
good government is impossible.   The influence of
defects of intelligence in obstructing all the elements of
good government requires no illustration.   Government consists of acts done by human beings ; and if
the agents, or those who choose the agents, or those
to whom the agents are responsible, or the lookers-on
whose opinion ought to influence and check all these,
are mere masses of ignorance, stupidity, and baleful
prejudice, every operation of government will go wrong :
while, in proportion as the men rise above this standard,
so will the government improve in quality ; up to the
point of excellence, attainable but nowhere attained,
where the officers of government, themselves persons
of superior virtue and intellect, are surrounded by the
atmosphere of a virtuous and enlightened, public
opinion.

The first element of good government, therefore,
being the virtue and intelligence of the human beings
composing the community, the most important point
of excellence which any form of government can
possess is to promote the virtue and intelligence of the
people themselves.   The first question in respect to
any political institutions is, how far they tend to
foster in the members of the community the various
desirable qualities, moral and intellectual ; or rather

(following Bentham's more complete classification) moral, intellectual, and active. The government which does this the best, has every likelihood of being the best in all other respects, since it is on these qualities, so far as they exist in the people, that all possibility of goodness in the practical operations of the government depends.

We may consider, then, as one criterion of the goodness of a government, the degree in which it tends to increase the sum of good qualities in the governed, collectively and individually; since, besides that their well-being is the sole object of government, their good qualities supply the moving force which works the machinery. This leaves, as the other constituent element of the merit of a government, the quality of the machinery itself; that is, the degree in which it is adapted to take advantage of the amount of good qualities which may at any time exist, and make them instrumental to the right purposes. Let us again take the subject of judicature as an example and illustration. The judicial system being given, the goodness of the administration of justice is in the compound ratio of the worth of the men composing the tribunals, and the worth of the public opinion which influences or controls them. But all the difference between a good and a bad system of judicature lies in the contrivances adopted for bringing whatever moral and intellectual worth exists in the community to bear upon the administration of justice, and making it duly operative on the result. The arrangements for rendering the choice of the judges such as to obtain the highest average of virtue and intelligence; the salutary forms of procedure; the publicity which allows observation and criticism of whatever is amiss; the liberty of discussion and censure through the press; the mode of taking evidence, according as it is well or ill adapted to elicit truth; the facilities, whatever be their amount, for obtaining access to the tribunals; the arrangements for detecting crimes and apprehending offenders;—all these things are not the power, but the machinery for bringing the power into contact with the obstacle : and the machinery has no action of itself, but without it the power, let it be ever so ample, would be wasted and of no effect.   A similar distinction exists in regard to the constitution of the executive departments of administration.   Their machinery is good, when the proper tests are prescribed for the qualifications of officers, the proper rules for their promotion ; when the business is conveniently distributed among those who are to transact it, a convenient and methodical order established for its transaction, a correct and intelligible record kept of it after being transacted ; when each individual knows for what he is responsible, and is known to others as responsible for it ; when the best-contrived checks are provided against negligence, favouritism, or jobbery, in any of the acts of the depart-ment.   But political checks will no more act of them-selves, than a bridle will direct a horse without a rider. If the checking functionaries are as corrupt or as negligent as those whom they ought to check, and if the public, the mainspring of the whole checking machinery, are too ignorant, too passive, or too careless and inattentive, to do their part, little benefit will be derived from the best administrative apparatus.   Yet a good apparatus is always preferable to a bad.   It enables such insufficient moving or checking power as exists, to act at the greatest advantage ; and without it, no amount of moving or checking power would be sufficient.   Publicity, for instance, is no impediment to evil nor stimulus to good if the public will not look at what is done ; but without publicity, how could they either check or encourage what they were not permitted to see ?   The ideally perfect constitution of a public office is that in which the interest of the functionary is entirely coincident with his duty.   No mere system will make it so, but still less can it be made so without a system, aptly devised for the purpose.

What we have said of the arrangements for the detailed administration of the government, is still more evidently true of its general constitution.   All government which aims at being good is an organization of some part of the good qualities existing in the individual members of the community, for the conduct of its collective affairs. A representative constitution is a means of bringing the general standard of intelligence and honesty existing in the community, and the individual intellect and virtue of its wisest members, more directly to bear upon the government, and investing them with greater influence in it, than they would in general have under any other mode of organization; though, under any, such influence as they do have is the source of all good that there is in the government, and the hindrance of every evil that there is not. The greater the amount of these good qualities which the institutions of a country succeed in organizing, and the better the mode of organization, the better will be the government.

We have now, therefore, obtained a foundation for a twofold division of the merit which any set of political institutions can possess. It consists partly of the degree in which they promote the general mental advancement of the community, including under that phrase advancement in intellect, in virtue, and in practical activity and efficiency; and partly of the degree of perfection with which they organize the moral, intellectual, and active worth already existing, so as to operate with the greatest effect on public affairs. A government is to be judged by its action upon men, and by its action upon things; by what it makes of the citizens, and what it does with them; its tendency to improve or deteriorate the people themselves, and the goodness or badness of the work it performs for them, and by means of them. Government is at once a great influence acting on the human mind, and a set of organized arrangements for public business: in the first capacity its beneficial action is chiefly indirect, but not therefore less vital, while its mischievous action may be direct.

The difference between these two functions of a government is not, like that between Order and Progress, a difference merely in degree, but in kind.   We must not, however, suppose that they have no intimate connexion with one another.   The institutions which ensure the best management of public affairs practicable in the existing state of cultivation, tend by this alone to the further improvement of that state.   A people which had the most just laws, the purest and most efficient judicature, the most enlightened administration, the most equitable and least onerous system of finance, compatible with the stage it had attained in moral and intellectual advancement, would be in a fair way to pass rapidly into a higher stage.   Nor is there any mode in which political institutions can contribute more effectually to the improvement of the people, than by doing their more direct work well. And, reversely, if their machinery is so badly constructed that they do their own particular business ill, the effect is felt in a thousand ways in lowering the morality and deadening the intelligence and activity of the people.   But the distinction is nevertheless real, because this is only one of the means by which political institutions improve or deteriorate the human mind, and the causes and modes of that beneficial or injurious influence remain a distinct and much wider subject of study.

Of the two modes of operation by which a form of government or set of political institutions affects the welfare of the community—its operation as an agency of national education, and its arrangements for conducting the collective affairs of the community in the state of education in which they already are ; the last evidently varies much less, from difference of country and state of civilization, than the first.   It has also much less to do with the fundamental constitution of the government.   The mode of conducting the practical business of government, which is best under a free constitution, would generally be best also in an absolute monarchy : only, an absolute monarchy is not so likely to practise it.   The laws of property, for example ; the principles of evidence and judicial procedure ; the system of taxation and of financial administration, need not necessarily be different in different forms of government. Each of these matters has principles and rules of its own, which are a subject of separate study. General jurisprudence, civil and penal legislation, financial and commercial policy, are sciences in themselves, or rather, separate members of the comprehensive science or art of government : and the most enlightened doctrines on all these subjects, though not equally likely to be understood or acted on under all forms of government, yet, if understood and acted on, would in general be equally beneficial under them all. It is true that these doctrines could not be applied without some modifications to all states of society and of the human mind : nevertheless, by far the greater number of them would require modifications solely of detail, to adapt them to any state of society sufficiently advanced to possess rulers capable of understanding them. A government to which they would be wholly unsuitable, must be one so bad in itself, or so opposed to public feeling, as to be unable to maintain itself in existence by honest means.

It is otherwise with that portion of the interests of the community which relate to the better or worse training of the people themselves. Considered as instrumental to this, institutions need to be radically different, according to the stage of advancement already reached. The recognition of this truth, though for the most part empirically rather than philosophically, may be regarded as the main point of superiority in the political theories of the present above those of the last age ; in which it was customary to claim representative democracy for England or France by arguments which would equally have proved it the only fit form of government for Bedouins or Malays. The state of different communities, in point of culture and development, ranges downwards to a condition very little above the highest of the beasts. The upward range, too, is considerable, and the future possible extension vastly greater. A community can only be developed out of one of these states into a higher, by a concourse of influences, among the principal of which is the government to which they are subject. In all states of human improvement ever yet attained, the nature and degree of authority exercised over individuals, the distribution of power, and the conditions of command and obedience, are the most powerful of the influences, except their religious belief, which make them what they are, and enable them to become what they can be. They may be stopped short at any point in their progress, by defective adaptation of their government to that particular stage of advancement. And the one indispensable merit of a government, in favour of which it may be forgiven almost any amount of other demerit compatible with progress, is that its operation on the people is favourable, or not unfavourable, to the next step which it is necessary for them to take, in order to raise themselves to a higher level.

Thus (to repeat a former example), a people in a state of savage independence, in which every one lives for himself, exempt, unless by fits, from any external control, is practically incapable of making any progress in civilization until it has learnt to obey. The indispensable virtue, therefore, in a government which establishes itself over a people of this sort is, that it make itself obeyed. To enable it to do this, the constitution of the government must be nearly, or quite, despotic. A constitution in any degree popular, dependent on the voluntary surrender by the different members of the community of their individual freedom of action, would fail to enforce the first lesson which the pupils, in this stage of their progress, require. Accordingly, the civilization of such tribes, when not the result of juxtaposition with others already civilized, is almost always the work of an absolute ruler, deriving his power either from religion or military prowess; very often from foreign arms.

Again, uncivilized races, and the bravest and most energetic still more than the rest, are averse to continuous labour of an unexciting kind. Yet all real civilization is at this price ; without such labour, neither can the mind be disciplined into the habits required by civilized society, nor the material world prepared to receive it.   There needs a rare concurrence of circumstances, and for that reason often a vast length of time, to reconcile such a people to industry, unless they are for a while compelled to it.   Hence even personal slavery, by giving a commencement to industrial life, and enforcing it as the exclusive occupation of the most numerous portion of the community, may accelerate the transition to a better freedom than that of fighting and rapine.   It is almost needless to say that this excuse for slavery is only available in a very early state of society.   A civilized people have far other means of imparting civilization to those under their influence ; and slavery is, in all its details, so repugnant to that government of law, which is the foundation of all modern life, and so corrupting to the master-class when they have once come under civilized influences, that its adoption under any circumstances whatever in modern society is a relapse into worse than barbarism.

At some period, however, of their history, almost every people, now civilized, have consisted, in majority, of slaves.   A people in that condition require to raise them out of it a very different polity from a nation of savages.   If they are energetic by nature, and especially if there be associated with them in the same community an industrious class who are neither slaves nor slave-owners (as was the case in Greece), they need, probably, no more to ensure their improvement than to make them free : when freed, they may often be fit, like Roman freedmen, to be admitted at once to the full rights of citizenship.   This, however, is not the normal condition of slavery, and is generally a sign that it is becoming obsolete.   A slave, properly so called, is a being who has not learnt to help himself. He is, no doubt, one step in advance of a savage.   He has not the first lesson of political society still to acquire. He has learnt to obey.   But what he obeys is only a direct command. It is the characteristic of *born* slaves to be incapable of conforming their conduct to a rule, or law. They can only do what they are ordered, and only when they are ordered to do it. If a man whom they fear is standing over them and threatening them with punishment, they obey ; but when his back is turned, the work remains undone. The motive determining them must appeal not to their interests, but to their instincts ; immediate hope or immediate terror. A despotism, which may tame the savage, will, in so far as it is a despotism, only confirm the slaves in their incapacities. Yet a government under their own control would be entirely unmanageable by them. Their improvement cannot come from themselves, but must be superinduced from without. The step which they have to take, and their only path to improvement, is to be raised from a government of will to one of law. They have to be taught self-government, and this, in its initial stage, means the capacity to act on general instructions. What they require is not a government of force, but one of guidance. Being, however, in too low a state to yield to the guidance of any but those to whom they look up as the possessors of force, the sort of government fittest for them is one which possesses force, but seldom uses it : a parental despotism or aristocracy, resembling the St. Simonian form of Socialism ; maintaining a general superintendence over all the operations of society, so as to keep before each the sense of a present force sufficient to compel his obedience to the rule laid down, but which, owing to the impossibility of descending to regulate all the minutiae of industry and life, necessarily leaves and induces individuals to do much of themselves. This, which may be termed the government of leading-strings, seems to be the one required to carry such a people the most rapidly through the next necessary step in social progress. Such appears to have been the idea of the government of the Incas of Peru; and such was that of the Jesuits of Paraguay. I need scarcely remark that leading-strings are only admissible as a means of gradually training the people to walk alone.

It would be out of place to carry the illustration further. To attempt to investigate what kind of government is suited to every known state of society would be to compose a treatise, not on representative government, but on political science at large. For our more limited purpose we borrow from political philosophy only its general principles. To determine the form of government most suited to any particular people, we must be able, among the defects and short-comings which belong to that people, to distinguish those that are the immediate impediment to progress ; to discover what it is which (as it were) stops the way. The best government for them is the one which tends most to give them that for want of which they cannot advance, or advance only in a lame and lopsided manner. We must not, however, forget the reservation necessary in all things which have for their object improvement, or Progress ; namely, that in seeking the good which is needed, no damage, or as little as possible, be done to that already possessed. A people of savages should be taught obedience, but not in such a manner as to convert them into a people of slaves. And (to give the observation a higher generality) the form of government which is most effectual for carrying a people through the next stage of progress, will still be very improper for them if it does this in such a manner as to obstruct, or positively unfit them for, the step next beyond. Such cases are frequent, and are among the most melancholy facts in history. The Egyptian hierarchy, the paternal despotism of China, were very fit instruments for carrying those nations up to the point of civilization which they attained. But having reached that point, they were brought to a permanent halt, for want of mental liberty and individuality ; requisites of improvement which the institutions that had carried them thus far, entirely inca-pacitated them from acquiring ; and as the institutions did not break down and give place to others, further improvement stopped.   In contrast with these nations, let us consider the example of an opposite character afforded by another and a comparatively insignificant Oriental people—the Jews.   They, too, had an absolute monarchy and a hierarchy, and their organized institutions were as obviously of sacerdotal origin as those of the Hindoos.   These did for them what was done for other Oriental races by their institutions—subdued them to industry and order, and gave them a national life.   But neither their kings nor their priests ever obtained, as in those other countries, the exclusive moulding of their character.   Their religion, which enabled persons of genius and a high religious tone to be regarded and to regard themselves as inspired from heaven, gave existence to an inestimably precious unorganized institution—the Order (if it may be so termed) of Prophets.   Under the protection, generally though not always effectual, of their sacred character, the Prophets were a power in the nation, often more than a match for kings and priests, and kept up, in that little corner of the earth, the antagonism of influences which is the only real security for continued progress.   Religion consequently was not there, what it has been in so many other places—a consecration of all that was once established, and a barrier against further improvement.   The remark of a distinguished Hebrew, M. Salvador, that the Prophets were, in Church and State, the equivalent of the modern liberty of the press, gives a just but not an adequate conception of the part fulfilled in national and universal history by this great element of Jewish life ; by means of which, the canon of inspiration never being complete, the persons most eminent in genius and moral feeling could not only denounce and reprobate, with the direct authority of the Almighty, whatever appeared to them deserving of such treatment, but could give forth better and higher interpretations of the national religion, which thenceforth became part of the religion.   Accordingly, whoever can divest himself of the habit of reading the Bible as if it was one book, which until lately was equally inveterate in Christians and in unbelievers, sees with admiration the vast interval between the morality and religion of the Pentateuch, or even of the historical books (the unmistakable work of Hebrew Conservatives of the sacerdotal order), and the morality and religion of the Prophecies: a distance as wide as between these last and the Gospels. Conditions more favourable to Progress could not easily exist: accordingly, the Jews, instead of being stationary like other Asiatics, were, next to the Greeks, the most progressive people of antiquity, and, jointly with them, have been the starting-point and main propelling agency of modern cultivation.

It is, then, impossible to understand the question of the adaptation of forms of government to states of society, without taking into account not only the next step, but all the steps which society has yet to make ; both those which can be foreseen, and the far wider indefinite range which is at present out of sight. It follows, that to judge of the merits of forms of government, an ideal must be constructed of the form of government most eligible in itself, that is, which, if the necessary conditions existed for giving effect to its beneficial tendencies, would, more than all others, favour and promote not some one improvement, but all forms and degrees of it. This having been done, we must consider what are the mental conditions of all sorts, necessary to enable this government to realize its tendencies, and what, therefore, are the various defects by which a people is made incapable of reaping its benefits. It would then be possible to construct a theorem of the circumstances in which that form of government may wisely be introduced ; and also to judge, in cases in which it had better not be introduced, what inferior forms of polity will best carry those communities through the intermediate stages which they must traverse before they can become fit for the best form of government.

Of these inquiries, the last does not concern us here ; but the first is an essential part of our subject : for we may, without rashness, at once enunciate a proposition, the proofs and illustrations of which will present themselves in the ensuing pages ; that this ideally best form of government will be found in some one or other variety of the Representative System.

CHAPTER III

THAT THE IDEALLY BEST FORM OF GOVERNMENT IS REPRESENTATIVE GOVERNMENT

It has long (perhaps throughout the entire duration of British freedom) been a common saying, that if a good despot could be ensured, despotic monarchy would be the best form of government. I look upon this as a radical and most pernicious misconception of what good government is ; which, until it can be got rid of, will fatally vitiate all our speculations on government.

The supposition is, that absolute power, in the hands of an eminent individual, would ensure a virtuous and intelligent performance of all the duties of government. Good laws would be established and enforced, bad laws would be reformed ; the best men would be placed in all situations of trust ; justice would be as well administered, the public burthens would be as light and as judiciously imposed, every branch of administration would be as purely and as intelligently conducted, as the circumstances of the country and its degree of intellectual and moral cultivation would admit. I am willing, for the sake of the argument, to concede all this : but I must point out how great the concession is ; how much more is needed to produce even an approximation to these results, than is conveyed in the simple expression, a good despot. Their realization would in fact imply, not merely a good monarch, but an all-seeing one. He must be at all times informed correctly, in considerable detail, of the conduct and working of every branch of administration, in every district of the country, and must be able, in the twenty-four hours per day which are all that is granted to a king as to the humblest labourer, to give an effective share of attention and superintendence to all parts of this vast field ; or he must at least be capable of discerning and choosing out, from among the mass of his subjects, not only a large abundance of honest and able men, fit to conduct every branch of public administration under supervision and control, but also the small number of men of eminent virtues and talents who can be trusted not only to do without that supervision, but to exercise it themselves over others.   So extraordinary are the faculties and energies required for performing this task in any supportable manner, that the good despot whom we are supposing can hardly be imagined as consenting to undertake it, unless as a refuge from intolerable evils, and a transitional preparation for something beyond.   But the argument can do without even this immense item in the account. Suppose the difficulty vanquished.   What should we then have ?   One man of superhuman mental activity managing the entire affairs of a mentally passive people. Their passivity is implied in the very idea of absolute power.   The nation as a whole, and every individual composing it, are without any potential voice in their own destiny.   They exercise no will in respect to their collective interests.   All is decided for them by a will not their own, which it is legally a crime for them to disobey.   What sort of human beings can be formed under such a regimen ?   What development can either their thinking or their active faculties attain under it ? On matters of pure theory they might perhaps be allowed to speculate, so long as their speculations either did not approach politics, or had not the remotest connexion with its practice.   On practical affairs they could at most be only suffered to suggest ; and even under the most moderate of despots, none but persons of already admitted or reputed superiority could hope that their suggestions would be known to, much less regarded by, those who had the management of affairs.

A person must have a very unusual taste for intellectual exercise in and for itself, who will put himself to the trouble of thought when it is to have no outward effect, or qualify himself for functions which he has no chance of being allowed to exercise. The only sufficient incitement to mental exertion, in any but a few minds in a generation, is the prospect of some practical use to be made of its results. It does not follow that the nation will be wholly destitute of intellectual power. The common business of life, which must necessarily be performed by each individual or family for themselves, will call forth some amount of intelligence and practical ability, within a certain narrow range of ideas. There may be a select class of *savants*, who cultivate science with a view to its physical uses, or for the pleasure of the pursuit. There will be a bureaucracy, and persons in training for the bureaucracy, who will be taught at least some empirical maxims of government and public administration. There may be, and often has been, a systematic organization of the best mental power in the country in some special direction (commonly military) to promote the grandeur of the despot. But the public at large remain without information and without interest on all the greater matters of practice; or, if they have any knowledge of them, it is but a *dilettante* knowledge, like that which people have of the mechanical arts who have never handled a tool. Nor is it only in their intelligence that they suffer. Their moral capacities are equally stunted. Wherever the sphere of action of human beings is artificially circumscribed, their sentiments are narrowed and dwarfed in the same proportion. The food of feeling is action : even domestic affection lives upon voluntary good offices. Let a person have nothing to do for his country, and he will not care for it. It has been said of old, that in a despotism there is at most but one patriot, the despot himself ; and the saying rests on a just appreciation of the effects of absolute subjection, even to a good and wise master. Religion remains : and here at least, it may be thought, is an agency that may be relied on for lifting men's eyes and minds above the dust at their feet. But religion, even supposing it to escape perversion for the purposes of despotism, ceases in these circumstances to be a social concern, and narrows into a personal affair between an individual and his Maker, in which the issue at stake is but his private salvation. Religion in this shape is quite consistent with the most selfish and contracted egoism, and identifies the votary as little in feeling with the rest of his kind as sensuality itself.

A good despotism means a government in which, so far as depends on the despot, there is no positive oppression by officers of state, but in which all the collective interests of the people are managed for them, all the thinking that has relation to collective interests done for them, and in which their minds are formed by, and consenting to, this abdication of their own energies. Leaving things to the Government, like leaving them to Providence, is synonymous with caring nothing about them, and accepting their results, when disagreeable, as visitations of Nature. With the exception, therefore, of a few studious men who take an intellectual interest in speculation for its own sake, the intelligence and sentiments of the whole people are given up to the material interests, and when these are provided for, to the amusement and ornamentation, of private life. But to say this is to say, if the whole testimony of history is worth anything, that the era of national decline has arrived : that is, if the nation had ever attained anything to decline from. If it has never risen above the condition of an Oriental people, in that condition it continues to stagnate. But if, like Greece or Rome, it had realized anything higher, through the energy, patriotism, and enlargement of mind, which as national qualities are the fruits solely of freedom, it relapses in a few generations into the Oriental state. And that state does not mean stupid tranquillity, with security against change for the worse ; it often means being overrun, conquered, and reduced to domestic slavery, either by a stronger despot, or by the nearest barbarous people who retain along with their savage rudeness the energies of freedom.

Such are not merely the natural tendencies, but the inherent necessities of despotic government; from which there is no outlet, unless in so far as the despotism consents not to be despotism; in so far as the supposed good despot abstains from exercising his power, and, though holding it in reserve, allows the general business of government to go on as if the people really governed themselves. However little probable it may be, we may imagine a despot observing many of the rules and restraints of constitutional government. He might allow such freedom of the press and of discussion as would enable a public opinion to form and express itself on national affairs. He might suffer local interests to be managed, without the interference of authority, by the people themselves. He might even surround himself with a council or councils of government, freely chosen by the whole or some portion of the nation; retaining in his own hands the power of taxation, and the supreme legislative as well as executive authority. Were he to act thus, and so far abdicate as a despot, he would do away with a considerable part of the evils characteristic of despotism. Political activity and capacity for public affairs would no longer be prevented from growing up in the body of the nation; and a public opinion would form itself, not the mere echo of the government. But such improvement would be the beginning of new difficulties. This public opinion, independent of the monarch's dictation, must be either with him or against him; if not the one, it will be the other. All governments must displease many persons, and these having now regular organs, and being able to express their sentiments, opinions adverse to the measures of government would often be expressed. What is the monarch to do when these unfavourable opinions happen to be in the majority? Is he to alter his course? Is he to defer to the nation? If so, he is no longer a despot, but a constitutional king; an organ or first minister of the people, distinguished only by being irremovable. If not, he must either put down opposition by his despotic power, or there will arise a permanent antagonism between the people and one man, which can have but one possible ending. Not even a religious principle of passive obedience and ' right divine ' would long ward off the natural consequences of such a position. The monarch would have to succumb, and conform to the conditions of constitutional royalty, or give place to some one who would. The despotism, being thus chiefly nominal, would possess few of the advantages supposed to belong to absolute monarchy; while it would realize in a very imperfect degree those of a free government; since however great an amount of liberty the citizens might practically enjoy, they could never forget that they held it on sufferance, and by a concession which under the existing constitution of the state might at any moment be resumed ; that they were legally slaves, though of a prudent, or indulgent, master.

It is not much to be wondered at, if impatient or disappointed reformers, groaning under the impediments opposed to the most salutary public improvements by the ignorance, the indifference, the intractableness, the perverse obstinacy of a people, and the corrupt combinations of selfish private interests armed with the powerful weapons afforded by free institutions, should at times sigh for a strong hand to bear down all these obstacles, and compel a recalcitrant people to be better governed. But (setting aside the fact, that for one despot who now and then reforms an abuse, there are ninety-nine who do nothing but create them) those who look in any such direction for the realization of their hopes leave out of the idea of good government its principal element, the improvement of the people themselves. One of the benefits of freedom is that under it the ruler cannot pass by the people's minds, and amend their affairs for them without amending them. If it were possible for the people to be well governed in spite of themselves, their

good government would last no longer than the freedom of a people usually lasts who have been liberated
by foreign arms without their own co-operation. It is
true, a despot may educate the people ; and to do so
really, would be the best apology for his despotism.
But any education which aims at making human beings
other than machines, in the long run makes them claim
to have the control of their own actions. The leaders
of French philosophy in the eighteenth century had
been educated by the Jesuits. Even Jesuit education,
it seems, was sufficiently real to call forth the appetite
for freedom. Whatever invigorates the faculties, in
however small a measure, creates an increased desire
for their more unimpeded exercise : and a popular
education is a failure, if it educates the people for any
state but that which it will certainly induce them to
desire, and most probably to demand.

I am far from condemning, in cases of extreme
exigency, the assumption of absolute power in the
form of a temporary dictatorship. Free nations have,
in times of old, conferred such power by their own
choice, as a necessary medicine for diseases of the body
politic which could not be got rid of by less violent
means. But its acceptance, even for a time strictly
limited, can only be excused, if, like Solon or Pittacus,
the dictator employs the whole power he assumes in
removing the obstacles which debar the nation from the
enjoyment of freedom. A good despotism is an
altogether false ideal, which practically (except as
a means to some temporary purpose) becomes the most
senseless and dangerous of chimeras. Evil for evil,
a good despotism, in a country at all advanced in
civilization, is more noxious than a bad one ; for it is
far more relaxing and enervating to the thoughts, feelings, and energies of the people. The despotism of
Augustus prepared the Romans for Tiberius. If the
whole tone of their character had not first been prostrated by nearly two generations of that mild slavery,
they would probably have had spirit enough left to
rebel against the more odious one.

There is no difficulty in showing that the ideally best form of government is that in which the sovereignty, or supreme controlling power in the last resort, is vested in the entire aggregate of the community; every citizen not only having a voice in the exercise of that ultimate sovereignty, but being, at least occasionally, called on to take an actual part in the government, by the personal discharge of some public function, local or general.

To test this proposition, it has to be examined in reference to the two branches into which, as pointed out in the last chapter, the inquiry into the goodness of a government conveniently divides itself, namely, how far it promotes the good management of the affairs of society by means of the existing faculties, moral, intellectual, and active, of its various members, and what is its effect in improving or deteriorating those faculties.

The ideally best form of government, it is scarcely necessary to say, does not mean one which is practicable or eligible in all states of civilization, but the one which, in the circumstances in which it is practicable and eligible, is attended with the greatest amount of beneficial consequences, immediate and prospective. A completely popular government is the only polity which can make out any claim to this character. It is pre-eminent in both the departments between which the excellence of a political constitution is divided. It is both more favourable to present good government, and promotes a better and higher form of national character, than any other polity whatsoever.

Its superiority in reference to present well-being rests upon two principles, of as universal truth and applicability as any general propositions which can be laid down respecting human affairs. The first is, that the rights and interests of every or any person are only secure from being disregarded, when the person interested is himself able, and habitually disposed, to stand up for them. The second is, that the general prosperity attains a greater height, and is more widely diffused, in proportion to the amount and variety of the personal energies enlisted in promoting it.

Putting these two propositions into a shape more special to their present application ; human beings are only secure from evil at the hands of others, in proportion as they have the power of being, and are, self-*protecting* ; and they only achieve a high degree of success in their struggle with Nature, in proportion as they are self-*dependent*, relying on what they themselves can do, either separately or in concert, rather than on what others do for them.

The former proposition—that each is the only safe guardian of his own rights and interests—is one of those elementary maxims of prudence, which every person, capable of conducting his own affairs, implicitly acts upon, wherever he himself is interested. Many, indeed, have a great dislike to it as a political doctrine, and are fond of holding it up to obloquy, as a doctrine of universal selfishness. To which we may answer, that whenever it ceases to be true that mankind, as a rule, prefer themselves to others, and those nearest to them to those more remote, from that moment Communism is not only practicable, but the only defensible form of society ; and will, when that time arrives, be assuredly carried into effect. For my own part, not believing in universal selfishness, I have no difficulty in admitting that Communism would even now be practicable among the *élite* of mankind, and may become so among the rest. But as this opinion is anything but popular with those defenders of existing institutions who find fault with the doctrine of the general predominance of self-interest, I am inclined to think they do in reality believe, that most men consider themselves before other people. It is not, however, necessary to affirm even thus much, in order to support the claim of all to participate in the sovereign power. We need not suppose that when power resides in an exclusive class, that class will knowingly and deliberately sacrifice the other classes to themselves : it suffices that, in the absence of its natural defenders, the interest of the excluded is always in danger of being overlooked; and, when looked at, is seen with very different eyes from those of the persons whom it directly concerns. In this country, for example, what are called the working classes may be considered as excluded from all direct participation in the government. I do not believe that the classes who do participate in it, have in general any intention of sacrificing the working classes to themselves. They once had that intention; witness the persevering attempts so long made to keep down wages by law. But in the present day, their ordinary disposition is the very opposite: they willingly make considerable sacrifices, especially of their pecuniary interest, for the benefit of the working classes, and err rather by too lavish and indiscriminating beneficence; nor do I believe that any rulers in history have been actuated by a more sincere desire to do their duty towards the poorer portion of their countrymen. Yet does Parliament, or almost any of the members composing it, ever for an instant look at any question with the eyes of a working man? When a subject arises in which the labourers as such have an interest, is it regarded from any point of view but that of the employers of labour? I do not say that the working men's view of these questions is in general nearer to the truth than the other: but it is sometimes quite as near; and in any case it ought to be respectfully listened to, instead of being, as it is, not merely turned away from, but ignored. On the question of strikes, for instance, it is doubtful if there is so much as one among the leading members of either House, who is not firmly convinced that the reason of the matter is unqualifiedly on the side of the masters, and that the men's view of it is simply absurd. Those who have studied the question, know well how far this is from being the case; and in how different, and how infinitely less superficial a manner the point would have to be argued, if the classes who strike were able to make themselves heard in Parliament.

It is an inherent condition of human affairs, that no intention, however sincere, of protecting the interests of others, can make it safe or salutary to tie up their own hands. Still more obviously true is it, that by their own hands only can any positive and durable improvement of their circumstances in life be worked out. Through the joint influence of these two principles, all free communities have both been more exempt from social injustice and crime, and have attained more brilliant prosperity, than any others, or than they themselves after they lost their freedom. Contrast the free states of the world, while their freedom lasted, with the cotemporary subjects of monarchical or oligarchical despotism : the Greek cities with the Persian satrapies ; the Italian republics, and the free towns of Flanders and Germany, with the feudal monarchies of Europe ; Switzerland, Holland, and England, with Austria or ante-revolutionary France. Their superior prosperity was too obvious ever to have been gainsaid : while their superiority in good government and social relations, is proved by the prosperity, and is manifest besides in every page of history. If we compare, not one age with another, but the different governments which coexisted in the same age, no amount of disorder which exaggeration itself can pretend to have existed amidst the publicity of the free states, can be compared for a moment with the contemptuous trampling upon the mass of the people which pervaded the whole life of the monarchical countries, or the disgusting individual tyranny which was of more than daily occurrence under the systems of plunder which they called fiscal arrangements, and in the secrecy of their frightful courts of justice.

It must be acknowledged that the benefits of freedom, so far as they have hitherto been enjoyed, were obtained by the extension of its privileges to a part only of the community ; and that a government in which they are extended impartially to all is a desideratum still unrealized. But though every approach to this has an independent value, and in many cases more than an approach could not, in the existing state of general improvement, be made, the participation of all in these benefits is the ideally perfect conception of free government. In proportion as any, no matter who, are excluded from it, the interests of the excluded are left without the guarantee accorded to the rest, and they themselves have less scope and encouragement than they might otherwise have to that exertion of their energies for the good of themselves and of the community, to which the general prosperity is always proportioned.

Thus stands the case as regards present well-being; the good management of the affairs of the existing generation. If we now pass to the influence of the form of government upon character, we shall find the superiority of popular government over every other to be, if possible, still more decided and indisputable.

This question really depends upon a still more fundamental one—viz. which of two common types of character, for the general good of humanity, it is most desirable should predominate—the active, or the passive type; that which struggles against evils, or that which endures them; that which bends to circumstances, or that which endeavours to make circumstances bend to itself.

The commonplaces of moralists, and the general sympathies of mankind, are in favour of the passive type. Energetic characters may be admired, but the acquiescent and submissive are those which most men personally prefer. The passiveness of our neighbours increases our sense of security, and plays into the hands of our wilfulness. Passive characters, if we do not happen to need their activity, seem an obstruction the less in our own path. A contented character is not a dangerous rival. Yet nothing is more certain, than that improvement in human affairs is wholly the work of the uncontented characters; and, moreover, that it is much easier for an active mind to acquire the virtues of patience, than for a passive one to assume those of energy.

Of the three varieties of mental excellence, intellectual, practical, and moral, there never could be any doubt in regard to the first two, which side had the advantage. All intellectual superiority is the fruit of active effort. Enterprise, the desire to keep moving, to be trying and accomplishing new things for our own benefit or that of others, is the parent even of speculative, and much more of practical, talent. The intellectual culture compatible with the other type is of that feeble and vague description, which belongs to a mind that stops at amusement, or at simple contemplation. The test of real and vigorous thinking, the thinking which ascertains truths instead of dreaming dreams, is successful application to practice. Where that purpose does not exist, to give definiteness, precision, and an intelligible meaning to thought, it generates nothing better than the mystical metaphysics of the Pythagoreans or the Vedas. With respect to practical improvement, the case is still more evident. The character which improves human life is that which struggles with natural powers and tendencies, not that which gives way to them. The self-benefiting qualities are all on the side of the active and energetic character : and the habits and conduct which promote the advantage of each individual member of the community, must be at least a part of those which conduce most in the end to the advancement of the community as a whole.

But on the point of moral preferability, there seems at first sight to be room for doubt. I am not referring to the religious feeling which has so generally existed in favour of the inactive character, as being more in harmony with the submission due to the divine will. Christianity as well as other religions has fostered this sentiment ; but it is the prerogative of Christianity, as regards this and many other perversions, that it is able to throw them off. Abstractedly from religious considerations, a passive character, which yields to obstacles instead of striving to overcome them, may not indeed be very useful to others, no more than to itself, but it might be expected to be at least inoffensive. Contentment is always counted among the moral virtues. But it is a complete error to suppose that contentment is necessarily or naturally attendant on passivity of character ; and unless it is, the moral consequences are mischievous. Where there exists a desire for advantages not possessed, the mind which does not potentially possess them by means of its own energies, is apt to look with hatred and malice on those who do. The person bestirring himself with hopeful prospects to improve his circumstances, is the one who feels goodwill towards others engaged in, or who have succeeded in, the same pursuit. And where the majority are so engaged, those who do not attain the object have had the tone given to their feelings by the general habit of the country, and ascribe their failure to want of effort or opportunity, or to their personal ill luck. But those who, while desiring what others possess, put no energy into striving for it, are either incessantly grumbling that fortune does not do for them what they do not attempt to do for themselves, or overflowing with envy and ill-will towards those who possess what they would like to have.

In proportion as success in life is seen or believed to be the fruit of fatality or accident, and not of exertion, in that same ratio does envy develop itself as a point of national character. The most envious of all mankind are the Orientals. In Oriental moralists, in Oriental tales, the envious man is remarkably prominent. In real life, he is the terror of all who possess anything desirable, be it a palace, a handsome child, or even good health and spirits : the supposed effect of his mere look constitutes the all-pervading superstition of the evil eye. Next to Orientals in envy, as in activity, are some of the Southern Europeans. The Spaniards pursued all their great men with it, embittered their lives, and generally succeeded in putting an early stop to their successes.[1] With the French, who are

[1] I limit the expression to past time, because I would say nothing derogatory of a great, and now at last a free, people, who are entering into the general movement of European progress with a vigour which bids fair to make

essentially a southern people, the double education of despotism and Catholicism has, in spite of their impulsive temperament, made submission and endurance the common character of the people, and their most received notion of wisdom and excellence : and if envy of one another, and of all superiority, is not more rife among them than it is, the circumstance must be ascribed to the many valuable counteracting elements in the French character, and most of all to the great individual energy which, though less persistent and more intermittent than in the self-helping and struggling Anglo-Saxons, has nevertheless manifested itself among the French in nearly every direction in which the operation of their institutions has been favourable to it.

There are, no doubt, in all countries, really contented characters, who not merely do not seek, but do not desire, what they do not already possess, and these naturally bear no ill-will towards such as have apparently a more favoured lot. But the great mass of seeming contentment is real discontent, combined with indolence or self-indulgence, which, while taking no legitimate means of raising itself, delights in bringing others down to its own level. And if we look narrowly even at the cases of innocent contentment, we perceive that they only win our admiration, when the indifference is solely to improvement in outward circumstances, and there is a striving for perpetual advancement in spiritual worth, or at least a disinterested zeal to benefit others. The contented man, or the contented family, who have no ambition to make any one else happier, to promote the good of their country or their neighbourhood, or to improve themselves in moral excellence, excite in us neither admiration nor approval. We rightly ascribe this sort of contentment to mere unmanliness and want of spirit. The content which

up rapidly the ground they have lost. No one can doubt what Spanish intellect and energy are capable of ; and their faults as a people are chiefly those for which freedom and industrial ardour are a real specific.

we approve, is an ability to do cheerfully without what cannot be had, a just appreciation of the comparative value of different objects of desire, and a willing renunciation of the less when incompatible with the greater. These, however, are excellences more natural to the character, in proportion as it is actively engaged in the attempt to improve its own or some other lot. He who is continually measuring his energy against difficulties, learns what are the difficulties insuperable to him, and what are those which though he might overcome, the success is not worth the cost. He whose thoughts and activities are all needed for, and habitually employed in, practicable and useful enterprises, is the person of all others least likely to let his mind dwell with brooding discontent upon things either not worth attaining, or which are not so to him. Thus the active, self-helping character is not only intrinsically the best, but is the likeliest to acquire all that is really excellent or desirable in the opposite type.

The striving, go-ahead character of England and the United States is only a fit subject of disapproving criticism, on account of the very secondary objects on which it commonly expends its strength. In itself it is the foundation of the best hopes for the general improvement of mankind. It has been acutely remarked, that whenever anything goes amiss, the habitual impulse of French people is to say, ' Il faut de la patience ; ' and of English people, ' What a shame.' The people who think it a shame when anything goes wrong—who rush to the conclusion that the evil could and ought to have been prevented, are those who, in the long run, do most to make the world better. If the desires are low placed, if they extend to little beyond physical comfort and the show of riches, the immediate results of the energy will not be much more than the continual extension of man's power over material objects ; but even this makes room, and prepares the mechanical appliances, for the greatest intellectual and social achievements ; and while the energy is there, some persons will apply it, and it will be applied more and more, to the perfecting not of outward circumstances alone, but of man's inward nature. Inactivity, unaspiringness, absence of desire, are a more fatal hindrance to improvement than any misdirection of energy; and are that through which alone, when existing in the mass, any very formidable misdirection by an energetic few becomes possible. It is this, mainly, which retains in a savage or semi-savage state the great majority of the human race.

Now there can be no kind of doubt that the passive type of character is favoured by the government of one or a few, and the active self-helping type by that of the Many. Irresponsible rulers need the quiescence of the ruled, more than they need any activity but that which they can compel. Submissiveness to the prescriptions of men as necessities of nature, is the lesson inculcated by all governments upon those who are wholly without participation in them. The will of superiors, and the law as the will of superiors, must be passively yielded to. But no men are mere instruments or materials in the hands of their rulers, who have will or spirit or a spring of internal activity in the rest of their proceedings : and any manifestation of these qualities, instead of receiving encouragement from despots, has to get itself forgiven by them. Even when irresponsible rulers are not sufficiently conscious of danger from the mental activity of their subjects to be desirous of repressing it, the position itself is a repression. Endeavour is even more effectually restrained by the certainty of its impotence, than by any positive discouragement. Between subjection to the will of others, and the virtues of self-help and self-government, there is a natural incompatibility. This is more or less complete, according as the bondage is strained or relaxed. Rulers differ very much in the length to which they carry the control of the free agency of their subjects, or the supersession of it by managing their business for them. But the difference is in degree, not in principle ; and the best despots often go the greatest lengths in chaining up the free agency of their subjects. A bad despot, when his own personal indulgences have been provided for, may sometimes be willing to let the people alone ; but a good despot insists on doing them good, by making them do their own business in a better way than they themselves know of. The regulations which restricted to fixed processes all the leading branches of French manufactures, were the work of the great Colbert.

Very different is the state of the human faculties where a human being feels himself under no other external restraint than the necessities of nature, or mandates of society which he has his share in imposing, and which it is open to him, if he thinks them wrong, publicly to dissent from, and exert himself actively to get altered. No doubt, under a government partially popular, this freedom may be exercised even by those who are not partakers in the full privileges of citizenship. But it is a great additional stimulus to any one's self-help and self-reliance when he starts from even ground, and has not to feel that his success depends on the impression he can make upon the sentiments and dispositions of a body of whom he is not one. It is a great discouragement to an individual, and a still greater one to a class, to be left out of the constitution ; to be reduced to plead from outside the door to the arbiters of their destiny, not taken into consultation within. The maximum of the invigorating effect of freedom upon the character is only obtained, when the person acted on either is, or is looking forward to becoming, a citizen as fully privileged as any other. What is still more important than even this matter of feeling, is the practical discipline which the character obtains, from the occasional demand made upon the citizens to exercise, for a time and in their turn, some social function. It is not sufficiently considered how little there is in most men's ordinary life to give any largeness either to their conceptions or to their sentiments. Their work is a routine ; not a labour of love, but of self-interest in the most elementary form, the satisfaction of daily wants ; neither the thing done,

nor the process of doing it, introduces the mind to
thoughts or feelings extending beyond individuals;
if instructive books are within their reach, there is no
stimulus to read them; and in most cases the individual has no access to any person of cultivation much
superior to his own. Giving him something to do for
the public, supplies, in a measure, all these deficiencies.
If circumstances allow the amount of public duty
assigned him to be considerable, it makes him an
educated man. Notwithstanding the defects of the
social system and moral ideas of antiquity, the practice
of the dicastery and the ecclesia raised the intellectual
standard of an average Athenian citizen far beyond
anything of which there is yet an example in any other
mass of men, ancient or modern. The proofs of this
are apparent in every page of our great historian of
Greece; but we need scarcely look further than to the
high quality of the addresses which their great orators
deemed best calculated to act with effect on their
understanding and will. A benefit of the same kind,
though far less in degree, is produced on Englishmen
of the lower middle class by their liability to be placed
on juries and to serve parish offices; which, though it
does not occur to so many, nor is so continuous, nor
introduces them to so great a variety of elevated considerations, as to admit of comparison with the public
education which every citizen of Athens obtained from
her democratic institutions, must make them nevertheless very different beings, in range of ideas and development of faculties, from those who have done nothing
in their lives but drive a quill, or sell goods over a
counter. Still more salutary is the moral part of the
instruction afforded by the participation of the private
citizen, if even rarely, in public functions. He is called
upon, while so engaged, to weigh interests not his own;
to be guided, in case of conflicting claims, by another
rule than his private partialities; to apply, at every
turn, principles and maxims which have for their
reason of existence the common good: and he usually
finds associated with him in the same work minds more

familiarized than his own with these ideas and operations, whose study it will be to supply reasons to his understanding, and stimulation to his feeling for the general interest. He is made to feel himself one of the public, and whatever is for their benefit to be for his benefit. Where this school of public spirit does not exist, scarcely any sense is entertained that private persons, in no eminent social situation, owe any duties to society, except to obey the laws and submit to the government. There is no unselfish sentiment of identification with the public. Every thought or feeling, either of interest or of duty, is absorbed in the individual and in the family. The man never thinks of any collective interest, of any objects to be pursued jointly with others, but only in competition with them, and in some measure at their expense. A neighbour, not being an ally or an associate, since he is never engaged in any common undertaking for joint benefit, is therefore only a rival. Thus even private morality suffers, while public is actually extinct. Were this the universal and only possible state of things, the utmost aspirations of the lawgiver or the moralist could only stretch to making the bulk of the community a flock of sheep innocently nibbling the grass side by side.

From these accumulated considerations it is evident, that the only government which can fully satisfy all the exigencies of the social state, is one in which the whole people participate ; that any participation, even in the smallest public function, is useful ; that the participation should everywhere be as great as the general degree of improvement of the community will allow ; and that nothing less can be ultimately desirable, than the admission of all to a share in the sovereign power of the state. But since all cannot, in a community exceeding a single small town, participate personally in any but some very minor portions of the public business, it follows that the ideal type of a perfect government must be representative.

CHAPTER IV

UNDER WHAT SOCIAL CONDITIONS REPRESENTATIVE GOVERNMENT IS INAPPLICABLE

WE have recognized in representative government the ideal type of the most perfect polity, for which, in consequence, any portion of mankind are better adapted in proportion to their degree of general improvement. As they range lower and lower in development, that form of government will be, generally speaking, less suitable to them; though this is not true universally: for the adaptation of a people to representative government does not depend so much upon the place they occupy in the general scale of humanity, as upon the degree in which they possess certain special requisites; requisites, however, so closely connected with their degree of general advancement, that any variation between the two is rather the exception than the rule. Let us examine at what point in the descending series representative government ceases altogether to be admissible, either through its own unfitness, or the superior fitness of some other regimen.

First, then, representative, like any other government, must be unsuitable in any case in which it cannot permanently subsist—i. e. in which it does not fulfil the three fundamental conditions enumerated in the first chapter. These were—(1) That the people should be willing to receive it. (2) That they should be willing and able to do what is necessary for its preservation. (3) That they should be willing and able to fulfil the duties and discharge the functions which it imposes on them.

The willingness of the people to accept representative government, only becomes a practical question, when an enlightened ruler, or a foreign nation or nations who have gained power over the country, are disposed to offer it the boon. To individual reformers the question is almost irrelevant, since, if no other objection can be made to their enterprise than that the opinion of the nation is not yet on their side, they have the ready and proper answer, that to bring it over to their side is the very end they aim at. When opinion is really adverse, its hostility is usually to the fact of change, rather than to representative government in itself. The contrary case is not indeed unexampled; there has sometimes been a religious repugnance to any limitation of the power of a particular line of rulers; but in general, the doctrine of passive obedience meant only submission to the will of the powers that be, whether monarchical or popular. In any case in which the attempt to introduce representative government is at all likely to be made, indifference to it, and inability to understand its processes and requirements, rather than positive opposition, are the obstacles to be expected. These, however, are as fatal, and may be as hard to be got rid of, as actual aversion; it being easier, in most cases, to change the direction of an active feeling, than to create one in a state previously passive. When a people have no sufficient value for, and attachment to, a representative constitution, they have next to no chance of retaining it. In every country, the executive is the branch of the government which wields the immediate power, and is in direct contact with the public; to it, principally, the hopes and fears of individuals are directed, and by it both the benefits, and the terrors and prestige, of government, are mainly represented to the public eye. Unless, therefore, the authorities whose office it is to check the executive are backed by an effective opinion and feeling in the country, the executive has always the means of setting them aside, or compelling them to subservience, and is sure to be well supported in doing so. Representative institutions necessarily depend for permanence upon the readiness of the people to fight for them in case of their being endangered. If too little valued for this, they seldom obtain a footing at all, and if they do, are almost sure to be overthrown, as soon as the head of the government, or any party leader who can muster force for a *coup de main*, is willing to run some small risk for absolute power.

These considerations relate to the first two causes of failure in a representative government. The third is, when the people want either the will or the capacity to fulfil the part which belongs to them in a representative constitution. When nobody, or only some small fraction, feels the degree of interest in the general affairs of the State necessary to the formation of a public opinion, the electors will seldom make any use of the right of suffrage but to serve their private interest, or the interest of their locality, or of some one with whom they are connected as adherents or dependents. The small class who, in this state of public feeling, gain the command of the representative body, for the most part use it solely as a means of seeking their fortune. If the executive is weak, the country is distracted by mere struggles for place; if strong, it makes itself despotic, at the cheap price of appeasing the representatives, or such of them as are capable of giving trouble, by a share of the spoil; and the only fruit produced by national representation is, that in addition to those who really govern, there is an assembly quartered on the public, and no abuse in which a portion of the assembly are interested is at all likely to be removed. When, however, the evil stops here, the price may be worth paying, for the publicity and discussion which, though not an invariable, are a natural accompaniment of any, even nominal, representation. In the modern kingdom of Greece, for example,[1] it can hardly be doubted, that the place-hunters who chiefly compose the representative assembly, though they contribute little or nothing

[1] Written before the salutary revolution of 1862, which, provoked by popular disgust at the system of governing by corruption, and the general demoralization of political men, has opened to that rapidly improving people a new and hopeful chance of real constitutional government.

directly to good government, nor even much temper the arbitrary power of the executive, yet keep up the idea of popular rights, and conduce greatly to the real liberty of the press which exists in that country. This benefit, however, is entirely dependent on the co-existence with the popular body of an hereditary king. If, instead of struggling for the favours of the chief ruler, these selfish and sordid factions struggled for the chief place itself, they would certainly, as in Spanish America, keep the country in a state of chronic revolution and civil war. A despotism, not even legal, but of illegal violence, would be alternately exercised by a succession of political adventurers, and the name and forms of representation would have no effect but to prevent despotism from attaining the stability and security by which alone its evils can be mitigated, or its few advantages realized.

The preceding are the cases in which representative government cannot permanently exist. There are others in which it possibly might exist, but in which some other form of government would be preferable. These are principally when the people, in order to advance in civilization, have some lesson to learn, some habit not yet acquired, to the acquisition of which representative government is likely to be an impediment.

The most obvious of these cases is the one already considered, in which the people have still to learn the first lesson of civilization, that of obedience. A race who have been trained in energy and courage by struggles with Nature and their neighbours, but who have not yet settled down into permanent obedience to any common superior, would be little likely to acquire this habit under the collective government of their own body. A representative assembly drawn from among themselves would simply reflect their own turbulent insubordination. It would refuse its authority to all proceedings which would impose, on their savage independence, any improving restraint. The mode in which such tribes are usually brought to submit to the primary conditions of civilized society, is through the necessities of warfare, and the despotic authority indispensable to military command. A military leader is the only superior to whom they will submit, except occasionally some prophet supposed to be inspired from above, or conjurer regarded as possessing miraculous power. These may exercise a temporary ascendancy, but as it is merely personal, it rarely effects any change in the general habits of the people, unless the prophet, like Mahomet, is also a military chief, and goes forth the armed apostle of a new religion; or unless the military chiefs ally themselves with his influence, and turn it into a prop for their own government.

A people are no less unfitted for representative government by the contrary fault to that last specified; by extreme passiveness, and ready submission to tyranny. If a people thus prostrated by character and circumstances could obtain representative institutions, they would inevitably choose their tyrants as their representatives, and the yoke would be made heavier on them by the contrivance which prima facie might be expected to lighten it. On the contrary, many a people has gradually emerged from this condition by the aid of a central authority, whose position has made it the rival, and has ended by making it the master, of the local despots, and which, above all, has been single. French history, from Hugh Capet to Richelieu and Louis XIV, is a continued example of this course of things. Even when the King was scarcely so powerful as many of his chief feudatories, the great advantage which he derived from being but one, has been recognized by French historians. To him the eyes of *all* the locally oppressed were turned; he was the object of hope and reliance throughout the kingdom; while each local potentate was only powerful within a more or less confined space. At his hands, refuge and protection were sought from every part of the country, against first one, then another, of the immediate oppressors. His progress to ascendancy was slow; but it resulted from successively taking advantage of opportunities which offered themselves only to him. It was, therefore, sure; and, in proportion as it was accomplished, it abated, in the oppressed portion of the community, the habit of submitting to oppression. The King's interest lay in encouraging all partial attempts on the part of the serfs to emancipate themselves from their masters, and place themselves in immediate subordination to himself. Under his protection numerous communities were formed which knew no one above them but the King. Obedience to a distant monarch is liberty itself, compared with the dominion of the lord of the neighbouring castle: and the monarch was long compelled by necessities of position to exert his authority as the ally, rather than the master, of the classes whom he had aided in effecting their liberation. In this manner a central power, despotic in principle though generally much restricted in practice, was mainly instrumental in carrying the people through a necessary stage of improvement, which representative government, if real, would most likely have prevented them from entering upon. Nothing short of despotic rule, or a general massacre, could have effected the emancipation of the serfs in the Russian Empire.

The same passages of history forcibly illustrate another mode in which unlimited monarchy overcomes obstacles to the progress of civilization which representative government would have had a decided tendency to aggravate. One of the strongest hindrances to improvement, up to a rather advanced stage, is an inveterate spirit of locality. Portions of mankind, in many other respects capable of, and prepared for, freedom, may be unqualified for amalgamating into even the smallest nation. Not only may jealousies and antipathies repel them from one another, and bar all possibility of voluntary union, but they may not yet have acquired any of the feelings or habits which would make the union real, supposing it to be nominally accomplished. They may, like the citizens of an ancient community, or those of an Asiatic village, have had considerable practice in exercising their faculties on village or town interests, and have even realized a tolerably effective popular government on that restricted scale, and may yet have but slender sympathies with anything beyond, and no habit or capacity of dealing with interests common to many such communities. I am not aware that history furnishes any example in which a number of these political atoms or corpuscles have coalesced into a body, and learnt to feel themselves one people, except through previous subjection to a central authority common to all.[1] It is through the habit of deferring to that authority, entering into its plans and subserving its purposes, that a people such as we have supposed, receive into their minds the conception of large interests, common to a considerable geographical extent. Such interests, on the contrary, are necessarily the predominant consideration in the mind of the central ruler; and through the relations, more or less intimate, which he progressively establishes with the localities, they become familiar to the general mind. The most favourable concurrence of circumstances under which this step in improvement could be made, would be one which should raise up representative institutions without representative government; a representative body, or bodies, drawn from the localities, making itself the auxiliary and instrument of the central power, but seldom attempting to thwart or control it. The people being thus taken, as it were, into council, though not sharing the supreme power, the political education given by the central authority is carried home, much more effectually than it could otherwise be, to the local chiefs and to the population generally; while, at the same time, a tradition is kept up of government by

[1] Italy, which alone can be quoted as an exception, is only so in regard to the final stage of its transformation. The more difficult previous advance from the city isolation of Florence, Pisa, or Milan, to the provincial unity of Tuscany or Lombardy, took place in the usual manner.

general consent, or at least, the sanction of tradition
is not given to government without it, which, when
consecrated by custom, has so often put a bad end to
a good beginning, and is one of the most frequent
causes of the sad fatality which in most countries has
stopped improvement in so early a stage, because the
work of some one period has been so done as to bar
the needful work of the ages following.   Meanwhile, it
may be laid down as a political truth, that by irresponsible monarchy rather than by representative government can a multitude of insignificant political units be
welded into a people, with common feelings of cohesion,
power enough to protect itself against conquest or
foreign aggression, and affairs sufficiently various and
considerable of its own to occupy worthily and expand
to fit proportions the social and political intelligence
of the population.

For these several reasons, kingly government, free
from the control (though perhaps strengthened by the
support) of representative institutions, is the most
suitable form of polity for the earliest stages of any
community, not excepting a city-community like those
of ancient Greece: where, accordingly, the government of kings, under some real but no ostensible or constitutional control by public opinion, did historically
precede by an unknown and probably great duration
all free institutions, and gave place at last, during
a considerable lapse of time, to oligarchies of a few
families.

A hundred other infirmities or shortcomings in a
people might be pointed out, which *pro tanto* disqualify
them from making the best use of representative
government; but in regard to these it is not equally
obvious that the government of One or a Few would
have any tendency to cure or alleviate the evil. Strong
prejudices of any kind; obstinate adherence to old
habits; positive defects of national character, or mere
ignorance, and deficiency of mental cultivation, if
prevalent in a people, will be in general faithfully
reflected in their representative assemblies: and should

it happen that the executive administration, the direct management of public affairs, is in the hands of persons comparatively free from these defects, more good would frequently be done by them when not hampered by the necessity of carrying with them the voluntary assent of such bodies. But the mere position of the rulers does not in these, as it does in the other cases which we have examined, of itself invest them with interests and tendencies operating in the beneficial direction. From the general weaknesses of the people or of the state of civilization, the One and his counsellors, or the Few, are not likely to be habitually exempt; except in the case of their being foreigners, belonging to a superior people or a more advanced state of society. Then, indeed, the rulers may be, to almost any extent, superior in civilization to those over whom they rule; and subjection to a foreign government of this description, notwithstanding its inevitable evils, is often of the greatest advantage to a people, carrying them rapidly through several stages of progress, and clearing away obstacles to improvement which might have lasted indefinitely if the subject population had been left unassisted to its native tendencies and chances. In a country not under the dominion of foreigners, the only cause adequate to producing similar benefits is the rare accident of a monarch of extraordinary genius. There have been in history a few of these, who, happily for humanity, have reigned long enough to render some of their improvements permanent, by leaving them under the guardianship of a generation which had grown up under their influence. Charlemagne may be cited as one instance; Peter the Great is another. Such examples however are so unfrequent that they can only be classed with the happy accidents, which have so often decided at a critical moment whether some leading portion of humanity should make a sudden start, or sink back towards barbarism: chances like the existence of Themistocles at the time of the Persian invasion, or of the first or third William of Orange.

It would be absurd to construct institutions for the mere purpose of taking advantage of such possibilities; especially as men of this calibre, in any distinguished position, do not require despotic power to enable them to exert great influence, as is evidenced by the three last mentioned. The case most requiring consideration in reference to institutions, is the not very uncommon one, in which a small but leading portion of the population, from difference of race, more civilized origin, or other peculiarities of circumstance, are markedly superior in civilization and general character to the remainder. Under these conditions, government by the representatives of the mass would stand a chance of depriving them of much of the benefit they might derive from the greater civilization of the superior ranks; while government by the representatives of those ranks would probably rivet the degradation of the multitude, and leave them no hope of decent treatment except by ridding themselves of one of the most valuable elements of future advancement. The best prospect of improvement for a people thus composed, lies in the existence of a constitutionally unlimited, or at least a practically preponderant, authority in the chief ruler of the dominant class. He alone has by his position an interest in raising and improving the mass, of whom he is not jealous, as a counterpoise to his associates, of whom he is. And if fortunate circumstances place beside him, not as controllers but as subordinates, a body representative of the superior caste, which by its objections and questionings, and by its occasional outbreaks of spirit, keeps alive habits of collective resistance, and may admit of being, in time and by degrees, expanded into a really national representation (which is in substance the history of the English Parliament), the nation has then the most favourable prospects of improvement, which can well occur to a community thus circumstanced and constituted.

Among the tendencies which, without absolutely rendering a people unfit for representative government, seriously incapacitate them from reaping the full benefit of it, one deserves particular notice. There are two states of the inclinations, intrinsically very different, but which have something in common, by virtue of which they often coincide in the direction they give to the efforts of individuals and of nations: one is, the desire to exercise power over others; the other is disinclination to have power exercised over themselves. The difference between different portions of mankind in the relative strength of these two dispositions, is one of the most important elements in their history. There are nations in whom the passion for governing others is so much stronger than the desire of personal independence, that for the mere shadow of the one they are found ready to sacrifice the whole of the other. Each one of their number is willing, like the private soldier in an army, to abdicate his personal freedom of action into the hands of his general, provided the army is triumphant and victorious, and he is able to flatter himself that he is one of a conquering host, though the notion that he has himself any share in the domination exercised over the conquered is an illusion. A government strictly limited in its powers and attributions, required to hold its hands from over-meddling, and to let most things go on without its assuming the part of guardian or director, is not to the taste of such a people. In their eyes the possessors of authority can hardly take too much upon themselves, provided the authority itself is open to general competition. An average individual among them prefers the chance, however distant or improbable, of wielding some share of power over his fellow-citizens, above the certainty, to himself and others, of having no unnecessary power exercised over them. These are the elements of a people of place-hunters; in whom the course of politics is mainly determined by place-hunting; where equality alone is cared for, but not liberty; where the contests of political parties are but struggles to decide whether the power of meddling in everything shall belong to one class or another, perhaps merely to one knot of public men or another; where the idea entertained of democracy is merely that of opening offices to the competition of all instead of a few; where, the more popular the institutions, the more innumerable are the places created, and the more monstrous the over-government exercised by all over each, and by the executive over all. It would be as unjust as it would be ungenerous to offer this, or anything approaching to it, as an unexaggerated picture of the French people; yet the degree in which they do participate in this type of character, has caused representative government by a limited class to break down by excess of corruption, and the attempt at representative government by the whole male population to end in giving one man the power of consigning any number of the rest, without trial, to Lambessa or Cayenne, provided he allows all of them to think themselves not excluded from the possibility of sharing his favours. The point of character which, beyond any other, fits the people of this country for representative government, is, that they have almost universally the contrary characteristic. They are very jealous of any attempt to exercise power over them, not sanctioned by long usage and by their own opinion of right; but they in general care very little for the exercise of power over others. Not having the smallest sympathy with the passion for governing, while they are but too well acquainted with the motives of private interest from which that office is sought, they prefer that it should be performed by those to whom it comes without seeking, as a consequence of social position. If foreigners understood this, it would account to them for some of the apparent contradictions in the political feelings of Englishmen; their unhesitating readiness to let themselves be governed by the higher classes, coupled with so little personal subservience to them, that no people are so fond of resisting authority when it oversteps certain prescribed limits, or so determined to make their rulers always remember that they will only be governed in the way they themselves like best.   Place-hunting, accordingly, is a form of ambition to which the English, considered nationally, are almost strangers.   If we except the few families or connexions of whom official employment lies directly in the way, Englishmen's views of advancement in life take an altogether different direction—that of success in business, or in a profession.   They have the strongest distaste for any mere struggle for office by political parties or individuals : and there are few things to which they have a greater aversion than to the multiplication of public employments : a thing, on the contrary, always popular with the bureaucracy-ridden nations of the Continent, who would rather pay higher taxes, than diminish by the smallest fraction their individual chances of a place for themselves or their relatives, and among whom a cry for retrenchment never means abolition of offices, but the reduction of the salaries of those which are too considerable for the ordinary citizen to have any chance of being appointed to them.

CHAPTER V

OF THE PROPER FUNCTIONS OF REPRESENTATIVE BODIES

In treating of representative government, it is above all necessary to keep in view the distinction between its idea or essence, and the particular forms in which the idea has been clothed by accidental historical developments, or by the notions current at some particular period.

The meaning of representative government is, that the whole people, or some numerous portion of them, exercise through deputies periodically elected by themselves, the ultimate controlling power, which, in every constitution, must reside somewhere.   This ultimate power they must possess in all its completeness.   They must be masters, whenever they please, of all the

operations of government. There is no need that the
constitutional law should itself give them this mastery.
It does not, in the British Constitution. But what it
does give, practically amounts to this. The power of
final control is as essentially single, in a mixed and
balanced government, as in a pure monarchy or democracy. This is the portion of truth in the opinion of
the ancients, revived by great authorities in our own
time, that a balanced constitution is impossible. There
is almost always a balance, but the scales never hang
exactly even. Which of them preponderates, is not
always apparent on the face of the political institutions. In the British Constitution, each of the three
co-ordinate members of the sovereignty is invested with
powers which, if fully exercised, would enable it to
stop all the machinery of government. Nominally,
therefore, each is invested with equal power of thwart-
ing and obstructing the others : and if, by exerting
that power, any of the three could hope to better its
position, the ordinary course of human affairs forbids
us to doubt that the power would be exercised. There
can be no question that the full powers of each would
be employed defensively, if it found itself assailed by
one or both of the others. What then prevents the
same powers from being exerted aggressively ? The
unwritten maxims of the Constitution—in other words,
the positive political morality of the country: and this
positive political morality is what we must look to, if
we would know in whom the really supreme power in
the Constitution resides.

By constitutional law, the Crown can refuse its assent
to any Act of Parliament, and can appoint to office
and maintain in it any Minister, in opposition to the
remonstrances of Parliament. But the constitutional
morality of the country nullifies these powers, preventing them from being ever used ; and, by requiring
that the head of the Administration should always be
virtually appointed by the House of Commons, makes
that body the real sovereign of the State. These
unwritten rules, which limit the use of lawful powers,

are, however, only effectual, and maintain themselves in existence, on condition of harmonizing with the actual distribution of real political strength. There is in every constitution a strongest power—one which would gain the victory, if the compromises by which the Constitution habitually works were suspended, and there came a trial of strength. Constitutional maxims are adhered to, and are practically operative, so long as they give the predominance in the Constitution to that one of the powers which has the preponderance of active power out of doors. This, in England, is the popular power. If, therefore, the legal provisions of the British Constitution, together with the unwritten maxims by which the conduct of the different political authorities is in fact regulated, did not give to the popular element in the Constitution that substantial supremacy over every department of the government, which corresponds to its real power in the country, the Constitution would not possess the stability which characterizes it; either the laws or the unwritten maxims would soon have to be changed. The British Government is thus a representative government in the correct sense of the term : and the powers which it leaves in hands not directly accountable to the people, can only be considered as precautions which the ruling power is willing should be taken against its own errors. Such precautions have existed in all well-constructed democracies. The Athenian Constitution had many such provisions ; and so has that of the United States.

But while it is essential to representative government that the practical supremacy in the state should reside in the representatives of the people, it is an open question what actual functions, what precise part in the machinery of government, shall be directly and personally discharged by the representative body. Great varieties in this respect are compatible with the essence of representative government, provided the functions are such as secure to the representative body the control of everything in the last resort.

There is a radical distinction between controlling the business of government, and actually doing it. The same person or body may be able to control everything, but cannot possibly do everything; and in many cases its control over everything will be more perfect, the less it personally attempts to do. The commander of an army could not direct its movements effectually if he himself fought in the ranks, or led an assault. It is the same with bodies of men. Some things cannot be done except by bodies; other things cannot be well done by them. It is one question, therefore, what a popular assembly should control, another what it should itself do. It should, as we have already seen, control all the operations of government. But in order to determine through what channel this general control may most expediently be exercised, and what portion of the business of government the representative assembly should hold in its own hands, it is necessary to consider what kinds of business a numerous body is competent to perform properly. That alone which it can do well, it ought to take personally upon itself. With regard to the rest, its proper province is not to do it, but to take means for having it well done by others.

For example, the duty which is considered as belonging more peculiarly than any other to an assembly representative of the people, is that of voting the taxes. Nevertheless, in no country does the representative body undertake, by itself or its delegated officers, to prepare the estimates. Though the supplies can only be voted by the House of Commons, and though the sanction of the House is also required for the appropriation of the revenues to the different items of the public expenditure, it is the maxim and the uniform practice of the Constitution that money can be granted only on the proposition of the Crown. It has, no doubt, been felt, that moderation as to the amount, and care and judgement in the detail of its application, can only be expected when the executive government, through whose hands it is to pass, is made responsible for the plans and calculations on which the disbursements are grounded. Parliament, accordingly, is not expected, nor even permitted, to originate directly either taxation or expenditure. All it is asked for is its consent, and the sole power it possesses is that of refusal.

The principles which are involved and recognized in this constitutional doctrine, if followed as far as they will go, are a guide to the limitation and definition of the general functions of representative assemblies. In the first place, it is admitted in all countries in which the representative system is practically understood, that numerous representative bodies ought not to administer. The maxim is grounded not only on the most essential principles of good government, but on those of the successful conduct of business of any description. No body of men, unless organized and under command, is fit for action, in the proper sense. Even a select board, composed of few members, and these specially conversant with the business to be done, is always an inferior instrument to some one individual who could be found among them, and would be improved in character if that one person were made the chief, and all the others reduced to subordinates. What can be done better by a body than by any individual, is deliberation. When it is necessary, or important to secure hearing and consideration to many conflicting opinions, a deliberative body is indispensable. Those bodies, therefore, are frequently useful, even for administrative business, but in general only as advisers; such business being, as a rule, better conducted under the responsibility of one. Even a joint-stock company has always in practice, if not in theory, a managing director; its good or bad management depends essentially on some one person's qualifications, and the remaining directors, when of any use, are so by their suggestions to him, or by the power they possess of watching him, and restraining or removing him in case of misconduct. That they are ostensibly equal sharers with him in the management is no advantage, but a considerable set-off against any good which they are capable of doing : it weakens greatly the sense in his own mind, and in those of other people, of that individual responsibility in which he should stand forth personally and undividedly.

But a popular assembly is still less fitted to administer, or to dictate in detail to those who have the charge of administration. Even when honestly meant, the interference is almost always injurious. Every branch of public administration is a skilled business, which has its own peculiar principles and traditional rules, many of them not even known, in any effectual way, except to those who have at some time had a hand in carrying on the business, and none of them likely to be duly appreciated by persons not practically acquainted with the department. I do not mean that the transaction of public business has esoteric mysteries, only to be understood by the initiated. Its principles are all intelligible to any person of good sense, who has in his mind a true picture of the circumstances and conditions to be dealt with : but to have this he must know those circumstances and conditions ; and the knowledge does not come by intuition. There are many rules of the greatest importance in every branch of public business (as there are in every private occupation), of which a person fresh to the subject neither knows the reason or even suspects the existence, because they are intended to meet dangers or provide against inconveniences which never entered into his thoughts. I have known public men, ministers, of more than ordinary natural capacity, who on their first introduction to a department of business new to them, have excited the mirth of their inferiors by the air with which they announced as a truth hitherto set at naught, and brought to light by themselves, something which was probably the first thought of everybody who ever looked at the subject, given up as soon as he had got on to a second. It is true that a great statesman is he who knows when to depart from traditions, as well as when to adhere to them. But it is a great mistake to suppose that he will do this better for being ignorant of the traditions. No one who does not thoroughly know the modes of action which common experience has sanctioned, is capable of judging of the circumstances which require a departure from those ordinary modes of action. The interests dependent on the acts done by a public department, the consequences liable to follow from any particular mode of conducting it, require for weighing and estimating them a kind of knowledge, and of specially exercised judgement, almost as rarely found in those not bred to it, as the capacity to reform the law in those who have not professionally studied it. All these difficulties are sure to be ignored by a representative assembly which attempts to decide on special acts of administration. At its best, it is inexperience sitting in judgement on experience, ignorance on knowledge : ignorance which never suspecting the existence of what it does not know, is equally careless and supercilious, making light of, if not resenting, all pretensions to have a judgement better worth attending to than its own. Thus it is when no interested motives intervene : but when they do, the result is jobbery more unblushing and audacious than the worst corruption which can well take place in a public office under a government of publicity. It is not necessary that the interested bias should extend to the majority of the assembly. In any particular case it is often enough that it affects two or three of their number. Those two or three will have a greater interest in misleading the body, than any other of its members are likely to have in putting it right. The bulk of the assembly may keep their hands clean, but they cannot keep their minds vigilant or their judgements discerning in matters they know nothing about : and an indolent majority, like an indolent individual, belongs to the person who takes most pains with it. The bad measures or bad appointments of a minister may be checked by Parliament ; and the interest of ministers in defending, and of rival partisans in attacking, secures a tolerably equal discussion: but *quis custodiet custodes?* who shall check the Parliament? A minister, a head of an office, feels himself under some responsibility. An assembly in such cases feels under no responsibility at all: for when did any member of Parliament lose his seat for the vote he gave on any detail of administration? To a minister, or the head of an office, it is of more importance what will be thought of his proceedings some time hence, than what is thought of them at the instant: but an assembly, if the cry of the moment goes with it, however hastily raised or artificially stirred up, thinks itself and is thought by everybody to be completely exculpated however disastrous may be the consequences. Besides, an assembly never personally experiences the inconveniences of its bad measures, until they have reached the dimensions of national evils. Ministers and administrators see them approaching, and have to bear all the annoyance and trouble of attempting to ward them off.

The proper duty of a representative assembly in regard to matters of administration, is not to decide them by its own vote, but to take care that the persons who have to decide them shall be the proper persons. Even this they cannot advantageously do by nominating the individuals. There is no act which more imperatively requires to be performed under a strong sense of individual responsibility than the nomination to employments. The experience of every person conversant with public affairs bears out the assertion, that there is scarcely any act respecting which the conscience of an average man is less sensitive; scarcely any case in which less consideration is paid to qualifications, partly because men do not know, and partly because they do not care for, the difference in qualifications between one person and another. When a minister makes what is meant to be an honest appointment, that is when he does not actually job it for his personal connexions or his party, an ignorant person might suppose that he would try to give it to the person best qualified. No such thing. An

ordinary minister thinks himself a miracle of virtue
if he gives it to a person of merit, or who has a claim
on the public on any account, though the claim or
the merit may be of the most opposite description to
that required. *Il fallait un calculateur, ce fut un danseur
qui l'obtint*, is hardly more of a caricature than in the
days of Figaro; and the minister doubtless thinks
himself not only blameless but meritorious if the man
dances well. Besides, the qualifications which fit special
individuals for special duties can only be recognized
by those who know the individuals, or who make it
their business to examine and judge of persons from
what they have done, or from the evidence of those
who are in a position to judge. When these conscientious obligations are so little regarded by great
public officers who can be made responsible for their
appointments, how must it be with assemblies who
cannot ? Even now, the worst appointments are those
which are made for the sake of gaining support or
disarming opposition in the representative body : what
might we expect if they were made by the body itself ?
Numerous bodies never regard special qualifications at
all. Unless a man is fit for the gallows, he is thought
to be about as fit as other people for almost anything
for which he can offer himself as a candidate. When
appointments made by a public body are not decided,
as they almost always are, by party connexion or
private jobbing, a man is appointed either because he
has a reputation, often quite undeserved, for *general*
ability, or frequently for no better reason than that
he is personally popular.

It has never been thought desirable that Parliament
should itself nominate even the members of a Cabinet.
It is enough that it virtually decides who shall be
prime minister, or who shall be the two or three
individuals from whom the prime minister shall be
chosen. In doing this it merely recognizes the fact
that a certain person is the candidate of the party
whose general policy commands its support. In reality,
the only thing which Parliament decides is, which of

two, or at most three, parties or bodies of men, shall furnish the executive government : the opinion of the party itself decides which of its members is fittest to be placed at the head. According to the existing practice of the British Constitution, these things seem to be on as good a footing as they can be. Parliament does not nominate any minister, but the Crown appoints the head of the administration in conformity to the general wishes and inclinations manifested by Parliament, and the other ministers on the recommendation of the chief ; while every minister has the undivided moral responsibility of appointing fit persons to the other offices of administration which are not permanent. In a republic, some other arrangement would be necessary : but the nearer it approached in practice to that which has long existed in England, the more likely it would be to work well. Either, as in the American republic, the head of the Executive must be elected by some agency entirely independent of the representative body ; or the body must content itself with naming the prime minister, and making him responsible for the choice of his associates and subordinates. To all these considerations, at least theoretically, I fully anticipate a general assent : though, practically, the tendency is strong in representative bodies to interfere more and more in the details of administration, by virtue of the general law, that whoever has the strongest power is more and more tempted to make an excessive use of it ; and this is one of the practical dangers to which the futurity of representative governments will be exposed.

But it is equally true, though only of late and slowly beginning to be acknowledged, that a numerous assembly is as little fitted for the direct business of legislation as for that of administration. There is hardly any kind of intellectual work which so much needs to be done not only by experienced and exercised minds, but by minds trained to the task through long and laborious study, as the business of making laws. This is a sufficient reason, were there no other, why they can never be well made but by a committee of very few persons. A reason no less conclusive is, that every provision of a law requires to be framed with the most accurate and long-sighted perception of its effect on all the other provisions ; and the law when made should be capable of fitting into a consistent whole with the previously existing laws. It is impossible that these conditions should be in any degree fulfilled when laws are voted clause by clause in a miscellaneous assembly. The incongruity of such a mode of legislating would strike all minds, were it not that our laws are already, as to form and construction, such a chaos, that the confusion and contradiction seem incapable of being made greater by any addition to the mass. Yet even now, the utter unfitness of our legislative machinery for its purpose is making itself practically felt every year more and more. The mere time necessarily occupied in getting through Bills, renders Parliament more and more incapable of passing any, except on detached and narrow points. If a Bill is prepared which even attempts to deal with the whole of any subject (and it is impossible to legislate properly on any part without having the whole present to the mind), it hangs over from session to session through sheer impossibility of finding time to dispose of it. It matters not though the Bill may have been deliberately drawn up by the authority deemed the best qualified, with all appliances and means to boot ; or by a select commission, chosen for their conversancy with the subject, and having employed years in considering and digesting the particular measure ; it cannot be passed, because the House of Commons will not forgo the precious privilege of tinkering it with their clumsy hands. The custom has of late been to some extent introduced, when the principle of a Bill has been affirmed on the second reading, of referring it for consideration in detail to a Select Committee : but it has not been found that this practice causes much less time to be lost afterwards in carrying it through the Committee of the whole House : the opinions or

private crotchets which have been overruled by knowledge, always insist on giving themselves a second
chance before the tribunal of ignorance. Indeed, the
practice itself has been adopted principally by the
House of Lords, the members of which are less busy
and fond of meddling, and less jealous of the importance of their individual voices, than those of the
elective House. And when a Bill of many clauses
does succeed in getting itself discussed in detail,
what can depict the state in which it comes out of
Committee ! Clauses omitted, which are essential to
the working of the rest ; incongruous ones inserted
to conciliate some private interest, or some crotchety
member who threatens to delay the Bill ; articles
foisted in on the motion of some sciolist with a mere
smattering of the subject, leading to consequences
which the member who introduced or those who supported the Bill did not at the moment foresee, and
which need an amending Act in the next session to
correct their mischiefs. It is one of the evils of the
present mode of managing these things, that the explaining and defending of a Bill, and of its various
provisions, is scarcely ever performed by the person
from whose mind they emanated, who probably has
not a seat in the House. Their defence rests upon
some minister or member of Parliament who did not
frame them, who is dependent on cramming for all
his arguments but those which are perfectly obvious,
who does not know the full strength of his case, nor
the best reasons by which to support it, and is wholly
incapable of meeting unforeseen objections. This evil,
as far as Government bills are concerned, admits of
remedy, and has been remedied in some representative
constitutions, by allowing the Government to be represented in either House by persons in its confidence,
having a right to speak, though not to vote.

If that, as yet considerable, majority of the House
of Commons who never desire to move an amendment
or make a speech, would no longer leave the whole
regulation of business to those who do ; if they would

bethink themselves that better qualifications for legislation exist, and may be found if sought for, than
a fluent tongue, and the faculty of getting elected by
a constituency; it would soon be recognized, that in
legislation as well as administration, the only task to
which a representative assembly can possibly be competent, is not that of doing the work, but of causing
it to be done; of determining to whom or to what
sort of people it shall be confided, and giving or withholding the national sanction to it when performed.
Any government fit for a high state of civilization,
would have as one of its fundamental elements a small
body, not exceeding in number the members of a
Cabinet, who should act as a Commission of legislation, having for its appointed office to make the laws.
If the laws of this country were, as surely they will
soon be, revised and put into a connected form, the
Commission of Codification by which this is effected
should remain as a permanent institution, to watch
over the work, protect it from deterioration, and make
further improvements as often as required. No one
would wish that this body should of itself have any
power of *enacting* laws: the Commission would only
embody the element of intelligence in their construction; Parliament would represent that of will. No
measure would become a law until expressly sanctioned
by Parliament; and Parliament, or either House,
would have the power not only of rejecting but of
sending back a Bill to the Commission for reconsideration or improvement. Either House might also exercise
its initiative, by referring any subject to the Commission, with directions to prepare a law. The Commission, of course, would have no power of refusing its
instrumentality to any legislation which the country
desired. Instructions, concurred in by both Houses, to
draw up a Bill which should effect a particular purpose, would be imperative on the Commissioners, unless
they preferred to resign their office. Once framed,
however, Parliament should have no power to alter
the measure, but solely to pass or reject it; or, if

partially disapproved of, remit it to the Commission for reconsideration. The Commissioners should be appointed by the Crown, but should hold their offices for a time certain, say five years, unless removed on an address from the two Houses of Parliament, grounded either on personal misconduct (as in the case of judges), or on refusal to draw up a Bill in obedience to the demands of Parliament. At the expiration of the five years a member should cease to hold office unless re-appointed, in order to provide a convenient mode of getting rid of those who had not been found equal to their duties, and of infusing new and younger blood into the body.

The necessity of some provision corresponding to this was felt even in the Athenian Democracy, where, in the time of its most complete ascendancy, the popular Ecclesia could pass Psephisms (mostly decrees on single matters of policy), but laws, so called, could only be made or altered by a different and less numerous body, renewed annually, called the Nomothetae, whose duty it also was to revise the whole of the laws, and keep them consistent with one another. In the English Constitution there is great difficulty in introducing any arrangement which is new both in form and in substance, but comparatively little repugnance is felt to the attainment of new purposes by an adaptation of existing forms and traditions. It appears to me that the means might be devised of enriching the Constitution with this great improvement through the machinery of the House of Lords. A Commission for preparing Bills would in itself be no more an innovation on the Constitution than the Board for the administration of the Poor Laws, or the Inclosure Commission. If, in consideration of the great importance and dignity of the trust, it were made a rule that every person appointed a member of the Legislative Commission, unless removed from office on an address from Parliament, should be a Peer for life, it is probable that the same good sense and taste which leave the judicial functions of the Peerage practically to the exclusive care of the law lords, would leave the business of legislation, except on questions involving political principles and interests, to the professional legislators ; that Bills originating in the Upper House would always be drawn up by them ; that the Government would devolve on them the framing of all its Bills ; and that private members of the House of Commons would gradually find it convenient, and likely to facilitate the passing of their measures through the two Houses, if instead of bringing in a Bill and submitting it directly to the House, they obtained leave to introduce it and have it referred to the Legislative Commission. For it would, of course, be open to the House to refer for the consideration of that body not a subject merely, but any specific proposal, or a Draft of a Bill *in extenso*, when any member thought himself capable of preparing one such as ought to pass ; and the House would doubtless refer every such draft to the Commission, if only as materials, and for the benefit of the suggestions it might contain : as they would, in like manner, refer every amendment or objection, which might be proposed in writing by any member of the House after a measure had left the Commissioners' hands. The alteration of Bills by a Committee of the whole House would cease, not by formal abolition, but by desuetude ; the right not being abandoned, but laid up in the same armoury with the royal veto, the right of withholding the supplies, and other ancient instruments of political warfare, which no one desires to see used, but no one likes to part with, lest they should at any time be found to be still needed in an extraordinary emergency. By such arrangements as these, legislation would assume its proper place as a work of skilled labour and special study and experience ; while the most important liberty of the nation, that of being governed only by laws assented to by its elected representatives, would be fully preserved, and made more valuable by being detached from the serious, but by no means unavoidable, drawbacks which now accompany it in the form of ignorant and ill-considered legislation.

Instead of the function of governing, for which it is radically unfit, the proper office of a representative assembly is to watch and control the government : to throw the light of publicity on its acts : to compel a full exposition and justification of all of them which any one considers questionable ; to censure them if found condemnable, and, if the men who compose the government abuse their trust, or fulfil it in a manner which conflicts with the deliberate sense of the nation, to expel them from office, and either expressly or virtually appoint their successors. This is surely ample power, and security enough for the liberty of the nation. In addition to this, the Parliament has an office, not inferior even to this in importance ; to be at once the nation's Committee of Grievances, and its Congress of Opinions ; an arena in which not only the general opinion of the nation, but that of every section of it, and as far as possible of every eminent individual whom it contains, can produce itself in full light and challenge discussion ; where every person in the country may count upon finding somebody who speaks his mind, as well or better than he could speak it himself—not to friends and partisans exclusively, but in the face of opponents, to be tested by adverse controversy ; where those whose opinion is overruled, feel satisfied that it is heard, and set aside not by a mere act of will, but for what are thought superior reasons, and commend themselves as such to the representatives of the majority of the nation ; where every party or opinion in the country can muster its strength, and be cured of any illusion concerning the number or power of its adherents ; where the opinion which prevails in the nation makes itself manifest as prevailing, and marshals its hosts in the presence of the government, which is thus enabled and compelled to give way to it on the mere manifestation, without the actual employment, of its strength ; where statesmen can assure themselves, far more certainly than by any other signs, what elements of opinion and power are growing, and what declining, and are enabled to shape their measures with some regard not solely to present exigencies, but to tendencies in progress. Representative assemblies are often taunted by their enemies with being places of mere talk and *bavardage*. There has seldom been more misplaced derision. I know not how a representative assembly can more usefully employ itself than in talk, when the subject of talk is the great public interests of the country, and every sentence of it represents the opinion either of some important body of persons in the nation, or of an individual in whom some such body have reposed their confidence. A place where every interest and shade of opinion in the country can have its cause even passionately pleaded, in the face of the government and of all other interests and opinions, can compel them to listen, and either comply, or state clearly why they do not, is in itself, if it answered no other purpose, one of the most important political institutions that can exist anywhere, and one of the foremost benefits of free government. Such ' talking ' would never be looked upon with disparagement if it were not allowed to stop ' doing ; ' which it never would, if assemblies knew and acknowledged that talking and discussion are their proper business, while *doing*, as the result of discussion, is the task not of a miscellaneous body, but of individuals specially trained to it ; that the fit office of an assembly is to see that those individuals are honestly and intelligently chosen, and to interfere no further with them, except by unlimited latitude of suggestion and criticism, and by applying or withholding the final seal of national assent. It is for want of this judicious reserve, that popular assemblies attempt to do what they cannot do well—to govern and legislate—and provide no machinery but their own for much of it, when of course every hour spent in talk is an hour withdrawn from actual business. But the very fact which most unfits such bodies for a Council of Legislation, qualifies them the more for their other office—namely, that they are not a selection of the greatest political minds in the country, from whose opinions little could with certainty be inferred concerning those of the nation, but are, when properly constituted, a fair sample of every grade of intellect among the people which is at all entitled to a voice in public affairs. Their part is to indicate wants, to be an organ for popular demands, and a place of adverse discussion for all opinions relating to public matters, both great and small; and, along with this, to check by criticism, and eventually by withdrawing their support, those high public officers who really conduct the public business, or who appoint those by whom it is conducted. Nothing but the restriction of the function of representative bodies within these rational limits, will enable the benefits of popular control to be enjoyed in conjunction with the no less important requisites (growing ever more important as human affairs increase in scale and in complexity) of skilled legislation and administration. There are no means of combining these benefits, except by separating the functions which guarantee the one from those which essentially require the other; by disjoining the office of control and criticism from the actual conduct of affairs, and devolving the former on the representatives of the Many, while securing for the latter, under strict responsibility to the nation, the acquired knowledge and practised intelligence of a specially trained and experienced Few.

The preceding discussion of the functions which ought to devolve on the sovereign representative assembly of the nation, would require to be followed by an inquiry into those properly vested in the minor representative bodies, which ought to exist for purposes that regard only localities. And such an inquiry forms an essential part of the present treatise; but many reasons require its postponement, until we have considered the most proper composition of the great representative body, destined to control as sovereign the enactment of laws and the administration of the general affairs of the nation.

CHAPTER VI

OF THE INFIRMITIES AND DANGERS TO WHICH REPRESENTATIVE GOVERNMENT IS LIABLE

THE defects of any form of government may be either negative or positive. It is negatively defective if it does not concentrate in the hands of the authorities, power sufficient to fulfil the necessary offices of a government; or if it does not sufficiently develop by exercise the active capacities and social feelings of the individual citizens. On neither of these points is it necessary that much should be said at this stage of our inquiry.

The want of an amount of power in the government, adequate to preserve order and allow of progress in the people, is incident rather to a wild and rude state of society generally, than to any particular form of political union. When the people are too much attached to savage independence, to be tolerant of the amount of power to which it is for their good that they should be subject, the state of society (as already observed) is not yet ripe for representative government. When the time for that government has arrived, sufficient power for all needful purposes is sure to reside in the sovereign assembly; and if enough of it is not entrusted to the executive, this can only arise from a jealous feeling on the part of the assembly towards the administration, never likely to exist but where the constitutional power of the assembly to turn them out of office has not yet sufficiently established itself. Wherever that constitutional right is admitted in principle, and fully operative in practice, there is no fear that the assembly will not be willing to trust its own ministers with any amount of power really desirable; the danger is, on the contrary, lest they should grant it too ungrudgingly, and too indefinite in extent, since the power of the minister is the power of the body who make and who keep him so. It is, however, very likely, and is one of the dangers of a controlling assembly, that it may be lavish of powers, but afterwards interfere with their exercise ; may give power by wholesale, and take it back in detail, by multiplied single acts of interference in the business of administration. The evils arising from this assumption of the actual function of governing, in lieu of that of criticizing and checking those who govern, have been sufficiently dwelt upon in the preceding chapter. No safeguard can in the nature of things be provided against this improper meddling, except a strong and general conviction of its injurious character.

The other negative defect which may reside in a government, that of not bringing into sufficient exercise the individual faculties, moral, intellectual, and active, of the people, has been exhibited generally in setting forth the distinctive mischiefs of despotism. As between one form of popular government and another, the advantage in this respect lies with that which most widely diffuses the exercise of public functions ; on the one hand, by excluding fewest from the suffrage; on the other, by opening to all classes of private citizens, so far as is consistent with other equally important objects, the widest participation in the details of judicial and administrative business ; as by jury trial, admission to municipal offices, and above all by the utmost possible publicity and liberty of discussion, whereby not merely a few individuals in succession, but the whole public, are made, to a certain extent, participants in the government, and sharers in the instruction and mental exercise derivable from it. The further illustration of these benefits, as well as of the limitations under which they must be aimed at, will be better deferred until we come to speak of the details of administration.

The *positive* evils and dangers of the representative, as of every other form of government, may be reduced to two heads : first, general ignorance and incapacity, or, to speak more moderately, insufficient mental qualifications, in the controlling body ; secondly, the danger of its being under the influence of interests not identical with the general welfare of the community.

The former of these evils, deficiency in high mental qualifications, is one to which it is generally supposed that popular government is liable in a greater degree than any other. The energy of a monarch, the steadiness and prudence of an aristocracy, are thought to contrast most favourably with the vacillation and short-sightedness of even a qualified democracy. These propositions, however, are not by any means so well founded as they at first sight appear.

Compared with simple monarchy, representative government is in these respects at no disadvantage. Except in a rude age, hereditary monarchy, when it is really such, and not aristocracy in disguise, far surpasses democracy in all the forms of incapacity supposed to be characteristic of the last. I say, except in a rude age, because in a really rude state of society there is a considerable guarantee for the intellectual and active capacities of the sovereign. His personal will is constantly encountering obstacles from the wilfulness of his subjects, and of powerful individuals among their number. The circumstances of society do not afford him much temptation to mere luxurious self-indulgence ; mental and bodily activity, especially political and military, are his principal excitements ; and among turbulent chiefs and lawless followers he has little authority, and is seldom long secure even of his throne, unless he possesses a considerable amount of personal daring, dexterity, and energy. The reason why the average of talent is so high among the Henries and Edwards of our history, may be read in the tragical fate of the second Edward and the second Richard, and the civil wars and disturbances of the reigns of John and his incapable successor. The troubled period of the Reformation also produced several eminent hereditary monarchs, Elizabeth, Henri Quatre, Gustavus Adolphus ; but they were mostly bred up in adversity, succeeded to the throne by the unexpected failure of nearer heirs, or had to contend with great difficulties in the commencement of their reign. Since European life assumed a settled aspect, anything above mediocrity in an hereditary king has become extremely rare, while the general average has been even below mediocrity, both in talent and in vigour of character. A monarchy constitutionally absolute now only maintains itself in existence (except temporarily in the hands of some active-minded usurper) through the mental qualifications of a permanent bureaucracy. The Russian and Austrian Governments, and even the French Government in its normal condition, are oligarchies of officials, of whom the head of the State does little more than select the chiefs. I am speaking of the regular course of their administration; for the will of the master of course determines many of their particular acts.

The governments which have been remarkable in history for sustained mental ability and vigour in the conduct of affairs, have generally been aristocracies. But they have been, without any exception, aristocracies of public functionaries. The ruling bodies have been so narrow, that each member, or at least each influential member, of the body, was able to make, and did make, public business an active profession, and the principal occupation of his life. The only aristocracies which have manifested high governing capacities, and acted on steady maxims of policy, through many generations, are those of Rome and Venice. But, at Venice, though the privileged order was numerous, the actual management of affairs was rigidly concentrated in a small oligarchy within the oligarchy, whose whole lives were devoted to the study and conduct of the affairs of the state. The Roman government partook more of the character of an open aristocracy like our own. But the really governing body, the Senate, was in general exclusively composed of persons who had exercised public functions, and had either already filled or were looking forward to fill the higher offices of the state, at the peril of a severe responsibility in case of incapacity and failure. When once members of the Senate, their lives were pledged to the conduct of public affairs; they were not permitted even to leave Italy except in the discharge of some public trust; and unless turned out of the Senate by the censors for character or conduct deemed disgraceful, they retained their powers and responsibilities to the end of life. In an aristocracy thus constituted, every member felt his personal importance entirely bound up with the dignity and estimation of the commonwealth which he administered, and with the part he was able to play in its councils. This dignity and estimation were quite different things from the prosperity or happiness of the general body of the citizens, and were often wholly incompatible with it. But they were closely linked with the external success and aggrandizement of the State: and it was, consequently, in the pursuit of that object almost exclusively, that either the Roman or the Venetian aristocracies manifested the systematically wise collective policy, and the great individual capacities for government, for which history has deservedly given them credit.

It thus appears that the only governments, not representative, in which high political skill and ability have been other than exceptional, whether under monarchical or aristocratic forms, have been essentially bureaucracies. The work of government has been in the hands of governors by profession; which is the essence and meaning of bureaucracy. Whether the work is done by them because they have been trained to it, or they are trained to it because it is to be done by them, makes a great difference in many respects, but none at all as to the essential character of the rule. Aristocracies, on the other hand, like that of England, in which the class who possessed the power derived it merely from their social position, without being specially trained or devoting themselves exclusively to it (and in which, therefore, the power was not exercised directly, but through representative institutions oligarchically constituted) have been, in respect to intellectual endowments, much on a par with democracies; that is, they have manifested such qualities in any considerable degree, only during the temporary ascendancy which great and popular talents, united with a distinguished position, have given to some one man. Themistocles and Pericles, Washington and Jefferson, were not more completely exceptions in their several democracies, and were assuredly much more splendid exceptions, than the Chathams and Peels of the representative aristocracy of Great Britain, or even the Sullys and Colberts of the aristocratic monarchy of France. A great minister, in the aristocratic governments of modern Europe, is almost as rare a phenomenon as a great king.

The comparison, therefore, as to the intellectual attributes of a government, has to be made between a representative democracy and a bureaucracy: all other governments may be left out of the account. And here it must be acknowledged that a bureaucratic government has, in some important respects, greatly the advantage. It accumulates experience, acquires well-tried and well-considered traditional maxims, and makes provision for appropriate practical knowledge in those who have the actual conduct of affairs. But it is not equally favourable to individual energy of mind. The disease which afflicts bureaucratic governments, and which they usually die of, is routine. They perish by the immutability of their maxims; and, still more, by the universal law that whatever becomes a routine loses its vital principle, and having no longer a mind acting within it, goes on revolving mechanically though the work it is intended to do remains undone. A bureaucracy always tends to become a pedantocracy. When the bureaucracy is the real government, the spirit of the corps (as with the Jesuits) bears down the individuality of its more distinguished members. In the profession of government, as in other professions, the sole idea of the majority is to do what they have been taught; and it requires a popular government to enable the conceptions of the man of original genius among them, to prevail over the obstructive spirit of trained mediocrity. Only in a popular government (setting apart the accident of a highly intelligent despot) could Sir Rowland Hill have been victorious over the Post Office. A popular government installed him *in* the Post Office, and made the body, in spite of itself, obey the impulse given by the man who united special knowledge with individual vigour and originality. That the Roman aristocracy escaped this characteristic disease of a bureaucracy, was evidently owing to its popular element. All special offices, both those which gave a seat in the Senate and those which were sought by senators, were conferred by popular election. The Russian Government is a characteristic exemplification of both the good and bad side of bureaucracy : its fixed maxims, directed with Roman perseverance to the same unflinchingly-pursued ends from age to age ; the remarkable skill with which those ends are generally pursued ; the frightful internal corruption, and the permanent organized hostility to improvements from without, which even the autocratic power of a vigorous-minded Emperor is seldom or never sufficient to overcome ; the patient obstructiveness of the body being in the long run more than a match for the fitful energy of one man. The Chinese Government, a bureaucracy of Mandarins, is, as far as known to us, another apparent example of the same qualities and defects.

In all human affairs, conflicting influences are required, to keep one another alive and efficient even for their own proper uses ; and the exclusive pursuit of one good object, apart from some other which should accompany it, ends not in excess of one and defect of the other, but in the decay and loss even of that which has been exclusively cared for. Government by trained officials cannot do, for a country, the things which can be done by a free government ; but it might be supposed capable of doing some things which free government, of itself, cannot do. We find, however, that an outside element of freedom is necessary to enable it to do effectually or permanently even its own business. And so, also, freedom cannot produce its best effects, and often breaks down altogether, unless means can be found of combining it with trained and skilled administration. There could not be a moment's hesitation between representative government, among a people in any degree ripe for it, and the most perfect imaginable bureaucracy. But it is, at the same time, one of the most important ends of political institutions, to attain as many of the qualities of the one as are consistent with the other ; to secure, as far as they can be made compatible, the great advantage of the conduct of affairs by skilled persons, bred to it as an intellectual profession, along with that of a general control vested in, and seriously exercised by, bodies representative of the entire people. Much would be done towards this end by recognizing the line of separation, discussed in the preceding chapter, between the work of government properly so called, which can only be well performed after special cultivation, and that of selecting, watching, and, when needful, controlling the governors, which in this case, as in others, properly devolves, not on those who do the work, but on those for whose benefit it ought to be done. No progress at all can be made towards obtaining a skilled democracy, unless the democracy are willing that the work which requires skill should be done by those who possess it. A democracy has enough to do in providing itself with an amount of mental competency sufficient for its own proper work, that of superintendence and check.

How to obtain and secure this amount, is one of the questions to be taken into consideration in judging of the proper constitution of a representative body. In proportion as its composition fails to secure this amount, the assembly will encroach, by special acts, on the province of the executive ; it will expel a good, or elevate and uphold a bad, ministry ; it will connive at, or overlook, in them, abuses of trust, will be deluded by their false pretences, or will withhold support from those who endeavour to fulfil their trust conscientiously; it will countenance, or impose, a selfish, a capricious and impulsive, a short-sighted, ignorant, and prejudiced general policy, foreign and domestic; it will abrogate good laws, or enact bad ones, let in new evils, or cling with perverse obstinacy to old; it will even, perhaps, under misleading impulses, momentary or permanent, emanating from itself or from its constituents, tolerate or connive at proceedings which set law aside altogether, in cases where equal justice would not be agreeable to popular feeling. Such are among the dangers of representative government, arising from a constitution of the representation which does not secure an adequate amount of intelligence and knowledge in the representative assembly.

We next proceed to the evils arising from the prevalence of modes of action in the representative body, dictated by sinister interests (to employ the useful phrase introduced by Bentham), that is, interests conflicting more or less with the general good of the community.

It is universally admitted, that, of the evils incident to monarchical and aristocratic governments, a large proportion arise from this cause. The interest of the monarch, or the interest of the aristocracy, either collective or that of its individual members, is promoted, or they themselves think that it will be promoted, by conduct opposed to that which the general interest of the community requires. The interest, for example, of the government is to tax heavily: that of the community is, to be as little taxed as the necessary expenses of good government permit. The interest of the king, and of the governing aristocracy, is to possess, and exercise, unlimited power over the people; to enforce, on their part, complete conformity to the will and preferences of the rulers. The interest of the people is, to have as little control exercised over them in any respect, as is consistent with attaining the legitimate ends of government. The interest, or apparent and supposed interest, of the king or aristocracy, is to permit no censure of themselves, at least in any form which they may consider either to threaten their power, or seriously to interfere with their free agency. The interest of the people is that there should be full liberty of censure on every public officer, and on every public act or measure. The interest of a ruling class, whether in an aristocracy or an aristocratic monarchy, is to assume to themselves an endless variety of unjust privileges, sometimes benefiting their pockets at the expense of the people, sometimes merely tending to exalt them above others, or, what is the same thing in different words, to degrade others below themselves. If the people are disaffected, which under such a government they are very likely to be, it is the interest of the king or aristocracy to keep them at a low level of intelligence and education, foment dissensions among them, and even prevent them from being too well off, lest they should ' wax fat, and kick '; agreeably to the maxim of Cardinal Richelieu in his celebrated ' Testament Politique.' All these things are for the interest of a king or aristocracy, in a purely selfish point of view, unless a sufficiently strong counter-interest is created by the fear of provoking resistance. All these evils have been, and many of them still are, produced by the sinister interests of kings and aristocracies, where their power is sufficient to raise them above the opinion of the rest of the community; nor is it rational to expect, as the consequence of such a position, any other conduct.

These things are superabundantly evident in the case of a monarchy or an aristocracy; but it is sometimes rather gratuitously assumed, that the same kind of injurious influences do not operate in a democracy. Looking at democracy in the way in which it is commonly conceived, as the rule of the numerical majority, it is surely possible that the ruling power may be under the dominion of sectional or class interests, pointing to conduct different from that which would be dictated by impartial regard for the interest of all. Suppose the majority to be whites, the minority negroes, or vice versa : is it likely that the majority would allow equal justice to the minority ?   Suppose the majority Catholics, the minority Protestants, or the reverse ; will there not be the same danger ?   Or let the majority be English, the minority Irish, or the contrary : is there not a great probability of similar evil ?   In all countries there is a majority of poor, a minority who, in contradistinction, may be called rich.   Between these two classes, on many questions, there is complete opposition of apparent interest.   We will suppose the majority sufficiently intelligent to be aware that it is not for their advantage to weaken the security of property, and that it would be weakened by any act of arbitrary spoliation.   But is there not a considerable danger lest they should throw upon the possessors of what is called realized property, and upon the larger incomes, an unfair share, or even the whole, of the burden of taxation, and having done so, add to the amount without scruple, expending the proceeds in modes supposed to conduce to the profit and advantage of the labouring class ?   Suppose, again, a minority of skilled labourers, a majority of unskilled : the experience of many Trade Unions, unless they are greatly calumniated, justifies the apprehension that equality of earnings might be imposed as an obligation, and that piecework, payment by the hour, and all practices which enable superior industry or abilities to gain a superior reward, might be put down.   Legislative attempts to raise wages, limitation of competition in the labour market, taxes or restrictions on machinery, and on improvements of all kinds tending to dispense with any of the existing labour—even, perhaps, protection of the home producer against foreign industry—are very natural (I do not venture to say whether probable) results of a feeling of class interest in a governing majority of manual labourers.

It will be said that none of these things are for the *real* interest of the most numerous class : to which I answer, that if the conduct of human beings was determined by no other interested considerations than those which constitute their 'real' interest, neither monarchy nor oligarchy would be such bad governments as they are; for assuredly very strong arguments may be, and often have been, adduced to show that either a king or a governing senate are in much the most enviable position, when ruling justly and vigilantly over an active, wealthy, enlightened, and high-minded people. But a king only now and then, and an oligarchy in no known instance, have taken this exalted view of their self-interest: and why should we expect a loftier mode of thinking from the labouring classes? It is not what their interest is, but what they suppose it to be, that is the important consideration with respect to their conduct: and it is quite conclusive against any theory of government, that it assumes the numerical majority to do habitually what is never done, nor expected to be done, save in very exceptional cases, by any other depositaries of power —namely, to direct their conduct by their real ultimate interest, in opposition to their immediate and apparent interest. No one, surely, can doubt that many of the pernicious measures above enumerated, and many others as bad, would be for the immediate interest of the general body of unskilled labourers. It is quite possible that they would be for the selfish interest of the whole existing generation of the class. The relaxation of industry and activity, and diminished encouragement to saving, which would be their ultimate consequence, might perhaps be little felt by the class of unskilled labourers in the space of a single lifetime. Some of the most fatal changes in human affairs have been, as to their more manifest immediate effects, beneficial. The establishment of the despotism of the Caesars was a great benefit to the entire generation in which it took place. It put a stop to civil war, abated a vast amount of malversation and tyranny by praetors and proconsuls; it fostered many of the graces of life, and intellectual cultivation in all departments not political; it produced monuments of literary

genius dazzling to the imaginations of shallow readers
of history, who do not reflect that the men to whom
the despotism of Augustus (as well as of Lorenzo de'
Medici and of Louis XIV) owes its brilliancy, were all
formed in the generation preceding. The accumulated
riches, and the mental energy and activity, produced
by centuries of freedom, remained for the benefit of the
first generation of slaves. Yet this was the commencement of a régime by whose gradual operation all the
civilization which had been gained, insensibly faded
away, until the Empire which had conquered and
embraced the world in its grasp, so completely lost
even its military efficiency, that invaders whom three
or four legions had always sufficed to coerce, were able
to overrun and occupy nearly the whole of its vast
territory. The fresh impulse given by Christianity
came but just in time to save arts and letters from
perishing, and the human race from sinking back into
perhaps endless night.

When we talk of the interest of a body of men, or
even of an individual man, as a principle determining
their actions, the question what would be considered
their interest by an unprejudiced observer, is one of
the least important parts of the whole matter. As
Coleridge observes, the man makes the motive, not the
motive the man. What it is the man's interest to do or
refrain from, depends less on any outward circumstances, than upon what sort of man he is. If you wish
to know what is practically a man's interest, you
must know the cast of his habitual feelings and thoughts.
Everybody has two kinds of interests, interests which
he cares for, and interests which he does not care for.
Everybody has selfish and unselfish interests, and
a selfish man has cultivated the habit of caring for the
former, and not caring for the latter. Every one has
present and distant interests, and the improvident
man is he who cares for the present interests and does
not care for the distant. It matters little that on any
correct calculation the latter may be the more considerable, if the habits of his mind lead him to fix his

thoughts and wishes solely on the former. It would be vain to attempt to persuade a man who beats his wife and illtreats his children, that he would be happier if he lived in love and kindness with them. He would be happier if he were the kind of person who *could* so live ; but he is not, and it is probably too late for him to become, that kind of person. Being what he is, the gratification of his love of domineering, and the indulgence of his ferocious temper, are to his perceptions a greater good to himself, than he would be capable of deriving from the pleasure and affection of those dependent on him. He has no pleasure in their pleasure, and does not care for their affection. His neighbour, who does, is probably a happier man than he ; but could he be persuaded of this, the persuasion would, most likely, only still further exasperate his malignity or his irritability. On the average, a person who cares for other people, for his country, or for mankind, is a happier man than one who does not ; but of what use is it to preach this doctrine to a man who cares for nothing but his own ease, or his own pocket ? He cannot care for other people if he would. It is like preaching to the worm who crawls on the ground, how much better it would be for him if he were an eagle.

Now it is an universally observed fact, that the two evil dispositions in question, the disposition to prefer a man's selfish interests to those which he shares with other people, and his immediate and direct interests to those which are indirect and remote, are characteristics most especially called forth and fostered by the possession of power. The moment a man, or a class of men, find themselves with power in their hands, the man's individual interest, or the class's separate interest, acquires an entirely new degree of importance in their eyes. Finding themselves worshipped by others, they become worshippers of themselves, and think themselves entitled to be counted at a hundred times the value of other people ; while the facility they acquire of doing as they like without regard to consequences, insensibly weakens the habits which make men look forward even to such consequences as affect themselves. This is the meaning of the universal tradition, grounded on universal experience, of men's being corrupted by power. Every one knows how absurd it would be to infer from what a man is or does when in a private station, that he will be and do exactly the like when a despot on a throne; where the bad parts of his human nature, instead of being restrained and kept in subordination by every circumstance of his life and by every person surrounding him, are courted by all persons, and ministered to by all circumstances. It would be quite as absurd to entertain a similar expectation in regard to a class of men; the Demos, or any other. Let them be ever so modest and amenable to reason while there is a power over them stronger than they, we ought to expect a total change in this respect when they themselves become the strongest power.

Governments must be made for human beings as they are, or as they are capable of speedily becoming: and in any state of cultivation which mankind, or any class among them, have yet attained, or are likely soon to attain, the interests by which they will be led, when they are thinking only of self-interest, will be almost exclusively those which are obvious at first sight, and which operate on their present condition. It is only a disinterested regard for others, and especially for what comes after them, for the idea of posterity, of their country, or of mankind, whether grounded on sympathy or on a conscientious feeling, which ever directs the minds and purposes of classes or bodies of men towards distant or unobvious interests. And it cannot be maintained that any form of government would be rational, which required as a condition that these exalted principles of action should be the guiding and master motives in the conduct of average human beings. A certain amount of conscience, and of disinterested public spirit, may fairly be calculated on in the citizens of any community ripe for representative government. But it would be ridiculous to expect such a degree of it, combined with such intellectual discernment, as would be proof against any plausible fallacy tending to make that which was for their class interest appear the dictate of justice and of the general good. We all know what specious fallacies may be urged in defence of every act of injustice yet proposed for the imaginary benefit of the mass. We know how many, not otherwise fools or bad men, have thought it justifiable to repudiate the national debt. We know how many, not destitute of ability, and of considerable popular influence, think it fair to throw the whole burden of taxation upon savings, under the name of realized property, allowing those whose progenitors and themselves have always spent all they received, to remain, as a reward for such exemplary conduct, wholly untaxed. We know what powerful arguments, the more dangerous because there is a portion of truth in them, may be brought against all inheritance, against the power of bequest, against every advantage which one person seems to have over another. We know how easily the uselessness of almost every branch of knowledge may be proved, to the complete satisfaction of those who do not possess it. How many, not altogether stupid men, think the scientific study of languages useless, think ancient literature useless, all erudition useless, logic and metaphysics useless, poetry and the fine arts idle and frivolous, political economy purely mischievous? Even history has been pronounced useless and mischievous by able men. Nothing but that acquaintance with external nature, empirically acquired, which serves directly for the production of objects necessary to existence or agreeable to the senses, would get its utility recognized if people had the least encouragement to disbelieve it. Is it reasonable to think that even much more cultivated minds than those of the numerical majority can be expected to be, will have so delicate a conscience, and so just an appreciation of what is against their own apparent interest, that they will reject these and the innumerable other fallacies which will press in upon them from all quarters as soon as they come into power, to induce them to follow their own selfish inclinations and short-sighted notions of their own good, in opposition to justice, at the expense of all other classes and of posterity ?

One of the greatest dangers, therefore, of democracy, as of all other forms of government, lies in the sinister interest of the holders of power : it is the danger of class legislation ; of government intended for (whether really effecting it or not) the immediate benefit of the dominant class, to the lasting detriment of the whole. And one of the most important questions demanding consideration, in determining the best constitution of a representative government, is how to provide efficacious securities against this evil.

If we consider as a class, politically speaking, any number of persons who have the same sinister interest, —that is, whose direct and apparent interest points towards the same description of bad measures ; the desirable object would be that no class, and no combination of classes likely to combine, should be able to exercise a preponderant influence in the government. A modern community, not divided within itself by strong antipathies of race, language, or nationality, may be considered as in the main divisible into two sections, which, in spite of partial variations, correspond on the whole with two divergent directions of apparent interest. Let us call them (in brief general terms) labourers on the one hand, employers of labour on the other : including however along with employers of labour, not only retired capitalists, and the possessors of inherited wealth, but all that highly paid description of labourers (such as the professions) whose education and way of life assimilate them with the rich, and whose prospect and ambition it is to raise themselves into that class. With the labourers, on the other hand, may be ranked those smaller employers of labour, who by interests, habits, and educational impressions, are assimilated in wishes, tastes, and objects to the labouring classes; comprehending a large proportion of petty tradesmen. In a state of society thus composed, if the representative system could be made ideally perfect, and if it were possible to maintain it in that state, its organization must be such, that these two classes, manual labourers and their affinities on one side, employers of labour and their affinities on the other, should be, in the arrangement of the representative system, equally balanced, each influencing about an equal number of votes in Parliament: since, assuming that the majority of each class, in any difference between them, would be mainly governed by their class interests, there would be a minority of each in whom that consideration would be subordinate to reason, justice, and the good of the whole; and this minority of either, joining with the whole of the other, would turn the scale against any demands of their own majority which were not such as ought to prevail. The reason why, in any tolerably constituted society, justice and the general interest mostly in the end carry their point, is that the separate and selfish interests of mankind are almost always divided; some are interested in what is wrong, but some, also, have their private interest on the side of what is right: and those who are governed by higher considerations, though too few and weak to prevail against the whole of the others, usually after sufficient discussion and agitation become strong enough to turn the balance in favour of the body of private interests which is on the same side with them. The representative system ought to be so constituted as to maintain this state of things: it ought not to allow any of the various sectional interests to be so powerful as to be capable of prevailing against truth and justice and the other sectional interests combined. There ought always to be such a balance preserved among personal interests, as may render any one of them dependent for its successes, on carrying with it at least a large proportion of those who act on higher motives, and more comprehensive and distant views.

CHAPTER VII

OF TRUE AND FALSE DEMOCRACY; REPRESENTATION
OF ALL, AND REPRESENTATION OF THE MAJORITY
ONLY

IT has been seen, that the dangers incident to a representative democracy are of two kinds: danger of a low grade of intelligence in the representative body, and in the popular opinion which controls it; and danger of class legislation on the part of the numerical majority, these being all composed of the same class. We have next to consider, how far it is possible so to organize the democracy, as, without interfering materially with the characteristic benefits of democratic government, to do away with these two great evils, or at least to abate them, in the utmost degree attainable by human contrivance.

The common mode of attempting this is by limiting the democratic character of the representation, through a more or less restricted suffrage. But there is a previous consideration which, duly kept in view, considerably modifies the circumstances which are supposed to render such a restriction necessary. A completely equal democracy, in a nation in which a single class composes the numerical majority, cannot be divested of certain evils; but those evils are greatly aggravated by the fact, that the democracies which at present exist are not equal, but systematically unequal in favour of the predominant class. Two very different ideas are usually confounded under the name democracy. The pure idea of democracy, according to its definition, is the government of the whole people by the whole people, equally represented. Democracy as commonly conceived and hitherto practised, is the government of the whole people by a mere majority of the people, exclusively represented. The former is synonymous with the equality of all citizens; the latter, strangely confounded with it, is a government of privilege, in favour of the numerical majority, who alone possess practically any voice in the State. This is the inevitable consequence of the manner in which the votes are now taken, to the complete disfranchisement of minorities.

The confusion of ideas here is great, but it is so easily cleared up, that one would suppose the slightest indication would be sufficient to place the matter in its true light before any mind of average intelligence. It would be so, but for the power of habit; owing to which the simplest idea, if unfamiliar, has as great difficulty in making its way to the mind as a far more complicated one. That the minority must yield to the majority, the smaller number to the greater, is a familiar idea; and accordingly men think there is no necessity for using their minds any further, and it does not occur to them that there is any medium between allowing the smaller number to be equally powerful with the greater, and blotting out the smaller number altogether. In a representative body actually deliberating, the minority must of course be overruled; and in an equal democracy (since the opinions of the constituents, when they insist on them, determine those of the representative body) the majority of the people, through their representatives, will outvote and prevail over the minority and their representatives. But does it follow that the minority should have no representatives at all? Because the majority ought to prevail over the minority, must the majority have all the votes, the minority none? Is it necessary that the minority should not even be heard? Nothing but habit and old association can reconcile any reasonable being to the needless injustice. In a really equal democracy, every or any section would be represented, not disproportionately, but proportionately. A majority of the electors would always have a majority of the representatives; but a minority of the electors would always have a minority of the representatives. Man for man, they would be as fully represented as the majority. Unless they are, there is not equal government, but a government of inequality and privilege : one part of the people rule over the rest : there is a part whose fair and equal share of influence in the representation is withheld from them ; contrary to all just government, but above all, contrary to the principle of democracy, which professes equality as its very root and foundation.

The injustice and violation of principle are not less flagrant because those who suffer by them are a minority ; for there is not equal suffrage where every single individual does not count for as much as any other single individual in the community. But it is not only a minority who suffer. Democracy, thus constituted, does not even attain its ostensible object, that of giving the powers of government in all cases to the numerical majority. It does something very different : it gives them to a majority of the majority ; who may be, and often are, but a minority of the whole. All principles are most effectually tested by extreme cases. Suppose then, that, in a country governed by equal and universal suffrage, there is a contested election in every constituency, and every election is carried by a small majority. The Parliament thus brought together represents little more than a bare majority of the people. This Parliament proceeds to legislate, and adopts important measures by a bare majority of itself. What guarantee is there that these measures accord with the wishes of a majority of the people ? Nearly half the electors, having been outvoted at the hustings, have had no influence at all in the decision ; and the whole of these may be, a majority of them probably are, hostile to the measures, having voted against those by whom they have been carried. Of the remaining electors, nearly half have chosen representatives who, by supposition, have voted against the measures. It is possible, therefore, and not at all improbable, that the opinion which has prevailed was agreeable only to a minority of the nation, though a majority of that portion of it, whom the institutions of the country have erected into a ruling class. If democracy means the certain ascendancy of the majority, there are no means of insuring that, but by allowing every individual figure to tell equally in the summing up. Any minority left out, either purposely or by the play of the machinery, gives the power not to the majority, but to a minority in some other part of the scale.

The only answer which can possibly be made to this reasoning is, that as different opinions predominate in different localities, the opinion which is in a minority in some places has a majority in others, and on the whole every opinion which exists in the constituencies obtains its fair share of voices in the representation. And this is roughly true in the present state of the constituency; if it were not, the discordance of the House with the general sentiment of the country would soon become evident. But it would be no longer true if the present constituency were much enlarged; still less, if made co-extensive with the whole population; for in that case the majority in every locality would consist of manual labourers; and when there was any question pending, on which these classes were at issue with the rest of the community, no other class could succeed in getting represented anywhere. Even now, is it not a great grievance, that in every Parliament a very numerous portion of the electors, willing and anxious to be represented, have no member in the House for whom they have voted? Is it just that every elector of Marylebone is obliged to be represented by two nominees of the vestries, every elector of Finsbury or Lambeth by those (as is generally believed) of the publicans? The constituencies to which most of the highly educated and public spirited persons in the country belong, those of the large towns, are now, in great part, either unrepresented or misrepresented. The electors who are on a different side in party politics from the local majority, are unrepresented. Of those who are on the same side, a large proportion are misrepresented; having been obliged to accept the man who had the greatest number of supporters in their political party, though his opinions may differ from theirs on every other point. The state of things is, in some respects, even worse than if the minority were not allowed to vote at all; for then, at least the majority might have a member who would represent their own best mind: while now, the necessity of not dividing the party, for fear of letting in its opponents, induces all to vote either for the first person who presents himself wearing their colours, or for the one brought forward by their local leaders; and these, if we pay them the compliment, which they very seldom deserve, of supposing their choice to be unbiassed by their personal interests, are compelled, that they may be sure of mustering their whole strength, to bring forward a candidate whom none of the party will strongly object to —that is, a man without any distinctive peculiarity, any known opinions except the shibboleth of the party. This is strikingly exemplified in the United States; where, at the election of President, the strongest party never dares put forward any of its strongest men, because every one of these, from the mere fact that he has been long in the public eye, has made himself objectionable to some portion or other of the party, and is therefore not so sure a card for rallying all their votes, as a person who has never been heard of by the public at all until he is produced as the candidate. Thus, the man who is chosen, even by the strongest party, represents perhaps the real wishes only of the narrow margin by which that party outnumbers the other. Any section whose support is necessary to success, possesses a veto on the candidate. Any section which holds out more obstinately than the rest, can compel all the others to adopt its nominee; and this superior pertinacity is unhappily more likely to be found among those who are holding out for their own interest, than for that of the public. The choice of the majority is therefore very likely to be determined by that portion of the body who are the most timid, the most narrow-minded and prejudiced, or who cling most tenaciously to the exclusive class-interest ; in which case the electoral rights of the minority, while useless for the purposes for which votes are given, serve only for compelling the majority to accept the candidate of the weakest or worst portion of themselves.

That, while recognizing these evils, many should consider them as the necessary price paid for a free government, is in no way surprising : it was the opinion of all the friends of freedom, up to a recent period. But the habit of passing them over as irremediable has become so inveterate, that many persons seem to have lost the capacity of looking at them as things which they would be glad to remedy if they could. From despairing of a cure, there is too often but one step to denying the disease ; and from this follows dislike to having a remedy proposed, as if the proposer were creating a mischief instead of offering relief from one. People are so inured to the evils, that they feel as if it were unreasonable, if not wrong, to complain of them. Yet, avoidable or not, he must be a purblind lover of liberty on whose mind they do not weigh ; who would not rejoice at the discovery that they could be dispensed with. Now, nothing is more certain, than that the virtual blotting-out of the minority is no necessary or natural consequence of freedom ; that, far from having any connexion with democracy, it is diametrically opposed to the first principle of democracy, representation in proportion to numbers. It is an essential part of democracy that minorities should be adequately represented. No real democracy, nothing but a false show of democracy, is possible without it.

Those who have seen and felt, in some degree, the force of these considerations, have proposed various expedients by which the evil may be, in a greater or less degree, mitigated. Lord John Russell, in one of his Reform Bills, introduced a provision, that certain constituencies should return three members, and that in these each elector should be allowed to vote only for two ; and Mr. Disraeli, in the recent debates, revived the memory of the fact by reproaching him for it; being of opinion, apparently, that it befits a Conservative statesman to regard only means, and to disown scornfully all fellow-feeling with any one who is betrayed, even once, into thinking of ends.[1] Others have proposed that each elector should be allowed to vote only for one. By either of these plans, a minority equalling or exceeding a third of the local constituency would be able, if it attempted no more, to return one out of three members. The same result might be attained in a still better way, if, as proposed in an able pamphlet by Mr. James Garth Marshall, the elector retained his three votes, but was at liberty to bestow them all upon the same candidate. These schemes, though infinitely better than none at all, are yet but makeshifts, and attain the end in a very imperfect manner; since all local minorities of less than a third, and all minorities, however numerous, which are made up from several constituencies, would remain unrepre-

[1] This blunder of Mr. Disraeli (from which, greatly to his credit, Sir John Pakington took an opportunity, soon after, of separating himself) is a speaking instance among many, how little the Conservative leaders understand Conservative principles. Without presuming to require from political parties such an amount of virtue and discernment as that they should comprehend, and know when to apply, the principles of their opponents, we may yet say that it would be a great improvement if each party understood and acted upon its own. Well would it be for England if Conservatives voted consistently for everything conservative, and Liberals for everything liberal. We should not then have to wait long for things which, like the present and many other great measures, are eminently both the one and the other. The Conservatives, as being by the law of their existence the stupidest party, have much the greatest sins of this description to answer for: and it is a melancholy truth, that if any measure were proposed, on any subject, truly, largely, and far-sightedly conservative, even if Liberals were willing to vote for it, the great bulk of the Conservative party would rush blindly in and prevent it from being carried.

sented. It is much to be lamented, however, that none of these plans have been carried into effect, as any of them would have recognized the right principle, and prepared the way for its more complete application. But real equality of representation is not obtained, unless any set of electors amounting to the average number of a constituency, wherever in the country they happen to reside, have the power of combining with one another to return a representative. This degree of perfection in representation appeared impracticable, until a man of great capacity, fitted alike for large general views and for the contrivance of practical details—Mr. Thomas Hare—had proved its possibility by drawing up a scheme for its accomplishment, embodied in a Draft of an Act of Parliament: a scheme which has the almost unparalleled merit, of carrying out a great principle of government in a manner approaching to ideal perfection as regards the special object in view, while it attains incidentally several other ends, of scarcely inferior importance.

According to this plan, the unit of representation, the quota of electors who would be entitled to have a member to themselves, would be ascertained by the ordinary process of taking averages, the number of voters being divided by the number of seats in the House: and every candidate who obtained that quota would be returned, from however great a number of local constituencies it might be gathered. The votes would, as at present, be given locally; but any elector would be at liberty to vote for any candidate, in whatever part of the country he might offer himself. Those electors, therefore, who did not wish to be represented by any of the local candidates, might aid by their vote in the return of the person they liked best among all those throughout the country, who had expressed a willingness to be chosen. This would, so far, give reality to the electoral rights of the otherwise virtually disfranchised minority. But it is important that not those alone who refuse to vote for any of the local candidates, but those also who vote for one of them

and are defeated, should be enabled to find elsewhere
the representation which they have not succeeded in
obtaining in their own district.   It is therefore provided that an elector may deliver a voting paper,
containing other names in addition to the one which
stands foremost in his preference.   His vote would
only be counted for one candidate ; but if the object
of his first choice failed to be returned, from not having
obtained the quota, his second perhaps might be more
fortunate.   He may extend his list to a greater number,
in the order of his preference, so that if the names
which stand near the top of the list either cannot make
up the quota, or are able to make it up without his
vote, the vote may still be used for some one whom it
may assist in returning.   To obtain the full number of
members required to complete the House, as well as to
prevent very popular candidates from engrossing nearly
all the suffrages, it is necessary, however many votes
a candidate may obtain, that no more of them than
the quota should be counted for his return : the remainder of those who voted for him would have their
votes counted for the next person on their respective
lists who needed them, and could by their aid complete
the quota.   To determine which of a candidate's votes
should be used for his return, and which set free for
others, several methods are proposed, into which we
shall not here enter.   He would of course retain the votes
of all those who would not otherwise be represented ;
and for the remainder, drawing lots, in default of better,
would be an unobjectionable expedient.   The voting
papers would be conveyed to a central office, where
the votes would be counted, the number of first, second,
third, and other votes given for each candidate ascertained, and the quota would be allotted to every one
who could make it up, until the number of the House
was complete ; first votes being preferred to second,
second to third, and so forth.   The voting papers, and
all the elements of the calculation, would be placed in
public repositories, accessible to all whom they concerned ; and if any one who had obtained the quota.

was not duly returned, it would be in his power easily
to prove it.

These are the main provisions of the scheme. For
a more minute knowledge of its very simple machinery,
I must refer to Mr. Hare's *Treatise on the Election of
Representatives* (a small volume published in 1859),[1]
and to a pamphlet by Mr. Henry Fawcett (now [1863]
Professor of Political Economy in the University of
Cambridge), published in 1860, and entitled *Mr. Hare's
Reform Bill simplified and explained*. This last is a
very clear and concise exposition of the plan, reduced
to its simplest elements, by the omission of some of
Mr. Hare's original provisions, which, though in themselves beneficial, were thought to take more from the
simplicity of the scheme than they added to its practical usefulness. The more these works are studied,
the stronger, I venture to predict, will be the impression of the perfect feasibility of the scheme, and its
transcendent advantages. Such and so numerous are
these, that, in my conviction, they place Mr. Hare's
plan among the very greatest improvements yet made
in the theory and practice of government.

In the first place, it secures a representation, in proportion to numbers, of every division of the electoral
body : not two great parties alone, with perhaps a few
large sectional minorities in particular places, but every
minority in the whole nation, consisting of a sufficiently large number to be, on principles of equal
justice, entitled to a representative. Secondly, no
elector would, as at present, be nominally represented
by some one whom he had not chosen. Every member
of the House would be the representative of an unanimous constituency. He would represent a thousand
electors, or two thousand, or five thousand, or ten
thousand, as the quota might be, every one of whom
would have not only voted for him, but selected him

---

[1] In a second edition, published recently [1861], Mr. Hare
has made important improvements in some of the detailed
provisions.

from the whole country; not merely from the assortment of two or three perhaps rotten oranges, which may be the only choice offered to him in his local market. Under this relation the tie between the elector and the representative would be of a strength, and a value, of which at present we have no experience. Every one of the electors would be personally identified with his representative, and the representative with his constituents. Every elector who voted for him, would have done so either because, among all the candidates for Parliament who are favourably known to a certain number of electors, he is the one who best expresses the voter's own opinions, or because he is one of those whose abilities and character the voter most respects, and whom he most willingly trusts to think for him. The member would represent persons, not the mere bricks and mortar of the town—the voters themselves, not a few vestrymen or parish notabilities merely. All, however, that is worth preserving in the representation of places would be preserved. Though the Parliament of the nation ought to have as little as possible to do with purely local affairs, yet, while it has to do with them, there ought to be members specially commissioned to look after the interests of every important locality: and these there would still be. In every locality which could make up the quota within itself, the majority would generally prefer to be represented by one of themselves; by a person of local knowledge, and residing in the locality, if there is any such person to be found among the candidates, who is otherwise well qualified to be their representative. It would be the minorities chiefly, who being unable to return the local member, would look out elsewhere for a candidate likely to obtain other votes in addition to their own.

Of all modes in which a national representation can possibly be constituted, this one affords the best security for the intellectual qualifications desirable in the representatives. At present, by universal admission, it is becoming more and more difficult for any one, who has only talents and character, to gain admission into the House of Commons. The only persons who can get elected are those who possess local influence, or make their way by lavish expenditure, or who, on the invitation of three or four tradesmen or attorneys, are sent down by one of the two great parties from their London clubs, as men whose votes the party can depend on under all circumstances. On Mr. Hare's system, those who did not like the local candidates, or who could not succeed in carrying the local candidate they preferred, would have the power to fill up their voting papers by a selection from all the persons of national reputation, on the list of candidates, with whose general political principles they were in sympathy. Almost every person, therefore, who had made himself in any way honourably distinguished, though devoid of local influence, and having sworn allegiance to no political party, would have a fair chance of making up the quota; and with this encouragement such persons might be expected to offer themselves, in numbers hitherto undreamt of. Hundreds of able men of independent thought, who would have no chance whatever of being chosen by the majority of any existing constituency, have by their writings, or their exertions in some field of public usefulness, made themselves known and approved by a few persons in almost every district of the kingdom; and if every vote that would be given for them in every place could be counted for their election, they might be able to complete the number of the quota. In no other way which it seems possible to suggest, would Parliament be so certain of containing the very *élite* of the country.

And it is not solely through the votes of minorities that this system of election would raise the intellectual standard of the House of Commons. Majorities would be compelled to look out for members of a much higher calibre. When the individuals composing the majority would no longer be reduced to Hobson's choice, of either voting for the person brought forward by their local leaders, or not voting at all; when the nominee of the leaders would have to encounter the competition not solely of the candidate of the minority, but of all the men of established reputation in the country who were willing to serve ; it would be impossible any longer to foist upon the electors the first person who presents himself with the catchwords of the party in his mouth, and three or four thousand pounds in his pocket. The majority would insist on having a candidate worthy of their choice, or they would carry their votes somewhere else, and the minority would prevail. The slavery of the majority to the least estimable portion of their number would be at an end : the very best and most capable of the local notabilities would be put forward by preference ; if possible, such as were known in some advantageous way beyond the locality, that their local strength might have a chance of being fortified by stray votes from elsewhere. Constituencies would become competitors for the best candidates, and would vie with one another in selecting from among the men of local knowledge and connexions those who were most distinguished in every other respect.

The natural tendency of representative government, as of modern civilization, is towards collective mediocrity : and this tendency is increased by all reductions and extensions of the franchise, their effect being to place the principal power in the hands of classes more and more below the highest level of instruction in the community. But though the superior intellects and characters will necessarily be outnumbered, it makes a great difference whether or not they are heard. In the false democracy which, instead of giving representation to all, gives it only to the local majorities, the voice of the instructed minority may have no organs at all in the representative body. It is an admitted fact that in the American democracy, which is constructed on this faulty model, the highly-cultivated members of the community, except such of them as are willing to sacrifice their own opinions and modes of judgement, and become the servile mouthpieces of their inferiors in knowledge, seldom even offer themselves for Congress or the State Legislatures, so little

likelihood have they of being returned. Had a plan
like Mr. Hare's by good fortune suggested itself to the
enlightened and patriotic founders of the American
Republic, the Federal and State Assemblies would
have contained many of these distinguished men, and
democracy would have been spared its greatest reproach and one of its most formidable evils. Against
this evil the system of personal representation, proposed by Mr. Hare, is almost a specific. The minority
of instructed minds scattered through the local constituencies, would unite to return a number, proportioned
to their own numbers, of the very ablest men the
country contains. They would be under the strongest
inducement to choose such men, since in no other mode
could they make their small numerical strength tell for
anything considerable. The representatives of the
majority, besides that they would themselves be improved in quality by the operation of the system,
would no longer have the whole field to themselves.
They would indeed outnumber the others, as much as
the one class of electors outnumbers the other in the
country: they could always outvote them, but they
would speak and vote in their presence, and subject
to their criticism. When any difference arose, they
would have to meet the arguments of the instructed
few, by reasons, at least apparently, as cogent; and
since they could not, as those do who are speaking to
persons already unanimous, simply assume that they
are in the right, it would occasionally happen to them
to become convinced that they were in the wrong. As
they would in general be well-meaning (for thus much
may reasonably be expected from a fairly-chosen
national representation), their own minds would be
insensibly raised by the influence of the minds with
which they were in contact, or even in conflict. The
champions of unpopular doctrines would not put forth
their arguments merely in books and periodicals, read
only by their own side; the opposing ranks would
meet face to face and hand to hand, and there would
be a fair comparison of their intellectual strength, in

the presence of the country. It would then be found out whether the opinion which prevailed by counting votes, would also prevail if the votes were weighed as well as counted. The multitude have often a true instinct for distinguishing an able man, when he has the means of displaying his ability in a fair field before them. If such a man fails to obtain at least some portion of his just weight, it is through institutions or usages which keep him out of sight. In the old democracies there were no means of keeping out of sight any able man: the bema was open to him; he needed nobody's consent to become a public adviser. It is not so in a representative government; and the best friends of representative democracy can hardly be without misgivings, that the Themistocles or Demosthenes whose counsels would have saved the nation, might be unable during his whole life ever to obtain a seat. But if the presence in the representative assembly can be insured, of even a few of the first minds in the country, though the remainder consist only of average minds, the influence of these leading spirits is sure to make itself sensibly felt in the general deliberations, even though they be known to be, in many respects, opposed to the tone of popular opinion and feeling. I am unable to conceive any mode by which the presence of such minds can be so positively insured, as by that proposed by Mr. Hare.

This portion of the Assembly would also be the appropriate organ of a great social function, for which there is no provision in any existing democracy, but which in no government can remain permanently unfulfilled without condemning that government to infallible degeneracy and decay. This may be called the function of Antagonism. In every government there is some power stronger than all the rest; and the power which is strongest tends perpetually to become the sole power. Partly by intention, and partly unconsciously, it is ever striving to make all other things bend to itself; and is not content while there is anything which makes permanent head against it, any influence not in agreement with its spirit. Yet if it succeeds in suppressing all rival influences, and moulding everything after its own model, improvement, in that country, is at an end, and decline commences. Human improvement is a product of many factors, and no power ever yet constituted among mankind includes them all : even the most beneficent power only contains in itself some of the requisites of good, and the remainder, if progress is to continue, must be derived from some other source. No community has ever long continued progressive, but while a conflict was going on between the strongest power in the community and some rival power ; between the spiritual and temporal authorities ; the military or territorial and the industrious classes ; the king and the people ; the orthodox, and religious reformers. When the victory on either side was so complete as to put an end to the strife, and no other conflict took its place, first stagnation followed, and then decay. The ascendancy of the numerical majority is less unjust, and on the whole less mischievous, than many others, but it is attended with the very same kind of dangers, and even more certainly ; for when the government is in the hands of One or a Few, the Many are always existent as a rival power, which may not be strong enough ever to control the other, but whose opinion and sentiment are a moral, and even a social, support to all who, either from conviction or contrariety of interest, are opposed to any of the tendencies of the ruling authority. But when the Democracy is supreme, there is no One or Few strong enough for dissentient opinions and injured or menaced interests to lean upon. The great difficulty of democratic government has hitherto seemed to be, how to provide, in a democratic society, what circumstances have provided hitherto in all the societies which have maintained themselves ahead of others—a social support, a *point d'appui*, for individual resistance to the tendencies of the ruling power ; a protection, a rallying point, for opinions and interests which the ascendant public opinion views with dis-

favour. For want of such a *point d'appui*, the older
societies, and all but a few modern ones, either fell into
dissolution or became stationary (which means slow deterioration) through the exclusive predominance of a part
only of the conditions of social and mental well-being.

Now, this great want the system of Personal Representation is fitted to supply, in the most perfect manner
which the circumstances of modern society admit of.
The only quarter in which to look for a supplement, or
completing corrective, to the instincts of a democratic
majority, is the instructed minority : but, in the
ordinary mode of constituting democracy, this minority
has no organ : Mr. Hare's system provides one. The
representatives who would be returned to Parliament
by the aggregate of minorities, would afford that organ
in its greatest perfection. A separate organization of
the instructed classes, even if practicable, would be
invidious, and could only escape from being offensive
by being totally without influence. But if the *élite* of
these classes formed part of the Parliament, by the
same title as any other of its members—by representing the same number of citizens, the same numerical
fraction of the national will—their presence could give
umbrage to nobody, while they would be in the position
of highest vantage, both for making their opinions and
counsels heard on all important subjects, and for taking
an active part in public business. Their abilities would
probably draw to them more than their numerical
share of the actual administration of government ; as
the Athenians did not confide responsible public functions to Cleon or Hyperbolus (the employment of Cleon
at Pylos and Amphipolis was purely exceptional), but
Nicias, and Theramenes, and Alcibiades, were in constant employment both at home and abroad, though
known to sympathize more with oligarchy than with
democracy. The instructed minority would, in the
actual voting, count only for their numbers, but as
a moral power they would count for much more, in
virtue of their knowledge, and of the influence it would
give them over the rest. An arrangement better adapted

to keep popular opinion within reason and justice, and to guard it from the various deteriorating influences which assail the weak side of democracy, could scarcely by human ingenuity be devised. A democratic people would in this way be provided with what in any other way it would almost certainly miss—leaders of a higher grade of intellect and character than itself. Modern democracy would have its occasional Pericles, and its habitual group of superior and guiding minds.

With all this array of reasons, of the most fundamental character, on the affirmative side of the question, what is there on the negative ? Nothing that will sustain examination, when people can once be induced to bestow any real examination upon a new thing. Those indeed, if any such there be, who under pretence of equal justice, aim only at substituting the class ascendancy of the poor for that of the rich, will of course be unfavourable to a scheme which places both on a level. But I do not believe that any such wish exists at present among the working classes of this country, though I would not answer for the effect which opportunity and demagogic artifices may hereafter have in exciting it. In the United States, where the numerical majority have long been in full possession of collective despotism, they would probably be as unwilling to part with it as a single despot, or an aristocracy. But I believe that the English democracy would as yet be content with protection against the class legislation of others, without claiming the power to exercise it in their turn.

Among the ostensible objectors to Mr. Hare's scheme, some profess to think the plan unworkable ; but these, it will be found, are generally people who have barely heard of it, or have given it a very slight and cursory examination. Others are unable to reconcile themselves to the loss of what they term the local character of the representation. A nation does not seem to them to consist of persons, but of artificial units, the creation of geography and statistics. Parliament must represent towns and counties, not human beings. But no

one seeks to annihilate towns and counties. Towns
and counties, it may be presumed, are represented,
when the human beings who inhabit them are represented. Local feelings cannot exist without somebody
who feels them; nor local interests without somebody
interested in them. If the human beings whose feelings
and interests these are, have their proper share of
representation, these feelings and interests are represented, in common with all other feelings and interests
of those persons. But I cannot see why the feelings
and interests which arrange mankind according to
localities, should be the only ones thought worthy of
being represented; or why people who have other
feelings and interests, which they value more than
they do their geographical ones, should be restricted
to these as the sole principle of their political classification. The notion that Yorkshire and Middlesex have
rights apart from those of their inhabitants, or that
Liverpool and Exeter are the proper objects of the
legislator's care, in contradistinction to the population
of those places, is a curious specimen of delusion produced by words.

In general, however, objectors cut the matter short
by affirming that the people of England will never
consent to such a system. What the people of England are likely to think of those who pass such a sum-
mary sentence on their capacity of understanding and
judgement, deeming it superfluous to consider whether
a thing is right or wrong before affirming that they are
certain to reject it, I will not undertake to say. For
my own part, I do not think that the people of England
have deserved to·be, without trial, stigmatized as
insurmountably prejudiced against anything which
can be proved to be good either for themselves or for
others. It also appears to me that when prejudices
persist obstinately, it is the fault of nobody so much
as of those who make a point of proclaiming them
insuperable, as an excuse to themselves for never
joining in an attempt to remove them. Any prejudice
whatever will be insurmountable, if those who do not

share it themselves, truckle to it, and flatter it, and accept it as a law of nature. I believe, however, that in this case there is in general, among those who have yet heard of the proposition, no other hostility to it, than the natural and healthy distrust attaching to all novelties which have not been sufficiently canvassed to make generally manifest all the pros and cons of the question. The only serious obstacle is the unfamiliarity : this indeed is a formidable one, for the imagination much more easily reconciles itself to a great alteration in substance, than to a very small one in names and forms. But unfamiliarity is a disadvantage which, when there is any real value in an idea, it only requires time to remove. And in these days of discussion, and generally awakened interest in improvement, what formerly was the work of centuries, often requires only years.

Since the first publication of this Treatise, several adverse criticisms have been made on Mr. Hare's plan, which indicate at least a careful examination of it, and a more intelligent consideration than had previously been given to its pretensions. This is the natural progress of the discussion of great improvements. They are at first met by a blind prejudice, and by arguments to which only blind prejudice could attach any value. As the prejudice weakens, the arguments it employs for some time increase in strength ; since, the plan being better understood, its inevitable inconveniences, and the circumstances which m litate against its at once producing all the benefits it is intrinsically capable of, come to light along with its merits. But, of all the objections, having any semblance of reason, which have come under my notice, there is not one which had not been foreseen, considered, and canvassed by the supporters of the plan, and found either unreal or easily surmountable.

The most serious, in appearance, of the objections, may be the most briefly answered ; the assumed impossibility of guarding against fraud, or suspicion of fraud, in the operations of the Central Office. Publicity, and complete liberty of inspecting the voting papers after the election, were the securities provided; but these, it is maintained, would be unavailing; because, to check the returns, a voter would have to go over all the work that had been done by the staff of clerks. This would be a very weighty objection, if there were any necessity that the returns should be verified individually by every voter. All that a simple voter could be expected to do in the way of verification, would be to check the use made of his own voting paper; for which purpose every paper would be returned, after a proper interval, to the place from whence it came. But what he could not do, would be done for him by the unsuccessful candidates and their agents. Those among the defeated, who thought that they ought to have been returned, would, singly or a number together, employ an agency for verifying the entire process of the election; and if they detected material error, the documents would be referred to a Committee of the House of Commons, by whom the entire electoral operations of the nation would be examined and verified, at a tenth part the expense of time and money necessary for the scrutiny of a single return before an Election Committee under the system now in force.

Assuming the plan to be workable, two modes have been alleged, in which its benefits might be frustrated, and injurious consequences produced in lieu of them. First, it is said that undue power would be given to knots or cliques; sectarian combinations; associations for special objects, such as the Maine Law League, the Ballot or Liberation Society; or bodies united by class interests or community of religious persuasion. It is in the second place objected, that the system would admit of being worked for party purposes. A central organ of each political party would send its list of 658 candidates all through the country, to be voted for by the whole of its supporters in every constituency. Their votes would far outnumber those which could ever be obtained by any independent candidate. The 'ticket' system, it is contended, would, as it does in America, operate solely in favour of the great organized parties, whose tickets would be accepted blindly, and voted for in their integrity ; and would hardly ever be outvoted, except occasionally by the sectarian groups, or knots of men bound together by a common crotchet, who have been already spoken of.

The answer to this appears to be conclusive. No one pretends that under Mr. Hare's or any other plan, organization would cease to be an advantage. Scattered elements are always at a disadvantage, compared with organized bodies. As Mr. Hare's plan cannot alter the nature of things, we must expect that all parties or sections, great or small, which possess organization, would avail themselves of it to the utmost to strengthen their influence. But under the existing system those influences are everything. The scattered elements are absolutely nothing. The voters who are neither bound to the great political nor to any of the little sectarian divisions, have no means of making their votes available. Mr. Hare's plan gives them the means. They might be more, or less, dexterous in using it. They might obtain their share of influence, or much less than their share. But whatever they did acquire would be clear gain. And when it is assumed that every petty interest, or combination for a petty object, would give itself an organization, why should we suppose that the great interest of national intellect and character would alone remain unorganized ? If there would be Temperance tickets, and Ragged School tickets, and the like, would not one public-spirited person in a constituency be sufficient to put forth a ' personal merit ' ticket, and circulate it through a whole neighbourhood ? And might not a few such persons, meeting in London, select from the list of candidates the most distinguished names, without regard to technical divisions of opinion, and publish them at a trifling expense through all the constituencies ? It must be remembered that the influence of the two great parties, under the present mode of election, is unlimited : in Mr. Hare's scheme it would be great, but confined within bounds. Neither they, nor any of the smaller knots, would be able to elect more members than in proportion to the relative number of their adherents. The ticket system in America operates under conditions the reverse of this. In America electors vote for the party ticket, because the election goes by a mere majority, and a vote for any one who is certain not to obtain the majority, is thrown away. But, on Mr. Hare's system, a vote given to a person of known worth has almost as much chance of obtaining its object, as one given to a party candidate. It might be hoped, therefore, that every Liberal or Conservative, who was anything besides a Liberal or a Conservative —who had any preferences of his own in addition to those of his party—would scratch through the names of the more obscure and insignificant party candidates, and inscribe in their stead some of the men who are an honour to the nation. And the probability of this fact would operate as a strong inducement with those who drew up the party lists, not to confine themselves to pledged party men, but to include along with these, in their respective tickets, such of the national notabilities as were more in sympathy with their side than with the opposite.

The real difficulty, for it is not to be dissembled that there is a difficulty, is that the independent voters, those who are desirous of voting for unpatronized persons of merit, would be apt to put down the names of a few such persons, and to fill up the remainder of their list with mere party candidates, thus helping to swell the numbers against those by whom they would prefer to be represented. There would be an easy remedy for this, should it be necessary to resort to it, namely, to impose a limit to the number of secondary or contingent votes. No voter is likely to have an independent preference, grounded on knowledge, for 658, or even for 100 candidates. There would be little objection to his being limited to twenty, fifty, or whatever might be the number in the selection of whom there was some probability that his own choice would be exercised—that he would vote as an individual, and not as one of the mere rank and file of a party. But even without this restriction, the evil would be likely to cure itself as soon as the system came to be well understood. To counteract it would become a paramount object with all the knots and cliques whose influence is so much deprecated. From these, each in itself a small minority, the word would go forth, ' Vote for your *special* candidates only ; or at least put their names foremost, so as to give them the full chance which your numerical strength warrants, of obtaining the quota by means of first votes, or without descending low in the scale.' And those voters who did not belong to any clique, would profit by the lesson.

The minor groups would have precisely the amount of power which they ought to have. The influence they could exercise would be exactly that which their number of voters entitled them to ; not a particle more ; while, to ensure even that, they would have a motive to put up, as representatives of their special objects, candidates whose other recommendations would enable them to obtain the suffrages of voters not of the sect or clique. It is curious to observe how the popular line of argument in defence of existing systems veers round, according to the nature of the attack made upon them. Not many years ago it was the favourite argument in support of the then existing system of representation, that under it all ' interests ' or ' classes ' were represented. And certainly, all interests or classes of any importance ought to be represented, that is, ought to have spokesmen, or advocates, in Parliament. But from thence it was argued that a system ought to be supported, which gave to the partial interests not advocates merely, but the tribunal itself. Now behold the change. Mr. Hare's system makes it impossible for partial interests to have the command of the tribunal, but it ensures them advocates, and for doing even this it is reproached. Because it unites the good points of class representation and the good points of numerical representation, it is attacked from both sides at once.

But it is not such objections as these that are the real difficulty in getting the system accepted; it is the exaggerated notion entertained of its complexity, and the consequent doubt whether it is capable of being carried into effect. The only complete answer to this objection would be actual trial. When the merits of the plan shall have become more generally known, and shall have gained for it a wider support among impartial thinkers, an effort should be made to obtain its introduction experimentally in some limited field, such as the municipal election of some great town. An opportunity was lost, when the decision was taken to divide the West Riding of Yorkshire for the purpose of giving it four members; instead of trying the new principle, by leaving the constituency undivided, and allowing a candidate to be returned on obtaining either in first or secondary votes, a fourth part of the whole number of votes given. Such experiments would be a very imperfect test of the worth of the plan: but they would be an exemplification of its mode of working; they would enable people to convince themselves that it is not impracticable; would familiarize them with its machinery, and afford some materials for judging whether the difficulties which are thought to be so formidable, are real or only imaginary. The day when such a partial trial shall be sanctioned by Parliament, will, I believe, inaugurate a new era of Parliamentary Reform; destined to give to Representative Government a shape fitted to its mature and triumphant period, when it shall have passed through the militant stage in which alone the world has yet seen it.[1]

[1] In the interval between the last and present editions of this treatise, it has become known that the experiment here suggested has actually been made on a larger than any municipal or provincial scale, and has been in course

CHAPTER VIII

OF THE EXTENSION OF THE SUFFRAGE

SUCH a representative democracy as has now been sketched, representative of all, and not solely of the majority—in which the interests, the opinions, the

of trial for several years. In the Danish Constitution (not that of Denmark proper, but the Constitution framed for the entire Danish kingdom) the equal representation of minorities was provided for on a plan so nearly identical with Mr. Hare's, as to add another to the many examples how the ideas which resolve difficulties arising out of a general situation of the human mind or of society, present themselves, without communication, to several superior minds at once. This feature of the Danish electoral law has been brought fully and clearly before the British public in an able paper by Mr. Robert Lytton, forming one of the valuable reports by Secretaries of Legation, printed by order of the House of Commons in 1864. Mr. Hare's plan, which may now be also called M. Andræ's, has thus advanced from the position of a simple project to that of a realized political fact.

Though Denmark is as yet the only country in which Personal Representation has become an institution, the progress of the idea among thinking minds has been very rapid. In almost all the countries in which universal suffrage is now regarded as a necessity, the scheme is rapidly making its way: with the friends of democracy, as a logical consequence of their principle; with those who rather accept than prefer democratic government, as an indispensable corrective of its inconveniences. The political thinkers of Switzerland led the way. Those of France followed. To mention no others, within a very recent period two of the most influential and authoritative political writers in France, one belonging to the moderate liberal and the other to the extreme democratic school, have given in a public adhesion to the plan. Among its German supporters is numbered one of the most eminent political thinkers in Germany, who is also a distinguished grades of intellect which are outnumbered would nevertheless be heard, and would have a chance of obtaining by weight of character and strength of argument, an influence which would not belong to their numerical force—this democracy, which is alone equal, alone impartial, alone the government of all by all, the only true type of democracy—would be free from the greatest evils of the falsely-called democracies which now prevail, and from which the current idea of democracy is exclusively derived. But even in this democracy, absolute power, if they chose to exercise it, would rest with the numerical majority; and these would be composed exclusively of a single class, alike in biases, prepossessions, and general modes of thinking, and a class, to say no more, not the most highly cultivated. The constitution would therefore still be liable to the characteristic evils of class government: in a far less degree, assuredly, than that exclusive government by a class, which now usurps the name of democracy; but still, under no effective restraint, except what might be found in the good sense, moderation, and forbearance, of the class itself. If checks of this description are sufficient, the philosophy of con-

member of the liberal Cabinet of the Grand Duke of Baden. This subject, among others, has its share in the important awakening of thought in the American republic, which is already one of the fruits of the great pending contest for human freedom. In the two principal of our Australian colonies Mr. Hare's plan has been brought under the consideration of their respective legislatures, and though not yet adopted, has already a strong party in its favour; while the clear and complete understanding of its principles, shown by the majority of the speakers both on the Conservative and on the Radical side of general politics, shows how unfounded is the notion of its being too complicated to be capable of being generally comprehended and acted on. Nothing is required to make both the plan and its advantages perfectly intelligible to all, except that the time should have come when they will think it worth their while to take the trouble of really attending to it.

stitutional government is but solemn trifling. All trust
in constitutions is grounded on the assurance they may
afford, not that the depositaries of power will not, but
that they cannot, misemploy it. Democracy is not
the ideally best form of government unless this weak
side of it can be strengthened; unless it can be so
organized that no class, not even the most numerous,
shall be able to reduce all but itself to political insig-
nificance, and direct the course of legislation and
administration by its exclusive class interest. The
problem is, to find the means of preventing this abuse,
without sacrificing the characteristic advantages of
popular government.

These twofold requisites are not fulfilled by the
expedient of a limitation of the suffrage, involving
the compulsory exclusion of any portion of the citizens
from a voice in the representation. Among the
foremost benefits of free government is that education of the intelligence and of the sentiments, which
is carried down to the very lowest ranks of the
people when they are called to take a part in acts
which directly affect the great interests of their country.
On this topic I have already dwelt so emphatically,
that I only return to it, because there are few who
seem to attach to this effect of popular institutions
all the importance to which it is entitled. People
think it fanciful to expect so much from what seems
so slight a cause—to recognize a potent instrument of
mental improvement in the exercise of political fran-
chises by manual labourers. Yet unless substantial
mental cultivation in the mass of mankind is to be
a mere vision, this is the road by which it must come.
If any one supposes that this road will not bring it,
I call to witness the entire contents of M. de Tocqueville's great work; and especially his estimate of the
Americans. Almost all travellers are struck by the
fact that every American is in some sense both a
patriot, and a person of cultivated intelligence; and
M. de Tocqueville has shown how close the connexion
is between these qualities and their democratic institu-

tions. No such wide diffusion of the ideas, tastes, and
sentiments of educated minds, has ever been seen elsewhere, or even conceived as attainable.[1] Yet this is
nothing to what we might look for in a government
equally democratic in its unexclusiveness, but better
organized in other important points. For political life
is indeed in America a most valuable school, but it is
a school from which the ablest teachers are excluded ;
the first minds in the country being as effectually shut
out from the national representation, and from public
functions generally, as if they were under a formal
disqualification. The Demos, too, being in America
the one source of power, all the selfish ambition of the
country gravitates towards it, as it does in despotic
countries towards the monarch : the people, like the
despot, is pursued with adulation and sycophancy,
and the corrupting effects of power fully keep
pace with its improving and ennobling influences. If,

---

[1] The following ' extract from the Report of the English
Commissioner to the New York Exhibition ', which I quote
from Mr. Carey's *Principles of Social Science*, bears striking
testimony to one part, at least, of the assertion in the
text :—

' We have a few great engineers and mechanics, and
a large body of clever workmen ; but the Americans seem
likely to become a whole nation of such people. Already,
their rivers swarm with steamboats ; their valleys are
becoming crowded with factories ; their towns, surpassing
those of every state of Europe, except Belgium, Holland,
and England, are the abodes of all the skill which now
distinguishes a town population ; and there is scarcely an
art in Europe not carried on in America with equal or
greater skill than in Europe, though it has been here
cultivated and improved through ages. A whole nation
of Franklins, Stephensons, and Watts in prospect, is
something wonderful for other nations to contemplate.
In contrast with the comparative inertness and ignorance
of the bulk of the people of Europe, whatever may be the
superiority of a few well-instructed and gifted persons,
the great intelligence of the whole people of America is
the circumstance most worthy of public attention.'

even with this alloy, democratic institutions produce so marked a superiority of mental development in the lowest class of Americans, compared with the corresponding classes in England and elsewhere, what would it be if the good portion of the influence could be retained without the bad? And this, to a certain extent, may be done; but not by excluding that portion of the people, who have fewest intellectual stimuli of other kinds, from so inestimable an introduction to large, distant, and complicated interests as is afforded by the attention they may be induced to bestow on political affairs. It is by political discussion that the manual labourer, whose employment is a routine, and whose way of life brings him in contact with no variety of impressions, circumstances, or ideas, is taught that remote causes, and events which take place far off, have a most sensible effect even on his personal interests; and it is from political discussion, and collective political action, that one whose daily occupations concentrate his interests in a small circle round himself, learns to feel for and with his fellow-citizens, and becomes consciously a member of a great community. But political discussions fly over the heads of those who have no votes, and are not endeavouring to acquire them. Their position, in comparison with the electors, is that of the audience in a court of justice, compared with the twelve men in the jury-box. It is not *their* suffrages that are asked, it is not their opinion that is sought to be influenced; the appeals are made, the arguments addressed, to others than them; nothing depends on the decision they may arrive at, and there is no necessity and very little inducement to them to come to any. Whoever, in an otherwise popular government, has no vote, and no prospect of obtaining it, will either be a permanent malcontent, or will feel as one whom the general affairs of society do not concern; for whom they are to be managed by others; who 'has no business with the laws except to obey them,' nor with public interests and concerns except as a looker-on. What he will know or care about them from this position, may partly be measured by what an average woman of the middle class knows and cares about politics, compared with her husband or brothers.

Independently of all these considerations, it is a personal injustice to withhold from any one, unless for the prevention of greater evils, the ordinary privilege of having his voice reckoned in the disposal of affairs in which he has the same interest as other people. If he is compelled to pay, if he may be compelled to fight, if he is required implicitly to obey, he should be legally entitled to be told what for; to have his consent asked, and his opinion counted at its worth, though not at more than its worth. There ought to be no pariahs in a full-grown and civilized nation; no persons disqualified, except through their own default. Every one is degraded, whether aware of it or not, when other people, without consulting him, take upon themselves unlimited power to regulate his destiny. And even in a much more improved state than the human mind has ever yet reached, it is not in nature that they who are thus disposed of should meet with as fair play as those who have a voice. Rulers and ruling classes are under a necessity of considering the interests and wishes of those who have the suffrage; but of those who are excluded, it is in their option whether they will do so or not; and however honestly disposed, they are in general too fully occupied with things which they *must* attend to, to have much room in their thoughts for anything which they can with impunity disregard. No arrangement of the suffrage, therefore, can be permanently satisfactory, in which any person or class is peremptorily excluded; in which the electoral privilege is not open to all persons of full age who desire to obtain it.

There are, however, certain exclusions, required by positive reasons, which do not conflict with this principle, and which, though an evil in themselves, are only to be got rid of by the cessation of the state of things which requires them. I regard it as wholly

inadmissible that any person should participate in the
suffrage, without being able to read, write, and, I will
add, perform the common operations of arithmetic.
Justice demands, even when the suffrage does not
depend on it, that the means of attaining these elementary acquirements should be within the reach of
every person, either gratuitously, or at an expense not
exceeding what the poorest, who earn their own living,
can afford. If this were really the case, people would
no more think of giving the suffrage to a man who
could not read, than of giving it to a child who could
not speak ; and it would not be society that would
exclude him, but his own laziness. When society has
not performed its duty, by rendering this amount of
instruction accessible to all, there is some hardship in
the case, but it is a hardship that ought to be borne.
If society has neglected to discharge two solemn obligations, the more important and more fundamental of
the two must be fulfilled first : universal teaching
must precede universal enfranchisement. No one but
those in whom an *a priori* theory has silenced common
sense, will maintain, that power over others, over the
whole community, should be imparted to people who
have not acquired the commonest and most essential
requisites for taking care of themselves ; for pursuing
intelligently their own interests, and those of the persons most nearly allied to them. This argument,
doubtless, might be pressed further, and made to prove
much more. It would be eminently desirable that
other things besides reading, writing, and arithmetic,
could be made necessary to the suffrage ; that some
knowledge of the conformation of the earth, its natural
and political divisions, the elements of general history,
and of the history and institutions of their own
country, could be required from all electors. But
these kinds of knowledge, however indispensable to
an intelligent use of the suffrage, are not, in this
country, nor probably anywhere save in the Northern
United States, accessible to the whole people ; nor
does there exist any trustworthy machinery for ascer-

taining whether they have been acquired or not. The attempt, at present, would lead to partiality, chicanery, and every kind of fraud. It is better that the suffrage should be conferred indiscriminately, or even withheld indiscriminately, than that it should be given to one and withheld from another at the discretion of a public officer. In regard, however, to reading, writing, and calculating, there need be no difficulty. It would be easy to require from every one who presented himself for registry, that he should, in the presence of the registrar, copy a sentence from an English book, and perform a sum in the rule of three ; and to secure, by fixed rules and complete publicity, the honest application of so very simple a test. This condition, therefore, should in all cases accompany universal suffrage ; and it would, after a few years, exclude none but those who cared so little for the privilege, that their vote, if given, would not in general be an indication of any real political opinion.

It is also important, that the assembly which votes the taxes, either general or local, should be elected exclusively by those who pay something towards the taxes imposed. Those who pay no taxes, disposing by their votes of other people's money, have every motive to be lavish, and none to economize. As far as money matters are concerned, any power of voting possessed by them is a violation of the fundamental principle of free government ; a severance of the power of control, from the interest in its beneficial exercise. It amounts to allowing them to put their hands into other people's pockets, for any purpose which they think fit to call a public one ; which in some of the great towns of the United States is known to have produced a scale of local taxation onerous beyond example, and wholly borne by the wealthier classes. That representation should be co-extensive with taxation, not stopping short of it, but also not going beyond it, is in accordance with the theory of British institutions. But to reconcile this, as a condition annexed to the representation, with universality, it is essential,

as it is on many other accounts desirable, that taxation, in a visible shape, should descend to the poorest
class. In this country, and in most others, there is
probably no labouring family which does not contribute
to the indirect taxes, by the purchase of tea, coffee,
sugar, not to mention narcotics or stimulants. But
this mode of defraying a share of the public expenses
is hardly felt: the payer, unless a person of education
and reflection, does not identify his interest with a low
scale of public expenditure, as closely as when money for
its support is demanded directly from himself; and even
supposing him to do so, he would doubtless take care
that, however lavish an expenditure he might, by his
vote, assist in imposing upon the government, it should
not be defrayed by any additional taxes on the articles
which he himself consumes. It would be better that
a direct tax, in the simple form of a capitation, should
be levied on every grown person in the community ;
or that every such person should be admitted an
elector, on allowing himself to be rated *extra ordinem*
to the assessed taxes ; or that a small annual payment,
rising and falling with the gross expenditure of the
country, should be required from every registered
elector ; that so every one might feel that the money
which he assisted in voting was partly his own, and
that he was interested in keeping down its amount.

However this may be, I regard it as required by
first principles, that the receipt of parish relief should
be a peremptory disqualification for the franchise. He
who cannot by his labour suffice for his own support,
has no claim to the privilege of helping himself to the
money of others. By becoming dependent on the
remaining members of the community for actual subsistence, he abdicates his claim to equal rights with
them in other respects. Those to whom he is indebted
for the continuance of his very existence, may justly
claim the exclusive management of those common concerns, to which he now brings nothing, or less than
he takes away. As a condition of the franchise, a term
should be fixed, say five years previous to the registry,

during which the applicant's name has not been on the parish books as a recipient of relief. To be an uncertified bankrupt, or to have taken the benefit of the Insolvent Act, should disqualify for the franchise until the person has paid his debts, or at least proved that he is not now, and has not for some long period been, dependent on eleemosynary support. Non-payment of taxes, when so long persisted in that it cannot have arisen from inadvertence, should disqualify while it lasts. These exclusions are not in their nature permanent. They exact such conditions only as all are able, or ought to be able, to fulfil if they choose. They leave the suffrage accessible to all who are in the normal condition of a human being: and if any one has to forgo it, he either does not care sufficiently for it, to do for its sake what he is already bound to do, or he is in a general condition of depression and degradation in which this slight addition, necessary for the security of others, would be unfelt, and on emerging from which, this mark of inferiority would disappear with the rest.

In the long run, therefore (supposing no restrictions to exist but those of which we have now treated), we might expect that all, except that (it is to be hoped) progressively diminishing class, the recipients of parish relief, would be in possession of votes, so that the suffrage would be, with that slight abatement, universal. That it should be thus widely expanded, is, as we have seen, absolutely necessary to an enlarged and elevated conception of good government. Yet in this state of things, the great majority of voters, in most countries, and emphatically in this, would be manual labourers; and the twofold danger, that of too low a standard of political intelligence, and that of class legislation, would still exist, in a very perilous degree. It remains to be seen whether any means exist by which these evils can be obviated.

They are capable of being obviated, if men sincerely wish it; not by any artificial contrivance, but by carrying out the natural order of human life, which recommends itself to every one in things in which he has no interest or traditional opinion running counter to it. In all human affairs, every person directly interested, and not under positive tutelage, has an admitted claim to a voice, and when his exercise of it is not inconsistent with the safety of the whole, cannot justly be excluded from it. But though every one ought to have a voice—that every one should have an equal voice is a totally different proposition. When two persons who have a joint interest in any business, differ in opinion, does justice require that both opinions should be held of exactly equal value ? If with equal virtue, one is superior to the other in knowledge and intelligence—or if with equal intelligence, one excels the other in virtue—the opinion, the judgement, of the higher moral or intellectual being, is worth more than that of the inferior : and if the institutions of the country virtually assert that they are of the same value, they assert a thing which is not. One of the two, as the wiser or better man, has a claim to superior weight : the difficulty is in ascertaining which of the two it is ; a thing impossible as between individuals, but, taking men in bodies and in numbers, it can be done with a certain approach to accuracy. There would be no pretence for applying this doctrine to any case which could with reason be considered as one of individual and private right. In an affair which concerns only one of two persons, that one is entitled to follow his own opinion, however much wiser the other may be than himself. But we are speaking of things which equally concern them both ; where, if the more ignorant does not yield his share of the matter to the guidance of the wiser man, the wiser man must resign his to that of the more ignorant. Which of these modes of getting over the difficulty is most for the interest of both, and most conformable to the general fitness of things ? If it be deemed unjust that either should have to give way, which injustice is greatest ? that the better judgement should give way to the worse, or the worse to the better ?

Now, national affairs are exactly such a joint concern, with the difference, that no one needs ever be called upon for a complete sacrifice of his own opinion. It can always be taken into the calculation, and counted at a certain figure, a higher figure being assigned to the suffrages of those whose opinion is entitled to greater weight. There is not, in this arrangement, anything necessarily invidious to those to whom it assigns the lower degrees of influence. Entire exclusion from a voice in the common concerns, is one thing: the concession to others of a more potential voice, on the ground of greater capacity for the management of the joint interests, is another. The two things are not merely different, they are incommensurable. Every one has a right to feel insulted by being made a nobody, and stamped as of no account at all. No one but a fool, and only a fool of a peculiar description, feels offended by the acknowledgement that there are others whose opinion, and even whose wish, is entitled to a greater amount of consideration than his. To have no voice in what are partly his own concerns, is a thing which nobody willingly submits to; but when what is partly his concern is also partly another's, and he feels the other to understand the subject better than himself, that the other's opinion should be counted for more than his own, accords with his expectations, and with the course of things which in all other affairs of life he is accustomed to acquiesce in. It is only necessary that this superior influence should be assigned on grounds which he can comprehend, and of which he is able to perceive the justice.

I hasten to say, that I consider it entirely inadmissible, unless as a temporary makeshift, that the superiority of influence should be conferred in consideration of property. I do not deny that property is a kind of test; education in most countries, though anything but proportional to riches, is on the average better in the richer half of society than in the poorer. But the criterion is so imperfect; accident has so much more to do than merit with enabling men to rise in the world; and it is so impossible for any one by acquiring any amount of instruction, to make sure of the corresponding rise in station, that this foundation of electoral privilege is always, and will continue to be, supremely odious. To connect plurality of votes with any pecuniary qualification would be not only objectionable in itself, but a sure mode of discrediting the principle, and making its permanent maintenance impracticable. The Democracy, at least of this country, are not at present jealous of personal superiority, but they are naturally and most justly so of that which is grounded on mere pecuniary circumstances. The only thing which can justify reckoning one person's opinion as equivalent to more than one, is individual mental superiority; and what is wanted is some approximate means of ascertaining that. If there existed such a thing as a really national education, or a trustworthy system of general examination, education might be tested directly. In the absence of these, the nature of a person's occupation is some test. An employer of labour is on the average more intelligent than a labourer; for he must labour with his head, and not solely with his hands. A foreman is generally more intelligent than an ordinary labourer, and a labourer in the skilled trades than in the unskilled. A banker, merchant, or manufacturer, is likely to be more intelligent than a tradesman, because he has larger and more complicated interests to manage. In all these cases it is not the having merely undertaken the superior function, but the successful performance of it, that tests the qualifications; for which reason, as well as to prevent persons from engaging nominally in an occupation for the sake of the vote, it would be proper to require that the occupation should have been persevered in for some length of time (say three years). Subject to some such condition, two or more votes might be allowed to every person who exercises any of these superior functions. The liberal professions, when really and not nominally practised, imply, of course, a still higher degree of instruction; and wherever a sufficient examination, or any serious conditions of education, are required before entering on a profession, its members could be admitted at once to a plurality of votes. The same rule might be applied to graduates of universities; and even to those who bring satisfactory certificates of having passed through the course of study required by any school at which the higher branches of knowledge are taught, under proper securities that the teaching is real, and not a mere pretence. The 'local' or 'middle class' examination for the degree of Associate, so laudably and public-spiritedly established by the Universities of Oxford and Cambridge, and any similar ones which may be instituted by other competent bodies (provided they are fairly open to all comers), afford a ground on which plurality of votes might with great advantage be accorded to those who have passed the test. All these suggestions are open to much discussion in the detail, and to objections which it is of no use to anticipate. The time is not come for giving to such plans a practical shape, nor should I wish to be bound by the particular proposals which I have made. But it is to me evident, that in this direction lies the true ideal of representative government; and that to work towards it, by the best practical contrivances which can be found, is the path of real political improvement.

If it be asked, to what length the principle admits of being carried, or how many votes might be accorded to an individual on the ground of superior qualifications, I answer, that this is not in itself very material, provided the distinctions and gradations are not made arbitrarily, but are such as can be understood and accepted by the general conscience and understanding. But it is an absolute condition, not to overpass the limit prescribed by the fundamental principle laid down in a former chapter as the condition of excellence in the constitution of a representative system. The plurality of votes must on no account be carried so far, that those who are privileged by it, or the class (if any) to which they mainly belong, shall outweigh by means of it all the rest of the community. The distinction in favour of education, right in itself, is further and strongly recommended by its preserving the educated from the class legislation of the uneducated; but it must stop short of enabling them to practise class legislation on their own account. Let me add, that I consider it an absolutely necessary part of the plurality scheme, that it be open to the poorest individual in the community to claim its privileges, if he can prove that, in spite of all difficulties and obstacles, he is, in point of intelligence, entitled to them. There ought to be voluntary examinations at which any person whatever might present himself, might prove that he came up to the standard of knowledge and ability laid down as sufficient, and be admitted, in consequence, to the plurality of votes. A privilege which is not refused to any one who can show that he has realized the conditions on which in theory and principle it is dependent, would not necessarily be repugnant to any one's sentiment of justice: but it would certainly be so, if, while conferred on general presumptions not always infallible, it were denied to direct proof.

Plural voting, though practised in vestry elections and those of poor-law guardians, is so unfamiliar in elections to Parliament, that it is not likely to be soon or willingly adopted: but as the time will certainly arrive when the only choice will be between this and equal universal suffrage, whoever does not desire the last, cannot too soon begin to reconcile himself to the former. In the meantime, though the suggestion, for the present, may not be a practical one, it will serve to mark what is best in principle, and enable us to judge of the eligibility of any indirect means, either existing or capable of being adopted, which may promote in a less perfect manner the same end. A person may have a double vote by other means than that of tendering two votes at the same hustings; he may have a vote in each of two different constituencies: and though this exceptional privilege at present belongs rather to superiority of means than of intelligence,

I would not abolish it where it exists, since until a truer test of education is adopted, it would be unwise to dispense with even so imperfect a one as is afforded by pecuniary circumstances. Means might be found of giving a further extension to the privilege, which would connect it in a more direct manner with superior education. In any future Reform Bill which lowers greatly the pecuniary conditions of the suffrage, it might be a wise provision to allow all graduates of universities, all persons who have passed creditably through the higher schools, all members of the liberal professions, and perhaps some others, to be registered specifically in those characters, and to give their votes as such in any constituency in which they choose to register: retaining, in addition, their votes as simple citizens in the localities in which they reside.

Until there shall have been devised, and until opinion is willing to accept, some mode of plural voting which may assign to education, as such, the degree of superior influence due to it, and sufficient as a counterpoise to the numerical weight of the least educated class; for so long, the benefits of completely universal suffrage cannot be obtained without bringing with them, as it appears to me, a chance of more than equivalent evils. It is possible, indeed (and this is perhaps one of the transitions through which we may have to pass in our progress to a really good representative system), that the barriers which restrict the suffrage might be entirely levelled in some particular constituencies, whose members, consequently, would be returned principally by manual labourers; the existing electoral qualification being maintained elsewhere, or any alteration in it being accompanied by such a grouping of the constituencies as to prevent the labouring class from becoming preponderant in Parliament. By such a compromise, the anomalies in the representation would not only be retained, but augmented: this however is not a conclusive objection; for if the country does not choose to pursue the right ends by a regular system directly leading to them, it must be content with an irregular makeshift, as being greatly preferable to a system free from irregularities, but regularly adapted to wrong ends, or in which some ends equally necessary with the others have been left out. It is a far graver objection, that this adjustment is incompatible with the inter-community of local constituencies which Mr. Hare's plan requires ; that under it every voter would remain imprisoned within the one or more constituencies in which his name is registered, and unless willing to be represented by one of the candidates for those localities, would not be represented at all.

So much importance do I attach to the emancipation of those who already have votes, but whose votes are useless, because always outnumbered ; so much should I hope from the natural influence of truth and reason, if only secured a hearing and a competent advocacy— that I should not despair of the operation even of equal and universal suffrage, if made real by the pro-portional representation of all minorities, on Mr. Hare's principle. But if the best hopes which can be formed on this subject were certainties, I should still contend for the principle of plural voting. I do not propose the plurality as a thing in itself undesirable, which, like the exclusion of part of the community from the suffrage, may be temporarily tolerated while necessary to prevent greater evils. I do not look upon equal voting as among the things which are good in them-selves, provided they can be guarded against incon-veniences. I look upon it as only relatively good ; less objectionable than inequality of privilege grounded on irrelevant or adventitious circumstances, but in principle wrong, because recognizing a wrong standard, and exercising a bad influence on the voter's mind. It is not useful, but hurtful, that the constitution of the country should declare ignorance to be entitled to as much political power as knowledge. The national institutions should place all things that they are con-cerned with, before the mind of the citizen in the light in which it is for his good that he should regard them : and as it is for his good that he should think that every one is entitled to some influence, but the better and wiser to more than others, it is important that this conviction should be professed by the State, and embodied in the national institutions. Such things constitute the *spirit* of the institutions of a country: that portion of their influence which is least regarded by common, and especially by English, thinkers; though the institutions of every country, not under great positive oppression, produce more effect by their spirit than by any of their direct provisions, since by it they shape the national character. The American institutions have imprinted strongly on the American mind, that any one man (with a white skin) is as good as any other; and it is felt that this false creed is nearly connected with some of the more unfavourable points in American character. It is not a small mischief that the constitution of any country should sanction this creed; for the belief in it, whether express or tacit, is almost as detrimental to moral and intellectual excellence, as any effect which most forms of government can produce.

It may, perhaps, be said, that a constitution which gives equal influence, man for man, to the most and to the least instructed, is nevertheless conducive to progress, because the appeals constantly made to the less instructed classes, the exercise given to their mental powers, and the exertions which the more instructed are obliged to make for enlightening their judgement and ridding them of errors and prejudices, are powerful stimulants to their advance in intelligence. That this most desirable effect really attends the admission of the less educated classes to some, and even to a large share of power, I admit, and have already strenuously maintained. But theory and experience alike prove that a counter current sets in when they are made the possessors of all power. Those who are supreme over everything, whether they be One, or Few, or Many, have no longer need of the arms of reason: they can make their mere will prevail; and those who cannot be resisted are usually far too well satisfied with their own opinions to be willing to change them, or listen without impatience to any one who tells them that they are in the wrong. The position which gives the strongest stimulus to the growth of intelligence, is that of rising into power, not that of having achieved it; and of all resting-points, temporary or permanent, in the way to ascendancy, the one which develops the best and highest qualities is the position of those who are strong enough to make reason prevail, but not strong enough to prevail against reason. This is the position in which, according to the principles we have laid down, the rich and the poor, the much and the little educated, and all the other classes and denominations which divide society between them, ought as far as practicable to be placed. And by combining this principle with the otherwise just one of allowing superiority of weight to superiority of mental qualities, a political constitution would realize that kind of relative perfection, which is alone compatible with the complicated nature of human affairs.

In the preceding argument for universal, but graduated suffrage, I have taken no account of difference of sex. I consider it to be as entirely irrelevant to political rights, as difference in height, or in the colour of the hair. All human beings have the same interest in good government; the welfare of all is alike affected by it, and they have equal need of a voice in it to secure their share of its benefits. If there be any difference, women require it more than men, since, being physically weaker, they are more dependent on law and society for protection. Mankind have long since abandoned the only premisses which will support the conclusion that women ought not to have votes. No one now holds that women should be in personal servitude; that they should have no thought, wish, or occupation, but to be the domestic drudges of husbands, fathers, or brothers. It is allowed to unmarried, and wants but little of being conceded to married women, to hold property, and have pecuniary and business interests, in the same manner as men.   It is considered suitable and proper that women should think, and write, and be teachers.   As soon as these things are admitted, the political disqualification has no principle to rest on. The whole mode of thought of the modern world is, with increasing emphasis, pronouncing against the claim of society to decide for individuals what they are and are not fit for, and what they shall and shall not be allowed to attempt.   If the principles of modern politics and political economy are good for anything, it is for proving that these points can only be rightly judged of by the individuals themselves : and that, under complete freedom of choice, wherever there are real diversities of aptitude, the great number will apply themselves to the things for which they are on the average fittest, and the exceptional course will only be taken by the exceptions.   Either the whole tendency of modern social improvements has been wrong, or it ought to be carried out to the total abolition of all exclusions and disabilities which close any honest employment to a human being.

But it is not even necessary to maintain so much, in order to prove that women should have the suffrage. Were it as right, as it is wrong, that they should be a subordinate class, confined to domestic occupations and subject to domestic authority, they would not the less require the protection of the suffrage to secure them from the abuse of that authority.   Men, as well as women, do not need political rights in order that they may govern, but in order that they may not be misgoverned.   The majority of the male sex are, and will be all their lives, nothing else than labourers in corn-fields or manufactories ; but this does not render the suffrage less desirable for them, nor their claim to it less irresistible, when not likely to make a bad use of it.   Nobody pretends to think that women would make a bad use of the suffrage.   The worst that is said is, that they would vote as mere dependents, at the bidding of their male relations.   If it be so, so let it be.   If they think for themselves, great good will be done, and if they do not, no harm. It is a benefit to human beings to take off their fetters, even if they do not desire to walk. It would already be a great improvement in the moral position of women, to be no longer declared by law incapable of an opinion, and not entitled to a preference, respecting the most important concerns of humanity. There would be some benefit to them individually in having something to bestow which their male relatives cannot exact, and are yet desirous to have. It would also be no small benefit that the husband would necessarily discuss the matter with his wife, and that the vote would not be his exclusive affair, but a joint concern. People do not sufficiently consider how markedly the fact, that she is able to have some action on the outward world independently of him, raises her dignity and value in a vulgar man's eyes, and makes her the object of a respect which no personal qualities would ever obtain for one whose social existence he can entirely appropriate. The vote itself, too, would be improved in quality. The man would often be obliged to find honest reasons for his vote, such as might induce a more upright and impartial character to serve with him under the same banner. The wife's influence would often keep him true to his own sincere opinion. Often, indeed, it would be used, not on the side of public principle, but of the personal interest or worldly vanity of the family. But wherever this would be the tendency of the wife's influence, it is exerted to the full already, in that bad direction; and with the more certainty, since under the present law and custom she is generally too utter a stranger to politics in any sense in which they involve principle, to be able to realize to herself that there is a point of honour in them; and most people have as little sympathy in the point of honour of others, when their own is not placed in the same thing, as they have in the religious feelings of those whose religion differs from theirs. Give the woman a vote, and she comes under the operation of the political point of honour. She learns to look on politics as a thing on which she is allowed to have an opinion, and in which if one has an opinion it ought to be acted upon ; she acquires a sense of personal accountability in the matter, and will no longer feel, as she does at present, that whatever amount of bad influence she may exercise, if the man can but be persuaded, all is right, and his responsibility covers all. It is only by being herself encouraged to form an opinion, and obtain an intelligent comprehension of the reasons which ought to prevail with the conscience against the temptations of personal or family interest, that she can ever cease to act as a disturbing force on the political conscience of the man. Her indirect agency can only be prevented from being politically mischievous, by being exchanged for direct.

I have supposed the right of suffrage to depend, as in a good state of things it would, on personal conditions. Where it depends, as in this and most other countries, on conditions of property, the contradiction is even more flagrant. There is something more than ordinarily irrational in the fact, that when a woman can give all the guarantees required from a male elector, independent circumstances, the position of a householder and head of a family, payment of taxes, or whatever may be the conditions imposed, the very principle and system of a representation based on property is set aside, and an exceptionally personal disqualification is created for the mere purpose of excluding her. When it is added that in the country where this is done, a woman now reigns, and that the most glorious ruler whom that country ever had was a woman, the picture of unreason, and scarcely disguised injustice, is complete. Let us hope that as the work proceeds of pulling down, one after another, the remains of the mouldering fabric of monopoly and tyranny, this one will not be the last to disappear ; that the opinion of Bentham, of Mr. Samuel Bailey, of Mr. Hare, and many other of the most powerful political thinkers of this age and country (not to speak of others), will make its way to all minds not rendered obdurate by selfishness or inveterate prejudice; and that, before the lapse of another generation, the accident of sex, no more than the accident of skin, will be deemed a sufficient justification for depriving its possessor of the equal protection and just privileges of a citizen.

CHAPTER IX

SHOULD THERE BE TWO STAGES OF ELECTION?

IN some representative constitutions, the plan has been adopted of choosing the members of the representative body by a double process, the primary electors only choosing other electors, and these electing the member of Parliament. This contrivance was probably intended as a slight impediment to the full sweep of popular feeling; giving the suffrage, and with it the complete ultimate power, to the Many, but compelling them to exercise it through the agency of a comparatively few, who, it was supposed, would be less moved than the Demos by the gusts of popular passion; and as the electors, being already a select body, might be expected to exceed in intellect and character the common level of their constituents, the choice made by them was thought likely to be more careful and enlightened, and would in any case be made under a greater feeling of responsibility, than election by the masses themselves. This plan of filtering, as it were, the popular suffrage through an intermediate body, admits of a very plausible defence; since it may be said, with great appearance of reason, that less intellect and instruction are required for judging who among our neighbours can be most safely trusted to choose a member of Parliament, than who is himself fittest to be one.

In the first place, however, if the dangers incident to popular power may be thought to be in some degree lessened by this indirect arrangement, so also are its benefits ; and the latter effect is much more certain than the former. To enable the system to work as desired, it must be carried into effect in the spirit in which it is planned ; the electors must use the suffrage in the manner supposed by the theory, that is, each of them must not ask himself who the member of Parliament should be, but only whom he would best like to choose one for him. It is evident, that the advantages which indirect is supposed to have over direct election, require this disposition of mind in the voter, and will only be realized by his taking the doctrine *au sérieux*, that his sole business is to choose the choosers, not the member himself. The supposition must be, that he will not occupy his thoughts with political opinions and measures, or political men, but will be guided by his personal respect for some private individual, to whom he will give a general power of attorney to act for him. Now if the primary electors adopt this view of their position, one of the principal uses of giving them a vote at all is defeated : the political function to which they are called fails of developing public spirit and political intelligence ; of making public affairs an object of interest to their feelings and of exercise to their faculties. The supposition, moreover, involves inconsistent conditions ; for if the voter feels no interest in the final result, how or why can he be expected to feel any in the process which leads to it ? To wish to have a particular individual for his representative in Parliament, is possible to a person of a very moderate degree of virtue and intelligence ; and to wish to choose an elector who will elect that individual, is a natural consequence : but for a person who does not care who is elected, or feels bound to put that consideration in abeyance, to take any interest whatever in merely naming the worthiest person to elect another according to his own judgement, implies a zeal for what is right in the abstract, an habitual principle of duty for the sake of duty, which is possible only to persons of a rather high grade of cultivation, who, by the very possession of it, show that they may be, and deserve to be, trusted with political power in a more direct shape. Of all public functions which it is possible to confer on the poorer members of the community, this surely is the least calculated to kindle their feelings, and holds out least natural inducement to care for it, other than a virtuous determination to discharge conscientiously whatever duty one has to perform : and if the mass of electors cared enough about political affairs to set any value on so limited a participation in them, they would not be likely to be satisfied without one much more extensive.

In the next place, admitting that a person who, from his narrow range of cultivation, cannot judge well of the qualifications of a candidate for Parliament, may be a sufficient judge of the honesty and general capacity of somebody whom he may depute to choose a member of Parliament for him ; I may remark, that if the voter acquiesces in this estimate of his capabilities, and really wishes to have the choice made for him by a person in whom he places reliance, there is no need of any constitutional provision for the purpose ; he has only to ask this confidential person privately what candidate he had better vote for. In that case the two modes of election coincide in their result, and every advantage of indirect election is obtained under direct. The systems only diverge in their operation, if we suppose that the voter would prefer to use his own judgement in the choice of a representative, and only lets another choose for him because the law does not allow him a more direct mode of action. But if this be his state of mind ; if his will does not go along with the limitation which the law imposes, and he desires to make a direct choice, he can do so notwithstanding the law. He has only to choose as elector a known partisan of the candidate he prefers, or some one who will pledge himself to vote for that candidate. And this is so much the natural working of election by two stages, that, except in a condition of complete political indifference, it can scarcely be expected to act otherwise.

It is in this way that the election of the President of the United States practically takes place. Nominally, the election is indirect: the population at large does not vote for the President; it votes for electors who choose the President. But the electors are always chosen under an express engagement to vote for a particular candidate: nor does a citizen ever vote for an elector because of any preference for the man; he votes for the Lincoln ticket, or the Breckenridge ticket. It must be remembered, that the electors are not chosen in order that they may search the country and find the fittest person in it to be President, or to be a member of Parliament. There would be something to be said for the practice if this were so: but it is not so; nor ever will be, until mankind in general are of opinion, with Plato, that the proper person to be entrusted with power is the person most unwilling to accept it. The electors are to make choice of one of those who have offered themselves as candidates: and those who choose the electors, already know who these are. If there is any political activity in the country, all electors, who care to vote at all, have made up their minds which of these candidates they would like to have; and will make that the sole consideration in giving their vote. The partisans of each candidate will have their list of electors ready, all pledged to vote for that individual; and the only question practically asked of the primary elector will be, which of these lists he will support.

The case in which election by two stages answers well in practice, is when the electors are not chosen solely as electors, but have other important functions to discharge, which precludes their being selected solely as delegates to give a particular vote. This combination of circumstances exemplifies itself in another American institution, the Senate of the United States. That assembly, the Upper House, as it were, of Congress, is considered to represent not the people directly, but the States as such, and to be the guardian of that portion of their sovereign rights which they have not alienated. As the internal sovereignty of each State is, by the nature of an equal federation, equally sacred whatever be the size or importance of the State, each returns to the Senate the same number of members (two), whether it be little Delaware, or the 'Empire State' of New York. These members are not chosen by the population, but by the State Legislatures, themselves elected by the people of each State ; but as the whole ordinary business of a legislative assembly, internal legislation and the control of the executive, devolves upon these bodies, they are elected with a view to those objects more than to the other ; and in naming two persons to represent the State in the Federal Senate, they for the most part exercise their own judgement, with only that general reference to public opinion necessary in all acts of the government of a democracy. The elections, thus made, have proved eminently successful, and are conspicuously the best of all the elections in the United States, the Senate invariably consisting of the most distinguished men among those who have made themselves sufficiently known in public life. After such an example, it cannot be said that indirect popular election is never advantageous. Under certain conditions, it is the very best system that can be adopted. But those conditions are hardly to be obtained in practice, except in a federal government like that of the United States, where the election can be entrusted to local bodies whose other functions extend to the most important concerns of the nation. The only bodies in any analogous position which exist, or are likely to exist, in this country, are the municipalities, or any other boards which have been or may be created for similar local purposes. Few persons, however, would think it any improvement in our parliamentary constitution, if the members for the City of London were chosen by the Aldermen and Common Council, and those for the borough of Marylebone avowedly, as they already are virtually, by the vestries of the component parishes. Even if those bodies, considered merely as local boards, were far less objectionable than they are, the qualities that would fit them for the limited and peculiar duties of municipal or parochial ædileship, are no guarantee of any special fitness to judge of the comparative qualifications of candidates for a seat in Parliament. They probably would not fulfil this duty any better than it is fulfilled by the inhabitants voting directly; while, on the other hand, if fitness for electing members of Parliament had to be taken into consideration in selecting persons for the office of vestrymen or town councillors, many of those who are fittest for that more limited duty would inevitably be excluded from it, if only by the necessity there would be of choosing persons whose sentiments in general politics agreed with those of the voters who elected them. The mere indirect political influence of town councils, has already led to a considerable perversion of municipal elections from their intended purpose, by making them a matter of party politics. If it were part of the duty of a man's book-keeper or steward to choose his physician, he would not be likely to have a better medical attendant than if he chose one for himself, while he would be restricted in his choice of a steward or book-keeper to such as might without too great danger to his health be entrusted with the other office.

It appears, therefore, that every benefit of indirect election which is attainable at all, is attainable under direct; that such of the benefits expected from it, as would not be obtained under direct election, will just as much fail to be obtained under indirect; while the latter has considerable disadvantages peculiar to itself. The mere fact that it is an additional and superfluous wheel in the machinery, is no trifling objection. Its decided inferiority as a means of cultivating public spirit and political intelligence, has already been dwelt upon: and if it had any effective operation at all—that is, if the primary electors did to any extent leave to their nominees the selection of their parliamentary representative,—the voter would be prevented from identifying himself with his member of Parliament,

and the member would feel a much less active sense
of responsibility to his constituents. In addition to
all this, the comparatively small number of persons in
whose hands, at last, the election of a member of
Parliament would reside, could not but afford great
additional facilities to intrigue, and to every form of
corruption compatible with the station in life of the
electors. The constituencies would universally be reduced, in point of conveniences for bribery, to the
condition of the small boroughs at present. It would
be sufficient to gain over a small number of persons,
to be certain of being returned. If it be said that the
electors would be responsible to those who elected
them, the answer is obvious, that, holding no permanent
office, or position in the public eye, they would risk
nothing by a corrupt vote except what they would
care little for, not to be appointed electors again : and
the main reliance must still be on the penalties for
bribery, the insufficiency of which reliance, in small
constituencies, experience has made notorious to all
the world. The evil would be exactly proportional to
the amount of discretion left to the chosen electors.
The only case in which they would probably be afraid
to employ their vote for the promotion of their personal interest, would be when they were elected under
an express pledge, as mere delegates, to carry, as it
were, the votes of their constituents to the hustings.
The moment the double stage of election began to
have any effect, it would begin to have a bad effect.
And this we shall find true of the principle of indirect
election however applied, except in circumstances
similar to those of the election of Senators in the
United States.

The best which could be said for this political contrivance is, that in some states of opinion it might be
a more practicable expedient than that of plural voting
for giving to every member of the community a vote
of some sort, without rendering the mere numerical
majority predominant in Parliament : as, for instance,
if the present constituency of this country were in-

creased by the addition of a numerous and select portion of the labouring classes, elected by the remainder.
Circumstances might render such a scheme a convenient
mode of temporary compromise, but it does not carry
out any principle sufficiently thoroughly to be likely
to recommend itself to any class of thinkers as a permanent arrangement.

CHAPTER X

OF THE MODE OF VOTING

THE question of greatest moment in regard to modes
of voting, is that of secrecy or publicity ; and to this
we will at once address ourselves.

It would be a great mistake to make the discussion
turn on sentimentalities about skulking or cowardice.
Secrecy is justifiable in many cases, imperative in
some, and it is not cowardice to seek protection against
evils which are honestly avoidable. Nor can it be
reasonably maintained that no cases are conceivable,
in which secret voting is preferable to public. But
I must contend that these cases, in affairs of a political
character, are the exception, not the rule.

The present is one of the many instances in which,
as I have already had occasion to remark, the *spirit*
of an institution, the impression it makes on the mind
of the citizen, is one of the most important parts of
its operation. The spirit of vote by ballot—the interpretation likely to be put on it in the mind of an
elector—is that the suffrage is given to him for himself ; for his particular use and benefit, and not as
a trust for the public. For if it is indeed a trust, if
the public are entitled to his vote, are not they entitled
to know his vote ? This false and pernicious impression may well be made on the generality, since it has
been made on most of those who of late years have
been conspicuous advocates of the ballot. The doctrine

was not so understood by its earlier promoters; but the effect of a doctrine on the mind is best shown, not in those who form it, but in those who are formed by it. Mr. Bright and his school of democrats think themselves greatly concerned in maintaining that the franchise is what they term a right, not a trust. Now this one idea, taking root in the general mind, does a moral mischief outweighing all the good that the ballot could do, at the highest possible estimate of it. In whatever way we define or understand the idea of a right, no person can have a right (except in the purely legal sense) to power over others: every such power, which he is allowed to possess, is morally, in the fullest force of the term, a trust. But the exercise of any political function, either as an elector or as a representative, is power over others. Those who say that the suffrage is not a trust but a right, will scarcely accept the conclusions to which their doctrine leads. If it is a right, if it belongs to the voter for his own sake, on what ground can we blame him for selling it, or using it to recommend himself to any one whom it is his interest to please? A person is not expected to consult exclusively the public benefit in the use he makes of his house, or his three per cent stock, or anything else to which he really has a right. The suffrage is indeed due to him, among other reasons, as a means to his own protection, but only against treatment from which he is equally bound, so far as depends on his vote, to protect every one of his fellow citizens. His vote is not a thing in which he has an option; it has no more to do with his personal wishes than the verdict of a juryman. It is strictly a matter of duty; he is bound to give it according to his best and most conscientious opinion of the public good. Whoever has any other idea of it is unfit to have the suffrage; its effect on him is to pervert, not to elevate his mind. Instead of opening his heart to an exalted patriotism and the obligation of public duty, it awakens and nourishes in him the disposition to use a public function for his own interest, pleasure, or caprice; the same feelings and purposes, on a humbler scale, which actuate a despot and oppressor. Now, an ordinary citizen in any public position, or on whom there devolves any social function, is certain to think and feel, respecting the obligations it imposes on him, exactly what society appears to think and feel in conferring it. What seems to be expected from him by society forms a standard which he may fall below, but which he will seldom rise above. And the interpretation which he is almost sure to put upon secret voting, is that he is not bound to give his vote with any reference to those who are not allowed to know how he gives it; but may bestow it simply as he feels inclined.

This is the decisive reason why the argument does not hold, from the use of the ballot in clubs and private societies, to its adoption in parliamentary elections. A member of a club is really, what the elector falsely believes himself to be, under no obligation to consider the wishes or interests of any one else. He declares nothing by his vote, but that he is or is not willing to associate, in a manner more or less close, with a particular person. This is a matter on which, by universal admission, his own pleasure or inclination is entitled to decide : and that he should be able so to decide it without risking a quarrel, is best for everybody, the rejected person included. An additional reason rendering the ballot unobjectionable in these cases, is that it does not necessarily or naturally lead to lying. The persons concerned are of the same class or rank, and it would be considered improper in one of them to press another with questions as to how he had voted. It is far otherwise in parliamentary elections, and is likely to remain so, as long as the social relations exist which produce the demand for the ballot; as long as one person is sufficiently the superior of another, to think himself entitled to dictate his vote. And while this is the case, silence or an evasive answer is certain to be construed as proof that the vote given has not been that which was desired.

In any political election, even by universal suffrage (and still more obviously in the case of a restricted suffrage), the voter is under an absolute moral obligation to consider the interest of the public, not his private advantage, and give his vote to the best of his judgement, exactly as he would be bound to do if he were the sole voter, and the election depended upon him alone. This being admitted, it is at least a prima facie consequence, that the duty of voting, like any other public duty, should be performed under the eye and criticism of the public ; every one of whom has not only an interest in its performance, but a good title to consider himself wronged if it is performed otherwise than honestly and carefully. Undoubtedly neither this nor any other maxim of political morality is absolutely inviolable ; it may be overruled by still more cogent considerations. But its weight is such that the cases which admit of a departure from it must be of a strikingly exceptional character.

It may, unquestionably, be the fact, that if we attempt, by publicity, to make the voter responsible to the public for his vote, he will practically be made responsible for it to some powerful individual, whose interest is more opposed to the general interest of the community, than that of the voter himself would be, if, by the shield of secrecy, he were released from responsibility altogether. When this is the condition, in a high degree, of a large proportion of the voters, the ballot may be the smaller evil. When the voters are slaves, anything may be tolerated which enables them to throw off the yoke. The strongest case for the ballot is when the mischievous power of the Few over the Many is increasing. In the decline of the Roman republic, the reasons for the ballot were irresistible. The oligarchy was yearly becoming richer and more tyrannical, the people poorer and more dependent, and it was necessary to erect stronger and stronger barriers against such abuse of the franchise as rendered it but an instrument the more in the hands of unprincipled persons of consequence. As little can it be doubted that the ballot, so far as it existed, had a beneficial operation in the Athenian constitution. Even in the least unstable of the Grecian common-wealths, freedom might be for the time destroyed by a single unfairly obtained popular vote: and though the Athenian voter was not sufficiently dependent to be habitually coerced, he might have been bribed, or intimidated by the lawless outrages of some knot of individuals, such as were not uncommon even at Athens among the youth of rank and fortune. The ballot was in these cases a valuable instrument of order, and conduced to the Eunomia by which Athens was distinguished among the ancient commonwealths.

But in the more advanced states of modern Europe, and especially in this country, the power of coercing voters has declined and is declining; and bad voting is now less to be apprehended from the influences to which the voter is subject at the hands of others, than from the sinister interests and discreditable feelings which belong to himself, either individually or as a member of a class. To secure him against the first, at the cost of removing all restraint from the last, would be to exchange a smaller and a diminishing evil for a greater and increasing one. On this topic, and on the question generally, as applicable to England at the present date, I have, in a pamphlet on Parliamentary Reform, expressed myself in terms which as I do not feel that I can improve upon, I will venture here to transcribe.

'Thirty years ago, it was still true that in the election of members of Parliament, the main evil to be guarded against was that which the ballot would exclude—coercion by landlords, employers, and customers. At present, I conceive, a much greater source of evil is the selfishness, or the selfish partialities, of the voter himself. A base and mischievous vote is now, I am convinced, much oftener given from the voter's personal interest, or class interest, or some mean feeling in his own mind, than from any fear of consequences at the hands of others: and to these influences the ballot would enable him to yield himself up, free from all sense of shame or responsibility.

' In times not long gone by, the higher and richer classes were in complete possession of the government. Their power was the master grievance of the country. The habit of voting at the bidding of an employer, or of a landlord, was so firmly established, that hardly anything was capable of shaking it but a strong popular enthusiasm, seldom known to exist but in a good cause. A vote given in opposition to these influences was therefore, in general, an honest, a public-spirited vote ; but in any case, and by whatever motive dictated, it was almost sure to be a good vote, for it was a vote against the monster evil, the overruling influence of oligarchy. Could the voter at that time have been enabled, with safety to himself, to exercise his privilege freely, even though neither honestly nor intelligently, it would have been a great gain to reform ; for it would have broken the yoke of the then ruling power in the country—the power which had created and which maintained all that was bad in the institutions and the administration of the State—the power of land-lords and boroughmongers.

' The ballot was not adopted ; but the progress of circumstances has done and is doing more and more, in this respect, the work of the ballot. Both the political and the social state of the country, as they affect this question, have greatly changed, and are changing every day. The higher classes are not now masters of the country. A person must be blind to all the signs of the times, who could think that the middle classes are as subservient to the higher, or the working classes as dependent on the higher and middle, as they were a quarter of a century ago. The events of that quarter of a century have not only taught each class to know its own collective strength, but have put the individuals of a lower class in a condition to show a much bolder front to those of a higher. In a majority of cases, the vote of the electors, whether in opposition to or in accordance with the wishes of their superiors, is not now the effect of coercion, which there are no longer the same means of applying, but the expression of their own personal or political partialities. The very vices of the present electoral system are a proof of this. The growth of bribery, so loudly complained of, and the spread of the contagion to places formerly free from it, are evidence that the local influences are no longer paramount; that the electors now vote to please themselves, and not other people. There is, no doubt, in counties, and in the smaller boroughs, a large amount of servile dependence still remaining; but the temper of the times is adverse to it, and the force of events is constantly tending to diminish it. A good tenant can now feel that he is as valuable to his landlord as his landlord is to him; a prosperous tradesman can afford to feel independent of any particular customer. At every election the votes are more and more the voter's own. It is their minds, far more than their personal circumstances, that now require to be emancipated. They are no longer passive instruments of other men's will—mere organs for putting power into the hands of a controlling oligarchy. The electors themselves are becoming the oligarchy.

'Exactly in proportion as the vote of the elector is determined by his own will, and not by that of somebody who is his master, his position is similar to that of a member of Parliament, and publicity is indispensable. So long as any portion of the community are unrepresented, the argument of the Chartists, against ballot in conjunction with a restricted suffrage, is unassailable. The present electors, and the bulk of those whom any probable Reform Bill would add to the number, are the middle class; and have as much a class interest, distinct from the working classes, as landlords or great manufacturers. Were the suffrage extended to all skilled labourers, even these would, or might, still have a class interest distinct from the unskilled. Suppose it extended to all men—suppose that what was formerly called by the misapplied name of universal suffrage, and now by the silly title of manhood suffrage, became the law ; the voters would still have a class interest, as distinguished from women. Suppose that there were a question before the Legislature specially affecting women ; as whether women should be allowed to graduate at Universities ; whether the mild penalties inflicted on ruffians who beat their wives daily almost to death's door, should be exchanged for something more effectual ; or suppose that any one should propose in the British Parliament, what one State after another in America is enacting not by a mere law, but by a provision of their revised Constitutions—that married women should have a right to their own property. Are not a man's wife and daughters entitled to know whether he votes for or against a candidate who will support these propositions ?

' It will of course be objected, that these arguments derive all their weight from the supposition of an unjust state of the suffrage : That if the opinion of the non-electors is likely to make the elector vote more honestly, or more beneficially, than he would vote if left to himself, they are more fit to be electors than he is, and ought to have the franchise : That whoever is fit to influence electors, is fit to be an elector : That those to whom voters ought to be responsible, should be themselves voters ; and being such, should have the safeguard of the ballot, to shield them from the undue influence of powerful individuals or classes to whom they ought not to be responsible.

' This argument is specious, and I once thought it conclusive. It now appears to me fallacious. All who are fit to influence electors are not, for that reason, fit to be themselves electors. This last is a much greater power than the former, and those may be ripe for the minor political function, who could not as yet be safely trusted with the superior. The opinions and wishes of the poorest and rudest class of labourers may be very useful as one influence among others on the minds of the voters, as well as on those of the Legislature ; and yet it might be highly mischievous to give them the preponderant influence, by admitting them, in their present state of morals and intelligence, to the full exercise of the suffrage. It is precisely this indirect influence of those who have not the suffrage over those who have, which, by its progressive growth, softens the transition to every fresh extension of the franchise, and is the means by which, when the time is ripe, the extension is peacefully brought about. But there is another and a still deeper consideration, which should never be left out of the account in political speculations. The notion is itself unfounded, that publicity, and the sense of being answerable to the public, are of no use unless the public are qualified to form a sound judgement. It is a very superficial view of the utility of public opinion, to suppose that it does good, only when it succeeds in enforcing a servile conformity to itself. To be under the eyes of others—to have to defend oneself to others—is never more important than to those who act in opposition to the opinion of others, for it obliges them to have sure ground of their own. Nothing has so steadying an influence as working against pressure. Unless when under the temporary sway of passionate excitement, no one will do that which he expects to be greatly blamed for, unless from a preconceived and fixed purpose of his own; which is always evidence of a thoughtful and deliberate character, and, except in radically bad men, generally proceeds from sincere and strong personal convictions. Even the bare fact of having to give an account of their conduct, is a powerful inducement to adhere to conduct of which at least some decent account can be given. If any one thinks that the mere obligation of preserving decency is not a very considerable check on the abuse of power, he has never had his attention called to the conduct of those who do not feel under the necessity of observing that restraint. Publicity is inappreciable even when it does no more than prevent that which can by no possibility be plausibly defended—than compel deliberation, and force every one to determine, before he acts, what he shall say if called to account for his actions.

' But, if not now (it may be said), at least hereafter, when all are fit to have votes, and when all men and women are admitted to vote in virtue of their fitness ; *then* there can no longer be danger of class legislation ; then the electors, being the nation, can have no interest apart from the general interest : even if individuals still vote according to private or class inducements, the majority will have no such inducement ; and as there will then be no non-electors to whom they ought to be responsible, the effect of the ballot, excluding none but the sinister influences, will be wholly bene-ficial.

' Even in this I do not agree. I cannot think that even if the people were fit for, and had obtained, universal suffrage, the ballot would be desirable. First, because it could not, in such circumstances, be sup-posed to be needful. Let us only conceive the state of things which the hypothesis implies ; a people universally educated, and every grown-up human being possessed of a vote. If, even when only a small proportion are electors, and the majority of the popula-tion almost uneducated, public opinion is already, as every one now sees that it is, the ruling power in the last resort ; it is a chimera to suppose that over a com-munity who all read, and who all have votes, any power could be exercised by landlords and rich people against their own inclination, which it would be at all difficult for them to throw off. But though the protection of secrecy would then be needless, the control of publicity would be as needful as ever. The universal observation of mankind has been very fallacious, if the mere fact of being one of the community, and not being in a position of pronounced contrariety of interest to the public at large, is enough to ensure the performance of a public duty, without either the stimulus or the restraint derived from the opinion of our fellow creatures. A man's own particular share of the public interest, even though he may have no private interest drawing him in the opposite direction, is not, as a general rule, found sufficient to make him do his duty to the public without other external inducements. Neither can it be admitted that even if all had votes, they would give their votes as honestly in secret as in public. The proposition that the electors, when they compose the whole of the community, cannot have an interest in voting against the interest of the community, will be found on examination to have more sound than meaning in it. Though the community as a whole can have (as the terms imply) no other interest than its collective interest, any or every individual in it may. A man's interest consists of whatever he takes an interest *in*. Everybody has as many different interests as he has feelings ; likings or dislikings, either of a selfish or of a better kind. It cannot be said that any of these, taken by itself, constitutes " his interest " : he is a good man or a bad, according as he prefers one class of his interests or another. A man who is a tyrant at home will be apt to sympathize with tyranny (when not exercised over himself) : he will be almost certain not to sympathize with resistance to tyranny. An envious man will vote against Aristides because he is called the Just. A selfish man will prefer even a trifling individual benefit, to his share of the advantage which his country would derive from a good law ; because interests peculiar to himself are those which the habits of his mind both dispose him to dwell on, and make him best able to estimate. A great number of the electors will have two sets of preferences—those on private, and those on public grounds. The last are the only ones which the elector would like to avow. The best side of their character is that which people are anxious to show, even to those who are no better than themselves. People will give dishonest or mean votes from lucre, from malice, from pique, from personal rivalry, even from the interests or prejudices of class or sect, more readily in secret than in public. And cases exist—they may come to be more frequent —in which almost the only restraint upon a majority of knaves consists in their involuntary respect for the opinion of an honest minority. In such a case as that of the repudiating States of North America, is there not some check to the unprincipled voter in the shame of looking an honest man in the face ? Since all this good would be sacrificed by the ballot, even in the circumstances most favourable to it, a much stronger case is requisite than can now be made out for its necessity (and the case is continually becoming still weaker) to make its adoption desirable.' [1]

On the other debateable points connected with the mode of voting, it is not necessary to expend so many words. The system of personal representation, as organized by Mr. Hare, renders necessary the employment of voting papers. But it appears to me indispensable that the signature of the elector should be affixed to the paper at a public polling place, or if there be no such place conveniently accessible, at some office open to all the world, and in the presence of a responsible public officer. The proposal which has been thrown out of allowing the voting papers to be filled up at the voter's own residence, and sent by the post, or called for by a public officer, I should regard as fatal. The act would be done in the absence of the salutary and the presence of all the pernicious influences. The briber might, in the shelter of privacy, behold with his own eyes his bargain fulfilled, and the intimidator could see the extorted obedience rendered irrevocably on the spot ; while the beneficent counter-influence of the presence of those who knew the voter's real sentiments, and the inspiring effect of the sympathy of those of his own party or opinion, would be shut out.[2]

---

[1] *Thoughts on Parliamentary Reform,* 2nd ed., pp. 32–36.
[2] ' This expedient has been recommended, both on the score of saving expense, and on that of obtaining the votes of many electors who otherwise would not vote, and who are regarded by the advocates of the plan as a particularly desirable class of voters. The scheme has been carried into practice in the election of poor-law guardians, and its success in that instance is appealed to in favour of adopting it in the more important case of voting for a

The polling places should be so numerous as to be within easy reach of every voter; and no expenses of conveyance, at the cost of the candidate, should be tolerated under any pretext. The infirm, and they only on medical certificate, should have the right of claiming suitable carriage conveyance, at the cost of the State, or of the locality. Hustings, poll clerks, and all the necessary machinery of elections, should be

member of the Legislature. But the two cases appear to me to differ in the point on which the benefits of the expedient depend. In a local election for a special kind of administrative business, which consists mainly in the dispensation of a public fund, it is an object to prevent the choice from being exclusively in the hands of those who actively concern themselves about it; for the public interest which attaches to the election being of a limited kind, and in most cases not very great in degree, the disposition to make themselves busy in the matter is apt to be in a great measure confined to persons who hope to turn their activity to their own private advantage; and it may be very desirable to render the intervention of other people as little onerous to them as possible, if only for the purpose of swamping these private interests. But when the matter in hand is the great business of national government, in which every one must take an interest who cares for anything out of himself, or who cares even for himself intelligently, it is much rather an object to prevent those from voting who are indifferent to the subject, than to induce them to vote by any other means than that of awakening their dormant minds. The voter who does not care enough about the election to go to the poll, is the very man who, if he can vote without that small trouble, will give his vote to the first person who asks for it, or on the most trifling or frivolous inducement. A man who does not care whether he votes, is not likely to care much which way he votes; and he who is in that state of mind has no moral right to vote at all; since, if he does so, a vote which is not the expression of a conviction, counts for as much, and goes as far in determining the result, as one which represents the thoughts and purposes of a life.'—*Thoughts*, &c., p. 39.

at the public charge. Not only the candidate should not be required, he should not be permitted, to incur any but a limited and trifling expense for his election. Mr. Hare thinks it desirable that a sum of £50 should be required from every one who places his name on the list of candidates, to prevent persons who have no chance of success, and no real intention of attempting it, from becoming candidates in wantonness or from mere love of notoriety, and perhaps carrying off a few votes which are needed for the return of more serious aspirants. There is one expense which a candidate or his supporters cannot help incurring, and which it can hardly be expected that the public should defray for every one who may choose to demand it ; that of making his claims known to the electors, by advertisements, placards, and circulars. For all necessary expenses of this kind the £50 proposed by Mr. Hare, if allowed to be drawn upon for these purposes (it might be made £100 if requisite), ought to be sufficient. If the friends of the candidate choose to go to expense for committees and canvassing, there are no means of preventing them ; but such expenses out of the candidate's own pocket, or any expenses whatever beyond the deposit of £50 (or £100) should be illegal and punishable. If there appeared any likelihood that opinion would refuse to connive at falsehood, a declaration on oath or honour should be required from every member on taking his seat, that he had not expended, nor would expend, money or money's worth, beyond the £50, directly or indirectly, for the purposes of his election ; and if the assertion were proved to be false or the pledge to have been broken, he should be liable to the penalties of perjury. It is probable that those penalties, by showing that the Legislature was in earnest, would turn the course of opinion in the same direction, and would hinder it from regarding, as it has hitherto done, this most serious crime against society as a venial peccadillo. When once this effect has been produced, there need be no doubt that the declaration on oath or honour

would be considered binding.[1] 'Opinion tolerates
a false disclaimer, only when it already tolerates the

[1] Several of the witnesses before the Committee of the
House of Commons in 1860, on the operation of the
Corrupt Practices Prevention Act, some of them of great
practical experience in election matters, were favourable
(either absolutely or as a last resort) to the principle of
requiring a declaration from members of Parliament ; and
were of opinion that, if supported by penalties, it would
be, to a great degree, effectual (*Evidence*, pp. 46, 54–7,
67, 123, 198–202, 208). The Chief Commissioner of the
Wakefield Inquiry said (in reference certainly to a different
proposal), ' If they see that the Legislature is earnest upon
the subject, the machinery will work. . . . I am quite sure
that if some personal stigma were applied upon conviction
of bribery, it would change the current of public opinion '
(pp. 26 and 32). A distinguished member of the Committee
(and of the present Cabinet) seemed to think it very
objectionable to attach the penalties of perjury to a
merely promissory as distinguished from an assertory oath :
but he was reminded, that the oath taken by a witness
in a court of justice is a promissory oath : and the re-
joinder (that the witness's promise relates to an act to be
done at once, while the member's would be a promise for
all future time) would only be to the purpose, if it could
be supposed that the swearer might forget the obligation
he had entered into, or could possibly violate it unawares :
contingencies which, in a case like the present, are out of
the question.

A more substantial difficulty is, that one of the forms
most frequently assumed by election expenditure, is that
of subscriptions to local charities, or other local objects ;
and it would be a strong measure to enact that money
should not be given in charity, within a place, by the
member for it. When such subscriptions are bona fide,
the popularity which may be derived from them is an
advantage which it seems hardly possible to deny to
superior riches. But the greatest part of the mischief
consists in the fact that money so contributed is employed
in bribery, under the euphemistic name of keeping up the
member's interest. To guard against this, it should be
part of the member's promissory declaration, that all sums
expended by him in the place, or for any purpose connected

thing disclaimed.' This is notoriously the case with
regard to electoral corruption. There has never yet
been, among political men, any real and serious attempt
to prevent bribery, because there has been no real
desire that elections should not be costly. Their costli-
ness is an advantage to those who can afford the expense, by excluding a multitude of competitors ; and
anything, however noxious, is cherished as having
a conservative tendency, if it limits the access to Parliament to rich men. This is a rooted feeling among
our legislators of both political parties, and is almost
the only point on which I believe them to be really ill-
intentioned. They care comparatively little who votes,
as long as they feel assured that none but persons of
their own class can be voted for. They know that they
can rely on the fellow-feeling of one of their class
with another, while the subservience of *nouveaux
enrichis* who are knocking at the door of the class, is
a still surer reliance ; and that nothing very hostile
to the class interests or feelings of the rich need be
apprehended under the most democratic suffrage, as
long as democratic persons can be prevented from
being elected to Parliament. But, even from their
own point of view, this balancing of evil by evil,
instead of combining good with good, is a wretched
policy. The object should be to bring together the
best members of both classes, under such a tenure as
shall induce them to lay aside their class preferences,
and pursue jointly the path traced by the common
interest ; instead of allowing the class feelings of the
Many to have full swing in the constituencies, subject

with it or with any of its inhabitants, (with the exception
perhaps of his own hotel expenses,) should pass through
the hands of the election auditor, and be by him (and not
by the member himself or his friends) applied to its
declared purpose.
The principle of making all lawful expenses of elections
a charge not upon the candidate, but upon the locality,
was upheld by two of the best witnesses (pp. 20, 65–70,
277).

to the impediment of having to act through persons imbued with the class feelings of the Few.

There is scarcely any mode in which political institutions are more morally mischievous—work greater evil through their spirit—than by representing political functions as a favour to be conferred, a thing which the depositary is to ask for as desiring it for himself, and even pay for as if it were designed for his pecuniary benefit. Men are not fond of paying large sums for leave to perform a laborious duty. Plato had a much juster view of the conditions of good government, when he asserted that the persons who should be sought out to be invested with political power are those who are personally most averse to it, and that the only motive which can be relied on for inducing the fittest men to take upon themselves the toils of government, is the fear of being governed by worse men. What must an elector think, when he sees three or four gentlemen, none of them previously observed to be lavish of their money on projects of disinterested beneficence, vying with one another in the sums they expend to be enabled to write M.P. after their names ? Is it likely he will suppose that it is for *his* interest they incur all this cost ? And if he forms an uncomplimentary opinion of their part in the affair, what moral obligation is he likely to feel as to his own ? Politicians are fond of treating it as the dream of enthusiasts, that the electoral body will ever be uncorrupt : truly enough, until they are willing to become so themselves : for the electors, assuredly, will take their moral tone from the candidates. So long as the elected member, in any shape or manner, pays for his seat, all endeavours will fail to make the business of election anything but a selfish bargain on all sides. ' So long as the candidate himself, and the customs of the world, seem to regard the function of a member of Parliament less as a duty to be discharged, than a personal favour to be solicited, no effort will avail to implant in an ordinary voter the feeling that the election of a member of Parliament is also a matter of duty, and that he is not at liberty to bestow his vote on any other consideration than that of personal fitness.'

The same principle which demands that no payment of money, for election purposes, should be either required or tolerated on the part of the person elected, dictates another conclusion, apparently of contrary tendency, but really directed to the same object. It negatives what has often been proposed as a means of rendering Parliament accessible to persons of all ranks and circumstances ; the payment of members of Parliament. If, as in some of our colonies, there are scarcely any fit persons who can afford to attend to an unpaid occupation, the payment should be an indemnity for loss of time or money, not a salary. The greater latitude of choice which a salary would give is an illusory advantage. No remuneration which any one would think of attaching to the post would attract to it those who were seriously engaged in other lucrative professions, with a prospect of succeeding in them. The business of a member of Parliament would therefore become an occupation in itself ; carried on, like other professions, with a view chiefly to its pecuniary returns, and under the demoralizing influences of an occupation essentially precarious. It would become an object of desire to adventurers of a low class ; and 658 persons in possession, with ten or twenty times as many in expectancy, would be incessantly bidding to attract or retain the suffrages of the electors, by promising all things, honest or dishonest, possible or impossible, and rivalling each other in pandering to the meanest feelings and most ignorant prejudices of the vulgarest part of the crowd. The auction between Cleon and the sausage-seller in Aristophanes is a fair caricature of what would be always going on. Such an institution would be a perpetual blister applied to the most peccant parts of human nature. It amounts to offering 658 prizes for the most successful flatterer, the most adroit misleader, of a body of his fellow countrymen. Under no despotism has there been such an organized system of tillage for raising a rich crop of vicious courtiership.[1] When, by reason of pre-eminent qualifications (as may at any time happen to be the case), it is desirable that a person entirely without independent means, either derived from property or from a trade or profession, should be brought into Parliament to render services which no other person accessible can render as well, there is the resource of a public subscription; he may be supported while in Parliament, like Andrew Marvell, by the contributions of his constituents. This mode is unobjectionable, for such an honour will never be paid to mere subserviency: bodies of men do not care so much for the difference between one sycophant and another, as to go to the expense of his maintenance in order to be flattered by that particular individual. Such a support will only be given in consideration of striking and impressive personal qualities, which though no absolute proof of fitness to be a national representative, are some presumption of it, and, at all events, some guarantee for the possession of an independent opinion and will.

[1] 'As Mr. Lorimer remarks, by creating a pecuniary inducement to persons of the lowest class to devote themselves to public affairs, the calling of the demagogue would be formally inaugurated. Nothing is more to be deprecated than making it the private interest of a number of active persons to urge the form of government in the direction of its natural perversion. The indications which either a multitude or an individual can give, when merely left to their own weaknesses, afford but a faint idea of what those weaknesses would become when played upon by a thousand flatterers. If there were 658 places of certain, however moderate, emolument, to be gained by persuading the multitude that ignorance is as good as knowledge, and better, it is terrible odds that they would believe and act upon the lesson' (Article in *Fraser's Magazine* for April 1859, headed 'Recent Writers on Reform').

CHAPTER XI

OF THE DURATION OF PARLIAMENTS

AFTER how long a term should members of Parliament be subject to re-election? The principles involved are here very obvious; the difficulty lies in their application. On the one hand, the member ought not to have so long a tenure of his seat as to make him forget his responsibility, take his duties easily, conduct them with a view to his own personal advantage, or neglect those free and public conferences with his constituents, which, whether he agrees or differs with them, are one of the benefits of representative government. On the other hand, he should have such a term of office to look forward to, as will enable him to be judged not by a single act, but by his course of action. It is important that he should have the greatest latitude of individual opinion and discretion, compatible with the popular control essential to free government; and for this purpose it is necessary that the control should be exercised, as in any case it is best exercised, after sufficient time has been given him to show all the qualities he possesses, and to prove that there is some other way than that of a mere obedient voter and advocate of their opinions, by which he can render himself in the eyes of his constituents a desirable and creditable representative.

It is impossible to fix, by any universal rule, the boundary between these principles. Where the democratic power in the constitution is weak or over-passive, and requires stimulation; where the representative, on leaving his constituents, enters at once into a courtly or aristocratic atmosphere, whose influences all tend to deflect his course into a different direction from the popular one, to tone down any democratic feelings which he may have brought with him, and make him forget the wishes and grow cool to

the interests of those who chose him; the obligation
of a frequent return to them for a renewal of his commission, is indispensable to keeping his temper and
character up to the right mark. Even three years, in
such circumstances, are almost too long a period; and
any longer term is absolutely inadmissible. Where,
on the contrary, democracy is the ascendant power,
and still tends to increase, requiring rather to be
moderated in its exercise than encouraged to any
abnormal activity; where unbounded publicity, and
an ever present newspaper press, give the representative assurance that his every act will be immediately
known, discussed, and judged by his constituents,
and that he is always either gaining or losing ground
in their estimation—while by the same means, the
influence of their sentiments, and all other democratic
influences, are kept constantly alive and active in his
own mind; less than five years would hardly be
a sufficient period to prevent timid subserviency. The
change which has taken place in English politics as to
all these features, explains why annual parliaments,
which forty years ago stood prominently in front of
the creed of the more advanced reformers, are so little
cared for and so seldom heard of at present. It deserves
consideration, that, whether the term is short or long,
during the last year of it the members are in the
position in which they would always be if parliaments
were annual: so that if the term were very brief, there
would virtually be annual parliaments during a great
proportion of all time. As things now are, the period
of seven years, though of unnecessary length, is hardly
worth altering for any benefit likely to be produced;
especially since the possibility, always impending, of an
earlier dissolution, keeps the motives for standing well
with constituents always before the member's eyes.

Whatever may be the term most eligible for the duration of the mandate, it might seem natural that the
individual member should vacate his seat at the expiration of that term from the day of his election, and that
there should be no general renewal of the whole House.

A great deal might be said for this system, if there were any practical object in recommending it.   But it is condemned by much stronger reasons than can be alleged in its support.   One is, that there would be no means of promptly getting rid of a majority which had pursued a course offensive to the nation.   The certainty of a general election after a limited, which would often be a nearly expired, period, and the possibility of it at any time when the minister either desires it for his own sake, or thinks that it would make him popular with the country, tend to prevent that wide divergence between the feelings of the assembly and those of the constituency, which might subsist indefinitely if the majority of the House had always several years of their term still to run—if it received new infusions drop by drop, which would be more likely to assume than to modify the qualities of the mass they were joined to.   It is as essential that the general sense of the House should accord in the main with that of the nation, as it is that distinguished individuals should be able, without forfeiting their seats, to give free utterance to the most unpopular sentiments. There is another reason, of much weight, against the gradual and partial renewal of a representative assembly.   It is useful that there should be a periodical general muster of opposing forces, to gauge the state of the national mind, and ascertain, beyond dispute, the relative strength of different parties and opinions. This is not done conclusively by any partial renewal, even where, as in some of the French constitutions, a large fraction, a fifth or a third, go out at once.

The reasons for allowing to the executive the power of dissolution, will be considered in a subsequent chapter, relating to the constitution and functions of the Executive in a representative government.

CHAPTER XII

OUGHT PLEDGES TO BE REQUIRED FROM MEMBERS OF
PARLIAMENT ?

SHOULD a member of the Legislature be bound by
the instructions of his constituents ? Should he be
the organ of their sentiments, or of his own ? their
ambassador to a congress, or their professional agent,
empowered not only to act for them, but to judge for
them what ought to be done ? These two theories of
the duty of a legislator in a representative government
have each its supporters, and each is the recognized
doctrine of some representative governments. In the
Dutch United Provinces, the members of the States
General were mere delegates ; and to such a length
was the doctrine carried, that when any important
question arose which had not been provided for in
their instructions, they had to refer back to their constituents, exactly as an ambassador does to the government from which he is accredited. In this and most
other countries which possess representative constitutions, law and custom warrant a member of Parliament in voting according to his opinion of right, however different from that of his constituents : but there
is a floating notion of the opposite kind, which has considerable practical operation on many minds, even of
members of Parliament, and often makes them, independently of desire for popularity, or concern for
their re-election, feel bound in conscience to let their
conduct, on questions on which their constituents have
a decided opinion, be the expression of that opinion
rather than of their own. Abstractedly from positive
law, and from the historical traditions of any particular
people, which of these notions of the duty of a representative is the true one ?

Unlike the questions which we have hitherto treated,
this is not a question of constitutional legislation, but
of what may more properly be called constitutional

morality—the ethics of representative government. It does not so much concern institutions, as the temper of mind which the electors ought to bring to the discharge of their functions; the ideas which should prevail as to the moral duties of an elector. For, let the system of representation be what it may, it will be converted into one of mere delegation if the electors so choose. As long as they are free not to vote, and free to vote as they like, they cannot be prevented from making their vote depend on any condition they think fit to annex to it. By refusing to elect any one who will not pledge himself to all their opinions, and even, if they please, to consult with them before voting on any important subject not foreseen, they can reduce their representative to their mere mouthpiece, or compel him in honour, when no longer willing to act in that capacity, to resign his seat. And since they have the power of doing this, the theory of the Constitution ought to suppose that they will wish to do it; since the very principle of constitutional government requires it to be assumed, that political power will be abused to promote the particular purposes of the holder; not because it always is so, but because such is the natural tendency of things, to guard against which is the especial use of free institutions. However wrong, therefore, or however foolish, we may think it in the electors to convert their representative into a delegate, that stretch of the electoral privilege being a natural and not improbable one, the same precautions ought to be taken as if it were certain. We may hope that the electors will not act on this notion of the use of the suffrage; but a representative government needs to be so framed that even if they do, they shall not be able to effect what ought not to be in the power of any body of persons—class legislation for their own benefit.

When it is said that the question is only one of political morality, this does not extenuate its importance. Questions of constitutional morality are of no less practical moment than those relating to the constitution itself. The very existence of some governments, and all that renders others endurable, rests on the practical observance of doctrines of constitutional morality; traditional notions in the minds of the several constituted authorities, which modify the use that might otherwise be made of their powers. In unbalanced governments— pure monarchy, pure aristocracy, pure democracy—such maxims are the only barrier which restrains the government from the utmost excesses in the direction of its characteristic tendency. In imperfectly balanced governments, where some attempt is made to set constitutional limits to the impulses of the strongest power, but where that power is strong enough to overstep them with at least temporary impunity, it is only by doctrines of constitutional morality, recognized and sustained by opinion, that any regard at all is preserved for the checks and limitations of the constitution. In well balanced governments, in which the supreme power is divided, and each sharer is protected against the usurpations of the others in the only manner possible—namely, by being armed for defence with weapons as strong as the others can wield for attack—the government can only be carried on by forbearance on all sides to exercise those extreme powers, unless provoked by conduct equally extreme on the part of some other sharer of power: and in this case we may truly say, that only by the regard paid to maxims of constitutional morality is the constitution kept in existence. The question of pledges is not one of those which vitally concern the existence of representative governments ; but it is very material to their beneficial operation. The laws cannot prescribe to the electors the principles by which they shall direct their choice ; but it makes a great practical difference by what principles they think they ought to direct it. And the whole of that great question is involved in the inquiry, whether they should make it a condition that the representative shall adhere to certain opinions laid down for him by his constituents. No reader of this treatise can doubt what conclusion, as to this matter, results from the general principles which it professes. We have from the first affirmed, and unvaryingly kept in view, the coequal importance of two great requisites of government: responsibility to those, for whose benefit political power ought to be, and always professes to be, employed; and jointly therewith, to obtain, in the greatest measure possible, for the function of government, the benefits of superior intellect, trained by long meditation and practical discipline to that special task. If this second purpose is worth attaining, it is worth the necessary price. Superior powers of mind and profound study are of no use, if they do not sometimes lead a person to different conclusions from those which are formed by ordinary powers of mind without study: and if it be an object to possess representatives in any intellectual respect superior to average electors, it must be counted upon that the representative will sometimes differ in opinion from the majority of his constituents, and that when he does, his opinion will be the oftenest right of the two. It follows, that the electors will not do wisely, if they insist on absolute conformity to their opinions, as the condition of his retaining his seat.

The principle is, thus far, obvious; but there are real difficulties in its application: and we will begin by stating them in their greatest force. If it is important that the electors should choose a representative more highly instructed than themselves, it is no less necessary that this wiser man should be responsible to them; in other words, they are the judges of the manner in which he fulfils his trust: and how are they to judge, except by the standard of their own opinions? How are they even to select him in the first instance, but by the same standard? It will not do to choose by mere brilliancy—by superiority of showy talent. The tests by which an ordinary man can judge beforehand of mere ability are very imperfect: such as they are, they have almost exclusive reference to the arts of expression, and little or none to the worth of what is expressed. The latter cannot be inferred from the former; and if the electors are to put their own opinions in abeyance, what criterion remains to them of the ability to govern well? Neither, if they could ascertain, even infallibly, the ablest man, ought they to allow him altogether to judge for them, without any reference to their own opinions. The ablest candidate may be a Tory, and the electors Liberals; or a Liberal, and they may be Tories. The political questions of the day may be Church questions, and he may be a High Churchman, or a Rationalist, while they may be Dissenters, or Evangelicals; and vice versa. His abilities, in these cases, might only enable him to go greater lengths, and act with greater effect, in what they may conscientiously believe to be a wrong course; and they may be bound, by their sincere convictions, to think it more important that their representative should be kept, on these points, to what they deem the dictate of duty, than that they should be represented by a person of more than average abilities. They may also have to consider, not solely how they can be most ably represented, but how their particular moral position and mental point of view shall be represented at all. The influence of every mode of thinking which is shared by numbers, ought to be felt in the Legislature: and the constitution being supposed to have made due provision that other and conflicting modes of thinking shall be represented likewise, to secure the proper representation for their own mode may be the most important matter which the electors on the particular occasion have to attend to. In some cases, too, it may be necessary that the representative should have his hands tied, to keep him true to their interest, or rather to the public interest as they conceive it. This would not be needful under a political system which assured them an indefinite choice of honest and unprejudiced candidates; but under the existing system, in which the electors are almost always obliged, by the expenses of election and the general circumstances of society, to select their representative from persons of a station in life widely different from theirs, and having a different class-interest, who will affirm that they ought to abandon themselves to his discretion ? Can we blame an elector of the poorer classes, who has only the choice among two or three rich men, for requiring from the one he votes for, a pledge to those measures which he considers as a test of emancipation from the class-interests of the rich ? It moreover always happens to some members of the electoral body, to be obliged to accept the representative selected by a majority of their own side. But though a candidate of their own choosing would have no chance, their votes may be necessary to the success of the one chosen for them ; and their only means of exerting their share of influence on his subsequent conduct, may be to make their support of him dependent on his pledging himself to certain conditions.

These considerations and counter-considerations are so intimately interwoven with one another ; it is so important that the electors should choose as their representatives wiser men than themselves, and should consent to be governed according to that superior wisdom, while it is impossible that conformity to their own opinions, when they have opinions, should not enter largely into their judgement as to who possesses the wisdom, and how far its presumed possessor has verified the presumption by his conduct ; that it seems quite impracticable to lay down for the elector any positive rule of duty : and the result will depend, less on any exact prescription, or authoritative doctrine of political morality, than on the general tone of mind of the electoral body, in respect to the important requisite, of deference to mental superiority. Individuals, and peoples, who are acutely sensible of the value of superior wisdom, are likely to recognize it, where it exists, by other signs than thinking exactly as they do, and even in spite of considerable differences of opinion : and when they have recognized it they will be far too desirous to secure it, at any admissible cost, to be prone to impose their own opinion as a law upon persons whom they look up to as wiser than themselves. On the other hand, there is a character of mind which does not look up to any one ; which thinks no other person's opinion much better than its own, or nearly so good as that of a hundred or a thousand persons like itself. Where this is the turn of mind of the electors, they will elect no one who is not, or at least who does not profess to be, the image of their own sentiments, and will continue him no longer than while he reflects those sentiments in his conduct : and all aspirants to political honours will endeavour, as Plato says in the Gorgias, to fashion themselves after the model of the Demos, and make themselves as like to it as possible. It cannot be denied, that a complete democracy has a strong tendency to cast the sentiments of the electors in this mould. Democracy is not favourable to the reverential spirit. That it destroys reverence for mere social position must be counted among the good, not the bad part of its influences ; though by doing this it closes the principal *school* of reverence (as to merely human relations) which exists in society. But also democracy, in its very essence, insists so much more forcibly on the things in which all are entitled to be considered equally, than on those in which one person is entitled to more consideration than another, that respect for even personal superiority is likely to be below the mark. It is for this, among other reasons, I hold it of so much importance that the institutions of the country should stamp the opinions of persons of a more educated class as entitled to greater weight than those of the less educated : and I should still contend for assigning plurality of votes to authenticated superiority of education, were it only to give the tone to public feeling, irrespective of any direct political consequences.

When there does exist in the electoral body an adequate sense of the extraordinary difference in value between one person and another, they will not lack signs by which to distinguish the persons whose worth

for their purposes is the greatest. Actual public services will naturally be the foremost indication: to
have filled posts of magnitude, and done important
things in them, of which the wisdom has been justified
by the results; to have been the author of measures
which appear from their effects to have been wisely
planned; to have made predictions which have been
often verified by the event, seldom or never falsified
by it; to have given advice, which when taken has
been followed by good consequences, when neglected,
by bad. There is doubtless a large portion of un-
certainty in these signs of wisdom; but we are seeking for such as can be applied by persons of ordinary
discernment. They will do well not to rely much on
any one indication, unless corroborated by the rest;
and, in their estimation of the success or merit of any
practical effort, to lay great stress on the general
opinion of disinterested persons conversant with the
subject matter. The tests which I have spoken of are
only applicable to tried men; among whom must be
reckoned those who, though untried practically, have
been tried speculatively; who, in public speech or in
print, have discussed public affairs in a manner which
proves that they have given serious study to them.
Such persons may, in the mere character of political
thinkers, have exhibited a considerable amount of the
same titles to confidence as those who have been
proved in the position of practical statesmen. When
it is necessary to choose persons wholly untried, the
best criteria are, reputation for ability among those
who personally know them, and the confidence placed
and recommendations given by persons already looked
up to. By tests like these, constituencies who sufficiently value mental ability, and eagerly seek for it,
will generally succeed in obtaining men beyond
mediocrity, and often men whom they can trust to
carry on public affairs according to their unfettered
judgement; to whom it would be an affront to require
that they should give up that judgement at the behest
of their inferiors in knowledge. If such persons, honestly

sought, are not to be found, then indeed the electors
are justified in taking other precautions; for they
cannot be expected to postpone their particular
opinions, unless in order that they may be served by
a person of superior knowledge to their own. They
would do well, indeed, even then, to remember, that
when once chosen, the representative, if he devotes
himself to his duty, has greater opportunities of correcting an original false judgement, than fall to the lot of
most of his constituents; a consideration which generally ought to prevent them (unless compelled by
necessity to choose some one whose impartiality they
do not fully trust) from exacting a pledge not to
change his opinion, or, if he does, to resign his seat.
But when an unknown person, not certified in unmistakable terms by some high authority, is elected
for the first time, the elector cannot be expected not
to make conformity to his own sentiments the primary
requisite. It is enough if he does not regard a subsequent change of those sentiments, honestly avowed,
with its grounds undisguisedly stated, as a peremptory
reason for withdrawing his confidence.

Even supposing the most tried ability and acknowledged eminence of character in the representative, the
private opinions of the electors are not to be placed
entirely in abeyance. Deference to mental superiority
is not to go the length of self-annihilation—abnegation
of any personal opinion. But when the difference does
not relate to the fundamentals of politics, however
decided the elector may be in his own sentiments,
he ought to consider that when an able man differs
from him there is at least a considerable chance of his
being in the wrong, and that even if otherwise, it is
worth while to give up his opinion in things not absolutely essential, for the sake of the inestimable advantage of having an able man to act for him in the many
matters in which he himself is not qualified to form
a judgement. In such cases he often endeavours to
reconcile both wishes, by inducing the able man to
sacrifice his own opinion on the points of difference;

but, for the able man to lend himself to this compromise, is treason against his especial office; abdication of the peculiar duties of mental superiority, of which it is one of the most sacred not to desert the cause which has the clamour against it, nor to deprive of his services those of his opinions which need them the most. A man of conscience and known ability should insist on full freedom to act as he in his own judgement deems best; and should not consent to serve on any other terms. But the electors are entitled to know how he means to act; what opinions, on all things which concern his public duty, he intends should guide his conduct. If some of these are unacceptable to them, it is for him to satisfy them that he nevertheless deserves to be their representative; and if they are wise, they will overlook, in favour of his general value, many and great differences between his opinions and their own. There are some differences, however, which they cannot be expected to overlook. Whoever feels the amount of interest in the government of his country which befits a freeman, has some convictions on national affairs which are like his life-blood; which the strength of his belief in their truth, together with the importance he attaches to them, forbid him to make a subject of compromise, or postpone to the judgement of any person, however greatly his superior. Such convictions, when they exist in a people, or in any appreciable portion of one, are entitled to influence in virtue of their mere existence, and not solely in that of the probability of their being grounded in truth. A people cannot be well governed in opposition to their primary notions of right, even though these may be in some points erroneous. A correct estimate of the relation which should subsist between governors and governed, does not require the electors to consent to be represented by one who intends to govern them in opposition to their fundamental convictions. If they avail themselves of his capacities of useful service in other respects, at a time when the points on which he is vitally at issue with them are not likely to be mooted, they are justified in dismissing him at the first moment when a question arises involving these, and on which there is not so assured a majority for what they deem right, as to make the dissenting voice of that particular individual unimportant. Thus (I mention names to illustrate my meaning, not for any personal application) the opinions supposed to be entertained by Mr. Cobden and Mr. Bright on resistance to foreign aggression, might be overlooked during the Crimean war, when there was an overwhelming national feeling on the contrary side, and might yet very properly lead to their rejection by the electors at the time of the Chinese quarrel (though in itself a more doubtful question), because it was then for some time a moot point whether their view of the case might not prevail.

As the general result of what precedes, we may affirm that actual pledges should not be required, unless, from unfavourable social circumstances or faulty institutions, the electors are so narrowed in their choice, as to be compelled to fix it on a person presumptively under the influence of partialities hostile to their interest: That they are entitled to a full knowledge of the political opinions and sentiments of the candidate; and not only entitled, but often bound, to reject one who differs from themselves on the few articles which are the foundation of their political belief: That in proportion to the opinion they entertain of the mental superiority of a candidate, they ought to put up with his expressing and acting on opinions different from theirs on any number of things not included in their fundamental articles of belief: That they ought to be unremitting in their search for a representative of such calibre as to be entrusted with full power of obeying the dictates of his own judgement: That they should consider it a duty which they owe to their fellow-countrymen, to do their utmost towards placing men of this quality in the Legislature: and that it is of much greater importance to themselves to be represented by such a man, than by one who professes agreement in a greater number of their opinions : for the benefits of his ability are certain, while the hypothesis of his being wrong and their being right on the points of difference is a very doubtful one.

I have discussed this question on the assumption that the electoral system, in all that depends on positive institution, conforms to the principles laid down in the preceding chapters. Even on this hypothesis, the delegation theory of representation seems to me false, and its practical operation hurtful, though the mischief would in that case be confined within certain bounds. But if the securities by which I have endeavoured to guard the representative principle are not recognized by the Constitution ; if provision is not made for the representation of minorities, nor any difference admitted in the numerical value of votes, according to some criterion of the amount of education possessed by the voters ; in that case no words can exaggerate the importance in principle of leaving an unfettered discretion to the representative ; for it would then be the only chance, under universal suffrage, for any other opinions than those of the majority to be heard in Parliament. In that falsely called democracy which is really the exclusive rule of the operative classes, all others being unrepresented and unheard, the only escape from class legislation in its narrowest, and political ignorance in its most dangerous, form, would lie in such disposition as the uneducated might have to choose educated representatives, and to defer to their opinions. Some willingness to do this might reasonably be expected, and everything would depend upon cultivating it to the highest point. But, once invested with political omnipotence, if the operative classes voluntarily concurred in imposing in this or any other manner, any considerable limitation upon their self-opinion and self-will, they would prove themselves wiser than any class, possessed of absolute power, has shown itself, or, we may venture to say, is ever likely to show itself, under that corrupting influence.

CHAPTER XIII

OF A SECOND CHAMBER

OF all topics relating to the theory of representative government, none has been the subject of more discussion, especially on the Continent, than what is known as the question of the Two Chambers. It has occupied a greater amount of the attention of thinkers than many questions of ten times its importance, and has been regarded as a sort of touchstone which distinguishes the partisans of limited from those of uncontrolled democracy. For my own part, I set little value on any check which a Second Chamber can apply to a democracy otherwise unchecked; and I am inclined to think that if all other constitutional questions are rightly decided, it is but of secondary importance whether the Parliament consists of two Chambers, or only of one.

If there are two Chambers, they may either be of similar, or of dissimilar composition. If of similar, both will obey the same influences, and whatever has a majority in one of the Houses will be likely to have it in the other. It is true that the necessity of obtaining the consent of both to the passing of any measure may at times be a material obstacle to improvement, since, assuming both the Houses to be representative, and equal in their numbers, a number slightly exceeding a fourth of the entire representation may prevent the passing of a Bill; while, if there is but one House, a Bill is secure of passing if it has a bare majority. But the case supposed is rather abstractedly possible than likely to occur in practice. It will not often happen that of two Houses similarly composed, one will be almost unanimous, and the other nearly equally divided: if a majority in one rejects a measure, there will generally have been a large minority unfavourable to it in the other; any improvement, therefore, which could be thus impeded, would in almost all cases be one which had not much more than a simple majority in the entire body, and the worst consequence that could ensue would be to delay for a short time the passing of the measure, or give rise to a fresh appeal to the electors to ascertain if the small majority in Parliament corresponded to an effective one in the country. The inconvenience of delay, and the advantage of the appeal to the nation, might be regarded in this case as about equally balanced.

I attach little weight to the argument oftenest urged for having two Chambers—to prevent precipitancy, and compel a second deliberation; for it must be a very ill-constituted representative assembly in which the established forms of business do not require many more than two deliberations. The consideration which tells most, in my judgement, in favour of two Chambers (and this I do regard as of some moment) is the evil effect produced upon the mind of any holder of power, whether an individual or an assembly, by the consciousness of having only themselves to consult. It is important that no set of persons should, in great affairs, be able, even temporarily, to make their *sic volo* prevail, without asking any one else for his consent. A majority in a single assembly, when it has assumed a permanent character—when composed of the same persons habitually acting together, and always assured of victory in their own House—easily becomes despotic and overweening, if released from the necessity of considering whether its acts will be concurred in by another constituted authority. The same reason which induced the Romans to have two consuls, makes it desirable there should be two Chambers: that neither of them may be exposed to the corrupting influence of undivided power, even for the space of a single year. One of the most indispensable requisites in the practical conduct of politics, especially in the management of free institutions, is conciliation: a readiness to compromise; a willingness to concede something to opponents, and to shape good measures so as to be as little offensive as possible to persons of opposite views; and of this salutary habit, the mutual give and take (as it has been called) between two Houses is a perpetual school; useful as such even now, and its utility would probably be even more felt, in a more democratic constitution of the Legislature.

But the Houses need not both be of the same composition; they may be intended as a check on one another. One being supposed democratic, the other will naturally be constituted with a view to its being some restraint upon the democracy. But its efficacy in this respect, wholly depends on the social support which it can command outside the House. An assembly which does not rest on the basis of some great power in the country, is ineffectual against one which does. An aristocratic House is only powerful in an aristocratic state of society. The House of Lords was once the strongest power in our Constitution, and the Commons only a checking body: but this was when the Barons were almost the only power out of doors. I cannot believe that, in a really democratic state of society, the House of Lords would be of any practical value as a moderator of democracy. When the force on one side is feeble in comparison with that on the other, the way to give it effect is not to draw both out in line, and muster their strength in open field over against one another. Such tactics would ensure the utter defeat of the less powerful. It can only act to advantage, by not holding itself apart, and compelling every one to declare himself either with or against it, but taking a position among, rather than in opposition to, the crowd, and drawing to itself the elements most capable of allying themselves with it on any given point; not appearing at all as an antagonist body, to provoke a general rally against it, but working as one of the elements in a mixed mass, infusing its leaven, and often making what would be the weaker part the stronger, by the addition of its influence. The really moderating power in a democratic constitution, must act in and through the democratic House.

That there should be, in every polity, a centre of resistance to the predominant power in the Constitution—and in a democratic constitution, therefore, a nucleus of resistance to the democracy—I have already maintained ; and I regard it as a fundamental maxim of government. If any people, who possess a democratic representation, are, from their historical antecedents, more willing to tolerate such a centre of resistance in the form of a Second Chamber or House of Lords than in any other shape, this constitutes a strong reason for having it in that shape. But it does not appear to me the best shape in itself, nor by any means the most efficacious for its object. If there are two Houses, one considered to represent the people, the other to represent only a class, or not to be representative at all, I cannot think that where democracy is the ruling power in society, the second House would have any real ability to resist even the aberrations of the first. It might be suffered to exist, in deference to habit and association, but not as an effective check. If it exercised an independent will, it would be required to do so in the same general spirit as the other House ; to be equally democratic with it, and to content itself with correcting the accidental oversights of the more popular branch of the Legislature, or competing with it in popular measures.

The practicability of any real check to the ascendancy of the majority, depends henceforth on the distribution of strength in the most popular branch of the governing body : and I have indicated the mode in which, to the best of my judgement, a balance of forces might most advantageously be established there. I have also pointed out, that even if the numerical majority were allowed to exercise complete predominance by means of a corresponding majority in Parliament, yet if minorities also are permitted to enjoy the equal right due to them on strictly democratic principles, of being represented proportionately to their numbers, this provision will ensure the perpetual presence in the House, by the same popular title as its

other members, of so many of the first intellects in
the country, that without being in any way banded
apart, or invested with any invidious prerogative, this
portion of the national representation will have a personal weight much more than in proportion to its
numerical strength, and will afford, in a most effective
form, the moral centre of resistance which is needed.
A second Chamber, therefore, is not required for this
purpose, and would not contribute to it, but might
even, in some conceivable modes, impede its attainment. If, however, for the other reasons already
mentioned, the decision were taken that there should
be such a Chamber, it is desirable that it should be
composed of elements which, without being open to
the imputation of class interests adverse to the majority,
would incline it to oppose itself to the class interests
of the majority, and qualify it to raise its voice with
authority against their errors and weaknesses. These
conditions evidently are not found in a body constituted in the manner of our House of Lords. So soon
as conventional rank and individual riches no longer
overawe the democracy, a House of Lords becomes
insignificant.

Of all principles on which a wisely conservative
body, destined to moderate and regulate democratic
ascendancy, could possibly be constructed, the best
seems to be that exemplified in the Roman Senate,
itself the most consistently prudent and sagacious body
that ever administered public affairs. The deficiencies
of a democratic assembly, which represents the general
public, are the deficiencies of the public itself, want of
special training and knowledge. The appropriate corrective is to associate with it a body of which special
training and knowledge should be the characteristics.
If one House represents popular feeling, the other
should represent personal merit, tested and guaranteed
by actual public service, and fortified by practical
experience. If one is the People's Chamber, the other
should be the Chamber of Statesmen; a council composed of all living public men who have passed through

important political offices or employments. Such a chamber would be fitted for much more than to be a merely moderating body. It would not be exclusively a check, but also an impelling force. In its hands, the power of holding the people back would be vested in those most competent, and who would generally be most inclined, to lead them forward in any right course. The council to whom the task would be entrusted of rectifying the people's mistakes, would not represent a class believed to be opposed to their interest, but would consist of their own natural leaders in the path of progress. No mode of composition could approach to this in giving weight and efficacy to their function of moderators. It would be impossible to cry down a body always foremost in promoting improvements, as a mere obstructive body, whatever amount-of mischief it might obstruct.

Were the place vacant in England for such a Senate (I need scarcely say that this is a mere hypothesis), it might be composed of some such elements as the following. All who were or had been members of the Legislative Commission described in a former chapter, and which I regard as an indispensable ingredient in a well-constituted popular government. All who were or had been Chief Justices, or heads of any of the superior courts of law or equity. All who had for five years filled the office of puisne judge. All who had held for two years any Cabinet office : but these should also be eligible to the House of Commons, and if elected members of it, their peerage or senatorial office should be held in suspense. The condition of time is needed to prevent persons from being named Cabinet Ministers merely to give them a seat in the Senate ; and the period of two years is suggested, that the same term which qualifies them for a pension might entitle them to a senatorship. All who had filled the office of Commander-in-Chief ; and all who, having commanded an army or a fleet, had been thanked by Parliament for military or naval successes. All who had held, during ten years, first-class diplomatic appointments.

All who had been Governors-General of India or British America, and all who had held for ten years any Colonial Governorships. The permanent civil service should also be represented ; all should be senators who had filled, during ten years, the important offices of Under-Secretary to the Treasury, permanent Under-Secretary of State, or any others equally high and responsible. If, along with the persons thus qualified by practical experience in the administration of public affairs, any representation of the speculative class were to be included—a thing in itself desirable—it would be worth consideration whether certain professorships, in certain national institutions, after a tenure of a few years, might confer a seat in the Senate. Mere scientific and literary eminence are too indefinite and disputable : they imply a power of selection, whereas the other qualifications speak for themselves ; if the writings by which reputation has been gained are unconnected with politics, they are no evidence of the special qualities required, while if political, they would enable successive Ministries to deluge the House with party tools.

The historical antecedents of England render it all but certain, that unless in the improbable case of a violent subversion of the existing Constitution, any second Chamber which could possibly exist would have to be built on the foundation of the House of Lords. It is out of the question to think practically of abolishing that assembly, to replace it by such a Senate as I have sketched, or by any other ; but there might not be the same insuperable difficulty in aggregating the classes or categories just spoken of to the existing body, in the character of Peers for life. An ulterior, and perhaps, on this supposition, a necessary step, might be, that the hereditary peerage should be present in the House by their representatives instead of personally; a practice already established in the case of the Scotch and Irish Peers, and which the mere multiplication of the order will probably at some time or other render inevitable. An easy adaptation of

Mr. Hare's plan would prevent the representative Peers from representing exclusively the party which has the majority in the Peerage. If, for example, one representative were allowed for every ten peers, any ten might be admitted to choose a representative, and the peers might be free to group themselves for that purpose as they pleased. The election might be thus conducted : All peers who were candidates for the representation of their order should be required to declare themselves such, and enter their names in a list. A day and place should be appointed at which peers desirous of voting should be present, either in person, or, in the usual parliamentary manner, by their proxies. The votes should be taken, each peer voting for only one. Every candidate who had as many as ten votes should be declared elected. If any one had more, all but ten should be allowed to withdraw their votes, or ten of the number should be selected by lot. These ten would form his constituency, and the remainder of his voters would be set free to give their votes over again for some one else. This process should be repeated until (so far as possible) every peer present either personally or by proxy was represented. When a number less than ten remained over, if amounting to five they might still be allowed to agree on a representative ; if fewer than five, their votes must be lost, or they might be permitted to record them in favour of somebody already elected. With this inconsiderable exception, every representative peer would represent ten members of the peerage, all of whom had not only voted for him, but selected him as the one, among all open to their choice, by whom they were most desirous to be represented. As a compensation to the peers who were not chosen representatives of their order, they should be eligible to the House of Commons ; a justice now refused to Scotch peers, and to Irish peers in their own part of the kingdom, while the representation in the House of Lords of any but the most numerous party in the peerage is denied equally to both.

The mode of composing a Senate, which has been here advocated, not only seems the best in itself, but is that for which historical precedent, and actual brilliant success, can to the greatest extent be pleaded. It is not, however, the only feasible plan that might be proposed. Another possible mode of forming a Second Chamber, would be to have it elected by the First; subject to the restriction, that they should not nominate any of their own members. Such an assembly, emanating like the American Senate from popular choice, only once removed, would not be considered to clash with democratic institutions, and would probably acquire considerable popular influence. From the mode of its nomination it would be peculiarly unlikely to excite the jealousy of, or to come into any hostile collision with, the popular House. It would, moreover (due provision being made for the representation of the minority), be almost sure to be well composed, and to comprise many of that class of highly capable men, who, either from accident or for want of showy qualities, had been unwilling to seek, or unable to obtain, the suffrages of a popular constituency.

The best constitution of a Second Chamber, is that which embodies the greatest number of elements exempt from the class interests and prejudices of the majority, but having in themselves nothing offensive to democratic feeling. I repeat, however, that the main reliance for tempering the ascendancy of the majority cannot be placed in a Second Chamber of any kind. The character of a representative government is fixed by the constitution of the popular House. Compared with this, all other questions relating to the form of government are insignificant.

CHAPTER XIV

OF THE EXECUTIVE IN A REPRESENTATIVE GOVERNMENT

It would be out of place, in this treatise, to discuss the question into what departments or branches the executive business of government may most conveniently be divided. In this respect the exigencies of different governments are different; and there is little probability that any great mistake will be made in the classification of the duties, when men are willing to begin at the beginning, and do not hold themselves bound by the series of accidents which, in an old government like ours, has produced the existing division of the public business. It may be sufficient to say, that the classification of functionaries should correspond to that of subjects, and that there should not be several departments independent of one another, to superintend different parts of the same natural whole; as in our own military administration down to a recent period, and in a less degree even at present. Where the object to be attained is single (such as that of having an efficient army), the authority commissioned to attend to it should be single likewise. The entire aggregate of means provided for one end, should be under one and the same control and responsibility. If they are divided among independent authorities, the means, with each of those authorities, become ends, and it is the business of nobody except the head of the Government, who is probably without the appropriate departmental experience, to take care of the real end. The different classes of means are not combined and adapted to one another under the guidance of any leading idea; and while every department pushes forward its own requirements, regardless of those of the rest, the purpose of the work is perpetually sacrificed to the work itself.

As a general rule, every executive function, whether superior or subordinate, should be the appointed duty of some given individual. It should be apparent to all the world, who did everything, and through whose default anything was left undone. Responsibility is null, when nobody knows who is responsible. Nor, even when real, can it be divided without being weakened. To maintain it at its highest, there must be one person who receives the whole praise of what is well done, the whole blame of what is ill. There are, however, two modes of sharing responsibility : by one it is only enfeebled, by the other, absolutely destroyed. It is enfeebled, when the concurrence of more than one functionary is required to the same act. Each one among them has still a real responsibility ; if a wrong has been done, none of them can say he did not do it ; he is as much a participant, as an accomplice is in an offence : if there has been legal criminality they may all be punished legally, and their punishment needs not be less severe than if there had been only one person concerned. But it is not so with the penalties, any more than with the rewards, of opinion : these are always diminished by being shared. Where there has been no definite legal offence, no corruption or malversation, only an error or an imprudence, or what may pass for such, every participator has an excuse to himself and to the world, in the fact that other persons are jointly involved with him. There is hardly anything, even to pecuniary dishonesty, for which men will not feel themselves almost absolved, if those whose duty it was to resist and remonstrate have failed to do it, still more if they have given a formal assent.

In this case, however, though responsibility is weakened, there still is responsibility : every one of those implicated has in his individual capacity assented to, and joined in, the act. Things are much worse when the act itself is only that of a majority—a Board, deliberating with closed doors, nobody knowing, or, except in some extreme case, being ever likely to

know, whether an individual member voted for the
act or against it. Responsibility in this case is a mere
name. ' Boards,' it is happily said by Bentham, ' are
screens.' What ' the Board ' does is the act of nobody ;
and nobody can be made to answer for it. The Board
suffers, even in reputation, only in its collective
character; and no individual member feels this;
further than his disposition leads him to identify
his own estimation with that of the body—a
feeling often very strong when the body is a permanent one, and he is wedded to it for better for
worse ; but the fluctuations of a modern official career
give no time for the formation of such an *esprit de
corps* ; which, if it exists at all, exists only in the
obscure ranks of the permanent subordinates. Boards,
therefore, are not a fit instrument for executive business ; and are only admissible in it, when, for other
reasons, to give full discretionary power to a single
minister would be worse.

On the other hand, it is also a maxim of experience,
that in the multitude of counsellors there is wisdom ;
and that a man seldom judges right, even in his own
concerns, still less in those of the public, when he
makes habitual use of no knowledge but his own, or
that of some single adviser. There is no necessary
incompatibility between this principle and the other.
It is easy to give the effective power, and the full
responsibility, to one, providing him when necessary
with advisers, each of whom is responsible only for
the opinion he gives.

In general, the head of a department of the executive
government is a mere politician. He may be a good
politician, and a man of merit ; and unless this is
usually the case, the government is bad. But his
general capacity, and the knowledge he ought to
possess of the general interests of the country, will
not, unless by occasional accident, be accompanied by
adequate, and what may be called professional, knowledge of the department over which he is called to
preside. Professional advisers must therefore be pro-

vided for him. Wherever mere experience and attainments are sufficient—wherever the qualities required in a professional adviser may possibly be united in a single well-selected individual (as in the case, for example, of a law officer), one such person for general purposes, and a staff of clerks to supply knowledge of details, meet the demands of the case. But, more frequently, it is not sufficient that the minister should consult some one competent person, and, when himself not conversant with the subject, act implicitly on that person's advice. It is often necessary that he should, not only occasionally but habitually, listen to a variety of opinions, and inform his judgement by the discussions among a body of advisers. This, for example, is emphatically necessary in military and naval affairs. The military and naval ministers, therefore, and probably several others, should be provided with a Council, composed, at least in those two departments, of able and experienced professional men. As a means of obtaining the best men for the purpose under every change of administration, they ought to be permanent: by which I mean, that they ought not, like the Lords of the Admiralty, to be expected to resign with the ministry by whom they were appointed: but it is a good rule that all who hold high appointments to which they have risen by selection, and not by the ordinary course of promotion, should retain their office only for a fixed term, unless reappointed; as is now the rule with Staff appointments in the British Army. This rule renders appointments somewhat less likely to be jobbed, not being a provision for life, and at the same time affords a means, without affront to any one, of getting rid of those who are least worth keeping, and bringing in highly qualified persons of younger standing, for whom there might never be room if death vacancies, or voluntary resignations, were waited for.

The Councils should be consultative merely, in this sense, that the ultimate decision should rest undividedly with the minister himself: but neither ought they to be looked upon, or to look upon themselves, as ciphers, or as capable of being reduced to such at his pleasure. The advisers attached to a powerful and perhaps self-willed man, ought to be placed under conditions which make it impossible for them, without discredit, not to express an opinion, and impossible for him not to listen to and consider their recommendations, whether he adopts them or not. The relation which ought to exist between a chief and this description of advisers is very accurately hit by the constitution of the Council of the Governor-General and those of the different Presidencies in India. These Councils are composed of persons who have professional knowledge of Indian affairs, which the Governor-General and Governors usually lack, and which it would not be desirable to require of them. As a rule, every member of Council is expected to give an opinion, which is of course very often a simple acquiescence : but if there is a difference of sentiment, it is at the option of every member, and is the invariable practice, to record the reasons of his opinion: the Governor-General, or Governor, doing the same. In ordinary cases the decision is according to the sense of the majority ; the Council, therefore, has a substantial part in the government : but if the Governor-General, or Governor, thinks fit, he may set aside even their unanimous opinion, recording his reasons. The result is, that the chief is individually and effectively responsible for every act of the Government. The members of Council have only the responsibility of advisers ; but it is always known, from documents capable of being produced, and which if called for by Parliament or public opinion always are produced, what each has advised, and what reasons he gave for his advice : while, from their dignified position, and ostensible participation in all acts of government, they have nearly as strong motives to apply themselves to the public business, and to form and express a well considered opinion on every part of it. as if the whole responsibility rested with themselves.

This mode of conducting the highest class of administrative business is one of the most successful instances of the adaptation of means to ends, which political history, not hitherto very prolific in works of skill and contrivance, has yet to show. It is one of the acquisitions with which the art of politics has been enriched by the experience of the East India Company's rule ; and, like most of the other wise contrivances by which India has been preserved to this country, and an amount of good government produced which is truly wonderful considering the circumstances and the materials, it is probably destined to perish in the general holocaust which the traditions of Indian government seem fated to undergo, since they have been placed at the mercy of public ignorance, and the presumptuous vanity of political men. Already an outcry is raised for abolishing the Councils, as a superfluous and expensive clog on the wheels of government: while the clamour has long been urgent, and is daily obtaining more countenance in the highest quarters, for the abrogation of the professional civil service, which breeds the men that compose the Councils, and the existence of which is the sole guarantee for their being of any value.

A most important principle of good government in a popular constitution, is that no executive functionaries should be appointed by popular election: neither by the votes of the people themselves, nor by those of their representatives. The entire business of government is skilled employment ; the qualifications for the discharge of it are of that special and professional kind, which cannot be properly judged of except by persons who have themselves some share of those qualifications, or some practical experience of them. The business of finding the fittest persons to fill public employments—not merely selecting the best who offer, but looking out for the absolutely best, and taking note of all fit persons who are met with, that they may be found when wanted—is very laborious, and requires a delicate as well as highly conscientious discernment; and as there is no public duty which is in general so badly performed, so there is none for which it is of greater importance to enforce the utmost practicable amount of personal responsibility, by imposing it as a special obligation on high functionaries in the several departments. All subordinate public officers who are not appointed by some mode of public competition, should be selected on the direct responsibility of the minister under whom they serve. The ministers, all but the chief, will naturally be selected by the chief; and the chief himself, though really designated by Parliament, should be, in a regal government, officially appointed by the Crown. The functionary who appoints should be the sole person empowered to remove any subordinate officer who is liable to removal; which the far greater number ought not to be, except for personal misconduct; since it would be vain to expect that the body of persons by whom the whole detail of the public business is transacted, and whose qualifications are generally of much more importance to the public than those of the minister himself, will devote themselves to their profession, and acquire the knowledge and skill on which the minister must often place entire dependence, if they are liable at any moment to be turned adrift for no fault, that the minister may gratify himself, or promote his political interest, by appointing somebody else.

To the principle which condemns the appointment of executive officers by popular suffrage, ought the chief of the executive, in a republican government, to be an exception? Is it a good rule, which, in the American constitution, provides for the election of the President once in every four years by the entire people? The question is not free from difficulty. There is unquestionably some advantage, in a country like America, where no apprehension needs be entertained of a *coup d'état*, in making the chief minister constitutionally independent of the legislative body, and rendering the two great branches of the government, while equally popular both in their origin and in their responsibility, an effective check on one another. The plan is in accordance with that sedulous avoidance of the concentration of great masses of power in the same hands, which is a marked characteristic of the American Federal Constitution. But the advantage, in this instance, is purchased at a price above all reasonable estimate of its value. It seems far better that the chief magistrate in a republic should be appointed avowedly, as the chief minister in a constitutional monarchy is virtually, by the representative body. In the first place, he is certain, when thus appointed, to be a more eminent man. The party which has the majority in Parliament would then, as a rule, appoint its own leader; who is always one of the foremost, and often the very foremost person in political life: while the President of the United States, since the last survivor of the founders of the republic disappeared from the scene, is almost always either an obscure man, or one who has gained any reputation he may possess in some other field than politics. And this, as I have before observed, is no accident, but the natural effect of the situation. The eminent men of a party, in an election extending to the whole country, are never its most available candidates. All eminent men have made personal enemies, or have done something, or at the lowest professed some opinion, obnoxious to some local or other considerable division of the community, and likely to tell with fatal effect upon the number of votes; whereas a man without antecedents, of whom nothing is known but that he professes the creed of the party, is readily voted for by its entire strength. Another important consideration is the great mischief of unintermitted electioneering. When the highest dignity in the State is to be conferred by popular election once in every few years, the whole intervening time is spent in what is virtually a canvass. President, ministers, chiefs of parties, and their followers, are all electioneerers: the whole community is kept intent on the mere personalities of politics, and every public question is discussed and decided with less reference to its merits than to its expected bearing on the presidential election. If a system had been devised to make party spirit the ruling principle of action in all public affairs, and create an inducement not only to make every question a party question, but to raise questions for the purpose of founding parties upon them, it would have been difficult to contrive any means better adapted to the purpose.

I will not affirm that it would at all times and places be desirable, that the head of the executive should be so completely dependent upon the votes of a representative assembly as the Prime Minister is in England, and is without inconvenience. If it were thought best to avoid this, he might, though appointed by Parliament, hold his office for a fixed period, independent of a parliamentary vote : which would be the American system, minus the popular election and its evils. There is another mode of giving the head of the administration as much independence of the Legislature, as is at all compatible with the essentials of free government. He never could be unduly dependent on a vote of Parliament, if he had, as the British Prime Minister practically has, the power to dissolve the House and appeal to the people : if instead of being turned out of office by a hostile vote, he could only be reduced by it to the alternative of resignation or dissolution. The power of dissolving Parliament is one which I think it desirable he should possess, even under the system by which his own tenure of office is secured to him for a fixed period. There ought not to be any possibility of that deadlock in politics, which would ensue on a quarrel breaking out between a President and an Assembly, neither of whom, during an interval which might amount to years, would have any legal means of ridding itself of the other. To get through such a period without a *coup d'état* being attempted, on either side or on both, requires such a combination of the love of liberty and the habit of self-restraint, as very few nations have yet shown themselves capable of : and though this extremity were avoided, to expect that the two authorities would not paralyse each other's operations, is to suppose that the political life of the country will always be pervaded by a spirit of mutual forbearance and compromise, imperturbable by the passions and excitements of the keenest party struggles. Such a spirit may exist, but even where it does, there is imprudence in trying it too far.

Other reasons make it desirable that some power in the state (which can only be the executive) should have the liberty of at any time, and at discretion, calling a new parliament. When there is a real doubt which of two contending parties has the strongest following, it is important that there should exist a constitutional means of immediately testing the point, and setting it at rest. No other political topic has a chance of being properly attended to while this is undecided : and such an interval is mostly an interregnum for purposes of legislative or administrative improvement ; neither party having sufficient confidence in its strength, to attempt things likely to promote opposition in any quarter that has either direct or indirect influence in the pending struggle.

I have not taken account of the case in which the vast power centralized in the chief magistrate, and the insufficient attachment of the mass of the people to free institutions, give him a chance of success in an attempt to subvert the Constitution, and usurp sovereign power. Where such peril exists, no first magistrate is admissible whom the Parliament cannot, by a single vote, reduce to a private station. In a state of things holding out any encouragement to that most audacious and profligate of all breaches of trust, even this entireness of constitutional dependence is but a weak protection.

Of all officers of government, those in whose appointment any participation of popular suffrage is the most objectionable, are judicial officers. While there are no functionaries whose special and professional qualifications the popular judgement is less fitted to estimate, there are none in whose case absolute impartiality, and freedom from connexion with politicians or sections of politicians, are of anything like equal importance. Some thinkers, among others Mr. Bentham, have been of opinion that, although it is better that judges should not be appointed by popular election, the people of their district ought to have the power, after sufficient experience, of removing them from their trust. It cannot be denied that the irremovability of any public officer, to whom great interests are entrusted, is in itself an evil. It is far from desirable that there should be no means of getting rid of a bad or incompetent judge, unless for such misconduct as he can be made to answer for in a criminal court; and that a functionary on whom so much depends, should have the feeling of being free from responsibility except to opinion and his own conscience. The question, however, is, whether in the peculiar position of a judge, and supposing that all practicable securities have been taken for an honest appointment, irresponsibility, except to his own and the public conscience, has not on the whole, less tendency to pervert his conduct, than responsibility to the government, or to a popular vote. Experience has long decided this point in the affirmative, as regards responsibility to the executive ; and the case is quite equally strong when the responsibility sought to be enforced is to the suffrages of electors. Among the good qualities of a popular constituency, those peculiarly incumbent upon a judge, calmness and impartiality, are not numbered. Happily, in that intervention of popular suffrage which is essential to freedom, they are not the qualities required. Even the quality of justice, though necessary to all human beings, and therefore to all electors, is not the inducement which decides any popular election. Justice and impartiality are as little wanted for electing a member of Parliament, as they can be in any transaction of men. The electors have not to award something which either candidate has a right to, nor to pass judgement on the general merits of the competitors, but to declare which of them has most of their personal confidence, or best represents their political convictions. A judge is bound to treat his political friend, or the person best known to him, exactly as he treats other people ; but it would be a breach of duty as well as an absurdity if an elector did so. No argument can be grounded on the beneficial effect produced on judges, as on all other functionaries, by the moral jurisdiction of opinion; for even in this respect, that which really exercises a useful control over the proceedings of a judge, when fit for the judicial office, is not (except sometimes in political cases) the opinion of the community generally, but that of the only public by whom his conduct or qualifications can be duly estimated, the bar of his own court. I must not be understood to say that the participation of the general public in the administration of justice is of no importance ; it is of the greatest : but in what manner ? By the actual discharge of a part of the judicial office, in the capacity of jurymen. This is one of the few cases in politics, in which it is better that the people should act directly and personally than through their representatives ; being almost the only case in which the errors that a person exercising authority may commit, can be better borne than the consequences of making him responsible for them. If a judge could be removed from office by a popular vote, whoever was desirous of supplanting him would make capital for that purpose out of all his judicial decisions ; would carry all of them, as far as he found practicable, by irregular appeal before a public opinion wholly incompetent, for want of having heard the case, or from having heard it without either the precautions or the impartiality belonging to a judicial hearing ; would play upon popular passion and prejudice where they existed, and take pains to arouse them where they did not. And in this, if the case were interesting, and he took sufficient trouble, he would infallibly be successful, unless the judge or his friends descended into the arena, and made equally powerful appeals on the other side.   Judges would end by feeling that they risked their office upon every decision they gave in a case susceptible of general interest, and that it was less essential for them to consider what decision was just, than what would be most applauded by the public, or would least admit of insidious misrepresentation.   The practice introduced by some of the new or revised State Constitutions in America, of submitting judicial officers to periodical popular re-election, will be found, I apprehend, to be one of the most dangerous errors ever yet committed by democracy : and, were it not that the practical good sense which never totally deserts the people of the United States, is said to be producing a reaction, likely in no long time to lead to the retractation of the error, it might with reason be regarded as the first great downward step in the degeneration of modern democratic government.[1]

With regard to that large and important body which constitutes the permanent strength of the public service, those who do not change with changes of politics, but remain, to aid every minister by their experience and traditions, inform him by their knowledge of business, and conduct official details under his general control ; those, in short, who form the class of professional

---

[1] I have been informed, however, that in the States which have made their judges elective, the choice is not really made by the people, but by the leaders of parties ; no elector ever thinking of voting for any one but the party candidate : and that, in consequence, the person elected is usually in effect the same who would have been appointed to the office by the President or by the Governor of the State.   Thus one bad practice limits and corrects another ; and the habit of voting *en masse* under a party banner, which is so full of evil in all cases in which the function of electing is rightly vested in the people, tends to alleviate a still greater mischief in a case where the officer to be elected is one who *ought* to be chosen not by the people but for them.

public servants, entering their profession as others do while young, in the hope of rising progressively to its higher grades as they advance in life ; it is evidently inadmissible that these should be liable to be turned out, and deprived of the whole benefit of their previous service, except for positive, proved, and serious misconduct. Not, of course, such delinquency only as makes them amenable to the law ; but voluntary neglect of duty, or conduct implying untrustworthiness for the purposes for which their trust is given them. Since, therefore, unless in case of personal culpability, there is no way of getting rid of them except by quartering them on the public as pensioners, it is of the greatest importance that the appointments should be well made in the first instance ; and it remains to be considered, by what mode of appointment this purpose can best be attained.

In making first appointments, little danger is to be apprehended from want of special skill and knowledge in the choosers, but much from partiality, and private or political interest. Being, as a rule, appointed at the commencement of manhood, not as having learnt, but in order that they may learn, their profession, the only thing by which the best candidates can be discriminated, is proficiency in the ordinary branches of liberal education : and this can be ascertained without difficulty, provided there be the requisite pains and the requisite impartiality in those who are appointed to inquire into it. Neither the one nor the other can reasonably be expected from a minister ; who must rely wholly on recommendations, and however disinterested as to his personal wishes, never will be proof against the solicitations of persons who have the power of influencing his own election, or whose political adherence is important to the ministry to which he belongs. These considerations have introduced the practice of submitting all candidates for first appointments to a public examination, conducted by persons not engaged in politics, and of the same class and quality with the examiners for honours at the Universities. This would probably be the best plan under any system; and under our parliamentary government it is the only one which affords a chance, I do not say of honest appointment, but even of abstinence from such as are manifestly and flagrantly profligate.

It is also absolutely necessary that the examinations should be competitive, and the appointments given to those who are most successful. A mere pass examination never, in the long run, does more than exclude absolute dunces. When the question, in the mind of an examiner, lies between blighting the prospects of an individual, and neglecting a duty to the public which, in the particular instance, seldom appears of first-rate importance; and when he is sure to be bitterly reproached for doing the first, while in general no one will either know or care whether he has done the latter; the balance, unless he is a man of very unusual stamp, inclines to the side of good nature. A relaxation in one instance establishes a claim to it in others, which every repetition of indulgence makes it more difficult to resist; each of these in succession becomes a precedent for more, until the standard of proficiency sinks gradually to something almost contemptible. Examinations for degrees at the two great Universities have generally been as slender in their requirements, as those for honours are trying and serious. Where there is no inducement to exceed a certain minimum, the minimum comes to be the maximum: it becomes the general practice not to aim at more, and as in everything there are some who do not attain all they aim at, however low the standard may be pitched there are always several who fall short of it. When, on the contrary, the appointments are given to those, among a great number of candidates, who most distinguish themselves, and where the successful competitors are classed in order of merit, not only each is stimulated to do his very utmost, but the influence is felt in every place of liberal education throughout the country. It becomes with every schoolmaster an object of ambition, and an avenue to success, to have furnished pupils who have gained a high place in these competitions; and there is hardly any other mode in which the State can do so much to raise the quality of educational institutions throughout the country. Though the principle of competitive examinations for public employment is of such recent introduction in this country, and is still so imperfectly carried out, the Indian service being as yet nearly the only case in which it exists in its completeness, a sensible effect has already begun to be produced on the places of middle-class education; notwithstanding the difficulties which the principle has encountered from the disgracefully low existing state of education in the country, which these very examinations have brought into strong light. So contemptible has the standard of acquirement been found to be, among the youths who obtain the nomination from the minister, which entitles them to offer themselves as candidates, that the competition of such candidates produces almost a poorer result, than would be obtained from a mere pass examination; for no one would think of fixing the conditions of a pass examination so low, as is actually found sufficient to enable a young man to surpass his fellow candidates. Accordingly, it is said that successive years show on the whole a decline of attainments, less effort being made, because the results of former examinations have proved that the exertions then used were greater than would have been sufficient to attain the object. Partly from this decrease of effort, and partly because, even at the examinations which do not require a previous nomination, conscious ignorance reduces the number of competitors to a mere handful, it has so happened that though there have always been a few instances of great proficiency, the lower part of the list of successful candidates represents but a very moderate amount of acquirement; and we have it on the word of the Commissioners that nearly all who have been unsuccessful have owed their failure to ignorance not of the higher branches of instruction, but of its very humblest elements—spelling and arithmetic.

The outcries which continue to be made against these examinations, by some of the organs of opinion, are often, I regret to say, as little creditable to the good faith as to the good sense of the assailants. They proceed partly by misrepresentation of the kind of ignorance, which, as a matter of fact, actually leads to failure in the examinations. They quote with emphasis the most recondite questions [1] which can be shown to have been ever asked, and make it appear as if unexceptionable answers to all these were made the *sine qua non* of success. Yet it has been repeated to satiety, that such questions are not put because it is expected of every one that he should answer them, but in order that whoever is able to do so may have the means of proving and availing himself of that portion of his knowledge. It is not as a ground of rejection, but as an additional means of success, that this opportunity is given. We are then asked whether the kind of knowledge supposed in this, that, or the other question, is calculated to be of any use to the candidate after he has attained his object. People differ greatly in opinion as to what knowledge is useful. There are persons in existence, and a late Foreign Secretary of State is one of them, who think English spelling a useless accomplishment in a diplomatic attaché, or a clerk in a Government office. About one thing the objectors seem to be unanimous, that general mental cultivation is not useful in these employments, whatever else may be so. If, however (as I presume to think), it is useful, or if any education at all is useful, it must be tested by the tests most likely to show whether the candidate possesses it or not. To ascertain whether he has been well educated, he must be interrogated in the things which he is likely to

[1] Not always, however, the most recondite ; for a late denouncer of competitive examination in the House of Commons had the *naïveté* to produce a set of almost elementary questions in algebra, history, and geography, as a proof of the exorbitant amount of high scientific attainment which the Commissioners were so wild as to exact.

know if he has been well educated, even though not directly pertinent to the work to which he is to be appointed. Will those who object to his being questioned in classics and mathematics, in a country where the only things regularly taught are classics and mathematics, tell us what they would have him questioned in ? There seems, however, to be equal objection to examining him in these, and to examining him in anything *but* these. If the Commissioners—anxious to open a door of admission to those who have not gone through the routine of a grammar school, or who make up for the smallness of their knowledge of what is there taught, by greater knowledge of something else—allow marks to be gained by proficiency in any other subject of real utility, they are reproached for that too. Nothing will satisfy the objectors, but free admission of total ignorance.

We are triumphantly told, that neither Clive nor Wellington could have passed the test which is prescribed for an aspirant to an engineer cadetship. As if, because Clive and Wellington did not do what was not required of them, they could not have done it if it had been required. If it be only meant to inform us that it is possible to be a great general without these things, so it is without many other things which are very useful to great generals. Alexander the Great had never heard of Vauban's rules, nor could Julius Caesar speak French. We are next informed that bookworms, a term which seems to be held applicable to whoever has the smallest tincture of book-knowledge, may not be good at bodily exercises, or have the habits of gentlemen. This is a very common line of remark with dunces of condition; but whatever the dunces may think, they have no monopoly of either gentlemanly habits or bodily activity. Wherever these are needed, let them be inquired into, and separately provided for, not to the exclusion of mental qualifications, but in addition. Meanwhile, I am credibly informed, that in the Military Academy at Woolwich, the competition cadets are as superior to those admitted on the old system of nomination in these respects as in all others; that they learn even their drill more quickly; as indeed might be expected, for an intelligent person learns all things sooner than a stupid one: and that in general demeanour they contrast so favourably with their predecessors, that the authorities of the institution are impatient for the day to arrive when the last remains of the old leaven shall have disappeared from the place. If this be so, and it is easy to ascertain whether it is so, it is to be hoped we shall soon have heard for the last time that ignorance is a better qualification than knowledge, for the military, and *a fortiori* for every other, profession; or that any one good-quality, however little apparently connected with liberal education, is at all likely to be promoted by going without it.

Though the first admission to government employment be decided by competitive examination, it would in most cases be impossible that subsequent promotion should be so decided: and it seems proper that this should take place, as it usually does at present, on a mixed system of seniority and selection. Those whose duties are of a routine character should rise by seniority to the highest point to which duties merely of that description can carry them; while those to whom functions of particular trust, and requiring special capacity, are confided, should be selected from the body on the discretion of the chief of the office. And this selection will generally be made honestly by him, if the original appointments take place by open competition: for under that system, his establishment will generally consist of individuals to whom, but for the official connexion, he would have been a stranger. If among them there be any in whom he, or his political friends and supporters, take an interest, it will be but occasionally, and only when, to this advantage of connexion, is added, as far as the initiatory examination could test it, at least equality of real merit. And, except when there is a very strong motive to job these appointments, there is always a strong one to appoint the fittest person; being the one who gives to his chief the most useful assistance, saves him most trouble, and helps most to build up that reputation for good management of public business, which necessarily and properly redounds to the credit of the minister, however much the qualities to which it is immediately owing may be those of his subordinates.

CHAPTER XV

OF LOCAL REPRESENTATIVE BODIES

It is but a small portion of the public business of a country, which can be well done, or safely attempted, by the central authorities; and even in our own government, the least centralized in Europe, the legislative portion at least of the governing body busies itself far too much with local affairs, employing the supreme power of the State in cutting small knots which there ought to be other and better means of untying. The enormous amount of private business which takes up the time of Parliament, and the thoughts of its individual members, distracting them from the proper occupations of the great council of the nation, is felt by all thinkers and observers as a serious evil, and what is worse, an increasing one.

It would not be appropriate to the limited design of this treatise, to discuss at large the great question, in no way peculiar to representative government, of the proper limits of governmental action. I have said elsewhere [1] what seemed to me most essential respecting the principles by which the extent of that action ought to be determined. But after subtracting from the functions performed by most European governments, those which ought not to be undertaken by public

[1] *On Liberty*, concluding chapter; and, at greater length, in the final chapter of *Principles of Political Economy*.

authorities at all, there still remains so great and various an aggregate of duties, that, if only on the principle of division of labour, it is indispensable to share them between central and local authorities. Not only are separate executive officers required for purely local duties (an amount of separation which exists under all governments), but the popular control over those officers can only be advantageously exerted through a separate organ. Their original appointment, the function of watching and checking them, the duty of providing, or the discretion of withholding, the supplies necessary for their operations, should rest, not with the national Parliament or the national executive, but with the people of the locality. In some of the New England States these functions are still exercised directly by the assembled people ; it is said, with better results than might be expected ; and those highly educated communities are so well satisfied with this primitive mode of local government, that they have no desire to exchange it for the only representative system they are acquainted with, by which all minorities are disfranchised. Such very peculiar circumstances, however, are required to make this arrangement work tolerably in practice, that recourse must generally be had to the plan of representative sub-Parliaments for local affairs. These exist in England, but very incompletely, and with great irregularity and want of system : in some other countries much less popularly governed, their constitution is far more rational. In England there has always been more liberty, but worse organization, while in other countries there is better organization, but less liberty. It is necessary, then, that in addition to the national representation, there should be municipal and provincial representations : and the two questions which remain to be resolved are, how the local representative bodies should be constituted, and what should be the extent of their functions.

In considering these questions, two points require an equal degree of our attention : how the local busi-

ness itself can be best done; and how its transaction
can be made most instrumental to the nourishment of
public spirit and the development of intelligence.   In
an earlier part of this inquiry, I have dwelt in strong
language—hardly any language is strong enough to
express the strength of my conviction—on the importance of that portion of the operation of free institutions, which may be called the public education of the
citizens.   Now, of this operation the local administrative institutions are the chief instrument.   Except by
the part they may take as jurymen in the administration of justice, the mass of the population have very
little opportunity of sharing personally in the conduct
of the general affairs of the community.   Reading
newspapers, and perhaps writing to them, public meet-
ings, and solicitations of different sorts addressed to
the political authorities, are the extent of the participation of private citizens in general politics, during
the interval between one parliamentary election and
another.   Though it is impossible to exaggerate the
importance of these various liberties, both as securities
for freedom and as means of general cultivation, the
practice which they give is more in thinking than in
action, and in thinking without the responsibilities of
action ; which with most people amounts to little more
than passively receiving the thoughts of some one else.
But in the case of local bodies, besides the function
of electing, many citizens in turn have the chance of
being elected, and many, either by selection or by
rotation, fill one or other of the numerous local executive offices.   In these positions they have to act, for
public interests, as well as to think and to speak, and
the thinking cannot all be done by proxy.   It may
be added, that these local functions, not being in
general sought by the higher ranks, carry down the
important political education which they are the means
of conferring, to a much lower grade in society.   The
mental discipline being thus a more important feature
in local concerns than in the general affairs of the
State, while there are not such vital interests depen-

dent on the quality of the administration, a greater weight may be given to the former consideration, and the latter admits much more frequently of being postponed to it, than in matters of general legislation, and the conduct of imperial affairs.

The proper constitution of local representative bodies does not present much difficulty. The principles which apply to it do not differ in any respect from those applicable to the national representation. The same obligation exists, as in the case of the more important function, for making the bodies elective ; and the same reasons operate as in that case, but with still greater force, for giving them a widely democratic basis : the dangers being less, and the advantages, in point of popular education and cultivation, in some respects even greater. As the principal duty of the local bodies consists of the imposition and expenditure of local taxation, the electoral franchise should vest in all who contribute to the local rates, to the exclusion of all who do not. I assume that there is no indirect taxation, no *octroi* duties, or that if there are, they are supplementary only ; those on whom their burthen falls being also rated to a direct assessment. The representation of minorities should be provided for in the same manner as in the national Parliament, and there are the same strong reasons for plurality of votes. Only, there is not so decisive an objection, in the inferior as in the higher body, to making the plural voting depend (as in some of the local elections of our own country) on a mere money qualification : for the honest and frugal dispensation of money forms so much larger a part of the business of the local, than of the national body, that there is more justice as well as policy in allowing a greater proportional influence to those who have a larger money interest at stake.

In the most recently established of our local representative institutions, the Boards of Guardians, the justices of peace of the district sit *ex officio* along with the elected members, in number limited by law to a third of the whole. In the peculiar constitution of

English society, I have no doubt of the beneficial effect of this provision. It secures the presence, in these bodies, of a more educated class than it would perhaps be practicable to attract thither on any other terms; and while the limitation in number of the *ex officio* members precludes them from acquiring predominance by mere numerical strength, they, as a virtual representation of another class, having sometimes a different interest from the rest, are a check upon the class interests of the farmers or petty shopkeepers who form the bulk of the elected Guardians. A similar commendation cannot be given to the constitution of the only provincial boards we possess, the Quarter Sessions, consisting of the justices of peace alone; on whom, over and above their judicial duties, some of the most important parts of the administrative business of the country depend for their performance. The mode of formation of these bodies is most anomalous, they being neither elected, nor, in any proper sense of the term, nominated, but holding their important functions, like the feudal lords to whom they succeeded, virtually by right of their acres: the appointment vested in the Crown (or, speaking practically, in one of themselves, the Lord Lieutenant) being made use of only as a means of excluding any one who it is thought would do discredit to the body, or, now and then, one who is on the wrong side in politics. The institution is the most aristocratic in principle which now remains in England; far more so than the House of Lords, for it grants public money and disposes of important public interests, not in conjunction with a popular assembly, but alone. It is clung to with proportionate tenacity by our aristocratic classes; but is obviously at variance with all the principles which are the foundation of representative government. In a County Board, there is not the same justification as in Boards of Guardians, for even an admixture of *ex officio* with elected members: since the business of a county being on a sufficiently large scale to be an object of interest and attraction to country gentlemen, they would have no more difficulty in getting themselves elected to the Board, than they have in being returned to Parliament as county members.

In regard to the proper circumscription of the constituencies which elect the local representative bodies ; the principle which, when applied as an exclusive and unbending rule to parliamentary representation, is inappropriate, namely community of local interests, is here the only just and applicable one. The very object of having a local representation, is in order that those who have any interest in common, which they do not share with the general body of their countrymen, may manage that joint interest by themselves : and the purpose is contradicted, if the distribution of the local representation follows any other rule than the grouping of those joint interests. There are local interests peculiar to every town, whether great or small, and common to all its inhabitants : every town, therefore, without distinction of size, ought to have its municipal council. It is equally obvious, that every town ought to have but one. The different quarters of the same town have seldom or never any material diversities of local interest ; they all require to have the same things done, the same expenses incurred ; and, except as to their churches, which it is probably desirable to leave under simply parochial management, the same arrangements may be made to serve for all. Paving, lighting, water supply, drainage, port and market regulations, cannot without great waste and inconvenience be different for different quarters of the same town. The subdivision of London into six or seven independent districts, each with its separate arrangements for local business (several of them without unity of administration even within themselves) prevents the possibility of consecutive or well regulated co-operation for common objects, precludes any uniform principle for the discharge of local duties, compels the general government to take things upon itself which would be best left to local authorities if there were any whose authority extended to the entire metropolis ; and answers no purpose but to keep up the fantastical trappings of that union of modern jobbing and antiquated foppery, the Corporation of the City of London.

Another equally important principle is, that in each local circumscription there should be but one elected body for all local business, not different bodies for different parts of it. Division of labour does not mean, cutting up every business into minute fractions; it means the union of such operations as are fit to be performed by the same persons, and the separation of such as can be better performed by different persons. The executive duties of the locality do indeed require to be divided into departments, for the same reason as those of the State; because they are of diverse kinds, each requiring knowledge peculiar to itself, and needing, for its due performance, the undivided attention of a specially qualified functionary. But the reasons for subdivision which apply to the execution, do not apply to the control. The business of the elective body is not to do the work, but to see that it is properly done, and that nothing necessary is left undone. This function can be fulfilled for all departments by the same superintending body; and by a collective and comprehensive far better than by a minute and microscopic view. It is as absurd in public affairs as it would be in private, that every workman should be looked after by a superintendent to himself. The Government of the Crown consists of many departments, and there are many ministers to conduct them, but those ministers have not a Parliament apiece to keep them to their duty. The local like the national Parliament, has for its proper business to consider the interest of the locality as a whole, composed of parts all of which must be adapted to one another, and attended to in the order and ratio of their importance. There is another very weighty reason for uniting the control of all the business of a locality under one body. The greatest imperfection of popular local institutions, and the chief cause of the failure which so often attends them, is the low calibre of the men by whom they are almost always carried on. That these should be of a very miscellaneous character is, indeed, part of the usefulness of the institution; it is that circumstance chiefly which renders it a school of political capacity and general intelligence. But a school supposes teachers as well as scholars: the utility of the instruction greatly depends on its bringing inferior minds into contact with superior, a contact which in the ordinary course of life is altogether exceptional, and the want of which contributes more than anything else to keep the generality of mankind on one level of contented ignorance. The school, moreover, is worthless, and a school of evil instead of good, if through the want of due surveillance, and of the presence within itself of a higher order of characters, the action of the body is allowed, as it so often is, to degenerate into an equally unscrupulous and stupid pursuit of the self-interest of its members. Now it is quite hopeless to induce persons of a high class, either socially or intellectually, to take a share of local administration in a corner by piecemeal, as members of a Paving Board or a Drainage Commission. The entire local business of their town is not more than a sufficient object, to induce men whose tastes incline them and whose knowledge qualifies them for national affairs, to become members of a mere local body, and devote to it the time and study which are necessary to render their presence anything more than a screen for the jobbing of inferior persons under the shelter of their responsibility. A mere Board of Works, though it comprehend the entire metropolis, is sure to be composed of the same class of persons as the vestries of the London parishes; nor is it practicable, or even desirable, that such should not form the majority; but it is important for every purpose which local bodies are designed to serve, whether it be the enlightened and honest performance of their special duties, or the cultivation of the political intelligence of the nation, that every such body should contain a portion of the very best minds of the locality:

who are thus brought into perpetual contact, of the most useful kind, with minds of a lower grade, receiving from them what local or professional knowledge they have to give, and in return inspiring them with a portion of their own more enlarged ideas, and higher and more enlightened purposes.

A mere village has no claim to a municipal representation. By a village I mean a place whose inhabitants are not markedly distinguished by occupation or social relations from those of the rural districts adjoining, and for whose local wants the arrangements made for the surrounding territory will suffice. Such small places have rarely a sufficient public to furnish a tolerable municipal council: if they contain any talent or knowledge applicable to public business, it is apt to be all concentrated in some one man, who thereby becomes the dominator of the place. It is better that such places should be merged in a larger circumscription. The local representation of rural districts will naturally be determined by geographical considerations ; with due regard to those sympathies of feeling by which human beings are so much aided to act in concert, and which partly follow historical boundaries, such as those of counties or provinces, and partly community of interest and occupation, as in agricultural, maritime, manufacturing, or mining districts. Different kinds of local business may require different areas of representation. The Unions of parishes have been fixed on as the most appropriate basis for the representative bodies which superintend the relief of indigence ; while, for the proper regulation of highways, or prisons, or police, a larger extent, like that of an average county, is not more than sufficient. In these large districts, therefore, the maxim, that an elective body constituted in any locality should have authority over all the local concerns common to the locality, requires modification from another principle ; as well as from the competing consideration, of the importance of obtaining for the discharge of the local duties the highest qualifications possible.

For example, if it be necessary (as I believe it to be) for the proper administration of the Poor Laws, that the area of rating should not be more extensive than most of the present Unions, a principle which requires a Board of Guardians for each Union; yet, as a much more highly qualified class of persons is likely to be obtainable for a County Board, than those who compose an average Board of Guardians, it may on that ground be expedient to reserve for the County Boards some higher descriptions of local business, which might otherwise have been conveniently managed within itself by each separate Union.

Besides the controlling Council, or local sub-Parliament, local business has its executive department. With respect to this, the same questions arise, as with respect to the executive authorities in the State; and they may, for the most part, be answered in the same manner. The principles applicable to all public trusts are in substance the same. In the first place, each executive officer should be single, and singly responsible for the whole of the duty committed to his charge. In the next place, he should be nominated, not elected. It is ridiculous that a surveyor, or a health officer, or even a collector of rates, should be appointed by popular suffrage. The popular choice usually depends on interest with a few local leaders, who, as they are not supposed to make the appointment, are not responsible for it; or on an appeal to sympathy, founded on having twelve children, and having been a ratepayer in the parish for thirty years. If in cases of this description election by the population is a farce, appointment by the local representative body is little less objectionable. Such bodies have a perpetual tendency to become joint-stock associations for carrying into effect the private jobs of their various members. Appointments should be made on the individual responsibility of the chairman of the body, let him be called mayor, chairman of Quarter Sessions, or by whatever other title. He occupies in the locality a position analogous to that of the Prime Minister in the State, and under a well-organized system the appointment and watching of the local officers would be the most important part of his duty: he himself being appointed by the Council from its own number, subject either to annual re-election, or to removal by a vote of the body.

From the constitution of the local bodies, I now pass to the equally important and more difficult subject of their proper attributions. This question divides itself into two parts: what should be their duties, and whether they should have full authority within the sphere of those duties, or should be liable to any, and what, interference on the part of the central government.

It is obvious, to begin with, that all business purely local—all which concerns only a single locality—should devolve upon the local authorities. The paving, lighting, and cleansing of the streets of a town, and in ordinary circumstances the draining of its houses, are of little consequence to any but its inhabitants. The nation at large is interested in them in no other way, than that in which it is interested in the private well-being of all its individual citizens. But among the duties classed as local, or performed by local functionaries, there are many which might with equal propriety be termed national, being the share, belonging to the locality, of some branch of the public administration in the efficiency of which the whole nation is alike interested: the gaols, for instance, most of which in this country are under county management; the local police; the local administration of justice, much of which, especially in corporate towns, is performed by officers elected by the locality, and paid from local funds. None of these can be said to be matters of local, as distinguished from national, importance. It would not be a matter personally indifferent to the rest of the country, if any part of it became a nest of robbers or a focus of demoralization, owing to the maladministration of its police; or if, through the bad regulations of its gaol, the punishment which the courts of justice intended to inflict on the criminals confined therein (who might have come from, or committed their offences in, any other district), might be doubled in intensity, or lowered to practical impunity. The points, moreover, which constitute good management of these things, are the same everywhere; there is no good reason why police, or gaols, or the administration of justice, should be differently managed in one part of the kingdom and in another; while there is great peril that in things so important, and to which the most instructed minds available to the State are not more than adequate, the lower average of capacities which alone can be counted on for the service of the localities, might commit errors of such magnitude as to be a serious blot upon the general administration of the country. Security of person and property, and equal justice between individuals, are the first needs of society, and the primary ends of government: if these things can be left to any responsibility below the highest, there is nothing, except war and treaties, which requires a general government at all. Whatever are the best arrangements for securing these primary objects should be made universally obligatory, and, to secure their enforcement, should be placed under central superintendence. It is often useful, and with the institutions of our own country even necessary, from the scarcity, in the localities, of officers representing the general government, that the execution of duties imposed by the central authority should be entrusted to functionaries appointed for local purposes by the locality. But experience is daily forcing upon the public a conviction of the necessity of having at least inspectors appointed by the general government, to see that the local officers do their duty. If prisons are under local management, the central government appoints inspectors of prisons, to take care that the rules laid down by Parliament are observed, and to suggest others if the state of the gaols shows them to be requisite: as there are inspectors of factories, and inspectors of schools, to watch over the observance of the Acts of Parliament relating to the first, and the fulfilment of the conditions on which State assistance is granted to the latter.

But, if the administration of justice, police and gaols included, is both so universal a concern, and so much a matter of general science independent of local peculiarities, that it may be, and ought to be, uniformly regulated throughout the country, and its regulation enforced by more trained and skilful hands than those of purely local authorities ; there is also business, such as the administration of the poor laws, sanitary regulation, and others, which, while really interesting to the whole country, cannot consistently with the very purposes of local administration, be managed otherwise than by the localities. In regard to such duties, the question arises, how far the local authorities ought to be trusted with discretionary power, free from any superintendence or control of the State.

To decide this question, it is essential to consider what is the comparative position of the central and the local authorities, as to capacity for the work, and security against negligence or abuse. In the first place, the local representative bodies and their officers are almost certain to be of a much lower grade of intelligence and knowledge, than Parliament and the national executive. Secondly, besides being themselves of inferior qualifications, they are watched by, and accountable to, an inferior public opinion. The public under whose eyes they act, and by whom they are criticized, is both more limited in extent, and generally far less enlightened, than that which surrounds and admonishes the highest authorities at the capital ; while the comparative smallness of the interests involved, causes even that inferior public to direct its thoughts to the subject less intently, and with less solicitude. Far less interference is exercised by the press and by public discussion, and that which is exercised may with much more impunity be disregarded, in the proceedings of local, than in those of national authorities. Thus far, the advantage seems wholly on the side of management by the central government. But, when we look more closely, these motives of preference are found to be balanced by others fully as substantial. If the local authorities and public are inferior to the central ones in knowledge of the principles of administration, they have the compensating advantage of a far more direct interest in the result. A man's neighbours or his landlord may be much cleverer than himself, and not without an indirect interest in his prosperity, but for all that, his interests will be better attended to in his own keeping than in theirs. It is further to be remembered, that even supposing the central government to administer through its own officers, its officers do not act at the centre, but in the locality: and however inferior the local public may be to the central, it is the local public alone which has any opportunity of watching them, and it is the local opinion alone which either acts directly upon their own conduct, or calls the attention of the government to the points in which they may require correction. It is but in extreme cases that the general opinion of the country is brought to bear at all upon details of local administration, and still more rarely has it the means of deciding upon them with any just appreciation of the case. Now, the local opinion necessarily acts far more forcibly upon purely local administrators. They, in the natural course of things, are permanent residents, not expecting to be withdrawn from the place when they cease to exercise authority in it; and their authority itself depends, by supposition, on the will of the local public. I need not dwell on the deficiencies of the central authority in detailed knowledge of local persons and things, and the too great engrossment of its time and thoughts by other concerns, to admit of its acquiring the quantity and quality of local knowledge necessary even for deciding on complaints, and enforcing responsibility from so great a number of local agents. In the details of management, therefore, the local bodies will generally have the advantage; but in comprehension of the principles even of purely local management, the superiority of the central government, when rightly constituted, ought to be prodigious: not only by reason of the probably great personal superiority of the individuals composing it, and the multitude of thinkers and writers who are at all times engaged in pressing useful ideas upon their notice, but also because the knowledge and experience of any local authority is but local knowledge and experience, confined to their own part of the country and its modes of management, whereas the central government has the means of knowing all that is to be learnt from the united experience of the whole kingdom, with the addition of easy access to that of foreign countries.

The practical conclusion from these premisses is not difficult to draw. The authority which is most conversant with principles should be supreme over principles, while that which is most competent in details should have the details left to it. The principal business of the central authority should be to give instruction, of the local authority to apply it. Power may be localized, but knowledge, to be most useful, must be centralized; there must be somewhere a focus at which all its scattered rays are collected, that the broken and coloured lights which exist elsewhere may find there what is necessary to complete and purify them. To every branch of local administration which affects the general interest, there should be a corresponding central organ, either a minister, or some specially appointed functionary under him; even if that functionary does no more than collect information from all quarters, and bring the experience acquired in one locality to the knowledge of another where it is wanted. But there is also something more than this for the central authority to do. It ought to keep open a perpetual communication with the localities: informing itself by their experience, and them by its own; giving advice freely when asked, volunteering it when seen to be required; compelling publicity and recordation of proceedings, and enforcing obedience to every general law which the legislature has laid down on the subject of local management. That some such laws ought to be laid down few are likely to deny. The localities may be allowed to mismanage their own interests, but not to prejudice those of others, nor violate those principles of justice between one person and another, of which it is the duty of the State to maintain the rigid observance. If the local majority attempts to oppress the minority, or one class another, the State is bound to interpose. For example, all local rates ought to be voted exclusively by the local representative body; but that body, though elected solely by ratepayers, may raise its revenues by imposts of such a kind, or assess them in such a manner, as to throw an unjust share of the burthen on the poor, the rich, or some particular class of the population: it is the duty, therefore, of the legislature, while leaving the mere amount of the local taxes to the discretion of the local body, to lay down authoritatively the modes of taxation, and rules of assessment, which alone the localities shall be permitted to use. Again, in the administration of public charity, the industry and morality of the whole labouring population depend, to a most serious extent, upon adherence to certain fixed principles in awarding relief. Though it belongs essentially to the local functionaries to determine who, according to those principles, is entitled to be relieved, the national Parliament is the proper authority to prescribe the principles themselves; and it would neglect a most important part of its duty if it did not, in a matter of such grave national concern, lay down imperative rules, and make effectual provision that those rules should not be departed from. What power of actual interference with the local administrators it may be necessary to retain, for the due enforcement of the laws, is a question of detail into which it would be useless to enter. The laws themselves will naturally define the penalties, and fix the mode of their enforcement. It may be requisite, to meet extreme cases, that the power of the central authority should extend to dissolving the local representative council, or dismissing the local executive: but not to making new appointments, or suspending the local institutions. Where Parliament has not interfered, neither ought any branch of the executive to interfere with authority; but as an adviser and critic, an enforcer of the laws, and a denouncer to Parliament or the local constituencies, of conduct which it deems condemnable, the functions of the executive are of the greatest possible value.

Some may think, that however much the central authority surpasses the local in knowledge of the principles of administration, the great object which has been so much insisted on, the social and political education of the citizens, requires that they should be left to manage these matters by their own, however imperfect, lights. To this it might be answered, that the education of the citizens is not the only thing to be considered; government and administration do not exist for that alone, great as its importance is. But the objection shows a very imperfect understanding of the function of popular institutions as a means of political instruction. It is but a poor education that associates ignorance with ignorance, and leaves them, if they care for knowledge, to grope their way to it without help, and to do without it if they do not. What is wanted is, the means of making ignorance aware of itself, and able to profit by knowledge; accustoming minds which know only routine, to act upon, and feel the value of, principles: teaching them to compare different modes of action, and learn, by the use of their reason, to distinguish the best. When we desire to have a good school, we do not eliminate the teacher. The old remark, ' as the schoolmaster is, so will be the school,' is as true of the indirect schooling of grown people by public business, as of the schooling of youth in academies and colleges. A government which attempts to do everything, is aptly compared by M. Charles de Rémusat to a schoolmaster who does all the pupils' tasks for them; he may be very popular

with the pupils, but he will teach them little. A
government, on the other hand, which neither does
anything itself that can possibly be done by any one
else, nor shows any one else how to do anything, is
like a school in which there is no schoolmaster, but
only pupil-teachers who have never themselves been
taught.

CHAPTER XVI

OF NATIONALITY, AS CONNECTED WITH REPRESENTATIVE
GOVERNMENT

A PORTION of mankind may be said to constitute
a Nationality, if they are united among themselves by
common sympathies, which do not exist between them
and any others—which make them co-operate with
each other more willingly than with other people,
desire to be under the same government, and desire
that it should be government by themselves or a portion
of themselves, exclusively. This feeling of nationality
may have been generated by various causes. Sometimes it is the effect of identity of race and descent.
Community of language, and community of religion,
greatly contribute to it. Geographical limits are one
of its causes. But the strongest of all is identity of
political antecedents ; the possession of a national
history, and consequent community of recollections ;
collective pride and humiliation, pleasure and regret,
connected with the same incidents in the past. None
of these circumstances however are either indispensable, or necessarily sufficient by themselves. Switzerland has a strong sentiment of nationality, though the
cantons are of different races, different languages, and
different religions. Sicily has, throughout history, felt
itself quite distinct in nationality from Naples, notwithstanding identity of religion, almost identity of
language, and a considerable amount of common

historical antecedents. The Flemish and the Walloon provinces of Belgium, notwithstanding diversity of race and language, have a much greater feeling of common nationality, than the former have with Holland, or the latter with France. Yet in general the national feeling is proportionally weakened by the failure of any of the causes which contribute to it. Identity of language, literature, and, to some extent, of race and recollections, have maintained the feeling of nationality in considerable strength among the different portions of the German name, though they have at no time been really united under the same government; but the feeling has never reached to making the separate States desire to get rid of their autonomy. Among Italians an identity far from complete, of language and literature, combined with a geographical position which separates them by a distinct line from other countries, and, perhaps more than everything else, the possession of a common name, which makes them all glory in the past achievements in arts, arms, politics, religious primacy, science, and literature, of any who share the same designation, give rise to an amount of national feeling in the population, which, though still imperfect, has been sufficient to produce the great events now passing before us, notwithstanding a great mixture of races, and although they have never, in either ancient or modern history, been under the same government, except while that government extended or was extending itself over the greater part of the known world.

Where the sentiment of nationality exists in any force, there is a prima facie case for uniting all the members of the nationality under the same government, and a government to themselves apart. This is merely saying that the question of government ought to be decided by the governed. One hardly knows what any division of the human race should be free to do, if not to determine, with which of the various collective bodies of human beings they choose to associate themselves. But, when a people are ripe for free institutions, there is a still more vital consideration. Free institutions are next to impossible in a country made up of different nationalities. Among a people without fellow-feeling, especially if they read and speak different languages, the united public opinion, necessary to the working of representative government, cannot exist. The influences which form opinions and decide political acts, are different in the different sections of the country. An altogether different set of leaders have the confidence of one part of the country and of another. The same books, newspapers, pamphlets, speeches, do not reach them. One section does not know what opinions, or what instigations, are circulating in another. The same incidents, the same acts, the same system of government, affect them in different ways ; and each fears more injury to itself from the other nationalities, than from the common arbiter, the State. Their mutual antipathies are generally much stronger than jealousy of the government. That any one of them feels aggrieved by the policy of the common ruler, is sufficient to determine another to support that policy. Even if all are aggrieved, none feel that they can rely on the others for fidelity in a joint resistance ; the strength of none is sufficient to resist alone, and each may reasonably think that it consults its own advantage most by bidding for the favour of the government against the rest. Above all, the grand and only effectual security in the last resort against the despotism of the government, is in that case wanting : the sympathy of the army with the people. The military are the part of every community in whom, from the nature of the case, the distinction between their fellow countrymen and foreigners is the deepest and strongest. To the rest of the people, foreigners are merely strangers ; to the soldier, they are men against whom he may be called, at a week's notice, to fight for life or death. The difference to him is that between friends and foes—we may almost say between fellow men and another kind of animals : for as respects the enemy, the only law is that of force, and the only mitigation, the same as in the case of other animals—that of simple humanity. Soldiers to whose feelings half or three-fourths of the subjects of the same government are foreigners, will have no more scruple in mowing them down, and no more desire to ask the reason why, than they would have in doing the same thing against declared enemies. An army composed of various nationalities has no other patriotism than devotion to the flag. Such armies have been the executioners of liberty through the whole duration of modern history. The sole bond which holds them together is their officers, and the government which they serve; and their only idea, if they have any, of public duty, is obedience to orders. A government thus supported, by keeping its Hungarian regiments in Italy and its Italian in Hungary, can long continue to rule in both places with the iron rod of foreign conquerors.

If it be said that so broadly marked a distinction between what is due to a fellow countryman and what is due merely to a human creature, is more worthy of savages than of civilized beings, and ought, with the utmost energy, to be contended against, no one holds that opinion more strongly than myself. But this object, one of the worthiest to which human endeavour can be directed, can never, in the present state of civilization, be promoted by keeping different nationalities of anything like equivalent strength, under the same government. In a barbarous state of society, the case is sometimes different. The government may then be interested in softening the antipathies of the races, that peace may be preserved, and the country more easily governed. But when there are either free institutions, or a desire for them, in any of the peoples artificially tied together, the interest of the government lies in an exactly opposite direction. It is then interested in keeping up and envenoming their antipathies; that they may be prevented from coalescing, and it may be enabled to use some of them as tools for the enslavement of others. The Austrian Court has now 'for a whole generation made these tactics its principal means of government; with what fatal success, at the time of the Vienna insurrection and the Hungarian contest, the world knows too well. Happily there are now signs that improvement is too far advanced, to permit this policy to be any longer successful.

For the preceding reasons, it is in general a necessary condition of free institutions, that the boundaries of governments should coincide in the main with those of nationalities. But several considerations are liable to conflict in practice with this general principle. In the first place, its application is often precluded by geographical hindrances. There are parts even of Europe, in which different nationalities are so locally intermingled, that it is not practicable for them to be under separate governments. The population of Hungary is composed of Magyars, Slovacks, Croats, Serbs, Roumans, and in some districts, Germans, so mixed up as to be incapable of local separation ; and there is no course open to them but to make a virtue of necessity, and reconcile themselves to living together under equal rights and laws. Their community of servitude, which dates only from the destruction of Hungarian independence in 1849, seems to be ripening and disposing them for such an equal union. The German colony of East Prussia is cut off from Germany by part of the ancient Poland, and being too weak to maintain separate independence, must, if geographical continuity is to be maintained, be either under a non-German government, or the intervening Polish territory must be under a German one. Another considerable region in which the dominant element of the population is German, the provinces of Courland, Esthonia, and Livonia, is condemned by its local situation to form part of a Slavonian state. In Eastern Germany itself there is a large Slavonic population : Bohemia is principally Slavonic, Silesia and other districts partially so. The most united country in

Europe, France, is far from being homogeneous: independently of the fragments of foreign nationalities at its remote extremities, it consists, as language and history prove, of two portions, one occupied almost exclusively by a Gallo-Roman population, while in the other the Frankish, Burgundian, and other Teutonic races form a considerable ingredient.

When proper allowance has been made for geographical exigencies, another more purely moral and social consideration offers itself. Experience proves, that it is possible for one nationality to merge and be absorbed in another: and when it was originally an inferior and more backward portion of the human race, the absorption is greatly to its advantage. Nobody can suppose that it is not more beneficial to a Breton, or a Basque of French Navarre, to be brought into the current of the ideas and feelings of a highly civilized and cultivated people—to be a member of the French nationality, admitted on equal terms to all the privileges of French citizenship, sharing the advantages of French protection, and the dignity and prestige of French power—than to sulk on his own rocks, the half-savage relic of past times, revolving in his own little mental orbit, without participation or interest in the general movement of the world. The same remark applies to the Welshman or the Scottish Highlander, as members of the British nation.

Whatever really tends to the admixture of nationalities, and the blending of their attributes and peculiarities in a common union, is a benefit to the human race. Not by extinguishing types, of which, in these cases, sufficient examples are sure to remain, but by softening their extreme forms, and filling up the intervals between them. The united people, like a crossed breed of animals (but in a still greater degree, because the influences in operation are moral as well as physical), inherits the special aptitudes and excellences of all its progenitors, protected by the admixture from being exaggerated into the neighbouring vices. But to render this admixture possible, there must be peculiar conditions. The combinations of circumstances which occur, and which affect the result, are various.

The nationalities brought together under the same government, may be about equal in numbers and strength, or they may be very unequal. If unequal, the least numerous of the two may either be the superior in civilization, or the inferior. Supposing it to be superior, it may either, through that superiority, be able to acquire ascendancy over the other, or it may be overcome by brute strength, and reduced to subjection. This last is a sheer mischief to the human race, and one which civilized humanity with one accord should rise in arms to prevent. The absorption of Greece by Macedonia was one of the greatest misfortunes which ever happened to the world: that of any of the principal countries of Europe by Russia would be a similar one.

If the smaller nationality, supposed to be the more advanced in improvement, is able to overcome the greater, as the Macedonians, reinforced by the Greeks, did Asia, and the English India, there is often a gain to civilization; but the conquerors and the conquered cannot in this case live together under the same free institutions. The absorption of the conquerors in the less advanced people would be an evil: these must be governed as subjects, and the state of things is either a benefit or a misfortune, according as the subjugated people have or have not reached the state in which it is an injury not to be under a free government, and according as the conquerors do or do not use their superiority in a manner calculated to fit the conquered for a higher stage of improvement. This topic will be particularly treated of in a subsequent chapter.

When the nationality which succeeds in overpowering the other, is both the most numerous and the most improved; and especially if the subdued nationality is small, and has no hope of reasserting its independence; then, if it is governed with any tolerable justice, and if the members of the more powerful nationality are not made odious by being invested with exclusive privileges, the smaller nationality is gradually reconciled to its position, and becomes amalgamated with the larger. No Bas-Breton, nor even any Alsatian, has the smallest wish at the present day to be separated from France. If all Irishmen have not yet arrived at the same disposition towards England, it is partly because they are sufficiently numerous to be capable of constituting a respectable nationality by themselves; but principally because, until of late years, they had been so atrociously governed, that all their best feelings combined with their bad ones in rousing bitter resentment against the Saxon rule. This disgrace to England, and calamity to the whole empire, has, it may be truly said, completely ceased for nearly a generation. No Irishman is now less free than an Anglo-Saxon, nor has a less share of every benefit either to his country or to his individual fortunes, than if he were sprung from any other portion of the British dominions. The only remaining real grievance of Ireland, that of the State Church, is one which half, or nearly half, the people of the larger island have in common with them. There is now next to nothing, except the memory of the past, and the difference in the predominant religion, to keep apart two races, perhaps the most fitted of any two in the world to be the completing counterpart of one another. The consciousness of being at last treated not only with equal justice but with equal consideration, is making such rapid way in the Irish nation, as to be wearing off all feelings that could make them insensible to the benefits which the less numerous and less wealthy people must necessarily derive, from being fellow citizens instead of foreigners to those who are not only their nearest neighbours, but the wealthiest, and one of the freest, as well as most civilized and powerful, nations of the earth.

The cases in which the greatest practical obstacles exist to the blending of nationalities, are when the nationalities which have been bound together are nearly equal in numbers, and in the other elements of power. In such cases, each, confiding in its strength, and feeling itself capable of maintaining an equal struggle with any of the others, is unwilling to be merged in it : each cultivates with party obstinacy its distinctive peculiarities ; obsolete customs, and even declining languages, are revived, to deepen the separation ; each deems itself tyrannized over if any authority is exercised within itself by functionaries of a rival race ; and whatever is given to one of the conflicting nationalities, is considered to be taken from all the rest. When nations, thus divided, are under a despotic government which is a stranger to all of them, or which, though sprung from one, yet feeling greater interest in its own power than in any sympathies of nationality, assigns no privilege to either nation, and chooses its instruments indifferently from all ; in the course of a few generations, identity of situation often produces harmony of feeling, and the different races come to feel towards each other as fellow countrymen ; particularly if they are dispersed over the same tract of country. But if the era of aspiration to free government arrives before this fusion has been effected, the opportunity has gone by for effecting it. From that time, if the unreconciled nationalities are geographically separate, and especially if their local position is such that there is no natural fitness or convenience in their being under the same government (as in the case of an Italian province under a French or German yoke), there is not only an obvious propriety, but, if either freedom or concord is cared for, a necessity, for breaking the connexion altogether. There may be cases in which the provinces, after separation, might usefully remain united by a federal tie : but it generally happens that if they are willing to forgo complete independence, and become members of a federation, each of them has other neighbours with whom it would prefer to connect itself, having more sympathies in common, if not also greater community of interest.

CHAPTER XVII

OF FEDERAL REPRESENTATIVE GOVERNMENTS

PORTIONS of mankind who are not fitted, or not disposed, to live under the same internal government, may often with advantage be federally united, as to their relations with foreigners : both to prevent wars among themselves, and for the sake of more effectual protection against the aggression of powerful States.

To render a federation advisable, several conditions are necessary. The first is, that there should be a sufficient amount of mutual sympathy among the populations. The federation binds them always to fight on the same side ; and if they have such feelings towards one another, or such diversity of feeling towards their neighbours, that they would generally prefer to fight on opposite sides, the federal tie is neither likely to be of long duration, nor to be well observed while it subsists. The sympathies available for the purpose are those of race, language, religion, and above all, of political institutions, as conducing most to a feeling of identity of political interest. When a few free states, separately insufficient for their own defence, are hemmed in on all sides by military or feudal monarchs, who hate and despise freedom even in a neighbour, those states have no chance for preserving liberty and its blessings, but by a federal union. The common interest arising from this cause has in Switzerland, for several centuries, been found adequate to maintain efficiently the federal bond, in spite not only of difference of religion when religion was the grand source of irreconcilable political enmity throughout Europe, but also in spite of great weakness in the constitution of the federation itself. In America, where all the conditions for the maintenance of union existed at the highest point, with the sole drawback of difference of institutions in the single but most important article of Slavery, this one difference has gone so far in alienating from each other's sympathies the two divisions of the Union, that the maintenance or disruption of a tie of so much value to them both, depends on the issue of an obstinate civil war.

A second condition of the stability of a federal government, is that the separate states be not so powerful, as to be able to rely, for protection against foreign encroachment, on their individual strength. If they are, they will be apt to think that they do not gain, by union with others, the equivalent of what they sacrifice in their own liberty of action; and consequently, whenever the policy of the Confederation, in things reserved to its cognizance, is different from that which any one of its members would separately pursue, the internal and sectional breach will, through absence of sufficient anxiety to preserve the union, be in danger of going so far as to dissolve it.

A third condition, not less important than the two others, is that there be not a very marked inequality of strength among the several contracting states. They cannot, indeed, be exactly equal in resources: in all federations there will be a gradation of power among the members; some will be more populous, rich, and civilized than others. There is a wide difference in wealth and population between New York and Rhode Island; between Bern, and Zug or Glaris. The essential is, that there should not be any one State so much more powerful than the rest, as to be capable of vying in strength with many of them combined. If there be such a one, and only one, it will insist on being master of the joint deliberations: if there be two, they will be irresistible when they agree; and whenever they differ, everything will be decided by a struggle for ascendancy between the rivals. This cause is alone enough to reduce the German Bund to almost a nullity, independently of its wretched internal constitution. It effects none of the real purposes of a confederation. It has never bestowed on Germany an uniform system of customs, nor so much as an uniform coinage; and has served only to give Austria and Prussia a legal right of pouring in their troops to assist the local sovereigns in keeping their subjects obedient to despotism: while in regard to external concerns, the Bund would make all Germany a dependency of Prussia, if there were no Austria, and of Austria if there were no Prussia: and in the meantime each petty prince has little choice but to be a partisan of one or the other, or to intrigue with foreign governments against both.

There are two different modes of organizing a Federal Union. The federal authorities may represent the Governments solely, and their acts may be obligatory only on the Governments as such; or they may have the power of enacting laws and issuing orders which are binding directly on individual citizens. The former is the plan of the German so-called Confederation, and of the Swiss Constitution previous to 1847. It was tried in America for a few years immediately following the War of Independence. The other principle is that of the existing Constitution of the United States, and has been adopted within the last dozen years by the Swiss Confederacy. The Federal Congress of the American Union is a substantive part of the government of every individual State. Within the limits of its attributions, it makes laws which are obeyed by every citizen individually, executes them through its own officers, and enforces them by its own tribunals. This is the only principle which has been found, or which is ever likely, to produce an effective federal government. An union between the governments only, is a mere alliance, and subject to all the contingencies which render alliances precarious. If the acts of the President and of Congress were binding solely on the Governments of New York, Virginia, or Pennsylvania, and could only be carried into effect through orders issued by those Governments to officers appointed by them, under responsibility to their own courts of justice, no mandates of the Federal Government which were disagreeable to a local majority would ever be executed. Requisitions issued to a government have no other sanction, or means of enforcement, than war : and a federal army would have to be always in readiness, to enforce the decrees of the Federation against any recalcitrant State ; subject to the probability that other States, sympathizing with the recusant, and perhaps sharing its sentiments on the particular point in dispute, would withhold their contingents, if not send them to fight in the ranks of the disobedient State. Such a federation is more likely to be a cause than a preventive of internal wars : and if such was not its effect in Switzerland until the events of the years immediately preceding 1847, it was only because the Federal Government felt its weakness so strongly, that it hardly ever attempted to exercise any real authority. In America, the experiment of a Federation on this principle broke down in the first few years of its existence ; happily while the men of enlarged knowledge and acquired ascendancy, who founded the independence of the Republic, were still alive to guide it through the difficult transition. The ' Federalist,' a collection of papers by three of these eminent men, written in explanation and defence of the new Federal Constitution while still awaiting the national acceptance, is even now the most instructive treatise we possess on federal government.[1] In Germany, the more imperfect kind of federation, as all know, has not even answered the purpose of maintaining an alliance. It has never, in any European war, prevented single members of the Confederation from allying themselves with foreign powers against the rest. Yet this is the only federation which seems possible among monarchical states. A king, who holds his power by inheritance, not by delegation, and who cannot be deprived of it, nor made responsible to any

---

[1] Mr. Freeman's *History of Federal Governments*, of which only the first volume has yet appeared, is already an accession to the literature of the subject, equally valuable by its enlightened principles and its mastery of historical details.

one for its use, is not likely to renounce having a separate army, or to brook the exercise of sovereign authority over his own subjects, not through him but directly, by another power. To enable two or more countries under kingly government to be joined together in an effectual confederation, it seems necessary that they should all be under the same king. England and Scotland were a federation of this description, during the interval of about a century between the union of the Crowns and that of the Parliaments. Even this was effective, not through federal institutions, for none existed, but because the regal power in both Constitutions was during the greater part of that time so nearly absolute, as to enable the foreign policy of both to be shaped according to a single will.

Under the more perfect mode of federation, where every citizen of each particular State owes obedience to two Governments, that of his own State, and that of the federation, it is evidently necessary not only that the constitutional limits of the authority of each should be precisely and clearly defined, but that the power to decide between them in any case of dispute should not reside in either of the Governments, or in any functionary subject to it, but in an umpire independent of both. There must be a Supreme Court of Justice, and a system of subordinate Courts in every State of the Union, before whom such questions shall be carried, and whose judgement on them, in the last stage of appeal, shall be final. Every State of the Union, and the Federal Government itself, as well as every functionary of each, must be liable to be sued in those Courts for exceeding their powers, or for non-performance of their federal duties, and must in general be obliged to employ those Courts as the instrument for enforcing their federal rights. This involves the remarkable consequence, actually realized in the United States, that a Court of Justice, the highest federal tribunal, is supreme over the various Governments, both State and Federal; having the right to declare that any law made, or act done by them, exceeds the powers assigned to them by the Federal Constitution, and, in consequence, has no legal validity. It was natural to feel strong doubts, before trial had been made, how such a provision would work ; whether the tribunal would have the courage to exercise its constitutional power ; if it did, whether it would exercise it wisely, and whether the Governments would consent to submit peaceably to its decision. The discussions on the American Constitution, before its final adoption, give evidence that these natural apprehensions were strongly felt ; but they are now entirely quieted, since, during the two generations and more which have subsequently elapsed, nothing has occurred to verify them, though there have at times been disputes of considerable acrimony, and which became the badges of parties, respecting the limits of the authority of the Federal and State Governments. The eminently beneficial working of so singular a provision, is probably, as M. de Tocqueville remarks, in a great measure attributable to the peculiarity inherent in a Court of Justice acting as such—namely, that it does not declare the law *eo nomine* and in the abstract, but waits until a case between man and man is brought before it judicially, involving the point in dispute : from which arises the happy effect, that its declarations are not made in a very early stage of the controversy ; that much popular discussion usually precedes them ; that the Court decides after hearing the point fully argued on both sides by lawyers of reputation ; decides only as much of the question at a time as is required by the case before it, and its decision, instead of being volunteered for political purposes, is drawn from it by the duty which it cannot refuse to fulfil, of dispensing justice impartially between adverse litigants. Even these grounds of confidence would not have sufficed to produce the respectful submission with which all authorities have yielded to the decisions of the Supreme Court on the interpretation of the Constitution, were it not that complete reliance has been felt, not only on the intellectual pre-eminence of the judges composing that exalted tribunal, but on their entire superiority over either private or sectional partialities. This reliance has been in the main justified; but there is nothing which more vitally imports the American people, than to guard with the most watchful solicitude against everything which has the remotest tendency to produce deterioration in the quality of this great national institution. The confidence on which depends the stability of federal institutions was for the first time impaired, by the judgement declaring slavery to be of common right, and consequently lawful in the Territories while not yet constituted as States, even against the will of a majority of their inhabitants. This memorable decision has probably done more than anything else to bring the sectional division to the crisis which has issued in civil war. The main pillar of the American Constitution is scarcely strong enough, to bear many more such shocks.

The tribunals which act as umpires between the Federal and the State Governments, naturally also decide all disputes between two States, or between a citizen of one State and the government of another. The usual remedies between nations, war and diplomacy, being precluded by the federal union, it is necessary that a judicial remedy should supply their place. The Supreme Court of the Federation dispenses international law, and is the first great example of what is now one of the most prominent wants of civilized society, a .real International Tribunal.

The powers of a Federal Government naturally extend not only to peace and war, and all questions which arise between the country and foreign governments, but to making any other arrangements which are, in the opinion of the States, necessary to their enjoyment of the full benefits of union. For example, it is a great advantage to them that their mutual commerce should be free, without the impediment of frontier duties and custom-houses. But this internal freedom cannot exist, if each State has the power of fixing the duties on interchange of commodities between itself and foreign countries; since every foreign product let in by one State, would be let into all the rest. And hence all custom duties and trade regulations, in the United States, are made or repealed by the Federal Government exclusively. Again, it is a great convenience to the States to have but one coinage, and but one system of weights and measures; which can only be ensured, if the regulation of these matters is entrusted to the Federal Government. The certainty and celerity of Post Office communication is impeded, and its expense increased, if a letter has to pass through half a dozen sets of public offices, subject to different supreme authorities: it is convenient, therefore, that all Post Offices should be under the Federal Government. But on such questions the feelings of different communities are liable to be different. One of the American States, under the guidance of a man who has displayed powers as a speculative political thinker superior to any who has appeared in American politics since the authors of the 'Federalist,'[1] claimed a veto for each State on the custom laws of the Federal Congress: and that statesman, in a posthumous work of great ability, which has been printed and widely circulated by the legislature of South Carolina, vindicated this pretension on the general principle of limiting the tyranny of the majority, and protecting minorities by admitting them to a substantial participation in political power. One of the most disputed topics in American politics, during the early part of this century, was whether the power of the Federal Government ought to extend, and whether by the Constitution it did extend, to making roads and canals at the cost of the Union. It is only in transactions with foreign powers that the authority of the Federal Government is of necessity complete. On every other subject, the question depends on how closely the

[1] Mr. Calhoun.

people in general wish to draw the federal tie; what portion of their local freedom of action they are willing to surrender, in order to enjoy more fully the benefit of being one nation.

Respecting the fitting constitution of a federal government within itself, much needs not be said. It of course consists of a legislative branch and an executive, and the constitution of each is amenable to the same principles as that of representative governments generally. As regards the mode of adapting these general principles to a federal government, the provision of the American Constitution seems exceedingly judicious, that Congress should consist of two Houses, and that while one of them is constituted according to population, each State being entitled to representatives in the ratio of the number of its inhabitants, the other should represent not the citizens, but the State Governments, and every State, whether large or small, should be represented in it by the same number of members. This provision precludes any undue power from being exercised by the more powerful States over the rest, and guarantees the reserved rights of the State Governments, by making it impossible, as far as the mode of representation can prevent, that any measure should pass Congress, unless approved not only by a majority of the citizens, but by a majority of the States. I have before adverted to the further incidental advantage obtained, of raising the standard of qualifications in one of the Houses. Being nominated by select bodies, the Legislatures of the various States, whose choice, for reasons already indicated, is more likely to fall on eminent men than any popular election—who have not only the power of electing such, but a strong motive to do so, because the influence of their State in the general deliberations must be materially affected by the personal weight and abilities of its representatives; the Senate of the United States, thus chosen, has always contained nearly all the political men of established and high reputation in the Union: while the Lower House of Congress has, in the opinion of competent observers, been generally as remarkable for the absence of conspicuous personal merit, as the Upper House for its presence.

When the conditions exist for the formation of efficient and durable Federal Unions, the multiplication of them is always a benefit to the world. It has the same salutary effect as any other extension of the practice of co-operation, through which the weak, by uniting, can meet on equal terms with the strong. By diminishing the number of those petty states which are not equal to their own defence, it weakens the temptations to an aggressive policy, whether working directly by arms, or through the prestige of superior power. It of course puts an end to war and diplomatic quarrels, and usually also to restrictions on commerce, between the States composing the Union; while, in reference to neighbouring nations, the increased military strength conferred by it is of a kind to be almost exclusively available for defensive, scarcely at all for aggressive, purposes. A federal government has not a sufficiently concentrated authority, to conduct with much efficiency any war but one of self-defence, in which it can rely on the voluntary co-operation of every citizen: nor is there anything very flattering to national vanity or ambition in acquiring, by a successful war, not subjects, nor even fellow citizens, but only new, and perhaps troublesome, independent members of the confederation. The warlike proceedings of the Americans in Mexico were purely exceptional, having been carried on principally by volunteers, under the influence of the migratory propensity which prompts individual Americans to possess themselves of unoccupied land; and stimulated, if by any public motive, not by that of national aggrandizement, but by the purely sectional purpose of extending slavery. There are few signs in the proceedings of Americans, nationally or individually, that the desire of territorial acquisition for their country as such, has any considerable power over them. Their hankering after Cuba is, in the same manner, merely sectional, and the northern States, those opposed to slavery, have never in any way favoured it.

The question may present itself (as in Italy at its present uprising) whether a country, which is determined to be united, should form a complete, or a merely federal union. The point is sometimes necessarily decided by the mere territorial magnitude of the united whole. There is a limit to the extent of country which can advantageously be governed, or even whose government can be conveniently superintended, from a single centre. There are vast countries so governed; but they, or at least their distant provinces, are in general deplorably ill administered, and it is only when the inhabitants are almost savages that they could not manage their affairs better separately. This obstacle does not exist in the case of Italy, the size of which does not come up to that of several very efficiently governed single states in past and present times. The question then is, whether the different parts of the nation require to be governed in a way so essentially different, that it is not probable the same Legislature, and the same ministry or administrative body, will give satisfaction to them all. Unless this be the case, which is a question of fact, it is better for them to be completely united. That a totally different system of laws, and very different administrative institutions, may exist in two portions of a country without being any obstacle to legislative unity, is proved by the case of England and Scotland. Perhaps, however, this undisturbed co-existence of two legal systems, under one united legislature, making different laws for the two sections of the country in adaptation to the previous differences, might not be so well preserved, or the same confidence might not be felt in its preservation, in a country whose legislators were more possessed (as is apt to be the case on the Continent) with the mania for uniformity. A people having that unbounded toleration which is characteristic of this country, for every description of anomaly, so long as those whose interests it concerns do not feel aggrieved by it, afforded an exceptionally advantageous field for trying this difficult experiment. In most countries, if it was an object to retain different systems of law, it might probably be necessary to retain distinct legislatures as guardians of them ; which is perfectly compatible with a national Parliament and King, or a national Parliament without a King, supreme over the external relations of all the members of the body.

Whenever it is not deemed necessary to maintain permanently, in the different provinces, different systems of jurisprudence, and fundamental institutions grounded on different principles, it is always practicable to reconcile minor diversities with the maintenance of unity of government. All that is needful is to give a sufficiently large sphere of action to the local authorities. Under one and the same central government there may be local governors, and provincial assemblies for local purposes. It may happen, for instance, that the people of different provinces may have preferences in favour of different modes of taxation. If the general legislature could not be depended on for being guided by the members for each province in modifying the general system of taxation to suit that province, the Constitution might provide that as many of the expenses of the government as could by any possibility be made local, should be defrayed by local rates imposed by the provincial assemblies, and that those which must of necessity be general, such as the support of an army and navy, should, in the estimates for the year, be apportioned among the different provinces according to some general estimate of their resources, the amount assigned to each being levied by the local assembly on the principles most acceptable to the locality, and paid *en bloc* into the national treasury. A practice approaching to this existed even in the old French monarchy, so far as regarded the *pays d' états* ; each of which, having consented or been required to furnish a fixed sum, was left to assess it upon the inhabitants by its own officers, thus escaping the grinding despotism of the royal *intendants* and *subdélégués* ;

and this privilege is always mentioned as one of the advantages which mainly contributed to render them, as some of them were, the most flourishing provinces of France.

Identity of central government is compatible with many different degrees of centralization, not only administrative, but even legislative. A people may have the desire, and the capacity, for a closer union than one merely federal, while yet their local peculiarities and antecedents render considerable diversities desirable in the details of their government. But if there is a real desire on all hands to make the experiment successful, there needs seldom be any difficulty in not only preserving these diversities, but giving them the guarantee of a constitutional provision against any attempt at assimilation, except by the voluntary act of those who would be affected by the change.

CHAPTER XVIII

OF THE GOVERNMENT OF DEPENDENCIES BY
A FREE STATE

FREE States, like all others, may possess dependencies, acquired either by conquest or by colonization; and our own is the greatest instance of the kind in modern history. It is a most important question, how such dependencies ought to be governed.

It is unnecessary to discuss the case of small posts, like Gibraltar, Aden, or Heligoland, which are held only as naval or military positions. The military or naval object is in this case paramount, and the inhabitants cannot, consistently with it, be admitted to the government of the place; though they ought to be allowed all liberties and privileges compatible with that restriction, including the free management of municipal affairs; and as a compensation for being locally sacrificed to the convenience of the governing State, should be admitted to equal rights with its native subjects in all other parts of the empire.

Outlying territories of some size and population, which are held as dependencies, that is, which are subject, more or less, to acts of sovereign power on the part of the paramount country, without being equally represented (if represented at all) in its legislature, may be divided into two classes. Some are composed of people of similar civilization to the ruling country; capable of, and ripe for, representative government: such as the British possessions in America and Australia. Others, like India, are still at a great distance from that state.

In the case of dependencies of the former class, this country has at length realized, in rare completeness, the true principle of government. England has always felt under a certain degree of obligation to bestow on such of her outlying populations as were of her own blood and language, and on some who were not, representative institutions formed in imitation of her own: but until the present generation, she has been on the same bad level with other countries as to the amount of self-government which she allowed them to exercise through the representative institutions that she conceded to them. She claimed to be the supreme arbiter even of their purely internal concerns, according to her own, not their, ideas of how those concerns could be best regulated. This practice was a natural corollary from the vicious theory of colonial policy—once common to all Europe, and not yet completely relinquished by any other people—which regarded colonies as valuable by affording markets for our commodities, that could be kept entirely to ourselves: a privilege we valued so highly, that we thought it worth purchasing by allowing to the colonies the same monopoly of our market for their own productions, which we claimed for our commodities in theirs. This notable plan for enriching them and ourselves, by making each pay enormous sums to the other, dropping the greatest part by the way, has been for some time abandoned.

But the bad habit of meddling in the internal government of the colonies, did not at once terminate when we relinquished the idea of making any profit by it. We continued to torment them, not for any benefit to ourselves, but for that of a section or faction among the colonists : and this persistence in domineering cost us a Canadian rebellion, before we had the happy thought of giving it up. England was like an ill brought-up elder brother, who persists in tyrannizing over the younger ones from mere habit, till one of them, by a spirited resistance, though with unequal strength, gives him notice to desist. We were wise enough not to require a second warning. A new era in the colonial policy of nations began with Lord Durham's Report ; the imperishable memorial of that nobleman's courage, patriotism, and enlightened liberality, and of the intellect and practical sagacity of its joint authors, Mr. Wakefield and the lamented Charles Buller.[1]

It is now a fixed principle of the policy of Great Britain, professed in theory and faithfully adhered to in practice, that her colonies of European race, equally with the parent country, possess the fullest measure of internal self-government. They have been allowed to make their own free representative constitutions, by altering in any manner they thought fit, the already very popular constitutions which we had given them. Each is governed by its own legislature and executive, constituted on highly democratic principles. The veto of the Crown and of Parliament, though nominally reserved, is only exercised (and that very rarely) on questions which concern the empire, and not solely the particular colony. How liberal a construction has been given to the distinction between imperial and colonial questions, is shown by the fact, that the whole of the

---

[1] I am speaking here of the *adoption* of this improved policy, not, of course, of its original suggestion. The honour of having been its earliest champion belongs unquestionably to Mr. Roebuck.

unappropriated lands in the regions behind our American and Australian colonies, have been given up to the uncontrolled disposal of the colonial communities ; though they might, without injustice, have been kept in the hands of the Imperial Government, to be administered for the greatest advantage of future emigrants from all parts of the empire. Every colony has thus as full power over its own affairs, as it could have if it were a member of even the loosest federation ; and much fuller than would belong to it under the Constitution of the United States, being free even to tax at its pleasure the commodities imported from the mother country. Their union with Great Britain is the slightest kind of federal union ; but not a strictly equal federation, the mother country retaining to itself the powers of a Federal Government, though reduced in practice to their very narrowest limits. This inequality is, of course, as far as it goes, a disadvantage to the dependencies, which have no voice in foreign policy, but are bound by the decisions of the superior country. They are compelled to join England in war, without being in any way consulted previous to engaging in it.

Those (now happily not a few) who think that justice is as binding on communities as it is on individuals, and that men are not warranted in doing to other countries, for the supposed benefit of their own country, what they would not be justified in doing to other men for their own benefit—feel even this limited amount of constitutional subordination on the part of the colonies to be a violation of principle, and have often occupied themselves in looking out for means by which it may be avoided. With this view it has been proposed by some, that the colonies should return representatives to the British legislature ; and by others, that the powers of our own, as well as of their Parliaments, should be confined to internal policy, and that there should be another representative body for foreign and imperial concerns, in which last the dependencies of Great Britain should be represented in the same

manner, and with the same completeness, as Great
Britain itself. On this system there would be a perfectly equal federation between the mother country
and her colonies, then no longer dependencies.

The feelings of equity, and conceptions of public
morality, from which these suggestions emanate, are
worthy of all praise ; but the suggestions themselves
are so inconsistent with rational principles of government, that it is doubtful if they have been seriously
accepted as a possibility by any reasonable thinker.
Countries separated by half the globe do not present
the natural conditions for being under one government,
or even members of one federation. If they had sufficiently the same interests, they have not, and never
can have, a sufficient habit of taking counsel together.
They are not part of the same public ; they do not
discuss and deliberate in the same arena, but apart,
and have only a most imperfect knowledge of what
passes in the minds of one another. They neither
know each other's objects, nor have confidence in each
other's principles of conduct. Let any Englishman
ask himself how he should like his destinies to depend
on an assembly of which one-third was British American, and another third South African and Australian.
Yet to this it must come, if there were anything like
fair or equal representation ; and would not every one
feel that the representatives of Canada and Australia,
even in matters of an imperial character, could not
know, or feel any sufficient concern for, the interests,
opinions, or wishes of English, Irish, and Scotch ?
Even for strictly federative purposes, the conditions
do not exist, which we have seen to be essential to
a federation. England is sufficient for her own protection without the colonies ; and would be in a much
stronger, as well as more dignified position, if separated
from them, than when reduced to be a single member
of an American, African, and Australian confederation.
Over and above the commerce which she might equally
enjoy after separation, England derives little advantage, except in prestige, from her dependencies ; and

the little she does derive is quite outweighed by the expense they cost her, and the dissemination they necessitate of her naval and military force, which in case of war, or any real apprehension of it, requires to be double or treble what would be deeded for the defence of this country alone.

But though Great Britain could do perfectly well without her colonies, and though on every principle of morality and justice she ought to consent to their separation, should the time come when, after full trial of the best form of union, they deliberately desire to be dissevered ; there are strong reasons for maintaining the present slight bond of connexion, so long as not disagreeable to the feelings of either party. It is a step, as far as it goes, towards universal peace, and general friendly co-operation among nations. It renders war impossible among a large number of otherwise independent communities ; and moreover hinders any of them from being absorbed into a foreign state, and becoming a source of additional aggressive strength to some rival power, either more despotic or closer at hand, which might not always be so unambitious or so pacific as Great Britain. It at least keeps the markets of the different countries open to one another, and prevents that mutual exclusion by hostile tariffs, which none of the great communities of mankind, except England, have yet completely outgrown. And in the case of the British possessions it has the advantage, specially valuable at the present time, of adding to the moral influence, and weight in the councils of the world, of the Power which, of all in existence, best understands liberty—and whatever may have been its errors in the past, has attained to more of conscience and moral principle in its dealings with foreigners, than any other great nation seems either to conceive as possible, or recognize as desirable. Since, then, the union can only continue, while it does continue, on the footing of an unequal federation, it is important to consider by what means this small amount of inequality can be prevented from being either onerous or humiliating to the communities occupying the less exalted position.

The only inferiority necessarily inherent in the case is, that the mother country decides, both for the colonies and for herself, on questions of peace and war. They gain, in return, the obligation on the mother country to repel aggressions directed against them : but, except when the minor community is so weak that the protection of a stronger power is indispensable to it, reciprocity of obligation is not a full equivalent for non-admission to a voice in the deliberations. It is essential, therefore, that in all wars, save those which, like the Caffre or New Zealand wars, are incurred for the sake of the particular colony, the colonists should not (without their own voluntary request) be called on to contribute anything to the expense, except what may be required for the specific local defence of their own ports, shores, and frontiers against invasion. Moreover, as the mother country claims the privilege, at her sole discretion, of taking measures or pursuing a policy which may expose them to attack, it is just that she should undertake a considerable portion of the cost of their military defence even in time of peace ; the whole of it so far as it depends upon a standing army.

But there is a means, still more effectual than these, by which, and in general by which alone, a full equivalent can be given to a smaller community for sinking its individuality, as a substantive power among nations, in the greater individuality of a wide and powerful empire. This one indispensable, and at the same time, sufficient, expedient, which meets at once the demands of justice and the growing exigencies of policy, is, to open the service of Government in all its departments, and in every part of the empire, on perfectly equal terms, to the inhabitants of the colonies. Why does no one ever hear a breath of disloyalty from the Islands in the British Channel ? By race, religion, and geographical position they belong less to England than to France. But, while they enjoy, like Canada and New

South Wales, complete control over their internal affairs and their taxation, every office or dignity in the gift of the Crown is freely open to the native of Guernsey or Jersey. Generals, admirals, peers of the United Kingdom, are made, and there is nothing which hinders prime ministers to be made, from those insignificant islands. The same system was commenced in reference to the colonies generally, by an enlightened Colonial Secretary, too early lost, Sir William Molesworth, when he appointed Mr. Hinckes, a leading Canadian politician, to a West Indian government. It is a very shallow view of the springs of political action in a community, which thinks such things unimportant because the number of those in a position actually to profit by the concession might not be very considerable. That limited number would be composed precisely of those' who have most moral power over the rest: and men are not so destitute of the sense of collective degradation, as not to feel the withholding of an advantage from even one person, because of a circumstance which they all have in common with him, an affront to all. If we prevent the leading men of a community from standing forth to the world as its chiefs and representatives in the general councils of mankind, we owe it both to their legitimate ambition, and to the just pride of the community, to give them in return an equal chance of occupying the same prominent position in a nation of greater power and importance.

Thus far, of the dependencies whose population is in a sufficiently advanced state to be fitted for representative government. But there are others which have not attained that state, and which, if held at all, must be governed by the dominant country, or by persons delegated for that purpose by it. This mode of government is as legitimate as any other, if it is the one which in the existing state of civilization of the subject people, most facilitates their transition to a higher stage of improvement. There are, as we have already seen, conditions of society in which a vigorous despotism is in itself the best mode of government for training the people in what is specifically wanting to render them capable of a higher civilization. There are others, in which the mere fact of despotism has indeed no beneficial effect, the lessons which it teaches having already been only too completely learnt; but in which, there being no spring of spontaneous improvement in the people themselves, their almost only hope of making any steps in advance depends on the chances of a good despot. Under a native despotism, a good despot is a rare and transitory accident: but when the dominion they are under is that of a more civilized people, that people ought to be able to supply it constantly. The ruling country ought to be able to do for its subjects all that could be done by a succession of absolute monarchs, guaranteed by irresistible force against the precariousness of tenure attendant on barbarous despotisms, and qualified by their genius to anticipate all that experience has taught to the more advanced nation. Such is the ideal rule of a free people over a barbarous or semi-barbarous one. We need not expect to see that ideal realized ; but unless some approach to it is, the rulers are guilty of a dereliction of the highest moral trust which can devolve upon a nation: and if they do not even aim at it, they are selfish usurpers, on a par in criminality with any of those whose ambition and rapacity have sported from age to age with the destiny of masses of mankind.

As it is already a common, and is rapidly tending to become the universal, condition of the more backward populations, to be either held in direct subjection by the more advanced, or to be under their complete political ascendancy ; there are in this age of the world few more important problems, than how to organize this rule, so as to make it a good instead of an evil to the subject people ; providing them with the best attainable present government, and with the conditions most favourable to future permanent improvement. But the mode of fitting the government for this purpose is by no means so well understood, as the conditions of good government in a people capable of governing themselves. We may even say, that it is not understood at all.

The thing appears perfectly easy to superficial observers. If India (for example) is not fit to govern itself, all that seems to them required is, that there should be a minister to govern it: and that this minister, like all other British ministers, should be responsible to the British Parliament. Unfortunately this, though the simplest mode of attempting to govern a dependency, is about the worst; and betrays in its advocates a total want of comprehension of the conditions of good government. To govern a country under responsibility to the people of that country, and to govern one country under responsibility to the people of another, are two very different things. What makes the excellence of the first, is that freedom is preferable to despotism: but the last *is* despotism. The only choice the case admits, is a choice of despotisms: and it is not certain that the despotism of twenty millions is necessarily better than that of a few, or of one. But it is quite certain, that the despotism of those who neither hear, nor see, nor know anything about their subjects, has many chances of being worse than that of those who do. It is not usually thought that the immediate agents of authority govern better because they govern in the name of an absent master, and of one who has a thousand more pressing interests to attend to. The master may hold them to a strict responsibility, enforced by heavy penalties; but it is very questionable if those penalties will often fall in the right place.

It is always under great difficulties, and very imperfectly, that a country can be governed by foreigners; even when there is no extreme disparity, in habits and ideas, between the rulers and the ruled. Foreigners do not feel with the people. They cannot judge, by the light in which a thing appears to their own minds, or the manner in which it affects their feelings, how it will affect the feelings or appear to the minds of the subject population. What a native of the country, of average practical ability, knows as it were by instinct, they have to learn slowly, and after all imperfectly, by study and experience. The laws, the customs, the social relations, for which they have to legislate, instead of being familiar to them from childhood, are all strange to them. For most of their detailed knowledge they must depend on the information of natives; and it is difficult for them to know whom to trust. They are feared, suspected, probably disliked by the population; seldom sought by them except for interested purposes; and they are prone to think that the servilely submissive are the trustworthy. Their danger is of despising the natives; that of the natives is, of disbelieving that anything the strangers do can be intended for their good. These are but a part of the difficulties that any rulers have to struggle with, who honestly attempt to govern well a country in which they are foreigners. To overcome these difficulties in any degree, will always be a work of much labour, requiring a very superior degree of capacity in the chief administrators, and a high average among the subordinates: and the best organization of such a government is that which will best ensure the labour, develop the capacity, and place the highest specimens of it in the situations of greatest trust. Responsibility to an authority which has gone through none of the labour, acquired none of the capacity, and for the most part is not even aware that either, in any peculiar degree, is required, cannot be regarded as a very effectual expedient for accomplishing these ends.

The government of a people by itself has a meaning, and a reality; but such a thing as government of one people by another, does not and cannot exist. One people may keep another as a warren or preserve for its own use, a place to make money in, a human cattle farm to be worked for the profit of its own inhabitants. But if the good of the governed is the proper business of a government, it is utterly impossible that a people should directly attend to it. The utmost they can do is to give some of their best men a commission to look after it; to whom the opinion of their own country can neither be much of a guide in the performance of their duty, nor a competent judge of the mode in which it has been performed. Let any one consider how the English themselves would be governed, if they knew and cared no more about their own affairs, than they know and care about the affairs of the Hindoos. Even this comparison gives no adequate idea of the state of the case; for a people thus indifferent to politics altogether, would probably be simply acquiescent, and let the government alone: whereas in the case of India, a politically active people like the English, amidst habitual acquiescence, are every now and then interfering, and almost always in the wrong place. The real causes which determine the prosperity or wretchedness, the improvement or deterioration, of the Hindoos, are too far off to be within their ken. They have not the knowledge necessary for suspecting the existence of those causes, much less for judging of their operation. The most essential interests of the country may be well administered without obtaining any of their approbation, or mismanaged to almost any excess without attracting their notice. The purposes for which they are principally tempted to interfere, and control the proceedings of their delegates, are of two kinds. One is, to force English ideas down the throats of the natives; for instance, by measures of proselytism, or acts intentionally or unintentionally offensive to the religious feelings of the people. This misdirection of opinion in the ruling country is instructively exemplified (the more so, because nothing is meant but justice and fairness, and as much impartiality as can be expected from persons really convinced) by the demand now so general in England for having the Bible taught, at the option of pupils or of their parents, in the Government schools. From the European point of view nothing can wear a fairer aspect, or seem less open to objection on the score of religious freedom. To Asiatic eyes it is quite another thing.   No Asiatic people ever believes that a government puts its paid officers and official machinery into motion unless it is bent upon an object; and when bent on an object, no Asiatic believes that any government, except a feeble and contemptible one, pursues it by halves.   If Government schools and schoolmasters taught Christianity, whatever pledges might be given of teaching it only to those who spontaneously sought it, no amount of evidence would ever persuade the parents that improper means were not used to make their children Christians, or at all events, outcasts from Hindooism.   If they could, in the end, be convinced of the contrary, it would only be by the entire failure of the schools, so conducted, to make any converts. If the teaching had the smallest effect in promoting its object, it would compromise not only the utility and even existence of the government education, but perhaps the safety of the government itself.   An English Protestant would not be easily induced, by disclaimers of proselytism, to place his children in a Roman Catholic seminary: Irish Catholics will not send their children to schools in which they can be made Protestants: and we expect that Hindoos, who believe that the privileges of Hindooism can be forfeited by a merely physical act, will expose theirs to the danger of being made Christians!

Such is one of the modes in which the opinion of the dominant country tends to act more injuriously than beneficially on the conduct of its deputed governors.   In other respects, its interference is likely to be oftenest exercised where it will be most pertinaciously demanded, and that is, on behalf of some interest of the English settlers.   English settlers have friends at home, have organs, have access to the public; they have a common language and common ideas with their countrymen: any complaint by an Englishman is more sympathetically heard, even if no unjust preference is intentionally accorded to it.   Now, if there be a fact to which all experience testifies, it is that when a country holds another in subjection, the individuals of the ruling people who resort to the foreign country to make their fortunes, are of all others those who most need to be held under powerful restraint. They are always one of the chief difficulties of the government. Armed with the prestige and filled with the scornful overbearingness of the conquering nation, they have the feelings inspired by absolute power, without its sense of responsibility. Among a people like that of India, the utmost efforts of the public authorities are not enough for the effectual protection of the weak against the strong : and of all the strong, the European settlers are the strongest. Wherever the demoralizing effect of the situation is not in a most remarkable degree corrected by the personal character of the individual, they think the people of the country mere dirt under their feet : it seems to them monstrous that any rights of the natives should stand in the way of their smallest pretensions : the simplest act of protection to the inhabitants against any act of power on their part which they may consider useful to their commercial objects, they denounce, and sincerely regard, as an injury. So natural is this state of feeling in a situation like theirs, that even under the discouragement which it has hitherto met with from the ruling authorities, it is impossible that more or less of the spirit should not perpetually break out. The Government, itself free from this spirit, is never able sufficiently to keep it down in the young and raw even of its own civil and military officers, over whom it has so much more control than over the independent residents. As it is with the English in India, so, according to trustworthy testimony, it is with the French in Algiers ; so with the Americans, in the countries conquered from Mexico ; so it seems to be with the Europeans in China, and already even in Japan : there is no necessity to recall how it was with the Spaniards in South America. In all these cases, the government to which these private adventurers are subject, is better than they, and does the most it can to protect the natives against them. Even the

Spanish Government did this, sincerely and earnestly, though ineffectually, as is known to every reader of Mr. Helps' instructive history. Had the Spanish Government been directly accountable to Spanish opinion, we may question if it would have made the attempt : for the Spaniards, doubtless, would have taken part with their Christian friends and relations rather than with Pagans. The settlers, not the natives, have the ear of the public at home ; it is they whose representations are likely to pass for truth, because they alone have both the means and the motive to press them perseveringly upon the inattentive and uninterested public mind. The distrustful criticism with which Englishmen, more than any other people, are in the habit of scanning the conduct of their country towards foreigners, they usually reserve for the proceedings of the public authorities. In all questions between a government and an individual, the presumption in every Englishman's mind is, that the government is in the wrong. And when the resident English bring the batteries of English political action to bear upon any of the bulwarks erected to protect the natives against their encroachments, the executive, with their real but faint velleities of something better, generally find it safer to their parliamentary interest, and at any rate less troublesome, to give up the disputed position, than to defend it.

What makes matters worse is, that when the public mind is invoked (as, to its credit, the English mind is extremely open to be) in the name of justice and philanthropy, in behalf of the subject community or race, there is the same probability of its missing the mark. For in the subject community also there are oppressors and oppressed ; powerful individuals or classes, and slaves prostrate before them ; and it is the former, not the latter, who have the means of access to the English public. A tyrant or sensualist who has been deprived of the power he had abused, and, instead of punishment, is supported in as great wealth and splendour as he ever enjoyed ; a knot of

privileged landholders, who demand that the State
should relinquish to them its reserved right to a rent
from their lands, or who resent as a wrong any attempt
to protect the masses from their extortion ; these have
no difficulty in procuring interested or sentimental
advocacy in the British Parliament and press. The
silent myriads obtain none.

The preceding observations exemplify the operation
of a principle—which might be called an obvious one,
were it not that scarcely anybody seems to be aware
of it—that, while responsibility to the governed is the
greatest of all securities for good government, responsibility to somebody else not only has no such tendency,
but is as likely to produce evil as good. The responsibility of the British rulers of India to the British nation
is chiefly useful because, when any acts of the government are called in question, it ensures publicity and
discussion ; the utility of which does not require that
the public at large should comprehend the point at
issue, provided there are any individuals among them
who do ; for, a merely moral responsibility not being
responsibility to the collective people, but to every
separate person among them who forms a judgement,
opinions may be weighed as well as counted, and the
approbation or disapprobation of one person well versed
in the subject may outweigh that of thousands who
know nothing about it at all. It is doubtless a useful
restraint upon the immediate rulers that they can be
put upon their defence, and that one or two of the jury
will form an opinion worth having about their conduct,
though that of the remainder will probably be several
degrees worse than none. Such as it is, this is the amount
of benefit to India, from the control exercised over the
Indian government by the British Parliament and people.

It is not by attempting to rule directly a country
like India, but by giving it good rulers, that the
English people can do their duty to that country ;
and they can scarcely give it a worse one than an
English Cabinet Minister, who is thinking of English,
not Indian politics ; who seldom remains long enough

in office to acquire an intelligent interest in so complicated a subject; upon whom the factitious public opinion got up in Parliament, consisting of two or three fluent speakers, acts with as much force as if it were genuine; while he is under none of the influences of training and position which would lead or qualify him to form an honest opinion of his own. A free country which attempts to govern a distant dependency, inhabited by a dissimilar people, by means of a branch of its own executive, will almost inevitably fail. The only mode which has any chance of tolerable success, is to govern through a delegated body, of a comparatively permanent character; allowing only a right of inspection, and a negative voice, to the changeable Administration of the State. Such a body did exist in the case of India; and I fear that both India and England will pay a severe penalty for the shortsighted policy by which this intermediate instrument of government was done away with.

It is of no avail to say that such a delegated body cannot have all the requisites of good government; above all, cannot have that complete and ever-operative identity of interest with the governed, which it is so difficult to obtain even where the people to be ruled are in some degree qualified to look after their own affairs. Real good government is not compatible with the conditions of the case. There is but a choice of imperfections. The problem is, so to construct the governing body that, under the difficulties of the position, it shall have as much interest as possible in good government, and as little in bad. Now these conditions are best found in an intermediate body. A delegated administration has always this advantage over a direct one, that it has, at all events, no duty to perform except to the governed. It has no interests to consider except theirs. Its own power of deriving profit from misgovernment may be reduced—in the latest constitution of the East India Company it was reduced —to a singularly small amount: and it can be kept entirely clear of bias from the individual or class interests of any one else. When the home government and Parliament are swayed by those partial influences in the exercise of the power reserved to them in the last resort, the intermediate body is the certain advocate and champion of the dependency before the imperial tribunal. The intermediate body, moreover, is, in the natural course of things, chiefly composed of persons who have acquired professional knowledge of this part of their country's concerns; who have been trained to it in the place itself, and have made its administration the main occupation of their lives. Furnished with these qualifications, and not being liable to lose their office from the accidents of home politics, they identify their character and consideration with their special trust, and have a much more permanent interest in the success of their administration, and in the prosperity of the country which they administer, than a member of a Cabinet under a representative constitution can possibly have in the good government of any country except the one which he serves. So far as the choice of those who carry on the management on the spot devolves upon this body, the appointments are kept out of the vortex of party and parliamentary jobbing, and freed from the influence of those motives to the abuse of patronage, for the reward of adherents, or to buy off those who would otherwise be opponents, which are always stronger, with statesmen of average honesty, than a conscientious sense of the duty of appointing the fittest man. To put this one class of appointments as far as possible out of harm's way, is of more consequence than the worst which can happen to all other offices in the state; for, in every other department, if the officer is unqualified, the general opinion of the community directs him in a certain degree what to do: but in the position of the administrators of a dependency where the people are not fit to have the control in their own hands, the character of the government entirely depends on the qualifications, moral and intellectual, of the individual functionaries.

It cannot be too often repeated, that in a country like India everything depends on the personal qualities and capacities of the agents of government. This truth is the cardinal principle of Indian administration. The day when it comes to be thought that the appointment of persons to situations of trust from motives of convenience, already so criminal in England, can be practised with impunity in India, will be the beginning of the decline and fall of our empire there. Even with a sincere intention of preferring the best candidate, it will not do to rely on chance for supplying fit persons. The system must be calculated to form them. It has done this hitherto; and because it has done so, our rule in India has lasted, and been one of constant, if not very rapid, improvement in prosperity and good administration. As much bitterness is now manifested against this system, and as much eagerness displayed to overthrow it, as if educating and training the officers of government for their work were a thing utterly unreasonable and indefensible, an unjustifiable interference with the rights of ignorance and inexperience. There is a tacit conspiracy between those who would like to job in first-rate Indian offices for their connexions here, and those who, being already in India, claim to be promoted from the indigo factory or the attorney's office, to administer justice or fix the payments due to government from millions of people. The ' monopoly' of the Civil Service, so much inveighed against, is like the monopoly of judicial offices by the bar ; and its abolition would be like opening the bench in Westminster Hall to the first comer whose friends certify that he has now and then looked into Blackstone. Were the course ever adopted of sending men from this country, or encouraging them in going out, to get themselves put into high appointments without having learnt their business by passing through the lower ones, the most important offices would be thrown to Scotch cousins and adventurers, connected by no professional feeling with the country or the work, held to no previous knowledge, and eager only to make money rapidly and return home. The safety of the country is, that those by whom it is administered be sent out in youth, as candidates only, to begin at the bottom of the ladder, and ascend higher or not, as, after a proper interval, they are proved qualified. The defect of the East India Company's system was, that though the best men were carefully sought out for the most important posts, yet if an officer remained in the service, promotion, though it might be delayed, came at last in some shape or other, to the least as well as to the most competent. Even the inferior in qualifications, among such a corps of functionaries, consisted, it must be remembered, of men who had been brought up to their duties, and had fulfilled them for many years, at lowest without disgrace, under the eye and authority of a superior. But though this diminished the evil, it was nevertheless considerable. A man who never becomes fit for more than an assistant's duty, should remain an assistant all his life, and his juniors should be promoted over him. With this exception, I am not aware of any real defect in the old system of Indian appointments. It had already received the greatest other improvement it was susceptible of, the choice of the original candidates by competitive examination: which, besides the advantage of recruiting from a higher grade of industry and capacity, has the recommendation, that under it, unless by accident, there are no personal ties between the candidates for offices and those who have a voice in conferring them.

It is in no way unjust, that public officers thus selected and trained should be exclusively eligible to offices which require specially Indian knowledge and experience. If any door to the higher appointments, without passing through the lower, be opened even for occasional use, there will be such incessant knocking at it by persons of influence, that it will be impossible ever to keep it closed. The only excepted appointment should be the highest one of all. The Viceroy of British India should be a person selected from all

Englishmen for his great general capacity for government. If he have this, he will be able to distinguish
in others, and turn to his own use, that special knowledge and judgement in local affairs which he has not
himself had the opportunity of acquiring. There are
good reasons why (saving exceptional cases) the Viceroy
should not be a member of the regular service. All
services have, more or less, their class prejudices, from
which the supreme ruler ought to be exempt. Neither
are men, however able and experienced, who have
passed their lives in Asia, so likely to possess the most
advanced European ideas in general statesmanship ;
which the chief ruler should carry out with him, and
blend with the results of Indian experience. Again,
being of a different class, and especially if chosen by
a different authority, he will seldom have any personal
partialities to warp his appointments to office. This
great security for honest bestowal of patronage existed
in rare perfection, under the mixed government of the
Crown and the East India Company. The supreme
dispensers of office, the Governor-General and Governors, were appointed, in fact though not formally, by
the Crown, that is, by the general Government, not
by the intermediate body ; and a great officer of the
Crown probably had not a single personal or political
connexion in the local service : while the delegated
body, most of whom had themselves served in the
country, had and were likely to have such connexions.
This guarantee for impartiality would be much impaired, if the civil servants of Government, even though
sent out in boyhood as mere candidates for employment, should come to be furnished, in any considerable
proportion, by the class of society which supplies viceroys and governors. Even the initiatory competitive
examination would then be an insufficient security.
It would exclude mere ignorance and incapacity ; it
would compel youths of family to start in the race
with the same amount of instruction and ability as
other people ; the stupidest son could not be put into
the Indian service, as he can be into the Church ; but

there would be nothing to prevent undue preference afterwards. No longer all equally unknown and unheard of by the arbiter of their lot, a portion of the service would be personally, and a still greater number politically, in close relation with him. Members of certain families, and of the higher classes and influential connexions generally, would rise more rapidly than their competitors, and be often kept in situations for which they were unfit, or placed in those for which others were fitter. The same influences would be brought into play, which affect promotions in the army : and those alone, if such miracles of simplicity there be, who believe that these are impartial, would expect impartiality in those of India. This evil is, I fear, irremediable by any general measures which can be taken under the present system. No such will afford a degree of security comparable to that which once flowed spontaneously from the so-called double government.

What is accounted so great an advantage in the case of the English system of government at home, has been its misfortune in India—that it grew up of itself, not from preconceived design, but by successive expedients, and by the adaptation of machinery originally created for a different purpose. As the country on which its maintenance depended, was not the one out of whose necessities it grew, its practical benefits did not come home to the mind of that country, and it would have required theoretic recommendations to render it acceptable. Unfortunately, these were exactly what it seemed to be destitute of : and undoubtedly the common theories of government did not furnish it with such, framed as those theories have been for states of circumstances differing in all the most important features from the case concerned. But in government, as in other departments of human agency, almost all principles which have been durable were first suggested by observation of some particular case, in which the general laws of nature acted in some new or previously unnoticed combination of

circumstances.   The institutions of Great Britain, and those of the United States, have had the distinction of suggesting most of the theories of government which, through good and evil fortune, are now, in the course of generations, reawakening political life in the nations of Europe.   It has been the destiny of the government of the East India Company, to suggest the true theory of the government of a semi-barbarous dependency by a civilized country, and after having done this, to perish.   It would be a singular fortune if, at the end of two or three more generations, this speculative result should be the only remaining fruit of our ascendancy in India ; if posterity should say of us, that having stumbled accidentally upon better arrangements than our wisdom would ever have devised, the first use we made of our awakened reason was to destroy them, and allow the good which had been in course of being realized to fall through and be lost, from ignorance of the principles on which it depended. *Di meliora* : but if a fate so disgraceful to England and to civilization can be averted, it must be through far wider political conceptions than merely English or European practice can supply, and through a much more profound study of Indian experience, and of the conditions of Indian government, than either English politicians, or those who supply the English public with opinions, have hitherto shown any willingness to undertake.

THE SUBJECTION

OF

WOMEN

CHAPTER I

THE object of this Essay is to explain, as clearly as I am able, the grounds of an opinion which I have held from the very earliest period when I had formed any opinions at all on social or political matters, and which, instead of being weakened or modified, has been constantly growing stronger by the progress of reflection and the experience of life : That the principle which regulates the existing social relations between the two sexes—the legal subordination of one sex to the other—is wrong in itself, and now one of the chief hindrances to human improvement ; and that it ought to be replaced by a principle of perfect equality, admitting no power or privilege on the one side, nor disability on the other.

The very words necessary to express the task I have undertaken, show how arduous it is. But it would be a mistake to suppose that the difficulty of the case must lie in the insufficiency or obscurity of the grounds of reason on which my conviction rests. The difficulty is that which exists in all cases in which there is a mass of feeling to be contended against. So long as an opinion is strongly rooted in the feelings, it gains rather than loses in stability by having a preponderating weight of argument against it. For if it were accepted as a result of argument, the refutation of the argument might shake the solidity of the conviction ; but when it rests solely on feeling, the worse it fares in argumentative contest, the more persuaded its adherents are that their feeling must have some deeper ground, which the arguments do not reach ; and while the feeling remains, it is always throwing up fresh entrenchments of argument to repair any breach made in the old. And there are so many causes tending to make the feelings connected with this subject the

most intense and most deeply-rooted of all those which
gather round and protect old institutions and customs,
that we need not wonder to find them as yet less
undermined and loosened than any of the rest by the
progress of the great modern spiritual and social transition ; nor suppose that the barbarisms to which men
cling longest must be less barbarisms than those which
they earlier shake off.

In every respect the burthen is hard on those who
attack an almost universal opinion. They must be
very fortunate as well as unusually capable if they
obtain a hearing at all. They have more difficulty in
obtaining a trial, than any other litigants have in
getting a verdict. If they do extort a hearing, they
are subjected to a set of logical requirements totally
different from those exacted from other people. In
all other cases, the burthen of proof is supposed to
lie with the affirmative. If a person is charged with
a murder, it rests with those who accuse him to give
proof of his guilt, not with himself to prove his innocence. If there is a difference of opinion about the
reality of any alleged historical event, in which the
feelings of men in general are not much interested, as
the Siege of Troy for example, those who maintain
that the event took place are expected to produce their
proofs, before those who take the other side can be
required to say anything ; and at no time are these
required to do more than show that the evidence produced by the others is of no value. Again, in practical
matters, the burthen of proof is supposed to be with
those who are against liberty ; who contend for any
restriction or prohibition ; either any limitation of
the general freedom of human action, or any disqualification or disparity of privilege affecting one person
or kind of persons, as compared with others. The
a priori presumption is in favour of freedom and
impartiality. It is held that there should be no restraint not required by the general good, and that the
law should be no respecter of persons, but should treat
all alike, save where dissimilarity of treatment is

required by positive reasons, either of justice or of policy. But of none of these rules of evidence will the benefit be allowed to those who maintain the opinion I profess. It is useless for me to say that those who maintain the doctrine that men have a right to command and women are under an obligation to obey, or that men are fit for government and women unfit, are on the affirmative side of the question, and that they are bound to show positive evidence for the assertions, or submit to their rejection. It is equally unavailing for me to say that those who deny to women any freedom or privilege rightly allowed to men, having the double presumption against them that they are opposing freedom and recommending partiality, must be held to the strictest proof of their case, and unless their success be such as to exclude all doubt, the judgement ought to go against them. These would be thought good pleas in any common case; but they will not be thought so in this instance. Before I could hope to make any impression, I should be expected not only to answer all that has ever been said by those who take the other side of the question, but to imagine all that could be said by them—to find them in reasons, as well as answer all I find: and besides refuting all arguments for the affirmative, I shall be called upon for invincible positive arguments to prove a negative. And even if I could do all this, and leave the opposite party with a host of unanswered arguments against them, and not a single unrefuted one on their side, I should be thought to have done little; for a cause supported on the one hand by universal usage, and on the other by so great a preponderance of popular sentiment, is supposed to have a presumption in its favour, superior to any conviction which an appeal to reason has power to produce in any intellects but those of a high class.

I do not mention these difficulties to complain of them; first, because it would be useless; they are inseparable from having to contend through people's understandings against the hostility of their feelings and practical tendencies : and truly the understandings of the majority of mankind would need to be much better cultivated than has ever yet been the case, before they can be asked to place such reliance in their own power of estimating arguments, as to give up practical principles in which they have been born and bred, and which are the basis of much of the existing order of the world, at the first argumentative attack which they are not capable of logically resisting. I do not therefore quarrel with them for having too little faith in argument, but for having too much faith in custom and the general feeling. It is one of the characteristic prejudices of the reaction of the nineteenth century against the eighteenth, to accord to the unreasoning elements in human nature the infallibility which the eighteenth century is supposed to have ascribed to the reasoning elements. For the apotheosis of Reason we have substituted that of Instinct ; and we call everything instinct which we find in ourselves and for which we cannot trace any rational foundation. This idolatry, infinitely more degrading than the other, and the most pernicious of the false worships of the present day, of all of which it is now the main support, will probably hold its ground until it gives way before a sound psychology, laying bare the real root of much that is bowed down to as the intention of Nature and the ordinance of God. As regards the present question, I am willing to accept the unfavourable conditions which the prejudice assigns to me. I consent that established custom, and the general feeling, should be deemed conclusive against me, unless that custom and feeling from age to age can be shown to have owed their existence to other causes than their soundness, and to have derived their power from the worse rather than the better parts of human nature. I am willing that judgement should go against me, unless I can show that my judge has been tampered with. The concession is not so great as it might appear ; for to prove this, is by far the easiest portion of my task.

The generality of a practice is in some cases a strong presumption that it is, or at all events once was, conducive to laudable ends. This is the case, when the practice was first adopted, or afterwards kept up, as a means to such ends, and was grounded on experience of the mode in which they could be most effectually attained. If the authority of men over women, when first established, had been the result of a conscientious comparison between different modes of constituting the government of society; if, after trying various other modes of social organization—the government of women over men, equality between the two, and such mixed and divided modes of government as might be invented—it had been decided, on the testimony of experience, that the mode in which women are wholly under the rule of men, having no share at all in public concerns, and each in private being under the legal obligation of obedience to the man with whom she has associated her destiny, was the arrangement most conducive to the happiness and well-being of both; its general adoption might then be fairly thought to be some evidence that, at the time when it was adopted, it was the best: though even then the considerations which recommended it may, like so many other primeval social facts of the greatest importance, have subsequently, in the course of ages, ceased to exist. But the state of the case is in every respect the reverse of this. In the first place, the opinion in favour of the present system, which entirely subordinates the weaker sex to the stronger, rests upon theory only; for there never has been trial made of any other: so that experience, in the sense in which it is vulgarly opposed to theory, cannot be pretended to have pronounced any verdict. And in the second place, the adoption of this system of inequality never was the result of deliberation, or forethought, or any social ideas, or any notion whatever of what conduced to the benefit of humanity or the good order of society. It arose simply from the fact that from the very earliest twilight of human society, every woman (owing to the value attached to her by men, combined with her inferiority in muscular strength) was found in a state of bondage to some man. Laws and systems of polity always begin by recognizing the relations they find already existing between individuals. They convert what was a mere physical fact into a legal right, give it the sanction of society, and principally aim at the substitution of public and organized means of asserting and protecting these rights, instead of the irregular and lawless conflict of physical strength. Those who had already been compelled to obedience became in this manner legally bound to it. Slavery, from being a mere affair of force between the master and the slave, became regularized and a matter of compact among the masters, who, binding themselves to one another for common protection, guaranteed by their collective strength the private possessions of each, including his slaves. In early times, the great majority of the male sex were slaves, as well as the whole of the female. And many ages elapsed, some of them ages of high cultivation, before any thinker was bold enough to question the rightfulness, and the absolute social necessity, either of the one slavery or of the other. By degrees such thinkers did arise: and (the general progress of society assisting) the slavery of the male sex has, in all the countries of Christian Europe at least (though, in one of them, only within the last few years) been at length abolished, and that of the female sex has been gradually changed into a milder form of dependence. But this dependence, as it exists at present, is not an original institution, taking a fresh start from considerations of justice and social expediency—it is the primitive state of slavery lasting on, through successive mitigations and modifications occasioned by the same causes which have softened the general manners, and brought all human relations more under the control of justice and the influence of humanity. It has not lost the taint of its brutal origin. No presumption in its favour, therefore, can be drawn from the fact of its existence. The only such presumption which it could be supposed to have, must be grounded on its having lasted till now, when so many other things which came down from the same odious source have been done away with. And this, indeed, is what makes it strange to ordinary ears, to hear it asserted that the inequality of rights between men and women has no other source than the law of the strongest.

That this statement should have the effect of a paradox, is in some respects creditable to the progress of civilization, and the improvement of the moral sentiments of mankind. We now live—that is to say, one or two of the most advanced nations of the world now live—in a state in which the law of the strongest seems to be entirely abandoned as the regulating principle of the world's affairs: nobody professes it, and, as regards most of the relations between human beings, nobody is permitted to practise it. When any one succeeds in doing so, it is under cover of some pretext which gives him the semblance of having some general social interest on his side. This being the ostensible state of things, people flatter themselves that the rule of mere force is ended; that the law of the strongest cannot be the reason of existence of anything which has remained in full operation down to the present time. However any of our present institutions may have begun, it can only, they think, have been preserved to this period of advanced civilization by a well-grounded feeling of its adaptation to human nature, and conduciveness to the general good. They do not understand the great vitality and durability of institutions which place right on the side of might; how intensely they are clung to; how the good as well as the bad propensities and sentiments of those who have power in their hands, become identified with retaining it; how slowly these bad institutions give way, one at a time, the weakest first, beginning with those which are least interwoven with the daily habits of life; and how very rarely those who have obtained legal power because they first had physical, have ever lost their hold of it until the physical power had passed over to the other side. Such shifting of the physical force not having taken place in the case of women; this fact, combined with all the peculiar and characteristic features of the particular case, made it certain from the first that this branch of the system of right founded on might, though softened in its most atrocious features at an earlier period than several of the others, would be the very last to disappear. It was inevitable that this one case of a social relation grounded on force would survive through generations of institutions grounded on equal justice, an almost solitary exception to the general character of their laws and customs; but which, so long as it does not proclaim its own origin, and as discussion has not brought out its true character, is not felt to jar with modern civilization, any more than domestic slavery among the Greeks jarred with their notion of themselves as a free people.

The truth is, that people of the present and the last two or three generations have lost all practical sense of the primitive condition of humanity; and only the few who have studied history accurately, or have much frequented the parts of the world occupied by the living representatives of ages long past, are able to form any mental picture of what society then was. People are not aware how entirely, in former ages, the law of superior strength was the rule of life; how publicly and openly it was avowed, I do not say cynically or shamelessly—for these words imply a feeling that there was something in it to be ashamed of, and no such notion could find a place in the faculties of any person in those ages, except a philosopher or a saint. History gives a cruel experience of human nature, in showing how exactly the regard due to the life, possessions, and entire earthly happiness of any class of persons, was measured by what they had the power of enforcing; how all who made any resistance to authorities that had arms in their hands, however dreadful might be the provocation, had not only the law of force but all other laws, and all the notions of social obligation against them; and, in the eyes of those whom they resisted, were not only guilty of crime, but of the worst of all crimes, deserving the most cruel chastisement which human beings could inflict. The first small vestige of a feeling of obligation in a superior to acknowledge any right in inferiors, began when he had been induced, for convenience, to make some promise to them. Though these promises, even when sanctioned by the most solemn oaths, were for many ages revoked or violated on the most trifling provocation or temptation, it is probable that this, except by persons of still worse than the average morality, was seldom done without some twinges of conscience. The ancient republics, being mostly grounded from the first upon some kind of mutual compact, or at any rate formed by an union of persons not very unequal in strength, afforded, in consequence, the first instance of a portion of human relations fenced round, and placed under the dominion of another law than that of force. And though the original law of force remained in full operation between them and their slaves, and also (except so far as limited by express compact) between a commonwealth and its subjects, or other independent commonwealths; the banishment of that primitive law, even from so narrow a field, commenced the regeneration of human nature, by giving birth to sentiments of which experience soon demonstrated the immense value even for material interests, and which thenceforward only required to be enlarged, not created. Though slaves were no part of the commonwealth, it was in the free states that slaves were first felt to have rights as human beings. The Stoics were, I believe, the first (except so far as the Jewish law constitutes an exception) who taught as a part of morality that men were bound by moral obligations to their slaves. No one, after Christianity became ascendant, could ever again have been a stranger to this belief, in theory; nor, after the rise of the Catholic Church, was it ever without persons to stand up for it. Yet to enforce it was the most arduous task which Christianity ever had to perform. For more than a thousand years the Church kept up the contest, with hardly any perceptible success. It was not for want of power over men's minds. Its power was prodigious. It could make kings and nobles resign their most valued possessions to enrich the Church. It could make thousands, in the prime of life and the height of worldly advantages, shut themselves up in convents to work out their salvation by poverty, fasting, and prayer. It could send hundreds of thousands across land and sea, Europe and Asia, to give their lives for the deliverance of the Holy Sepulchre. It could make kings relinquish wives who were the objects of their passionate attachment, because the Church declared that they were within the seventh (by our calculation the fourteenth) degree of relationship. All this it did; but it could not make men fight less with one another, nor tyrannize less cruelly over the serfs, and, when they were able, over burgesses. It could not make them renounce either of the applications of force; force militant, or force triumphant. This they could never be induced to do until they were themselves in their turn compelled by superior force. Only by the growing power of kings was an end put to fighting except between kings, or competitors for kingship; only by the growth of a wealthy and warlike bourgeoisie in the fortified towns, and of a plebeian infantry which proved more powerful in the field than the undisciplined chivalry, was the insolent tyranny of the nobles over the bourgeoisie and peasantry brought within some bounds. It was persisted in not only until, but long after, the oppressed had obtained a power enabling them often to take conspicuous vengeance; and on the Continent much of it continued to the time of the French Revolution, though in England the earlier and better organization of the democratic classes put an end to it sooner, by establishing equal laws and free national institutions.

If people are mostly so little aware how completely,

during the greater part of the duration of our species, the law of force was the avowed rule of general conduct, any other being only a special and exceptional consequence of peculiar ties—and from how very recent a date it is that the affairs of society in general have been even pretended to be regulated according to any moral law; as little do people remember or consider, how institutions and customs which never had any ground but the law of force, last on into ages and states of general opinion which never would have permitted their first establishment. Less than forty years ago, Englishmen might still by law hold human beings in bondage as saleable property: within the present century they might kidnap them and carry them off, and work them literally to death. This absolutely extreme case of the law of force, condemned by those who can tolerate almost every other form of arbitrary power, and which, of all others, presents features the most revolting to the feelings of all who look at it from an impartial position, was the law of civilized and Christian England within the memory of persons now living: and in one half of Anglo-Saxon America three or four years ago, not only did slavery exist, but the slave trade, and the breeding of slaves expressly for it, was a general practice between slave states. Yet not only was there a greater strength of sentiment against it, but, in England at least, a less amount either of feeling or of interest in favour of it, than of any other of the customary abuses of force: for its motive was the love of gain, unmixed and undisguised; and those who profited by it were a very small numerical fraction of the country, while the natural feeling of all who were not personally interested in it, was unmitigated abhorrence. So extreme an instance makes it almost superfluous to refer to any other: but consider the long duration of absolute monarchy. In England at present it is the almost universal conviction that military despotism is a case of the law of force, having no other origin or justification. Yet in all the great nations of Europe except England it either still exists, or has only just ceased to exist, and has even now a strong party favourable to it in all ranks of the people, especially among persons of station and consequence. Such is the power of an established system, even when far from universal; when not only in almost every period of history there have been great and well-known examples of the contrary system, but these have almost invariably been afforded by the most illustrious and most prosperous communities. In this case, too, the possessor of the undue power, the person directly interested in it, is only one person, while those who are subject to it and suffer from it are literally all the rest. The yoke is naturally and necessarily humiliating to all persons, except the one who is on the throne, together with, at most, the one who expects to succeed to it. How different are these cases from that of the power of men over women! I am not now prejudging the question of its justifiableness. I am showing how vastly more permanent it could not but be, even if not justifiable, than these other dominations which have nevertheless lasted down to our own time. Whatever gratification of pride there is in the possession of power, and whatever personal interest in its exercise, is in this case not confined to a limited class, but common to the whole male sex. Instead of being, to most of its supporters, a thing desirable chiefly in the abstract, or, like the political ends usually contended for by factions, of little private importance to any but the leaders; it comes home to the person and hearth of every male head of a family, and of every one who looks forward to being so. The clodhopper exercises, or is to exercise, his share of the power equally with the highest nobleman. And the case is that in which the desire of power is the strongest: for every one who desires power, desires it most over those who are nearest to him, with whom his life is passed, with whom he has most concerns in common, and in whom any independence of his authority is oftenest likely to interfere with his individual preferences. If, in the other cases specified,

powers manifestly grounded only on force, and having
so much less to support them, are so slowly and with
so much difficulty got rid of, much more must it be so
with this, even if it rests on no better foundation than
those. We must consider, too, that the possessors of
the power have facilities in this case, greater than in
any other, to prevent any uprising against it. Every
one of the subjects lives under the very eye, and almost,
it may be said, in the hands, of one of the masters—
in closer intimacy with him than with any of her
fellow subjects; with no means of combining against
him, no power of even locally overmastering him, and,
on the other hand, with the strongest motives for
seeking his favour and avoiding to give him offence.
In struggles for political emancipation, everybody
knows how often its champions are bought off by
bribes, or daunted by terrors. In the case of women,
each individual of the subject-class is in a chronic
state of bribery and intimidation combined. In setting
up the standard of resistance, a large number of the
leaders, and still more of the followers, must make an
almost complete sacrifice of the pleasures or the
alleviations of their own individual lot. If ever any
system of privilege and enforced subjection had its
yoke tightly riveted on the necks of those who are
kept down by it, this has. I have not yet shown that
it is a wrong system: but every one who is capable
of thinking on the subject must see that even if it is,
it was certain to outlast all other forms of unjust
authority. And when some of the grossest of the other
forms still exist in many civilized countries, and have
only recently been got rid of in others, it would be
strange if that which is so much the deepest-rooted
had yet been perceptibly shaken anywhere. There is
more reason to wonder that the protests and testi-
monies against it should have been so numerous and
so weighty as they are.

Some will object, that a comparison cannot fairly
be made between the government of the male sex and
the forms of unjust power which I have adduced in

illustration of it, since these are arbitrary, and the effect of mere usurpation, while it on the contrary is natural. But was there ever any domination which did not appear natural to those who possessed it? There was a time when the division of mankind into two classes, a small one of masters and a numerous one of slaves, appeared, even to the most cultivated minds, to be a natural, and the only natural, condition of the human race. No less an intellect, and one which contributed no less to the progress of human thought, than Aristotle, held this opinion without doubt or misgiving; and rested it on the same premisses on which the same assertion in regard to the dominion of men over women is usually based, namely that there are different natures among mankind, free natures, and slave natures; that the Greeks were of a free nature, the barbarian races of Thracians and Asiatics of a slave nature. But why need I go back to Aristotle? Did not the slave-owners of the Southern United States maintain the same doctrine, with all the fanaticism with which men cling to the theories that justify their passions and legitimate their personal interests? Did they not call heaven and earth to witness that the dominion of the white man over the black is natural, that the black race is by nature incapable of freedom, and marked out for slavery?—some even going so far as to say that the freedom of manual labourers is an unnatural order of things anywhere. Again, the theorists of absolute monarchy have always affirmed it to be the only natural form of government; issuing from the patriarchal, which was the primitive and spontaneous form of society, framed on the model of the paternal, which is anterior to society itself, and, as they contend, the most natural authority of all. Nay, for that matter, the law of force itself, to those who could not plead any other, has always seemed the most natural of all grounds for the exercise of authority. Conquering races hold it to be Nature's own dictate that the conquered should obey the conquerors, or, as they euphoniously paraphrase it, that the feebler and

more unwarlike races should submit to the braver and
manlier. The smallest acquaintance with human life
in the Middle Ages shows how supremely natural the
dominion of the feudal nobility over men of low condition appeared to the nobility themselves, and how
unnatural the conception seemed, of a person of the
inferior class claiming equality with them, or exercising authority over them. It hardly seemed less so to
the class held in subjection. The emancipated serfs
and burgesses, even in their most vigorous struggles,
never made any pretension to a share of authority;
they only demanded more or less of limitation to the
power of tyrannizing over them. So true is it that
unnatural generally means only uncustomary, and
that everything which is usual appears natural. The
subjection of women to men being a universal custom,
any departure from it quite naturally appears unnatural. But how entirely, even in this case, the feeling is dependent on custom, appears by ample experience. Nothing so much astonishes the people of distant
parts of the world, when they first learn anything
about England, as to be told that it is under a queen:
the thing seems to them so unnatural as to be almost
incredible. To Englishmen this does not seem in the
least degree unnatural, because they are used to it;
but they do feel it unnatural that women should be
soldiers or members of Parliament. In the feudal ages,
on the contrary, war and politics were not thought
unnatural to women, because not unusual; it seemed
natural that women of the privileged classes should be
of manly character, inferior in nothing but bodily
strength to their husbands and fathers. The independence of women seemed rather less unnatural
to the Greeks than to other ancients, on account of
the fabulous Amazons (whom they believed to be historical), and the partial example afforded by the
Spartan women; who, though no less subordinate by
law than in other Greek states, were more free in
fact, and being trained to bodily exercises in the same
manner with men, gave ample proof that they were

not naturally disqualified for them.   There can be little doubt that Spartan experience suggested to Plato, among many other of his doctrines, that of the social and political equality of the two sexes.

But, it will be said, the rule of men over women differs from all these others in not being a rule of force: it is accepted voluntarily; women make no complaint, and are consenting parties to it.   In the first place, a great number of women do not accept it.   Ever since there have been women able to make their sentiments known by their writings (the only mode of publicity which society permits to them), an increasing number of them have recorded protests against their present social condition: and recently many thousands of them, headed by the most eminent women known to the public, have petitioned Parliament for their admission to the Parliamentary Suffrage.   The claim of women to be educated as solidly, and in the same branches of knowledge, as men, is urged with growing intensity, and with a great prospect of success; while the demand for their admission into professions and occupations hitherto closed against them, becomes every year more urgent.   Though there are not in this country, as there are in the United States, periodical Conventions and an organized party to agitate for the Rights of Women, there is a numerous and active Society organized and managed by women, for the more limited object of obtaining the political franchise. Nor is it only in our own country and in America that women are beginning to protest, more or less collectively, against the disabilities under which they labour. France, and Italy, and Switzerland, and Russia now afford examples of the same thing.   How many more women there are who silently cherish similar aspirations, no one can possibly know; but there are abundant tokens how many *would* cherish them, were they not so strenuously taught to repress them as contrary to the proprieties of their sex.   It must be remembered, also, that no enslaved class ever asked for complete liberty at once.   When Simon de Montfort called the deputies of the commons to sit for the first time in Parliament, did any of them dream of demanding that an assembly, elected by their constituents, should make and destroy ministries, and dictate to the king in affairs of State ? No such thought entered into the imagination of the most ambitious of them. The nobility had already these pretensions ; the commons pretended to nothing but to be exempt from arbitrary taxation, and from the gross individual oppression of the king's officers. It is a political law of nature that those who are under any power of ancient origin never begin by complaining of the power itself, but only of its oppressive exercise. There is never any want of women who complain of ill usage by their husbands. There would be infinitely more, if complaint were not the greatest of all provocatives to a repetition and increase of the ill usage. It is this which frustrates all attempts to maintain the power but protect the woman against its abuses. In no other case (except that of a child) is the person who has been proved judicially to have suffered an injury, replaced under the physical power of the culprit who inflicted it. Accordingly wives, even in the most extreme and protracted cases of bodily ill usage, hardly ever dare avail themselves of the laws made for their protection : and if, in a moment of irrepressible indignation, or by the interference of neighbours, they are induced to do so, their whole effort afterwards is to disclose as little as they can, and to beg off their tyrant from his merited chastisement.

All causes, social and natural, combine to make it unlikely that women should be collectively rebellious to the power of men. They are so far in a position different from all other subject classes, that their masters require something more from them than actual service. Men do not want solely the obedience of women, they want their sentiments. All men, except the most brutish, desire to have, in the woman most nearly connected with them, not a forced slave but a willing one; not a slave merely, but a favourite.

They have therefore put everything in practice to enslave their minds. The masters of all other slaves rely, for maintaining obedience, on fear; either fear of themselves, or religious fears. The masters of women wanted more than simple obedience, and they turned the whole force of education to effect their purpose. All women are brought up from the very earliest years in the belief that their ideal of character is the very opposite to that of men; not self-will, and government by self-control, but submission, and yielding to the control of others. All the moralities tell them that it is the duty of women, and all the current sentimentalities that it is their nature, to live for others; to make complete abnegation of themselves, and to have no life but in their affections. And by their affections are meant the only ones they are allowed to have—those to the men with whom they are connected, or to the children who constitute an additional and indefeasible tie between them and a man. When we put together three things—first, the natural attraction between opposite sexes; secondly, the wife's entire dependence on the husband, every privilege or pleasure she has being either his gift, or depending entirely on his will; and lastly, that the principal object of human pursuit, consideration, and all objects of social ambition, can in general be sought or obtained by her only through him—it would be a miracle if the object of being attractive to men had not become the polar star of feminine education and formation of character. And, this great means of influence over the minds of women having been acquired, an instinct of selfishness made men avail themselves of it to the utmost as a means of holding women in subjection, by representing to them meekness, submissiveness, and resignation of all individual will into the hands of a man, as an essential part of sexual attractiveness. Can it be doubted that any of the other yokes which mankind have succeeded in breaking, would have subsisted till now if the same means had existed, and had been as sedulously used,

to bow down their minds to it ?   If it had been made
the object of the life of every young plebeian to find
personal favour in the eyes of some patrician, of every
young serf with some seigneur ; if domestication with
him, and a share of his personal affections, had been
held out as the prize which they all should look out
for, the most gifted and aspiring being able to reckon
on the most desirable prizes ; and if, when this prize
had been obtained, they had been shut out by a wall
of brass from all interests not centring in him, all
feelings and desires but those which he shared or
inculcated ; would not serfs and seigneurs, plebeians
and patricians, have been as broadly distinguished at
this day as men and women are ? and would not all
but a thinker here and there have believed the distinction to be a fundamental and unalterable fact in
human nature ?

The preceding considerations are amply sufficient to
show that custom, however universal it may be, affords
in this case no presumption, and ought not to create
any prejudice, in favour of the arrangements which
place women in social and political subjection to men.
But I may go farther, and maintain that the course
of history, and the tendencies of progressive human
society, afford not only no presumption in favour of
this system of inequality of rights, but a strong one
against it ; and that, so far as the whole course of
human improvement up to this time, the whole stream
of modern tendencies, warrants any inference on the
subject, it is, that this relic of the past is discordant
with the future, and must necessarily disappear.

For what is the peculiar character of the modern
world—the difference which chiefly distinguishes
modern institutions, modern social ideas, modern
life itself, from those of times long past ? It is, that
human beings are no longer born to their place in life,
and chained down by an inexorable bond to the place
they are born to, but are free to employ their faculties,
and such favourable chances as offer, to achieve the
lot which may appear to them most desirable.   Human

society of old was constituted on a very different principle. All were born to a fixed social position, and were mostly kept in it by law, or interdicted from any means by which they could emerge from it. As some men are born white and others black, so some were born slaves and others freemen and citizens; some were born patricians, others plebeians; some were born feudal nobles, others commoners and *roturiers*. A slave or serf could never make himself free, nor, except by the will of his master, become so. In most European countries it was not till towards the close of the Middle Ages, and as a consequence of the growth of regal power, that commoners could be ennobled. Even among nobles, the eldest son was born the exclusive heir to the paternal possessions, and a long time elapsed before it was fully established that the father could disinherit him. Among the industrious classes, only those who were born members of a guild, or were admitted into it by its members, could lawfully practise their calling within its local limits; and nobody could practise any calling deemed important, in any but the legal manner—by processes authoritatively prescribed. Manufacturers have stood in the pillory for presuming to carry on their business by new and improved methods. In modern Europe, and most in those parts of it which have participated most largely in all other modern improvements, diametrically opposite doctrines now prevail. Law and government do not undertake to prescribe by whom any social or industrial operation shall or shall not be conducted, or what modes of conducting them shall be lawful. These things are left to the unfettered choice of individuals. Even the laws which required that workmen should serve an apprenticeship, have in this country been repealed: there being ample assurance that in all cases in which an apprenticeship is necessary, its necessity will suffice to enforce it. The old theory was, that the least possible should be left to the choice of the individual agent; that all he had to do should, as far as practicable, be laid down for him by superior wisdom.   Left to himself he was sure to go wrong. The modern conviction, the fruit of a thousand years of experience, is, that things in which the individual is the person directly interested, never go right but as they are left to his own discretion ; and that any regulation of them by authority, except to protect the rights of others, is sure to be mischievous.   This conclusion, slowly arrived at, and not adopted until almost every possible application of the contrary theory had been made with disastrous result, now (in the industrial department) prevails universally in the most advanced countries, almost universally in all that have pretensions to any sort of advancement.   It is not that all processes are supposed to be equally good, or all persons to be equally qualified for everything ; but that freedom of individual choice is now known to be the only thing which procures the adoption of the best processes, and throws each operation into the hands of those who are best qualified for it.   Nobody thinks it necessary to make a law that only a strong-armed man shall be a blacksmith.   Freedom and competition suffice to make blacksmiths strong armed men, because the weak-armed can earn more by engaging in occupations for which they are more fit.   In consonance with this doctrine, it is felt to be an overstepping of the proper bounds of authority to fix beforehand, on some general presumption, that certain persons are not fit to do certain things.   It is now thoroughly known and admitted that if some such presumptions exist, no such presumption is infallible.   Even if it be well grounded in a majority of cases, which it is very likely not to be, there will be a minority of exceptional cases in which it does not hold : and in those it is both an injustice to the individuals, and a detriment to society, to place barriers in the way of their using their faculties for their own benefit and for that of others.   In the cases, on the other hand, in which the unfitness is real, the ordinary motives of human conduct will on the whole suffice to prevent the incompetent person from making, or from persisting in, the attempt.

If this general principle of social and economical science is not true ; if individuals, with such help as they can derive from the opinion of those who know them, are not better judges than the law and the government, of their own capacities and vocation ; the world cannot too soon abandon this principle, and return to the old system of regulations and disabilities. But if the principle is true, we ought to act as if we believed it, and not to ordain that to be born a girl instead of a boy, any more than to be born black instead of white, or a commoner instead of a nobleman, shall decide the person's position through all life—shall interdict people from all the more elevated social positions, and from all, except a few, respectable occupations. Even were we to admit the utmost that is ever pretended as to the superior fitness of men for all the functions now reserved to them, the same argument applies which forbids a legal qualification for members of Parliament. If only once in a dozen years the conditions of eligibility exclude a fit person, there is a real loss, while the exclusion of thousands of unfit persons is no gain; for if the constitution of the electoral body disposes them to choose unfit persons, there are always plenty of such persons to choose from. In all things of any difficulty and importance, those who can do them well are fewer than the need, even with the most unrestricted latitude of choice : and any limitation of the field of selection deprives society of some chances of being served by the competent, without ever saving it from the incompetent.

At present, in the more improved countries, the disabilities of women are the only case, save one, in which laws and institutions take persons at their birth, and ordain that they shall never in all their lives be allowed to compete for certain things. The one exception is that of royalty. Persons still are born to the throne ; no one, not of the reigning family, can ever occupy it, and no one even of that family can, by any means but the course of hereditary succession, attain it. All other dignities and social advantages are open to the whole male sex: many indeed are only attainable by wealth, but wealth may be striven for by any one, and is actually obtained by many men of the very humblest origin. The difficulties, to the majority, are indeed insuperable without the aid of fortunate accidents; but no male human being is under any legal ban: neither law nor opinion superadd artificial obstacles to the natural ones. Royalty, as I have said, is excepted: but in this case every one feels it to be an exception—an anomaly in the modern world, in marked opposition to its customs and principles, and to be justified only by extraordinary special expediencies, which, though individuals and nations differ in estimating their weight, unquestionably do in fact exist. But in this exceptional case, in which a high social function is, for important reasons, bestowed on birth instead of being put up to competition, all free nations contrive to adhere in substance to the principle from which they nominally derogate; for they circumscribe this high function by conditions avowedly intended to prevent the person to whom it ostensibly belongs from really performing it; while the person by whom it is performed, the responsible minister, does obtain the post by a competition from which no full-grown citizen of the male sex is legally excluded. The disabilities, therefore, to which women are subject from the mere fact of their birth, are the solitary examples of the kind in modern legislation. In no instance except this, which comprehends half the human race, are the higher social functions closed against any one by a fatality of birth which no exertions, and no change of circumstances, can overcome; for even religious disabilities (besides that in England and in Europe they have practically almost ceased to exist) do not close any career to the disqualified person in case of conversion.

The social subordination of women thus stands out an isolated fact in modern social institutions; a solitary breach of what has become their fundamental law; a single relic of an old world of thought and practice exploded in everything else, but retained in the one thing of most universal interest ; as if a gigantic dolmen, or a vast temple of Jupiter Olympius, occupied the site of St. Paul's and received daily worship, while the surrounding Christian churches were only resorted to on fasts and festivals. This entire discrepancy between one social fact and all those which accompany it, and the radical opposition between its nature and the progressive movement which is the boast of the modern world, and which has successively swept away everything else of an analogous character, surely affords, to a conscientious observer of human tendencies, serious matter for reflection. It raises a prima facie presumption on the unfavourable side, far outweighing any which custom and usage could in such circumstances create on the favourable ; and should at least suffice to make this, like the choice between republicanism and royalty, a balanced question.

The least that can be demanded is, that the question should not be considered as prejudged by existing fact and existing opinion, but open to discussion on its merits, as a question of justice and expediency : the decision on this, as on any of the other social arrangements of mankind, depending on what an enlightened estimate of tendencies and consequences may show to be most advantageous to humanity in general, without distinction of sex. And the discussion must be a real discussion, descending to foundations, and not resting satisfied with vague and general assertions. It will not do, for instance, to assert in general terms, that the experience of mankind has pronounced in favour of the existing system. Experience cannot possibly have decided between two courses, so long as there has only been experience of one. If it be said that the doctrine of the equality of the sexes rests only on theory, it must be remembered that the contrary doctrine also has only theory to rest upon. All that is proved in its favour by direct experience, is that mankind have been able to exist under it, and to attain the degree of improvement and prosperity which we now see ; but whether that prosperity has been attained sooner, or is now greater, than it would have been under the other system, experience does not say. On the other hand, experience does say, that every step in improvement has been so invariably accompanied by a step made in raising the social position of women, that historians and philosophers have been led to adopt their elevation or debasement as on the whole the surest test and most correct measure of the civilization of a people or an age. Through all the progressive period of human history, the condition of women has been approaching nearer to equality with men. This does not of itself prove that the assimilation must go on to complete equality ; but it assuredly affords some presumption that such is the case.

Neither does it avail anything to say that the *nature* of the two sexes adapts them to their present functions and position, and renders these appropriate to them. Standing on the ground of common sense and the constitution of the human mind, I deny that any one knows, or can know, the nature of the two sexes, as long as they have only been seen in their present relation to one another. If men had ever been found in society without women, or women without men, or if there had been a society of men and women in which the women were not under the control of the men, something might have been positively known about the mental and moral differences which may be inherent in the nature of each. What is now called the nature of women is an eminently artificial thing— the result of forced repression in some directions, un- natural stimulation in others. It may be asserted without scruple, that no other class of dependents have had their character so entirely distorted from its natural proportions by their relation with their masters ; for, if conquered and slave races have been, in some respects, more forcibly repressed, whatever in them has not been crushed down by an iron heel has generally been let alone, and if left with any liberty of development, it has developed itself according to its own laws ; but in the case of women, a hot-house and stove cultivation has always been carried on of some of the capabilities of their nature, for the benefit and pleasure of their masters. Then, because certain products of the general vital force sprout luxuriantly and reach a great development in this heated atmosphere and under this active nurture and watering, while other shoots from the same root, which are left outside in the wintry air, with ice purposely heaped all round them, have a stunted growth, and some are burnt off with fire and disappear; men, with that inability to recognize their own work which distinguishes the unanalytic mind, indolently believe that the tree grows of itself in the way they have made it grow, and that it would die if one half of it were not kept in a vapour bath and the other half in the snow.

Of all difficulties which impede the progress of thought, and the formation of well-grounded opinions on life and social arrangements, the greatest is now the unspeakable ignorance and inattention of mankind in respect to the influences which form human character. Whatever any portion of the human species now are, or seem to be, such, it is supposed, they have a natural tendency to be: even when the most elementary knowledge of the circumstances in which they have been placed, clearly points out the causes that made them what they are. Because a cottier deeply in arrears to his landlord is not industrious, there are people who think that the Irish are naturally idle. Because constitutions can be overthrown when the authorities appointed to execute them turn their arms against them, there are people who think the French incapable of free government. Because the Greeks cheated the Turks, and the Turks only plundered the Greeks, there are persons who think that the Turks are naturally more sincere: and because women, as is often said, care nothing about politics except their personalities, it is supposed that the general good is naturally less interesting to women than to men. History, which is now so much better understood than formerly, teaches another lesson: if only by showing the extraordinary susceptibility of human nature to external influences, and the extreme variableness of those of its manifestations which are supposed to be most universal and uniform. But in history, as in travelling, men usually see only what they already had in their own minds ; and few learn much from history, who do not bring much with them to its study.

Hence, in regard to that most difficult question, what are the natural differences between the two sexes—a subject on which it is impossible in the present state of society to obtain complete and correct knowledge—while almost everybody dogmatizes upon it, almost all neglect and make light of the only means by which any partial insight can be obtained into it. This is, an analytic study of the most important department of psychology, the laws of the influence of circumstances on character. For, however great and apparently ineradicable the moral and intellectual differences between men and women might be, the evidence of their being natural differences could only be negative. Those only could be inferred to be natural which could not possibly be artificial—the residuum, after deducting every characteristic of either sex which can admit of being explained from education or external circumstances. The profoundest knowledge of the laws of the formation of character is indispensable to entitle any one to affirm even that there is any difference, much more what the difference is, between the two sexes considered as moral and rational beings ; and since no one, as yet, has that knowledge (for there is hardly any subject which, in proportion to its importance, has been so little studied), no one is thus far entitled to any positive opinion on the subject. Conjectures are all that can at present be made ; conjectures more or less probable, according as more or less authorized by such knowledge as we yet have of the laws of psychology, as applied to the formation of character.

Even the preliminary knowledge, what the differences between the sexes now are, apart from all question as to how they are made what they are, is still in the crudest and most incomplete state. Medical practitioners and physiologists have ascertained, to some extent, the differences in bodily constitution; and this is an important element to the psychologist: but hardly any medical practitioner is a psychologist. Respecting the mental characteristics of women; their observations are of no more worth than those of common men. It is a subject on which nothing final can be known, so long as those who alone can really know it, women themselves, have given but little testimony, and that little, mostly suborned. It is easy to know stupid women. Stupidity is much the same all the world over. A stupid person's notions and feelings may confidently be inferred from those which prevail in the circle by which the person is surrounded. Not so with those whose opinions and feelings are an emanation from their own nature and faculties. It is only a man here and there who has any tolerable knowledge of the character even of the women of his own family. I do not mean, of their capabilities; these nobody knows, not even themselves, because most of them have never been called out. I mean their actually existing thoughts and feelings. Many a man thinks he perfectly understands women, because he has had amatory relations with several, perhaps with many of them. If he is a good observer, and his experience extends to quality as well as quantity, he may have learnt something of one narrow department of their nature—an important department, no doubt. But of all the rest of it, few persons are generally more ignorant, because there are few from whom it is so carefully hidden. The most favourable case which a man can generally have for studying the character of a woman, is that of his own wife: for the opportunities are greater, and the cases of complete sympathy not so unspeakably rare. And in fact, this is the source from which any knowledge worth having on the subject has, I believe, generally come. But most men have not had the opportunity of studying in this way more than a single case : accordingly one can, to an almost laughable degree, infer what a man's wife is like, from his opinions about women in general. To make even this one case yield any result, the woman must be worth knowing, and the man not only a competent judge, but of a character so sympathetic in itself, and so well adapted to hers, that he can either read her mind by sympathetic intuition, or has nothing in himself which makes her shy of disclosing it. Hardly anything, I believe, can be more rare than this conjunction. It often happens that there is the most complete unity of feeling and community of interests as to all external things, yet the one has as little admission into the internal life of the other as if they were common acquaintance. Even with true affection, authority on the one side and subordination on the other prevent perfect confidence. Though nothing may be intentionally withheld, much is not shown. In the analogous relation of parent and child, the corresponding phenomenon must have been in the observation of every one. As between father and son, how many are the cases in which the father, in spite of real affection on both sides, obviously to all the world does not know, nor suspect, parts of the son's character familiar to his companions and equals. The truth is, that the position of looking up to another is extremely unpropitious to complete sincerity and openness with him. The fear of losing ground in his opinion or in his feelings is so strong, that even in an upright character, there is an unconscious tendency to show only the best side, or the side which, though not the best, is that which he most likes to see : and it may be confidently said that thorough knowledge of one another hardly ever exists, but between persons who, besides being intimates, are equals. How much more true, then, must all this be, when the one is not only under the authority of the other, but has it inculcated on her as a duty to reckon everything else subordinate to his comfort and pleasure, and to let him neither see nor feel anything coming from her, except what is agreeable to him. All these difficulties stand in the way of a man's obtaining any thorough knowledge even of the one woman whom alone, in general, he has sufficient opportunity of studying. When we further consider that to understand one woman is not necessarily to understand any other woman; that even if he could study many women of one rank, or of one country, he would not thereby understand women of other ranks or countries; and even if he did, they are still only the women of a single period of history; we may safely assert that the knowledge which men can acquire of women, even as they have been and are, without reference to what they might be, is wretchedly imperfect and superficial, and always will be so, until women themselves have told all that they have to tell.

And this time has not come; nor will it come otherwise than gradually. It is but of yesterday that women have either been qualified by literary accomplishments, or permitted by society, to tell anything to the general public. As yet very few of them dare tell anything, which men, on whom their literary success depends, are unwilling to hear. Let us remember in what manner, up to a very recent time, the expression, even by a male author, of uncustomary opinions, or what are deemed eccentric feelings, usually was, and in some degree still is, received; and we may form some faint conception under what impediments a woman, who is brought up to think custom and opinion her sovereign rule, attempts to express in books anything drawn from the depths of her own nature. The greatest woman who has left writings behind her sufficient to give her an eminent rank in the literature of her country, thought it necessary to prefix as a motto to her boldest work, ' Un homme peut braver l'opinion ; une femme doit s'y soumettre.' [1] The greater part of what women write about women is mere sycophancy to men. In the case of unmarried women, much of

---

[1] Title-page of Mme de Staël's *Delphine.*

it seems only intended to increase their chance of a husband. Many, both married and unmarried, overstep the mark, and inculcate a servility beyond what is desired or relished by any man, except the very vulgarest. But this is not so often the case as, even at a quite late period, it still was. Literary women are becoming more freespoken, and more willing to express their real sentiments. Unfortunately, in this country especially, they are themselves such artificial products, that their sentiments are compounded of a small element of individual observation and consciousness, and a very large one of acquired associations. This will be less and less the case, but it will remain true to a great extent, as long as social institutions do not admit the same free development of originality in women which is possible to men. When that time comes, and not before, we shall see, and not merely hear, as much as it is necessary to know of the nature of women, and the adaptation of other things to it.

I have dwelt so much on the difficulties which at present obstruct any real knowledge by men of the true nature of women, because in this as in so many other things ' opinio copiae inter maximas causas inopiae est ' ; and there is little chance of reasonable thinking on the matter, while people flatter themselves that they perfectly understand a subject of which most men know absolutely nothing, and of which it is at present impossible that any man, or all men taken together, should have knowledge which can qualify them to lay down the law to women as to what is, or is not, their vocation. Happily, no such knowledge is necessary for any practical purpose connected with the position of women in relation to society and life. For, according to all the principles involved in modern society, the question rests with women themselves— to be decided by their own experience, and by the use of their own faculties. There are no means of finding what either one person or many can do, but by trying— and no means by which any one else can discover for them what it is for their happiness to do or leave undone.

One thing we may be certain of—that what is contrary to women's nature to do, they never will be made to do by simply giving their nature free play. The anxiety of mankind to interfere in behalf of nature, for fear lest nature should not succeed in effecting its purpose, is an altogether unnecessary solicitude. What women by nature cannot do, it is quite superfluous to forbid them from doing. What they can do, but not so well as the men who are their competitors, competition suffices to exclude them from ; since nobody asks for protective duties and bounties in favour of women ; it is only asked that the present bounties and protective duties in favour of men should be recalled. If women have a greater natural inclination for some things than for others, there is no need of laws or social inculcation to make the majority of them do the former in preference to the latter. Whatever women's services are most wanted for, the free play of competition will hold out the strongest inducements to them to undertake. And, as the words imply, they are most wanted for the things for which they are most fit ; by the apportionment of which to them, the collective faculties of the two sexes can be applied on the whole with the greatest sum of valuable result.

The general opinion of men is supposed to be, that the natural vocation of a woman is that of a wife and mother. I say, is supposed to be, because, judging from acts—from the whole of the present constitution of society—one might infer that their opinion was the direct contrary. They might be supposed to think that the alleged natural vocation of women was of all things the most repugnant to their nature ; insomuch that if they are free to do anything else—if any other means of living, or occupation of their time and faculties, is open, which has any chance of appearing desirable to them—there will not be enough of them who will be willing to accept the condition said to be natural to them. If this is the real opinion of men in general, it would be well that it should be spoken out. I should like to hear somebody openly enunciating the doctrine (it is already implied in much that is written on the subject)—'It is necessary to society that women should marry and produce children. They will not do so unless they are compelled. Therefore it is necessary to compel them.' The merits of the case would then be clearly defined. It would be exactly that of the slaveholders of South Carolina and Louisiana. 'It is necessary that cotton and sugar should be grown. White men cannot produce them. Negroes will not, for any wages which we choose to give. *Ergo* they must be compelled.' An illustration still closer to the point is that of impressment. Sailors must absolutely be had to defend the country. It often happens that they will not voluntarily enlist. Therefore there must be the power of forcing them. How often has this logic been used ! and, but for one flaw in it, without doubt it would have been successful up to this day. But it is open to the retort—First pay the sailors the honest value of their labour. When you have made it as well worth their while to serve you, as to work for other employers, you will have no more difficulty than others have in obtaining their services. To this there is no logical answer except 'I will not': and as people are now not only ashamed, but are not desirous, to rob the labourer of his hire, impressment is no longer advocated. Those who attempt to force women into marriage by closing all other doors against them, lay themselves open to a similar retort. If they mean what they say, their opinion must evidently be, that men do not render the married condition so desirable to women, as to induce them to accept it for its own recommendations. It is not a sign of one's thinking the boon one offers very attractive, when one allows only Hobson's choice, 'that or none.' And here, I believe, is the clue to the feelings of those men, who have a real antipathy to the equal freedom of women. I believe they are afraid, not lest women should be unwilling to marry, for I do not think that any one in reality has that apprehension; but lest they should insist that marriage should be on equal conditions; lest all women of spirit and capacity should prefer doing almost anything else, not in their own eyes degrading, rather than marry, when marrying is giving themselves a master, and a master too of all their earthly possessions. And truly, if this consequence were necessarily incident to marriage, I think that the apprehension would be very well founded. I agree in thinking it probable that few women, capable of anything else, would, unless under an irresistible *entraînement*, rendering them for the time insensible to anything but itself, choose such a lot, when any other means were open to them of filling a conventionally honourable place in life: and if men are determined that the law of marriage shall be a law of despotism, they are quite right, in point of mere policy, in leaving to women only Hobson's choice. But, in that case, all that has been done in the modern world to relax the chain on the minds of women, has been a mistake. They never should have been allowed to receive a literary education. Women who read, much more women who write, are, in the existing constitution of things, a contradiction and a disturbing element: and it was wrong to bring women up with any acquirements but those of an odalisque, or of a domestic servant.

CHAPTER II

IT will be well to commence the detailed discussion of the subject by the particular branch of it to which the course of our observations has led us: the conditions which the laws of this and all other countries annex to the marriage contract. Marriage being the destination appointed by society for women, the prospect they are brought up to, and the object which it is intended should be sought by all of them, except those who are too little attractive to be chosen by any man as his companion; one might have supposed that everything would have been done to make this condition as eligible to them as possible, that they might have no cause to regret being denied the option of any other. Society, however, both in this, and, at first, in all other cases, has preferred to attain its object by foul rather than fair means: but this is the only case in which it has substantially persisted in them even to the present day. Originally women were taken by force, or regularly sold by their father to the husband. Until a late period in European history, the father had the power to dispose of his daughter in marriage at his own will and pleasure, without any regard to hers. · The Church, indeed, was so far faithful to a better morality as to require a formal ' yes ' from the woman at the marriage ceremony; but there was nothing to show that the consent was other than compulsory; and it was practically impossible for the girl to refuse compliance if the father persevered, except perhaps when she might obtain the protection of religion by a determined resolution to take monastic vows. After marriage, the man had anciently (but this was anterior to Christianity) the power of life and death over his wife. She could invoke no law against him; he was her sole tribunal and law. For a long time he could repudiate her, but she had no corresponding power in regard to him. By the old laws of England, the husband was called the *lord* of the wife; he was literally regarded as her sovereign, inasmuch that the murder of a man by his wife was called treason (*petty* as distinguished from *high* treason), and was more cruelly avenged than was usually the case with high treason, for the penalty was burning to death. Because these various enormities have fallen into disuse (for most of them were never formally abolished, or not until they had long ceased to be practised) men suppose that all is now as it should be in regard to the marriage contract; and we are continually told that civilization and Christianity have restored to the woman her just rights. Meanwhile the wife is the actual bond-servant of her husband : no less so, as far as legal obligation goes, than slaves commonly so called. She vows a lifelong obedience to him at the altar, and is held to it all through her life by law. Casuists may say that the obligation of obedience stops short of participation in crime, but it certainly extends to everything else. She can do no act whatever but by his permission, at least tacit. She can acquire no property but for him ; the instant it becomes hers, even if by inheritance, it becomes *ipso facto* his.   In this respect the wife's position under the common law of England is worse than that of slaves in the laws of many countries : by the Roman law, for example, a slave might have his peculium, which to a certain extent the law guaranteed to him for his exclusive use. The higher classes in this country have given an analogous advantage to their women, through special contracts setting aside the law, by conditions of pin-money, &c. : since parental feeling being stronger with fathers than the class feeling of their own sex, a father generally prefers his own daughter to a son-in-law who is a stranger to him. By means of settlements, the rich usually contrive to withdraw the whole or part of the inherited property of the wife from the absolute control of the husband : but they do not succeed in keeping it under her own control ; the utmost they can do only prevents the husband from squandering it, at the same time debarring the rightful owner from its use. The property itself is out of the reach of both ; and as to the income derived from it, the form of settlement most favourable to the wife (that called 'to her separate use') only precludes the husband from receiving it instead of her : it must pass through her hands, but if he takes it from her by personal violence as soon as she receives it, he can neither be punished, nor compelled to restitution. This is the amount of the protection which, under the laws of this country, the most powerful nobleman can give his own daughter as respects her

husband. In the immense majority of cases there is
no settlement: and the absorption of all rights, all
property, as well as all freedom of action, is complete.
The two are called 'one person in law', for the purpose of inferring that whatever is hers is his, but the
parallel inference is never drawn that whatever is his
is hers; the maxim is not applied against the man,
except to make him responsible to third parties for
her acts, as a master is for the acts of his slaves or of
his cattle. I am far from pretending that wives are in
general no better treated than slaves; but no slave
is a slave to the same lengths, and in so full a sense
of the word, as a wife is. Hardly any slave, except
one immediately attached to the master's person, is
a slave at all hours and all minutes; in general he
has, like a soldier, his fixed task, and when it is done,
or when he is off duty, he disposes, within certain
limits, of his own time, and has a family life into
which the master rarely intrudes. 'Uncle Tom'
under his first master had his own life in his 'cabin',
almost as much as any man whose work takes him
away from home, is able to have in his own family.
But it cannot be so with the wife. Above all, a female
slave has (in Christian countries) an admitted right,
and is considered under a moral obligation, to refuse
to her master the last familiarity. Not so the wife:
however brutal a tyrant she may unfortunately be
chained to—though she may know that he hates her,
though it may be his daily pleasure to torture her,
and though she may feel it impossible not to loathe
him—he can claim from her and enforce the lowest
degradation of a human being, that of being made
the instrument of an animal function contrary to her
inclinations. While she is held in this worst description of slavery as to her own person, what is her
position in regard to the children in whom she and
her master have a joint interest ? They are by law *his*
children. He alone has any legal rights over them.
Not one act can she do towards or in relation to them,
except by delegation from him. Even after he is dead

she is not their legal guardian, unless he by will has made her so. He could even send them away from her, and deprive her of the means of seeing or corresponding with them, until this power was in some degree restricted by Serjeant Talfourd's Act. This is her legal state. And from this state she has no means of withdrawing herself. If she leaves her husband, she can take nothing with her, neither her children nor anything which is rightfully her own. If he chooses, he can compel her to return, by law, or by physical force ; or he may content himself with seizing for his own use anything which she may earn, or which may be given to her by her relations. It is only legal separation by a decree of a court of justice, which entitles her to live apart, without being forced back into the custody of an exasperated jailer—or which empowers her to apply any earnings to her own use, without fear that a man whom perhaps she has not seen for twenty years will pounce upon her some day and carry all off. This legal separation, until lately, the courts of justice would only give at an expense which made it inaccessible to any one out of the higher ranks. Even now it is only given in cases of desertion, or of the extreme of cruelty ; and yet complaints are made every day that it is granted too easily. Surely, if a woman is denied any lot in life but that of being the personal body-servant of a despot, and is dependent for everything upon the chance of finding one who may be disposed to make a favourite of her instead of merely a drudge, it is a very cruel aggravation of her fate that she should be allowed to try this chance only once. The natural sequel and corollary from this state of things would be, that since her all in life depends upon obtaining a good master, she should be allowed to change again and again until she finds one. I am not saying that she ought to be allowed this privilege. That is a totally different consideration. The question of divorce, in the sense involving liberty of remarriage, is one into which it is foreign to my purpose to enter. All I now say is, that to those to whom nothing but servitude is allowed, the free choice of servitude is the only, though a most insufficient, alleviation. Its refusal completes the assimilation of the wife to the slave—and the slave under not the mildest form of slavery: for in some slave codes the slave could, under certain circumstances of ill usage, legally compel the master to sell him. But no amount of ill usage, without adultery superadded, will in England free a wife from her tormentor.

I have no desire to exaggerate, nor does the case stand in any need of exaggeration. I have described the wife's legal position, not her actual treatment. The laws of most countries are far worse than the people who execute them, and many of them are only able to remain laws by being seldom or never carried into effect. If married life were all that it might be expected to be, looking to the laws alone, society would be a hell upon earth. Happily there are both feelings and interests which in many men exclude, and in most, greatly temper, the impulses and propensities which lead to tyranny: and of those feelings, the tie which connects a man with his wife affords, in a normal state of things, incomparably the strongest example. The only tie which at all approaches to it, that between him and his children, tends, in all save exceptional cases, to strengthen, instead of conflicting with, the first. Because this is true; because men in general do not inflict, nor women suffer, all the misery which could be inflicted and suffered if the full power of tyranny with which the man is legally invested were acted on; the defenders of the existing form of the institution think that all its iniquity is justified, and that any complaint is merely quarrelling with the evil which is the price paid for every great good. But the mitigations in practice, which are compatible with maintaining in full legal force this or any other kind of tyranny, instead of being any apology for despotism, only serve to prove what power human nature possesses of reacting against the vilest institutions, and with what vitality the seeds of good as well as those of evil in human character diffuse and propagate themselves. Not a word can be said for despotism in the family which cannot be said for political despotism. Every absolute king does not sit at his window to enjoy the groans of his tortured subjects, nor strips them of their last rag and turns them out to shiver in the road. The despotism of Louis XVI was not the despotism of Philippe le Bel, or of Nadir Shah, or of Caligula; but it was bad enough to justify the French Revolution, and to palliate even its horrors. If an appeal be made to the intense attachments which exist between wives and their husbands, exactly as much may be said of domestic slavery. It was quite an ordinary fact in Greece and Rome for slaves to submit to death by torture rather than betray their masters. In the proscriptions of the Roman civil wars it was remarked that wives and slaves were heroically faithful, sons very commonly treacherous. Yet we know how cruelly many Romans treated their slaves. But in truth these intense individual feelings nowhere rise to such a luxuriant height as under the most atrocious institutions. It is part of the irony of life, that the strongest feelings of devoted gratitude of which human nature seems to be susceptible, are called forth in human beings towards those who, having the power entirely to crush their earthly existence, voluntarily refrain from using that power. How great a place in most men this sentiment fills, even in religious devotion, it would be cruel to inquire. We daily see how much their gratitude to Heaven appears to be stimulated by the contemplation of fellow creatures to whom God has not been so merciful as he has to themselves.

Whether the institution to be defended is slavery, political absolutism, or the absolutism of the head of a family, we are always expected to judge of it from its best instances; and we are presented with pictures of loving exercise of authority on one side, loving submission to it on the other—superior wisdom ordering all things for the greatest good of the dependants, and surrounded by their smiles and benedictions. All this would be very much to the purpose if any one pretended that there are no such things as good men. Who doubts that there may be great goodness, and great happiness, and great affection, under the absolute government of a good man? Meanwhile, laws and institutions require to be adapted, not to good men, but to bad. Marriage is not an institution designed for a select few. Men are not required, as a preliminary to the marriage ceremony, to prove by testimonials that they are fit to be trusted with the exercise of absolute power. The tie of affection and obligation to a wife and children is very strong with those whose general social feelings are strong, and with many who are little sensible to any other social ties; but there are all degrees of sensibility and insensibility to it, as there are all grades of goodness and wickedness in men, down to those whom no ties will bind, and on whom society has no action but through its *ultima ratio*, the penalties of the law. In every grade of this descending scale are men to whom are committed all the legal powers of a husband. The vilest malefactor has some wretched woman tied to him, against whom he can commit any atrocity except killing her, and, if tolerably cautious, can do that without much danger of the legal penalty. And how many thousands are there among the lowest classes in every country, who, without being in a legal sense malefactors in any other respect, because in every other quarter their aggressions meet with resistance, indulge the utmost habitual excesses of bodily violence towards the unhappy wife, who alone, at least of grown persons, can neither repel nor escape from their brutality; and towards whom the excess of dependence inspires their mean and savage natures, not with a generous forbearance, and a point of honour to behave well to one whose lot in life is trusted entirely to their kindness, but on the contrary with a notion that the law has delivered her to them as their thing, to be used at their pleasure, and that they are not expected to practise the consideration

towards her which is required from them towards everybody else. The law, which till lately left even these
atrocious extremes of domestic oppression practically
unpunished, has within these few years made some
feeble attempts to repress them. But its attempts
have done little, and cannot be expected to do much,
because it is contrary to reason and experience to suppose that there can be any real check to brutality,
consistent with leaving the victim still in the power
of the executioner. Until a conviction for personal
violence, or at all events a repetition of it after a first
conviction, entitles the woman *ipso facto* to a divorce,
or at least to a judicial separation, the attempt to
repress these ' aggravated assaults ' by legal penalties
will break down for want of a prosecutor, or for want
of a witness.

When we consider how vast is the number of men,
in any great country, who are little higher than brutes,
and that this never prevents them from being able,
through the law of marriage, to obtain a victim, the
breadth and depth of human misery caused in this
shape alone by the abuse of the institution swells to
something appalling. Yet these are only the extreme
cases. They are the lowest abysses, but there is a sad
succession of depth after depth before reaching them.
In domestic as in political tyranny, the case of absolute
monsters chiefly illustrates the institution by showing
that there is scarcely any horror which may not occur
under it if the despot pleases, and thus setting in
a strong light what must be the terrible frequency of
things only a little less atrocious. Absolute fiends are
as rare as angels, perhaps rarer : ferocious savages,
with occasional touches of humanity, are, however, very
frequent : and in the wide interval which separates
these from any worthy representatives of the human
species, how many are the forms and gradations of
animalism and selfishness, often under an outward
varnish of civilization and even cultivation, living at
peace with the law, maintaining a creditable appearance to all who are not under their power, yet sufficient

often to make the lives of all who are so, a torment
and a burthen to them! It would be tiresome
to repeat the commonplaces about the unfitness of
men in general for power, which, after the political
discussions of centuries, every one knows by heart,
were it not that hardly any one thinks of applying
these maxims to the case in which above all others
they are applicable, that of power, not placed in the
hands of a man here and there, but offered to every
adult male, down to the basest and most ferocious. It
is not because a man is not known to have broken any
of the Ten Commandments, or because he maintains
a respectable character in his dealings with those
whom he cannot compel to have intercourse with him,
or because he does not fly out into violent bursts of
ill temper against those who are not obliged to bear
with him, that it is possible to surmise of what sort his
conduct will be in the unrestraint of home. Even
the commonest men reserve the violent, the sulky, the
undisguisedly selfish side of their character for those
who have no power to withstand it. The relation of
superiors to dependants is the nursery of these vices
of character, which, wherever else they exist, are an
overflowing from that source. A man who is morose
or violent to his equals, is sure to be one who has lived
among inferiors, whom he could frighten or worry into
submission. If the family in its best forms is, as it is
often said to be, a school of sympathy, tenderness,
and loving forgetfulness of self, it is still oftener, as
respects its chief, a school of wilfulness, overbearingness, unbounded self-indulgence, and a double-dyed
and idealized selfishness, of which sacrifice itself is
only a particular form: the care for the wife and
children being only care for them as parts of the man's
own interests and belongings, and their individual
happiness being immolated in every shape to his
smallest preferences. What better is to be looked for
under the existing form of the institution? We know
that the bad propensities of human nature are only
kept within bounds when they are allowed no scope

for their indulgence. We know that from impulse and habit, when not from deliberate purpose, almost every one to whom others yield, goes on encroaching upon them, until a point is reached at which they are compelled to resist. Such being the common tendency of human nature; the almost unlimited power which present social institutions give to the man over at least one human being—the one with whom he resides, and whom he has always present—this power seeks out and evokes the latent germs of selfishness in the remotest corners of his nature—fans its faintest sparks and smouldering embers—offers to him a licence for the indulgence of those points of his original character which in all other relations he would have found it necessary to repress and conceal, and the repression of which would in time have become a second nature. I know that there is another side to the question. I grant that the wife, if she cannot effectually resist, can at least retaliate ; she, too, can make the man's life extremely uncomfortable, and by that power is able to carry many points which she ought, and many which she ought not,'to prevail in. But this instrument of self-protection—which may be called the power of the scold, or the shrewish sanction—has the fatal defect, that it avails most against the least tyrannical superiors, and in favour of the least deserving dependants. It is the weapon of irritable and self-willed women ; of those who would make the worst use of power if they themselves had it, and who generally turn this power to a bad use. The amiable cannot use such an instrument, the high-minded disdain it. And on the other hand, the husbands against whom it is used most effectively are the gentler and more inoffensive ; those who cannot be induced, even by provocation, to resort to any very harsh exercise of authority. The wife's power of being disagreeable generally only establishes a counter-tyranny, and makes victims in their turn chiefly of those husbands who are least inclined to be tyrants.

What is it, then, which really tempers the corrupting

effects of the power, and makes it compatible with such amount of good as we actually see ? Mere feminine blandishments, though of great effect in individual instances, have very little effect in modifying the general tendencies of the situation; for their power only lasts while the woman is young and attractive, often only while her charm is new, and not dimmed by familiarity; and on many men they have not much influence at any time. The real mitigating causes are, the personal affection which is the growth of time, in so far as the man's nature is susceptible of it, and the woman's character sufficiently congenial with his to excite it; their common interests as regards the children, and their general community of interest as concerns third persons (to which however there are very great limitations); the real importance of the wife to his daily comforts and enjoyments, and the value he consequently attaches to her on his personal account, which, in a man capable of feeling for others, lays the foundation of caring for her on her own; and lastly, the influence naturally acquired over almost all human beings by those near to their persons (if not actually disagreeable to them): who, both by their direct entreaties, and by the insensible contagion of their feelings and dispositions, are often able, unless counteracted by some equally strong personal influence, to obtain a degree of command over the conduct of the superior, altogether excessive and unreasonable. Through these various means, the wife frequently exercises even too much power over the man; she is able to affect his conduct in things in which she may not be qualified to influence it for good—in which her influence may be not only unenlightened, but employed on the morally wrong side; and in which he would act better if left to his own prompting. But neither in the affairs of families nor in those of states is power a compensation for the loss of freedom. Her power often gives her what she has no right to, but does not enable her to assert her own rights. A Sultan's favourite slave has slaves under her, over whom she tyrannizes;

but the desirable thing would be that she should neither have slaves nor be a slave. By entirely sinking her own existence in her husband; by having no will (or persuading him that she has no will) but his, in anything which regards their joint relation, and by making it the business of her life to work upon his sentiments, a wife may gratify herself by influencing, and very probably perverting, his conduct, in those of his external relations which she has never qualified herself to judge of, or in which she is herself wholly influenced by some personal or other partiality or prejudice. Accordingly, as things now are, those who act most kindly to their wives are quite as often made worse, as better, by the wife's influence, in respect to all interests extending beyond the family. She is taught that she has no business with things out of that sphere; and accordingly she seldom has any honest and conscientious opinion on them; and therefore hardly ever meddles with them for any legitimate purpose, but generally for an interested one. She neither knows nor cares which is the right side in politics, but she knows what will bring in money or invitations, give her husband a title, her son a place, or her daughter a good marriage.

But how, it will be asked, can any society exist without government? In a family, as in a state, some one person must be the ultimate ruler. Who shall decide when married people differ in opinion? Both cannot have their way, yet a decision one way or the other must be come to.

It is not true that in all voluntary association between two people, one of them must be absolute master: still less that the law must determine which of them it shall be. The most frequent case of voluntary association, next to marriage, is partnership in business: and it is not found or thought necessary to enact that, in every partnership, one partner shall have entire control over the concern, and the others shall be bound to obey his orders. No one would enter into partnership on terms which would subject him to the responsibilities of a principal, with only the powers and privileges of a clerk or agent. If the law dealt with other contracts as it does with marriage, it would ordain that one partner should administer the common business as if it was his private concern; that the others should have only delegated powers; and that this one should be designated by some general presumption of law, for example as being the eldest. The law never does this: nor does experience show it to be necessary that any theoretical inequality of power should exist between the partners, or that the partnership should have any other conditions than what they may themselves appoint by their articles of agreement. Yet it might seem that the exclusive power might be conceded with less danger to the rights and interests of the inferior, in the case of partnership than in that of marriage, since he is free to cancel the power by withdrawing from the connexion. The wife has no such power, and even if she had, it is almost always desirable that she should try all measures before resorting to it.

It is quite true that things which have to be decided every day, and cannot adjust themselves gradually, or wait for a compromise, ought to depend on one will: one person must have their sole control. But it does not follow that this should always be the same person. The natural arrangement is a division of powers between the two; each being absolute in the executive branch of their own department, and any change of system and principle requiring the consent of both. The division neither can nor should be pre-established by the law, since it must depend on individual capacities and suitabilities. If the two persons chose, they might pre-appoint it by the marriage contract, as pecuniary arrangements are now often pre-appointed. There would seldom be any difficulty in deciding such things by mutual consent, unless the marriage was one of those unhappy ones in which all other things, as well as this, become subjects of bickering and dispute. The division of rights would naturally follow the division of duties and functions; and that is already made by consent, or at all events not by law, but by general custom, modified and modifiable at the pleasure of the persons concerned.

The real practical decision of affairs, to whichever may be given the legal authority, will greatly depend, as it even now does, upon comparative qualifications. The mere fact that he is usually the eldest, will in most cases give the preponderance to the man; at least until they both attain a time of life at which the difference in their years is of no importance. There will naturally also be a more potential voice on the side, whichever it is, that brings the means of support. Inequality from this source does not depend on the law of marriage, but on the general conditions of human society, as now constituted. The influence of mental superiority, either general or special, and of superior decision of character, will necessarily tell for much. It always does so at present. And this fact shows how little foundation there is for the apprehension that the powers and responsibilities of partners in life (as of partners in business) cannot be satisfactorily apportioned by agreement between themselves. They always are so apportioned, except in cases in which the marriage institution is a failure. Things never come to an issue of downright power on one side, and obedience on the other, except where the connexion altogether has been a mistake, and it would be a blessing to both parties to be relieved from it. Some may say that the very thing by which an amicable settlement of differences becomes possible, is the power of legal compulsion known to be in reserve; as people submit to an arbitration because there is a court of law in the background, which they know that they can be forced to obey. But to make the cases parallel, we must suppose that the rule of the court of law was, not to try the cause, but to give judgement always for the same side, suppose the defendant. If so, the amenability to it would be a motive with the plaintiff to agree to almost any arbitration, but it would be just the reverse with the defendant. The despotic power which the law gives to the husband may be a reason to make the wife assent to any compromise by which power is practically shared between the two, but it cannot be the reason why the husband does. That there is always among decently conducted people a practical compromise, though one of them at least is under no physical or moral necessity of making it, shows that the natural motives which lead to a voluntary adjustment of the united life of two persons in a manner acceptable to both, do, on the whole, except in unfavourable cases, prevail. The matter is certainly not improved by laying down as an ordinance of law, that the superstructure of free government shall be raised upon a legal basis of despotism on one side and subjection on the other, and that every concession which the despot makes may, at his mere pleasure, and without any warning, be recalled. Besides that no freedom is worth much when held on so precarious a tenure, its conditions are not likely to be the most equitable when the law throws so prodigious a weight into one scale; when the adjustment rests between two persons one of whom is declared to be entitled to everything, the other not only entitled to nothing except during the good pleasure of the first, but under the strongest moral and religious obligation not to rebel under any excess of oppression.

A pertinacious adversary, pushed to extremities, may say, that husbands indeed are willing to be reasonable, and to make fair concessions to their partners without being compelled to it, but that wives are not : that if allowed any rights of their own, they will acknowledge no rights at all in any one else, and never will yield in anything, unless they can be compelled, by the man's mere authority, to yield in everything. This would have been said by many persons some generations ago, when satires on women were in vogue, and men thought it a clever thing to insult women for being what men made them. But it will be said by no one now who is worth replying to. It is not the doctrine of the present day that women are less susceptible of good feeling, and consideration for those with whom they are united by the strongest ties, than men are. On the contrary, we are perpetually told that women are better than men, by those who are totally opposed to treating them as if they were as good; so that the saying has passed into a piece of tiresome cant, intended to put a complimentary face upon an injury, and resembling those celebrations of royal clemency which, according to Gulliver, the king of Lilliput always prefixed to his most sanguinary decrees. If women are better than men in anything, it surely is in individual self-sacrifice for those of their own family. But I lay little stress on this, so long as they are universally taught that they are born and created for self-sacrifice. I believe that equality of rights would abate the exaggerated self-abnegation which is the present artificial ideal of feminine character, and that a good woman would not be more self-sacrificing than the best man: but on the other hand, men would be much more unselfish and self-sacrificing than at present, because they would no longer be taught to worship their own will as such a grand thing that it is actually the law for another rational being. There is nothing which men so easily learn as this self-worship: all privileged persons, and all privileged classes, have had it. The more we descend in the scale of humanity, the intenser it is; and most of all in those who are not, and can never expect to be, raised above any one except an unfortunate wife and children. The honourable exceptions are proportionally fewer than in the case of almost any other human infirmity. Philosophy and religion, instead of keeping it in check, are generally suborned to defend it; and nothing controls it but that practical feeling of the equality of human beings, which is the theory of Christianity, but which Christianity will never practically teach, while it sanctions institutions grounded on an arbitrary preference of one human being over another.

There are, no doubt, women, as there are men, whom equality of consideration will not satisfy; with whom there is no peace while any will or wish is regarded but their own. Such persons are a proper subject for the law of divorce. They are only fit to live alone, and no human beings ought to be compelled to associate their lives with them. But the legal subordination tends to make such characters among women more, rather than less, frequent. If the man exerts his whole power, the woman is of course crushed: but if she is treated with indulgence, and permitted to assume power, there is no rule to set limits to her encroachments. The law, not determining her rights, but theoretically allowing her none at all, practically declares that the measure of what she has a right to, is what she can contrive to get.

The equality of married persons before the law is not only the sole mode in which that particular relation can be made consistent with justice to both sides, and conducive to the happiness of both, but it is the only means of rendering the daily life of mankind, in any high sense, a school of moral cultivation. Though the truth may not be felt or generally acknowledged for generations to come, the only school of genuine moral sentiment is society between equals. The moral education of mankind has hitherto emanated chiefly from the law of force, and is adapted almost solely to the relations which force creates. In the less advanced states of society, people hardly recognize any relation with their equals. To be an equal is to be an enemy. Society, from its highest place to its lowest, is one long chain, or rather ladder, where every individual is either above or below his nearest neighbour, and wherever he does not command he must obey. Existing moralities, accordingly, are mainly fitted to a relation of command and obedience. Yet command and obedience are but unfortunate necessities of human life: society in equality is its normal state. Already in modern life, and more and more as it progressively improves, command and obedience become exceptional

facts in life, equal association its general rule.   The
morality of the first ages rested on the obligation to
submit to power ; that of the ages next following, on
the right of the weak to the forbearance and protection
of the strong.   How much longer is one form of society
and life to content itself with the morality made for
another ?   We have had the morality of submission,
and the morality of chivalry and generosity ; the time
is now come for the morality of justice.   Whenever,
in former ages, any approach has been made to society
in equality, Justice has asserted its claims as the
foundation of virtue.   It was thus in the free republics of antiquity.   But even in the best of these,
the equals were limited to the free male citizens ;
slaves, women, and the unenfranchised residents were
under the law of force.   The joint influence of Roman
civilization and of Christianity obliterated these distinctions, and in theory (if only partially in practice)
declared the claims of the human being, as such, to be
paramount to those of sex, class, or social position.
The barriers which had begun to be levelled were
raised again by the northern conquests ; and the whole
of modern history consists of the slow process by which
they have since been wearing away.   We are entering
into an order of things in which justice will again be
the primary virtue ; grounded as before on equal, but
now also on sympathetic association ; having its root
no longer in the instinct of equals for self-protection,
but in a cultivated sympathy between them ; and no
one being now left out, but an equal measure being
extended to all.   It is no novelty that mankind do not
distinctly foresee their own changes, and that their
sentiments are adapted to past, not to coming ages.
To see the futurity of the species has always been the
privilege of the intellectual *élite*, or of those who have
learnt from them ; to have the feelings of that futurity
has been the distinction, and usually the martyrdom,
of a still rarer *élite*.   Institutions, books, education,
society, all go on training human beings for the old,
long after the new has come ; much more when it is

only coming. But the true virtue of human beings is fitness to live together as equals; claiming nothing for themselves but what they as freely concede to every one else; regarding command of any kind as an exceptional necessity, and in all cases a temporary one; and preferring, whenever possible, the society of those with whom leading and following can be alternate and reciprocal. To these virtues, nothing in life as at present constituted gives cultivation by exercise. The family is a school of despotism, in which the virtues of despotism, but also its vices, are largely nourished. Citizenship, in free countries, is partly a school of society in equality; but citizenship fills only a small place in modern life, and does not come near the daily habits or inmost sentiments. The family, justly constituted, would be the real school of the virtues of freedom. It is sure to be a sufficient one of everything else. It will always be a school of obedience for the children, of command for the parents. What is needed is, that it should be a school of sympathy in equality, of living together in love, without power on one side or obedience on the other. This it ought to be between the parents. It would then be an exercise of those virtues which each requires to fit them for all other association, and a model to the children of the feelings and conduct which their temporary training by means of obedience is designed to render habitual, and therefore natural, to them. The moral training of mankind will never be adapted to the conditions of the life for which all other human progress is a preparation, until they practise in the family the same moral rule which is adapted to the normal constitution of human society. Any sentiment of freedom which can exist in a man whose nearest and dearest intimacies are with those of whom he is absolute master, is not the genuine or Christian love of freedom, but, what the love of freedom generally was in the ancients and in the Middle Ages—an intense feeling of the dignity and importance of his own personality; making him disdain a yoke for himself, of which he has no abhorrence whatever in the abstract, but which he is abundantly ready to impose on others for his own interest or glorification.

I readily admit (and it is the very foundation of my hopes) that numbers of married people even under the present law (in the higher classes of England probably a great majority) live in the spirit of a just law of equality. Laws never would be improved, if there were not numerous persons whose moral sentiments are better than the existing laws. Such persons ought to support the principles here advocated; of which the only object is to make all other married couples similar to what these are now. But persons even of considerable moral worth, unless they are also thinkers, are very ready to believe that laws or practices, the evils of which they have not personally experienced, do not produce any evils, but (if seeming to be generally approved of) probably do good, and that it is wrong to object to them. It would, however, be a great mistake in such married people to suppose, because the legal conditions of the tie which unites them do not occur to their thoughts once in a twelvemonth, and because they live and feel in all respects as if they were legally equals, that the same is the case with all other married couples, wherever the husband is not a notorious ruffian. To suppose this, would be to show equal ignorance of human nature and of fact. The less fit a man is for the possession of power—the less likely to be allowed to exercise it over any person with that person's voluntary consent—the more does he hug himself in the consciousness of the power the law gives him, exact its legal rights to the utmost point which custom (the custom of men like himself) will tolerate, and take pleasure in using the power, merely to enliven the agreeable sense of possessing it. What is more; in the most naturally brutal and morally uneducated part of the lower classes, the legal slavery of the woman, and something in the merely physical subjection to their will as an instrument, causes them to feel a sort of disrespect and contempt towards their own wife which they do not feel towards any other woman, or any other human being, with whom they come in contact; and which makes her seem to them an appropriate subject for any kind of indignity. Let an acute observer of the signs of feeling, who has the requisite opportunities, judge for himself whether this is not the case: and if he finds that it is, let him not wonder at any amount of disgust and indignation that can be felt against institutions which lead naturally to this depraved state of the human mind.

We shall be told, perhaps, that religion imposes the duty of obedience; as every established fact which is too bad to admit of any other defence, is always presented to us as an injunction of religion. The Church, it is very true, enjoins it in her formularies, but it would be difficult to derive any such injunction from Christianity. We are told that St. Paul said, ' Wives, obey your husbands:' but he also said, ' Slaves, obey your masters.' It was not St. Paul's business, nor was it consistent with his object, the propagation of Christianity, to incite any one to rebellion against existing laws. The apostle's acceptance of all social institutions as he found them, is no more to be construed as a disapproval of attempts to improve them at the proper time, than his declaration, ' The powers that be are ordained of God,' gives his sanction to military despotism, and to that alone, as the Christian form of political government, or commands passive obedience to it. To pretend that Christianity was intended to stereotype existing forms of government and society, and protect them against change, is to reduce it to the level of Islamism or of Brahminism. It is precisely because Christianity has not done this, that it has been the religion of the progressive portion of mankind, and Islamism, Brahminism, &c., have been those of the stationary portions; or rather (for there is no such thing as a really stationary society) of the declining portions. There have been abundance of people, in all ages of Christianity, who tried to make it something of the same kind; to convert us into a sort of Christian Mussulmans, with the Bible for a Koran, prohibiting all improvement: and great has been their power, and many have had to sacrifice their lives in resisting them. But they have been resisted, and the resistance has made us what we are, and will yet make us what we are to be.

After what has been said respecting the obligation of obedience, it is almost superfluous to say anything concerning the more special point included in the general one—a woman's right to her own property; for I need not hope that this treatise can make any impression upon those who need anything to convince them that a woman's inheritance or gains ought to be as much her own after marriage as before. The rule is simple: whatever would be the husband's or wife's if they were not married, should be under their exclusive control during marriage; which need not interfere with the power to tie up property by settlement, in order to preserve it for children. Some people are sentimentally shocked at the idea of a separate interest in money matters, as inconsistent with the ideal fusion of two lives into one. For my own part, I am one of the strongest supporters of community of goods, when resulting from an entire unity of feeling in the owners, which makes all things common between them. But I have no relish for a community of goods resting on the doctrine, that what is mine is yours but what is yours is not mine; and I should prefer to decline entering into such a compact with any one, though I were myself the person to profit by it.

This particular injustice and oppression to women, which is, to common apprehensions, more obvious than all the rest, admits of remedy without interfering with any other mischiefs: and there can be little doubt that it will be one of the earliest remedied. Already, in many of the new and several of the old States of the American Confederation, provisions have been inserted even in the written Constitutions, securing to women equality of rights in this respect: and thereby improving materially the position, in the marriage relation, of those women at least who have property, by leaving them one instrument of power which they have not signed away ; and preventing also the scandalous abuse of the marriage institution, which is perpetrated when a man entraps a girl into marrying him without a settlement, for the sole purpose of getting possession of her money. When the support of the family depends, not on property, but on earnings, the common arrangement, by which the man earns the income and the wife superintends the domestic expenditure, seems to me in general the most suitable division of labour between the two persons. If, in addition to the physical suffering of bearing children, and the whole responsibility of their care and education in early years, the wife undertakes the careful and economical application of the husband's earnings to the general comfort of the family ; she takes not only her fair share, but usually the larger share, of the bodily and mental exertion required by their joint existence. If she undertakes any additional portion, it seldom relieves her from this, but only prevents her from performing it properly. The care which she is herself disabled from taking of the children and the household, nobody else takes ; those of the children who do not die, grow up as they best can, and the management of the household is likely to be so bad, as even in point of economy to be a great drawback from the value of the wife's earnings. In an otherwise just state of things, it is not, therefore, I think, a desirable custom, that the wife should contribute by her labour to the income of the family. In an unjust state of things, her doing so may be useful to her, by making her of more value in the eyes of the man who is legally her master ; but, on the other hand, it enables him still farther to abuse his power, by forcing her to work, and leaving the support of the family to her exertions, while he spends most of his time in drinking and idleness. The *power* of earning is essential to the dignity of a woman, if she has not independent property. But if marriage were an equal contract, not implying the obligation of

obedience; if the connexion were no longer enforced
to the oppression of those to whom it is purely a mischief, but a separation, on just terms (I do not now
speak of a divorce), could be obtained by any woman
who was morally entitled to it ; and if she would then
find all honourable employments as freely open to her
as to men ; it would not be necessary for her protection, that during marriage she should make this particular use of her faculties. Like a man when he
chooses a profession, so, when a woman marries, it
may in general be understood that she makes choice
of the management of a household, and the bringing
up of a family, as the first call upon her exertions,
during as many years of her life as may be required
for the purpose ; and that she renounces, not all other
objects and occupations, but all which are not consistent with the requirements of this. The actual
exercise, in a habitual or systematic manner, of out-
door occupations, or such as cannot be carried on at
home, would by this principle be practically interdicted
to the greater number of married women. But the
utmost latitude ought to exist for the adaptation of
general rules to individual suitabilities ; and there
ought to be nothing to prevent faculties exceptionally
adapted to any other pursuit, from obeying their vocation notwithstanding marriage : due provision being
made for supplying otherwise any falling-short which
might become inevitable, in her full performance of
the ordinary functions of mistress of a family. These
things, if once opinion were rightly directed on the
subject, might with perfect safety be left to be regulated
by opinion, without any interference of law.

CHAPTER III

On the other point which is involved in the just
equality of women, their admissibility to all the functions and occupations hitherto retained as the monopoly
of the stronger sex, I should anticipate no difficulty in

convincing any one who has gone with me on the subject of the equality of women in the family. I believe that their disabilities elsewhere are only clung to in order to maintain their subordination in domestic life; because the generality of the male sex cannot yet tolerate the idea of living with an equal. Were it not for that, I think that almost every one, in the existing state of opinion in politics and political economy, would admit the injustice of excluding half the human race from the greater number of lucrative occupations, and from almost all high social functions; ordaining from their birth either that they are not, and cannot by any possibility become, fit for employments which are legally open to the stupidest and basest of the other sex, or else that however fit they may be, those employments shall be interdicted to them, in order to be preserved for the exclusive benefit of males. In the last two centuries, when (which was seldom the case) any reason beyond the mere existence of the fact was thought to be required to justify the disabilities of women, people seldom assigned as a reason their inferior mental capacity; which, in times when there was a real trial of personal faculties (from which all women were not excluded) in the struggles of public life, no one really believed in. The reason given in those days was not women's unfitness, but the interest of society, by which was meant the interest of men: just as the *raison d'état*, meaning the convenience of the government, and the support of existing authority, was deemed a sufficient explanation and excuse for the most flagitious crimes. In the present day, power holds a smoother language, and whomsoever it oppresses, always pretends to do so for their own good: accordingly, when anything is forbidden to women, it is thought necessary to say, and desirable to believe, that they are incapable of doing it, and that they depart from their real path of success and happiness when they aspire to it. But to make this reason plausible (I do not say valid), those by whom it is urged must be prepared to carry it to a much

greater length than any one ventures to do in the face
of present experience. It is not sufficient to maintain
that women on the average are less gifted than men
on the average, with certain of the higher mental
faculties, or that a smaller number of women than of
men are fit for occupations and functions of the highest
intellectual character. It is necessary to maintain that
no women at all are fit for them, and that the most
eminent women are inferior in mental faculties to the
most mediocre of the men on whom those functions
at present devolve. For if the performance of the
function is decided either by competition, or by any
mode of choice which secures regard to the public
interest, there needs be no apprehension that any important employments will fall into the hands of women
inferior to average men, or to the average of their
male competitors. The only result would be that there
would be fewer women than men in such employments ;
a result certain to happen in any case, if only from the
preference always likely to be felt by the majority of
women for the one vocation in which there is nobody
to compete with them. Now, the most determined
depreciator of women will not venture to deny, that
when we add the experience of recent times to that of
ages past, women, and not a few merely, but many
women, have proved themselves capable of everything,
perhaps without a single exception, which is done by
men, and of doing it successfully and creditably. The
utmost that can be said is, that there are many things
which none of them have succeeded in doing as well
as they have been done by some men—many in which
they have not reached the very highest rank. But
there are extremely few, dependent only on mental
faculties, in which they have not attained the rank
next to the highest. Is not this enough, and much
more than enough, to make it a tyranny to them, and
a detriment to society, that they should not be allowed
to compete with men for the exercise of these functions ? Is it not a mere truism to say, that such
functions are often filled by men far less fit for them

than numbers of women, and who would be beaten by women in any fair field of competition? What difference does it make that there may be men somewhere, fully employed about other things, who may be still better qualified for the things in question than these women? Does not this take place in all competitions? Is there so great a superfluity of men fit for high duties, that society can afford to reject the service of any competent person? Are we so certain of always finding a man made to our hands for any duty or function of social importance which falls vacant, that we lose nothing by putting a ban upon one-half of mankind, and refusing beforehand to make their faculties available, however distinguished they may be? And even if we could do without them, would it be consistent with justice to refuse to them their fair share of honour and distinction, or to deny to them the equal moral right of all human beings to choose their occupation (short of injury to others) according to their own preferences, at their own risk? Nor is the injustice confined to them: it is shared by those who are in a position to benefit by their services. To ordain that any kind of persons shall not be physicians, or shall not be advocates, or shall not be members of parliament, is to injure not them only, but all who employ physicians or advocates, or elect members of parliament, and who are deprived of the stimulating effect of greater competition on the exertions of the competitors, as well as restricted to a narrower range of individual choice.

It will perhaps be sufficient if I confine myself, in the details of my argument, to functions of a public nature: since, if I am successful as to those, it probably will be readily granted that women should be admissible to all other occupations to which it is at all material whether they are admitted or not. And here let me begin by marking out one function, broadly distinguished from all others, their right to which is entirely independent of any question which can be raised concerning their faculties. I mean the suffrage, both parliamentary and municipal. The right to share in the choice of those who are to exercise a public trust, is altogether a distinct thing from that of competing for the trust itself. If no one could vote for a member of parliament who was not fit to be a candidate, the government would be a narrow oligarchy indeed. To have a voice in choosing those by whom one is to be governed, is a means of self-protection due to every one, though he were to remain for ever excluded from the function of governing: and that women are considered fit to have such a choice, may be presumed from the fact, that the law already gives it to women in the most important of all cases to themselves: for the choice of the man who is to govern a woman to the end of life, is always supposed to be voluntarily made by herself. In the case of election to public trusts, it is the business of constitutional law to surround the right of suffrage with all needful securities and limitations; but whatever securities are sufficient in the case of the male sex, no others need be required in the case of women. Under whatever conditions, and within whatever limits, men are admitted to the suffrage, there is not a shadow of justification for not admitting women under the same. The majority of the women of any class are not likely to differ in political opinion from the majority of the men of the same class, unless the question be one in which the interests of women, as such, are in some way involved; and if they are so, women require the suffrage, as their guarantee of just and equal consideration. This ought to be obvious even to those who coincide in no other of the doctrines for which I contend. Even if every woman were a wife, and if every wife ought to be a slave, all the more would these slaves stand in need of legal protection: and we know what legal protection the slaves have, where the laws are made by their masters.

With regard to the fitness of women, not only to participate in elections, but themselves to hold offices or practise professions involving important public responsibilities; I have already observed that this consideration is not essential to the practical question in dispute: since any woman, who succeeds in an open profession, proves by that very fact that she is qualified for it. And in the case of public offices, if the political system of the country is such as to exclude unfit men, it will equally exclude unfit women: while if it is not, there is no additional evil in the fact that the unfit persons whom it admits may be either women or men. As long therefore as it is acknowledged that even a few women may be fit for these duties, the laws which shut the door on those exceptions cannot be justified by any opinion which can be held respecting the capacities of women in general. But, though this last consideration is not essential, it is far from being irrelevant. An unprejudiced view of it gives additional strength to the arguments against the disabilities of women, and reinforces them by high considerations of practical utility.

Let us at first make entire abstraction of all psychological considerations tending to show, that any of the mental differences supposed to exist between women and men are but the natural effect of the differences in their education and circumstances, and indicate no radical difference, far less radical inferiority, of nature. Let us consider women only as they already are, or as they are known to have been; and the capacities which they have already practically shown. What they have done, that at least, if nothing else, it is proved that they can do. When we consider how sedulously they are all trained away from, instead of being trained towards, any of the occupations or objects reserved for men, it is evident that I am taking a very humble ground for them, when I rest their case on what they have actually achieved. For, in this case, negative evidence is worth little, while any positive evidence is conclusive. It cannot be inferred to be impossible that a woman should be a Homer, or an Aristotle, or a Michael Angelo, or a Beethoven, because no woman has yet actually produced works comparable to theirs in any of those lines of excellence. This negative fact at most leaves the question uncertain, and open to psychological discussion. But it is quite certain that a woman can be a Queen Elizabeth, or a Deborah, or a Joan of Arc, since this is not inference, but fact. Now it is a curious consideration, that the only things which the existing law excludes women from doing, are the things which they have proved that they are able to do. There is no law to prevent a woman from having written all the plays of Shakespeare, or composed all the operas of Mozart. But Queen Elizabeth or Queen Victoria, had they not inherited the throne, could not have been entrusted with the smallest of the political duties, of which the former showed herself equal to the greatest.

If anything conclusive could be inferred from experience, without psychological analysis, it would be that the things which women are not allowed to do are the very ones for which they are peculiarly qualified; since their vocation for government has made its way, and become conspicuous, through the very few opportunities which have been given; while in the lines of distinction which apparently were freely open to them, they have by no means so eminently distinguished themselves. We know how small a number of reigning queens history presents, in comparison with that of kings. Of this smaller number a far larger proportion have shown talents for rule; though many of them have occupied the throne in difficult periods. It is remarkable, too, that they have, in a great number of instances, been distinguished by merits the most opposite to the imaginary and conventional character of women: they have been as much remarked for the firmness and vigour of their rule, as for its intelligence. When, to queens and empresses, we add regents, and viceroys of provinces, the list of women who have been eminent rulers of mankind swells to a great length.[1] This fact is so undeniable,

[1] Especially is this true if we take into consideration Asia as well as Europe. If a Hindoo principality is strongly,

that some one, long ago, tried to retort the argument, and turned the admitted truth into an additional insult, by saying that queens are better than kings, because under kings women govern, but under queens, men.

It may seem a waste of reasoning to argue against a bad joke; but such things do affect people's minds; and I have heard men quote this saying, with an air as if they thought that there was something in it. At any rate, it will serve as well as anything else for a starting-point in discussion. I say, then, that it is not true that under kings, women govern. Such cases are entirely exceptional: and weak kings have quite as often governed ill through the influence of male favourites, as of female. When a king is governed by a woman merely through his amatory propensities, good government is not probable, though even then there are exceptions. But French history counts two kings who have voluntarily given the direction of affairs during many years, the one to his mother, the other to his sister: one of them, Charles VIII, was a mere boy, but in doing so he followed the intentions of his father Louis XI, the ablest monarch of his age. The other, Saint Louis, was the best, and one of the most vigorous

vigilantly, and economically governed; if order is preserved without oppression; if cultivation is extending, and the people prosperous, in three cases out of four that principality is under a woman's rule. This fact, to me an entirely unexpected one, I have collected from a long official knowledge of Hindoo governments. There are many such instances: for though, by Hindoo institutions, a woman cannot reign, she is the legal regent of a kingdom during the minority of the heir; and minorities are frequent, the lives of the male rulers being so often prematurely terminated through the effect of inactivity and sensual excesses. When we consider that these princesses have never been seen in public, have never conversed with any man not of their own family except from behind a curtain, that they do not read, and if they did, there is no book in their languages which can give them the smallest instruction on political affairs; the example they afford of the natural capacity of women for government is very striking.

rulers, since the time of Charlemagne. Both these princesses ruled in a manner hardly equalled by any prince among their cotemporaries. The emperor Charles the Fifth, the most politic prince of his time, who had as great a number of able men in his service as a ruler ever had, and was one of the least likely of all sovereigns to sacrifice his interest to personal feelings, made two princesses of his family successively Governors of the Netherlands, and kept one or other of them in that post during his whole life (they were afterwards succeeded by a third). Both ruled very successfully, and one of them, Margaret of Austria, was one of the ablest politicians of the age. So much for one side of the question. Now as to the other. When it is said that under queens men govern, is the same meaning to be understood as when kings are said to be governed by women? Is it meant that queens choose as their instruments of government, the associates of their personal pleasures? The case is rare even with those who are as unscrupulous on the latter point as Catherine II: and it is not in these cases that the good government, alleged to arise from male influence, is to be found. If it be true, then, that the administration is in the hands of better men under a queen than under an average king, it must be that queens have a superior capacity for choosing them; and women must be better qualified than men both for the position of sovereign, and for that of chief minister; for the principal business of a prime minister is not to govern in person, but to find the fittest persons to conduct every department of public affairs. The more rapid insight into character, which is one of the admitted points of superiority in women over men, must certainly make them, with anything like parity of qualifications in other respects, more apt than men in that choice of instruments, which is nearly the most important business of every one who has to do with governing mankind. Even the unprincipled Catherine de' Medici could feel the value of a Chancellor de l'Hôpital. But it is also true that most great queens have been great by their own talents for government, and have been well served precisely for that reason. They retained the supreme direction of affairs in their own hands : and if they listened to good advisers, they gave by that fact the strongest proof that their judgement fitted them for dealing with the great questions of government.

Is it reasonable to think that those who are fit for the greater functions of politics, are incapable of qualifying themselves for the less ?   Is there any reason in the nature of things, that the wives and sisters of princes should, whenever called on, be found as competent as the princes themselves to *their* business, but that the wives and sisters of statesmen, and administrators, and directors of companies, and managers of public institutions, should be unable to do what is done by their brothers and husbands ?   The real reason is plain enough ; it is that princesses, being more raised above the generality of men by their rank than placed below them by their sex, have never been taught that it was improper for them to concern themselves with politics ; but have been allowed to feel the liberal interest natural to any cultivated human being, in the great transactions which took place around them, and in which they might be called on to take a part.   The ladies of reigning families are the only women who are allowed the same range of interests and freedom of development as men ; and it is precisely in their case that there is not found to be any inferiority.   Exactly where and in proportion as women's capacities for government have been tried, in that proportion have they been found adequate.

This fact is in accordance with the best general conclusions which the world's imperfect experience seems as yet to suggest, concerning the peculiar tendencies and aptitudes characteristic of women, as women have hitherto been.   I do not say, as they will continue to be ; for, as I have already said more than once, I consider it presumption in any one to pretend to decide what women are or are not, can or cannot be, by natural constitution. They have always hitherto been kept, as far as regards spontaneous development, in so unnatural a state, that their nature cannot but have been greatly distorted and disguised ; and no one can safely pronounce that if women's nature were left to choose its direction as freely as men's, and if no artificial bent were attempted to be given to it except that required by the conditions of human society, and given to both sexes alike, there would be any material difference, or perhaps any difference at all, in the character and capacities which would unfold themselves. I shall presently show, that even the least contestable of the differences which now exist, are such as may very well have been produced merely by circumstances, without any difference of natural capacity. But, looking at women as they are known in experience, it may be said of them, with more truth than belongs to most other generalizations on the subject, that the general bent of their talents is towards the practical. This statement is conformable to all the public history of women, in the present and the past. It is no less borne out by common and daily experience. Let us consider the special nature of the mental capacities most characteristic of a woman of talent. They are all of a kind which fits them for practice, and makes them tend towards it. What is meant by a woman's capacity of intuitive perception ? It means, a rapid and correct insight into present fact. It has nothing to do with general principles. Nobody ever perceived a scientific law of nature by intuition, nor arrived at a general rule of duty or prudence by it. These are results of slow and careful collection and comparison of experience ; and neither the men nor the women of intuition usually shine in this department, unless, indeed, the experience necessary is such as they can acquire by themselves. For what is called their intuitive sagacity makes them peculiarly apt in gathering such general truths as can be collected from their individual means of observation. When, consequently, they chance to be as well provided as men are with

the results of other people's experience, by reading
and education (I use the word chance advisedly, for,
in respect to the knowledge that tends to fit them
for the greater concerns of life, the only educated
women are the self-educated), they are better furnished
than men in general with the essential requisites of
skilful and successful practice. Men who have been
much taught, are apt to be deficient in the sense of
present fact ; they do not see, in the facts which they
are called upon to deal with, what is really there, but
what they have been taught to expect. This is seldom
the case with women of any ability. Their capacity
of ' intuition ' preserves them from it. With equality
of experience and of general faculties, a woman usually
sees much more than a man of what is immediately
before her. Now this sensibility to the present, is the
main quality on which the capacity for practice, as distinguished from theory, depends. To discover general
principles, belongs to the speculative faculty : to dis-
cern and discriminate the particular cases in which
they are and are not applicable, constitutes practical
talent : and for this, women as they now are have
a peculiar aptitude. I admit that there can be no
good practice without principles, and that the predominant place which quickness of observation holds
among a woman's faculties, makes her particularly apt
to build over-hasty generalizations upon her own observation ; though at the same time no less ready in
rectifying those generalizations, as her observation
takes a wider range. But the corrective to this defect,
is access to the experience of the human race ; general
knowledge—exactly the thing which education can
best supply. A woman's mistakes are specifically those
of a clever self-educated man, who often sees what
men trained in routine do not see, but falls into errors
for want of knowing things which have long been
known. Of course he has acquired much of the pre-
existing knowledge, or he could not have got on at
all ; but what he knows of it he has picked up in
fragments and at random, as women do.

But this gravitation of women's minds to the present, to the real, to actual fact, while in its exclusiveness it is a source of errors, is also a most useful counteractive of the contrary error. The principal and most characteristic aberration of speculative minds as such, consists precisely in the deficiency of this lively perception and ever-present sense of objective fact. For want of this, they often not only overlook the contradiction which outward facts oppose to their theories, but lose sight of the legitimate purpose of speculation altogether, and let their speculative faculties go astray into regions not peopled with real beings, animate or inanimate, even idealized, but with personified shadows created by the illusions of metaphysics or by the mere entanglement of words, and think these shadows the proper objects of the highest, the most transcendant, philosophy. Hardly anything can be of greater value to a man of theory and speculation who employs himself not in collecting materials of knowledge by observation, but in working them up by processes of thought into comprehensive truths of science and laws of conduct, than to carry on his speculations in the companionship, and under the criticism, of a really superior woman. There is nothing comparable to it for keeping his thoughts within the limits of real things, and the actual facts of nature. A woman seldom runs wild after an abstraction. The habitual direction of her mind to dealing with things as individuals rather than in groups, and (what is closely connected with it) her more lively interest in the present feelings of persons, which makes her consider first of all, in anything which claims to be applied to practice, in what manner persons will be affected by it—these two things make her extremely unlikely to put faith in any speculation which loses sight of individuals, and deals with things as if they existed for the benefit of some imaginary entity, some mere creation of the mind, not resolvable into the feelings of living beings. Women's thoughts are thus as useful in giving reality to those of thinking men, as men's thoughts in giving width and largeness to those of women.   In depth, as distinguished from breadth, I greatly doubt if even now, women, compared with men, are at any disadvantage.

If the existing mental characteristics of women are thus valuable even in aid of speculation, they are still more important, when speculation has done its work, for carrying out the results of speculation into practice. For the reasons already given, women are comparatively unlikely to fall into the common error of men, that of sticking to their rules in a case whose specialities either take it out of the class to which the rules are applicable, or require a special adaptation of them. Let us now consider another of the admitted superiorities of clever women, greater quickness of apprehension. Is not this pre-eminently a quality which fits a person for practice ?   In action, everything continually depends upon deciding promptly.   In speculation, nothing does.   A mere thinker can wait, can take time to consider, can collect additional evidence ; he is not obliged to complete his philosophy at once, lest the opportunity should go by.   The power of drawing the best conclusion possible from insufficient data is not indeed useless in philosophy ; the construction of a provisional hypothesis consistent with all known facts is often the needful basis for further inquiry.   But this faculty is rather serviceable in philosophy, than the main qualification for it :   and, for the auxiliary as well as for the main operation, the philosopher can allow himself any time he pleases.   He is in no need of the capacity of doing rapidly what he does ;   what he rather needs is patience, to work on slowly until imperfect lights have become perfect, and a conjecture has ripened into a theorem.   For those, on the contrary, whose business is with the fugitive and perishable—with individual facts, not kinds of facts—rapidity of thought is a qualification next only in importance to the power of thought itself.   He who has not his faculties under immediate command, in the contingencies of action, might as well not have them at all.   He may be fit to criticize, but he is not fit to act.   Now it is in this that women, and the men who are most like women, confessedly excel. The other sort of man, however pre-eminent may be his faculties, arrives slowly at complete command of them: rapidity of judgement and promptitude of judicious action, even in the things he knows best, are the gradual and late result of strenuous effort grown into habit.

It will be said, perhaps, that the greater nervous susceptibility of women is a disqualification for practice, in anything but domestic life, by rendering them mobile, changeable, too vehemently under the influence of the moment, incapable of dogged perseverance, unequal and uncertain in the power of using their faculties. I think that these phrases sum up the greater part of the objections commonly made to the fitness of women for the higher class of serious business. Much of all this is the mere overflow of nervous energy run to waste, and would cease when the energy was directed to a definite end. Much is also the result of conscious or unconscious cultivation; as we see by the almost total disappearance of 'hysterics' and fainting fits, since they have gone out of fashion. Moreover, when people are brought up, like many women of the higher classes (though less so in our own country than in any other), a kind of hot-house plants, shielded from the wholesome vicissitudes of air and temperature, and untrained in any of the occupations and exercises which give stimulus and development to the circulatory and muscular system, while their nervous system, especially in its emotional department, is kept in unnaturally active play; it is no wonder if those of them who do not die of consumption, grow up with constitutions liable to derangement from slight causes, both internal and external, and without stamina to support any task, physical or mental, requiring continuity of effort. But women brought up to work for their livelihood show none of these morbid characteristics, unless indeed they are chained to an excess of sedentary work in confined and unhealthy rooms. Women who in their early years have shared in the healthful physical education and bodily freedom of their brothers, and who obtain a sufficiency of pure air and exercise in after-life, very rarely have any excessive susceptibility of nerves which can disqualify them for active pursuits. There is indeed a certain proportion of persons, in both sexes, in whom an unusual degree of nervous sensibility is constitutional, and of so marked a character as to be the feature of their organization which exercises the greatest influence over the whole character of the vital phenomena. This constitution, like other physical conformations, is hereditary, and is transmitted to sons as well as daughters ; but it is possible, and probable, that the nervous temperament (as it is called) is inherited by a greater number of women than of men. We will assume this as a fact : and let me then ask, are men of nervous temperament found to be unfit for the duties and pursuits usually followed by men ? If not, why should women of the same temperament be unfit for them ? The peculiarities of the temperament are, no doubt, within certain limits, an obstacle to success in some employments, though an aid to it in others. But when the occupation is suitable to the temperament, and sometimes even when it is unsuitable, the most brilliant examples of success are continually given by the men of high nervous sensibility. They are distinguished in their practical manifestations chiefly by this, that being susceptible of a higher degree of excitement than those of another physical constitution, their powers when excited differ more than in the case of other people, from those shown in their ordinary state : they are raised, as it were, above themselves, and do things with ease which they are wholly incapable of at other times. But this lofty excitement is not, except in weak bodily constitutions, a mere flash, which passes away immediately, leaving no permanent traces, and incompatible with persistent and steady pursuit of an object. It is the character of the nervous temperament to be capable of *sustained* excitement, holding out through long continued efforts. It is what is meant by *spirit*. It is what makes the high-bred racehorse run without slackening speed till he drops down dead. It is what has enabled so many delicate women to maintain the most sublime constancy not only at the stake, but through a long preliminary succession of mental and bodily tortures. It is evident that people of this temperament are particularly apt for what may be called the executive department of the leadership of mankind. They are the material of great orators, great preachers, impressive diffusers of moral influences. Their constitution might be deemed less favourable to the qualities required from a statesman in the cabinet, or from a judge. It would be so, if the consequence necessarily followed that because people are excitable they must always be in a state of excitement. But this is wholly a question of training. Strong feeling is the instrument and element of strong self-control: but it requires to be cultivated in that direction. When it is, it forms not the heroes of impulse only, but those also of self-conquest. History and experience prove that the most passionate characters are the most fanatic-ally rigid in their feelings of duty, when their passion has been trained to act in that direction. The judge who gives a just decision in a case where his feelings are intensely interested on the other side, derives from that same strength of feeling the determined sense of the obligation of justice, which enables him to achieve this victory over himself. The capability of that lofty enthusiasm which takes the human being out of his every-day character, reacts upon the daily character itself. His aspirations and powers when he is in this exceptional state, become the type with which he com-pares, and by which he estimates, his sentiments and proceedings at other times: and his habitual purposes assume a character moulded by and assimilated to the moments of lofty excitement, although those, from the physical nature of a human being, can only be transient. Experience of races, as well as of individuals, does not show those of excitable temperament to be less fit, on the average, either for speculation or practice, than

the more unexcitable. The French, and the Italians,
are undoubtedly by nature more nervously excitable
than the Teutonic races. and, compared at least with
the English, they have a much greater habitual and
daily emotional life : but have they been less great in
science, in public business, in legal and judicial eminence, or in war ? There is abundant evidence that the
Greeks were of old, as their descendants and successors
still are, one of the most excitable of the races of
mankind. It is superfluous to ask, what among the
achievements of men they did not excel in. The
Romans, probably, as an equally southern people, had
the same original temperament : but the stern character
of their national discipline, like that of the Spartans,
made them an example of the opposite type of national
character ; the greater strength of their natural feelings
being chiefly apparent in the intensity which the same
original temperament made it possible to give to the
artificial. If these cases exemplify what a naturally
excitable people may be made, the Irish Celts afford
one of the aptest examples of what they are when left
to themselves (if those can be said to be left to themselves who have been for centuries under the indirect
influence of bad government, and the direct training
of a Catholic hierarchy and of a sincere belief in the
Catholic religion). The Irish character must be considered, therefore, as an unfavourable case : yet, whenever the circumstances of the individual have been at
all favourable, what people have shown greater capacity
for the most varied and multifarious individual eminence ? Like the French compared with the English,
the Irish with the Swiss, the Greeks or Italians compared with the German races, so women compared
with men may be found, on the average, to do the
same things with some variety in the particular kind
of excellence. But, that they would do them fully as
well on the whole, if their education and cultivation
were adapted to correcting instead of aggravating the
infirmities incident to their temperament, I see not the
smallest reason to doubt.

Supposing it, however, to be true that women's minds are by nature more mobile than those of men, less capable of persisting long in the same continuous effort, more fitted for dividing their faculties among many things than for travelling in any one path to the highest point which can be reached by it: this may be true of women as they now are (though not without great and numerous exceptions), and may account for their having remained behind the highest order of men in precisely the things in which this absorption of the whole mind in one set of ideas and occupations may seem to be most requisite. Still, this difference is one which can only affect the kind of excellence, not the excellence itself, or its practical worth: and it remains to be shown whether this exclusive working of a part of the mind, this absorption of the whole thinking faculty in a single subject, and concentration of it on a single work, is the normal and healthful condition of the human faculties, even for speculative uses. I believe that what is gained in special development by this concentration, is lost in the capacity of the mind for the other purposes of life; and even in abstract thought, it is my decided opinion that the mind does more by frequently returning to a difficult problem, than by sticking to it without interruption. For the purposes, at all events, of practice, from its highest to its humblest departments, the capacity of passing promptly from one subject of consideration to another, without letting the active spring of the intellect run down between the two, is a power far more valuable; and this power women pre-eminently possess, by virtue of the very mobility of which they are accused. They perhaps have it from nature, but they certainly have it by training and education; for nearly the whole of the occupations of women consist in the management of small but multitudinous details, on each of which the mind cannot dwell even for a minute, but must pass on to other things, and if anything requires longer thought, must steal time at odd moments for thinking

of it. The capacity indeed which women show for
doing their thinking in circumstances and at times
which almost any man would make an excuse to himself for not attempting it, has often been noticed:
and a woman's mind, though it may be occupied only
with small things, can hardly ever permit itself to be
vacant, as a man's so often is when not engaged in
what he chooses to consider the business of his life.
The business of a woman's ordinary life is things in
general, and can as little cease to go on as the world
to go round.

But (it is said) there is anatomical evidence of the
superior mental capacity of men compared with women:
they have a larger brain. I reply, that in the first
place the fact itself is doubtful. It is by no means
established that the brain of a woman is smaller than
that of a man. If it is inferred merely because a
woman's bodily frame generally is of less dimensions
than a man's, this criterion would lead to strange consequences. A tall and large-boned man must on this
showing be wonderfully superior in intelligence to
a small man, and an elephant or a whale must prodigiously excel mankind. The size of the brain in
human beings, anatomists say, varies much less than
the size of the body, or even of the head, and the one
cannot be at all inferred from the other. It is certain
that some women have as large a brain as any man.
It is within my knowledge that a man who had weighed
many human brains, said that the heaviest he knew
of, heavier even than Cuvier's (the heaviest previously
recorded), was that of a woman. Next, I must observe
that the precise relation which exists between the
brain and the intellectual powers is not yet well understood, but is a subject of great dispute. That there is
a very close relation we cannot doubt. The brain is
certainly the material organ of thought and feeling:
and (making abstraction of the great unsettled controversy respecting the appropriation of different parts
of the brain to different mental faculties) I admit
that it would be an anomaly, and an exception to all

we know of the general laws of life and organization, if the size of the organ were wholly indifferent to the function; if no accession of power were derived from the greater magnitude of the instrument. But the exception and the anomaly would be fully as great if the organ exercised influence by its magnitude *only*. In all the more delicate operations of nature—of which those of the animated creation are the most delicate, and those of the nervous system by far the most delicate of these—differences in the effect depend as much on differences of quality in the physical agents, as on their quantity: and if the quality of an instrument is to be tested by the nicety and delicacy of the work it can do, the indications point to a greater average fineness of quality in the brain and nervous system of women than of men. Dismissing abstract difference of quality, a thing difficult to verify, the efficiency of an organ is known to depend not solely on its size but on its activity: and of this we have an approximate measure in the energy with which the blood circulates through it, both the stimulus and the reparative force being mainly dependent on the circulation. It would not be surprising—it is indeed an hypothesis which accords well with the differences actually observed between the mental operations of the two sexes—if men on the average should have the advantage in the size of the brain, and women in activity of cerebral circulation. The results which conjecture, founded on analogy, would lead us to expect from this difference of organization, would correspond to some of those which we most commonly see. In the first place, the mental operations of men might be expected to be slower. They would neither be so prompt as women in thinking, nor so quick to feel. Large bodies take more time to get into full action. On the other hand, when once got thoroughly into play, men's brain would bear more work. It would be more persistent in the line first taken; it would have more difficulty in changing from one mode of action to another, but, in the one thing it was doing, it could go on longer without loss of power or sense of fatigue. And do we not find that the things in which men most excel women are those which require most plodding and long hammering at a single thought, while women do best what must be done rapidly ? A woman's brain is sooner fatigued, sooner exhausted ; but given the degree of exhaustion, we should expect to find that it would recover itself sooner. I repeat that this speculation is entirely hypothetical ; it pretends to no more than to suggest a line of inquiry. I have before repudiated the notion of its being yet certainly known that there is any natural difference at all in the average strength or direction of the mental capacities of the two sexes, much less what that difference is. Nor is it possible that this should be known, so long as the psychological laws of the formation of character have been so little studied, even in a general way, and in the particular case never scientifically applied at all ; so long as the most obvious external causes of difference of character are habitually disregarded—left unnoticed by the observer, and looked down upon with a kind of supercilious contempt by the prevalent schools both of natural history and of mental philosophy: who, whether they look for the source of what mainly distinguishes human beings from one another, in the world of matter or in that of spirit, agree in running down those who prefer to explain these differences by the different relations of human beings to society and life.

To so ridiculous an extent are the notions formed of the nature of women, mere empirical generalizations, framed, without philosophy or analysis, upon the first instances which present themselves, that the popular idea of it is different in different countries, according as the opinions and social circumstances of the country have given to the women living in it any speciality of development or non-development. An Oriental thinks that women are by nature peculiarly voluptuous ; see the violent abuse of them on this ground in Hindoo writings. An Englishman usually thinks that they are by nature cold. The sayings about women's fickleness are mostly of French origin ; from the famous distich of Francis the First, upward and downward. In England it is a common remark, how much more constant women are than men. Inconstancy has been longer reckoned discreditable to a woman, in England than in France ; and Englishwomen are besides, in their inmost nature, much more subdued to opinion. It may be remarked by the way, that Englishmen are in peculiarly unfavourable circumstances for attempting to judge what is or is not natural, not merely to women, but to men, or to human beings altogether, at least if they have only English experience to go upon : because there is no place where human nature shows so little of its original lineaments. Both in a good and a bad sense, the English are farther from a state of nature than any other modern people. They are, more than any other people, a product of civilization and discipline. England is the country in which social discipline has most succeeded, not so much in conquering, as in suppressing, whatever is liable to conflict with it. The English, more than any other people, not only act but feel according to rule. In other countries, the taught opinion, or the requirement of society, may be the stronger power, but the promptings of the individual nature are always visible under it, and often resisting it : rule may be stronger than nature, but nature is still there. In England, rule has to a great degree substituted itself for nature. The greater part of life is carried on, not by following inclination under the control of rule, but by having no inclination but that of following a rule. Now this has its good side doubtless, though it has also a wretchedly bad one ; but it must render an Englishman peculiarly ill-qualified to pass a judgement on the original tendencies of human nature from his own experience. The errors to which observers elsewhere are liable on the subject, are of a different character. An Englishman is ignorant respecting human nature, a Frenchman is prejudiced. An Englishman's errors are negative, a Frenchman's positive. An Englishman fancies that things do not exist, because he never sees them ; a Frenchman thinks they must always and necessarily exist, because he does see them. An Englishman does not know nature, because he has had no opportunity of observing it ; a Frenchman generally knows a great deal of it, but often mistakes it, because he has only seen it sophisticated and distorted. For the artificial state superinduced by society disguises the natural tendencies of the thing which is the subject of observation, in two different ways : by extinguishing the nature, or by transforming it. In the one case there is but a starved residuum of nature remaining to be studied ; in the other case there is much, but it may have expanded in any direction rather than that in which it would spontaneously grow.

I have said that it cannot now be known how much of the existing mental differences between men and women is natural, and how much artificial ; whether there are any natural differences at all ; or, supposing all artificial causes of difference to be withdrawn, what natural character would be revealed. I am not about to attempt what I have pronounced impossible : but doubt does not forbid conjecture, and where certainty is unattainable, there may yet be the means of arriving at some degree of probability. The first point, the origin of the differences actually observed, is the one most accessible to speculation ; and I shall attempt to approach it, by the only path by which it can be reached ; by tracing the mental consequences of external influences. We cannot isolate a human being from the circumstances of his condition, so as to ascertain experimentally what he would have been by nature ; but we can consider what he is, and what his circumstances have been, and whether the one would have been capable of producing the other.

Let us take, then, the only marked case which observation affords, of apparent inferiority of women to men, if we except the merely physical one of bodily strength. No production in philosophy, science, or art, entitled to the first rank, has been the work of a woman. Is there any mode of accounting for this, without supposing that women are naturally incapable of producing them ?

In the first place, we may fairly question whether experience has afforded sufficient grounds for an induction. It is scarcely three generations since women, saving very rare exceptions, have begun to try their capacity in philosophy, science, or art. It is only in the present generation that their attempts have been at all numerous ; and they are even now extremely few, everywhere but in England and France. It is a relevant question, whether a mind possessing the requisites of first-rate eminence in speculation or creative art could have been expected, on the mere calculation of chances, to turn up during that lapse of time, among the women whose tastes and personal position admitted of their devoting themselves to these pursuits. In all things which there has yet been time for—in all but the very highest grades in the scale of excellence, especially in the department in which they have been longest engaged, literature (both prose and poetry)—women have done quite as much, have obtained fully as high prizes and as many of them, as could be expected from the length of time and the number of competitors. If we go back to the earlier period when very few women made the attempt, yet some of those few made it with distinguished success. The Greeks always accounted Sappho among their great poets ; and we may well suppose that Myrtis, said to have been the teacher of Pindar, and Corinna, who five times bore away from him the prize of poetry, must at least have had sufficient merit to admit of being compared with that great name. Aspasia did not leave any philosophical writings ; but it is an admitted fact that Socrates resorted to her for instruction, and avowed himself to have obtained it.

If we consider the works of women in modern times,

and contrast them with those of men, either in the literary or the artistic department, such inferiority as may be observed resolves itself essentially into one thing: but that is a most material one; deficiency of originality. Not total deficiency; for every production of mind which is of any substantive value, has an originality of its own—is a conception of the mind itself, not a copy of something else. Thoughts original, in the sense of being unborrowed—of being derived from the thinker's own observations or intellectual processes—are abundant in the writings of women. But they have not yet produced any of those great and luminous new ideas which form an era in thought, nor those fundamentally new conceptions in art, which open a vista of possible effects not before thought of, and found a new school. Their compositions are mostly grounded on the existing fund of thought, and their creations do not deviate widely from existing types. This is the sort of inferiority which their works manifest: for in point of execution, in the detailed application of thought, and the perfection of style, there is no inferiority. Our best novelists in point of composition, and of the management of detail, have mostly been women; and there is not in all modern literature a more eloquent vehicle of thought than the style of Madame de Staël, nor, as a specimen of purely artistic excellence, anything superior to the prose of Madame Sand, whose style acts upon the nervous system like a symphony of Haydn or Mozart. High originality of conception is, as I have said, what is chiefly wanting. And now to examine if there is any manner in which this deficiency can be accounted for.

Let us remember, then, so far as regards mere thought, that during all that period in the world's existence, and in the progress of cultivation, in which great and fruitful new truths could be arrived at by mere force of genius, with little previous study and accumulation of knowledge—during all that time women did not concern themselves with speculation at all. From the days of Hypatia to those of the

Reformation, the illustrious Heloisa is almost the only woman to whom any such achievement might have been possible ; and we know not how great a capacity of speculation in her may have been lost to mankind by the misfortunes of her life. Never since any considerable number of women have began to cultivate serious thought, has originality been possible on easy terms. Nearly all the thoughts which can be reached by mere strength of original faculties, have long since been arrived at ; and originality, in any high sense of the word, is now scarcely ever attained but by minds which have undergone elaborate discipline, and are deeply versed in the results of previous thinking. It is Mr. Maurice, I think, who has remarked on the present age, that its most original thinkers are those who have known most thoroughly what had been thought by their predecessors : and this will always henceforth be the case. Every fresh stone in the edifice has now to be placed on the top of so many others, that a long process of climbing, and of carrying up materials, has to be gone through by whoever aspires to take a share in the present stage of the work. How many women are there who have gone through any such process ? Mrs. Somerville, alone perhaps of women, knows as much of mathematics as is now needful for making any considerable mathematical discovery : is it any proof of inferiority in women, that she has not happened to be one of the two or three persons who in her lifetime have associated their names with some striking advancement of the science ? Two women, since political economy has been made a science, have known enough of it to write usefully on the subject : of how many of the innumerable men who have written on it during the same time, is it possible with truth to say more ? If no woman has hitherto been a great historian, what woman has had the necessary erudition ? If no woman is a great philologist, what woman has studied Sanscrit and Slavonic, the Gothic of Ulphila and the Persic of the Zendavesta ? Even in practical matters we all know what is the value of the originality of untaught geniuses. It means, inventing over again in its rudimentary form something already invented and improved upon by many successive inventors. When women have had the preparation which all men now require to be eminently original, it will be time enough to begin judging by experience of their capacity for originality.

It no doubt often happens that a person, who has not widely and accurately studied the thoughts of others on a subject, has by natural sagacity a happy intuition, which he can suggest, but cannot prove, which yet when matured may be an important addition to knowledge : but even then, no justice can be done to it until some other person, who does possess the previous acquirements, takes it in hand, tests it, gives it a scientific or practical form, and fits it into its place among the existing truths of philosophy or science. Is it supposed that such felicitous thoughts do not occur to women ? They occur by hundreds to every woman of intellect. But they are mostly lost, for want of a husband or friend who has the other knowledge which can enable him to estimate them properly and bring them before the world : and even when they are brought before it, they generally appear as his ideas, not their real author's. Who can tell how many of the most original thoughts put forth by male writers, belong to a woman by suggestion, to themselves only by verifying and working out ? If I may judge by my own case, a very large proportion indeed.

If we turn from pure speculation to literature in the narrow sense of the term, and the fine arts, there is a very obvious reason why women's literature is, in its general conception and in its main features, an imitation of men's. Why is the Roman literature, as critics proclaim to satiety, not original, but an imitation of the Greek ? Simply because the Greeks came first. If women lived in a different country from men, and had never read any of their writings, they would have had a literature of their own. As it is, they have not created one, because they found a highly advanced literature already created. If there had been no suspension of the knowledge of antiquity, or if the Renaissance had occurred before the Gothic cathedrals were built, they never would have been built. We see that, in France and Italy, imitation of the ancient literature stopped the original development even after it had commenced. All women who write are pupils of the great male writers. A painter's early pictures, even if he be a Raffaelle, are undistinguishable in style from those of his master. Even a Mozart does not display his powerful originality in his earliest pieces. What years are to a gifted individual, generations are to a mass. If women's literature is destined to have a different collective character from that of men, depending on any difference of natural tendencies, much longer time is necessary than has yet elapsed, before it can emancipate itself from the influence of accepted models, and guide itself by its own impulses. But if, as I believe, there will not prove to be any natural tendencies common to women, and distinguishing their genius from that of men, yet every individual writer among them has her individual tendencies, which at present are still subdued by the influence of precedent and example: and it will require generations more, before their individuality is sufficiently developed to make head against that influence.

It is in the fine arts, properly so called, that the prima facie evidence of inferior original powers in women at first sight appears the strongest: since opinion (it may be said) does not exclude them from these, but rather encourages them, and their education, instead of passing over this department, is in the affluent classes mainly composed of it. Yet in this line of exertion they have fallen still more short than in many others, of the highest eminence attained by men. This shortcoming, however, needs no other explanation than the familiar fact, more universally true in the fine arts than in anything else; the vast superiority of professional persons over amateurs.

Women in the educated classes are almost universally taught more or less of some branch or other of the fine arts, but not that they may gain their living or their social consequence by it. Women artists are all amateurs. The exceptions are only of the kind which confirm the general truth. Women are taught music, but not for the purpose of composing, only of executing it : and accordingly it is only as composers, that men, in music, are superior to women. The only one of the fine arts which women do follow, to any extent, as a profession, and an occupation for life, is the histrionic ; and in that they are confessedly equal, if not superior, to men. To make the comparison fair, it should be made between the productions of women in any branch of art, and those of men not following it as a profession. In musical composition, for example, women surely have produced fully as good things as have ever been produced by male amateurs. There are now a few women, a very few, who practise painting as a profession, and these are already beginning to show quite as much talent as could be expected. Even male painters (*pace* Mr. Ruskin) have not made any very remarkable figure these last centuries, and it will be long before they do so. The reason why the old painters were so greatly superior to the modern, is that a greatly superior class of men applied themselves to the art. In the fourteenth and fifteenth centuries the Italian painters were the most accomplished men of their age. The greatest of them were men of encyclopaedical acquirements and powers, like the great men of Greece. But in their times fine art was, to men's feelings and conceptions, among the grandest things in which a human being could excel; and by it men were made, what only political or military distinction now makes them, the companions of sovereigns, and the equals of the highest nobility. In the present age, men of anything like similar calibre find something more important to do, for their own fame and the uses of the modern world, than painting : and it is only now and then that a Reynolds or a Turner (of whose relative rank among eminent men I do not pretend to an opinion) applies himself to that art. Music belongs to a different order of things; it does not require the same general powers of mind, but seems more dependent on a natural gift: and it may be thought surprising that no one of the great musical composers has been a woman. But even this natural gift, to be made available for great creations, requires study, and professional devotion to the pursuit. The only countries which have produced first-rate composers, even of the male sex, are Germany and Italy—countries in which, both in point of special and of general cultivation, women have remained far behind France and England, being generally (it may be said without exaggeration) very little educated, and having scarcely cultivated at all any of the higher faculties of mind. And in those countries the men who are acquainted with the principles of musical composition must be counted by hundreds, or more probably by thousands, the women barely by scores: so that here again, on the doctrine of averages, we cannot reasonably expect to see more than one eminent woman to fifty eminent men; and the last three centuries have not produced fifty eminent male composers either in Germany or in Italy.

There are other reasons, besides those which we have now given, that help to explain why women remain behind men, even in the pursuits which are open to both. For one thing, very few women have time for them. This may seem a paradox; it is an undoubted social fact. The time and thoughts of every woman have to satisfy great previous demands on them for things practical. There is, first, the superintendence of the family and the domestic expenditure, which occupies at least one woman in every family, generally the one of mature years and acquired experience; unless the family is so rich as to admit of delegating that task to hired agency, and submitting to all the waste and malversation inseparable from that mode of conducting it. The superintendence of a household, even when not in other respects laborious, is extremely onerous to the thoughts; it requires incessant vigilance, an eye which no detail escapes, and presents questions for consideration and solution, foreseen and unforeseen, at every hour of the day, from which the person responsible for them can hardly ever shake herself free. If a woman is of a rank and circumstances which relieve her in a measure from these cares, she has still devolving on her the management for the whole family of its intercourse with others—of what is called society, and the less the call made on her by the former duty, the greater is always the development of the latter: the dinner parties, concerts, evening parties, morning visits, letter-writing, and all that goes with them. All this is over and above the engrossing duty which society imposes exclusively on women, of making themselves charming. A clever woman of the higher ranks finds nearly a sufficient employment of her talents in cultivating the graces of manner and the arts of conversation. To look only at the outward side of the subject: the great and continual exercise of thought which all women who attach any value to dressing well (I do not mean expensively, but with taste, and perception of natural and of artificial *convenance*) must bestow upon their own dress, perhaps also upon that of their daughters, would alone go a great way towards achieving respectable results in art, or science, or literature, and does actually exhaust much of the time and mental power they might have to spare for either.[1] If it were possible that all this

---

[1] 'It appears to be the same right turn of mind which enables a man to acquire the *truth*, or the just idea of what is right, in the ornaments, as in the more stable principles of art. It has still the same centre of perfection, though it is the centre of a smaller circle.—To illustrate this by the fashion of dress, in which there is allowed to be a good or bad taste. The component parts of dress are continually changing from great to little, from short to long.; but the general form still remains; it is still the same general dress, which is comparatively fixed, though

number of little practical interests (which are made great to them) should leave them either much leisure, or much energy and freedom of mind, to be devoted to art or speculation, they must have a much greater original supply of active faculty than the vast majority of men. But this is not all. Independently of the regular offices of life which devolve upon a woman, she is expected to have her time and faculties always at the disposal of everybody. If a man has not a profession to exempt him from such demands, still, if he has a pursuit, he offends nobody by devoting his time to it; occupation is received as a valid excuse for his not answering to every casual demand which may be made on him. Are a woman's occupations, especially her chosen and voluntary ones, ever regarded as excusing her from any of what are termed the calls of society? Scarcely are her most necessary and recognized duties allowed as an exemption. It requires an illness in the family, or something else out of the common way, to entitle her to give her own business the precedence over other people's amusement. She must always be at the beck and call of somebody, generally of everybody. If she has a study or a pursuit, she must snatch any short interval which accidentally occurs to be employed in it. A celebrated woman, in a work which I hope will some day be published, remarks truly that everything a woman does is done at odd times. Is it wonderful, then, if she does not attain the highest eminence in things which require consecutive attention, and the concentration on them of the chief interest of life? Such is philosophy, and such, above all, is art, in which, besides the devotion of the thoughts and feelings, the hand

on a very slender foundation; but it ,is on this which fashion must rest. He who invents with the most success, or dresses in the best taste, would probably, from the same sagacity employed to greater purposes, have discovered equal skill, or have formed the same correct taste, in the highest labours of art.'—*Sir Joshua Reynolds's Discourses.* Disc. vii.

also must be kept in constant exercise to attain high skill.

There is another consideration to be added to all these. In the various arts and intellectual occupations, there is a degree of proficiency sufficient for living by it, and there is a higher degree on which depend the great productions which immortalize a name. To the attainment of the former, there are adequate motives in the case of all who follow the pursuit professionally : the other is hardly ever attained where there is not, or where there has not been at some period of life, an ardent desire of celebrity. Nothing less is commonly a sufficient stimulus to undergo the long and patient drudgery, which, in the case even of the greatest natural gifts, is absolutely required for great eminence in pursuits in which we already possess so many splendid memorials of the highest genius. Now, whether the cause be natural or artificial, women seldom have this eagerness for fame. Their ambition is generally confined within narrower bounds. The influence they seek is over those who immediately surround them. Their desire is to be liked, loved, or admired, by those whom they see with their eyes : and the proficiency in knowledge, arts, and accomplishments, which is sufficient for that, almost always contents them. This is a trait of character which cannot be left out of the account in judging of women as they are. I do not at all believe that it is inherent in women. It is only the natural result of their circumstances. The love of fame in men is encouraged by education and opinion : to ' scorn delights and live laborious days ' for its sake, is accounted the part of ' noble minds ', even if spoken of as their ' last infirmity ', and is stimulated by the access which fame gives to all objects of ambition, including even the favour of women; while to women themselves all these objects are closed, and the desire of fame itself considered daring and unfeminine. Besides, how could it be that a woman's interests should not be all concentrated upon the impressions made on those who come into her daily life, when society has ordained that all her duties should be to them, and has contrived that all her comforts should depend on them? The natural desire of consideration from our fellow creatures is as strong in a woman as in a man; but society has so ordered things that public consideration is, in all ordinary cases, only attainable by her through the consideration of her husband or of her male relations, while her private consideration is forfeited by making herself individually prominent, or appearing in any other character than that of an appendage to men. Whoever is in the least capable of estimating the influence on the mind of the entire domestic and social position and the whole habit of a life, must easily recognize in that influence a complete explanation of nearly all the apparent differences between women and men, including the whole of those which imply any inferiority.

As for moral differences, considered as distinguished from intellectual, the distinction commonly drawn is to the advantage of women. They are declared to be better than men; an empty compliment, which must provoke a bitter smile from every woman of spirit, since there is no other situation in life in which it is the established order, and considered quite natural and suitable, that the better should obey the worse. If this piece of idle talk is good for anything, it is only as an admission by men, of the corrupting influence of power; for that is certainly the only truth which the fact, if it be a fact, either proves or illustrates. And it *is* true that servitude, except when it actually brutalizes, though corrupting to both, is less so to the slaves than to the slave-masters. It is wholesomer for the moral nature to be restrained, even by arbitrary power, than to be allowed to exercise arbitrary power without restraint. Women, it is said, seldomer fall under the penal law—contribute a much smaller number of offenders to the criminal calendar, than men. I doubt not that the same thing may be said, with the same truth, of negro slaves. Those who are under the control of others cannot often commit crimes, unless at the command and for the purposes of their masters. I do not know a more signal instance of the blindness with which the world, including the herd of studious men, ignore and pass over all the influences of social circumstances, than their silly depreciation of the intellectual, and silly panegyrics on the moral, nature of women.

The complimentary dictum about women's superior moral goodness may be allowed to pair off with the disparaging one respecting their greater liability to moral bias. Women, we are told, are not capable of resisting their personal partialities: their judgement in grave affairs is warped by their sympathies and antipathies. Assuming it to be so, it is still to be proved that women are oftener misled by their personal feelings than men by their personal interests. The chief difference would seem in that case to be, that men are led from the course of duty and the public interest by their regard for themselves, women (not being allowed to have private interests of their own) by their regard for somebody else. It is also to be considered, that all the education which women receive from society inculcates on them the feeling that the individuals connected with them are the only ones to whom they owe any duty—the only ones whose interest they are called upon to care for; while, as far as education is concerned, they are left strangers even to the elementary ideas which are presupposed in any intelligent regard for larger interests or higher moral objects. The complaint against them resolves itself merely into this, that they fulfil only too faithfully the sole duty which they are taught, and almost the only one which they are permitted to practise.

The concessions of the privileged to the unprivileged are so seldom brought about by any better motive than the power of the unprivileged to extort them, that any arguments against the prerogative of sex are likely to be little attended to by the generality, as long as they are able to say to themselves that women do not complain of it. That fact certainly enables men to retain the unjust privilege some time longer; but does not render it less unjust. Exactly the same thing may be said of the women in the harem of an Oriental: they do not complain of not being allowed the freedom of European women. They think our women insufferably bold and unfeminine. How rarely it is that even men complain of the general order of society; and how much rarer still would such complaint be, if they did not know of any different order existing anywhere else. Women do not complain of the general lot of women; or rather they do, for plaintive elegies on it are very common in the writings of women, and were still more so as long as the lamentations could not be suspected of having any practical object. Their complaints are like the complaints which men make of the general unsatisfactoriness of human life; they are not meant to imply blame, or to plead for any change. But though women do not complain of the power of husbands, each complains of her own husband, or of the husbands of her friends. It is the same in all other cases of servitude, at least in the commencement of the emancipatory movement. The serfs did not at first complain of the power of their lords, but only of their tyranny. The Commons began by claiming a few municipal privileges; they next asked an exemption for themselves from being taxed without their own consent; but they would at that time have thought it a great presumption to claim any share in the king's sovereign authority. The case of women is now the only case in which to rebel against established rules is still looked upon with the same eyes as was formerly a subject's claim to the right of rebelling against his king. A woman who joins in any movement which her husband disapproves, makes herself a martyr, without even being able to be an apostle, for the husband can legally put a stop to her apostleship. Women cannot be expected to devote themselves to the emancipation of women, until men in considerable number are prepared to join with them in the undertaking.

CHAPTER IV

THERE remains a question, not of less importance than those already discussed, and which will be asked the most importunately by those opponents whose conviction is somewhat shaken on the main point. What good are we to expect from the changes proposed in our customs and institutions ? Would mankind be at all better off if women were free ? If not, why disturb their minds, and attempt to make a social revolution in the name of an abstract right ?

It is hardly to be expected that this question will be asked in respect to the change proposed in the condition of women in marriage. The sufferings, immoralities, evils of all sorts, produced in innumerable cases by the subjection of individual women to individual men, are far too terrible to be overlooked. Unthinking or uncandid persons, counting those cases alone which are extreme, or which attain publicity, may say that the evils are exceptional; but no one can be blind to their existence, nor, in many cases, to their intensity. And it is perfectly obvious that the abuse of the power cannot be very much checked while the power remains. It is a power given, or offered, not to good men, or to decently respectable men, but to all men; the most brutal, and the most criminal. There is no check but that of opinion, and such men are in general within the reach of no opinion but that of men like themselves. If such men did not brutally tyrannize over the one human being whom the law compels to bear everything from them, society must already have reached a paradisaical state. There could be no need any longer of laws to curb men's vicious propensities. Astraea must not only have returned to earth, but the heart of the worst man must have become her temple. The law of servitude in marriage is a monstrous contradiction to all the principles of the modern world, and to all the experience through which those principles have been slowly and painfully worked out. It is the sole case, now that negro slavery has been abolished, in which a human being in the plenitude of every faculty is delivered up to the tender mercies of another human being, in the hope forsooth that this other will use the power solely for the good of the person subjected to it. Marriage is the only actual bondage known to our law. There remain no legal slaves, except the mistress of every house.

It is not, therefore, on this part of the subject, that the question is likely to be asked, *Cui bono ?* We may be told that the evil would outweigh the good, but the reality of the good admits of no dispute. In regard, however, to the larger question, the removal of women's disabilities—their recognition as the equals of men in all that belongs to citizenship—the opening to them of all honourable employments, and of the training and education which qualifies for those employments— there are many persons for whom it is not enough that the inequality has no just or legitimate defence ; they require to be told what express advantage would be obtained by abolishing it.

To which let me first answer, the advantage of having the most universal and pervading of all human rela- tions regulated by justice instead of injustice. The vast amount of this gain to human nature, it is hardly possible, by any explanation or illustration, to place in a stronger light than it is placed by the bare state- ment, to any one who attaches a moral meaning to words. All the selfish propensities, the self-worship, the unjust self-preference, which exist among mankind, have their source and root in, and derive their principal nourishment from, the present constitution of the rela- tion between men and women. Think what it is to a boy, to grow up to manhood in the belief that with- out any merit or any exertion of his own, though he may be the most frivolous and empty or the most ignorant and stolid of mankind, by the mere fact of being born a male he is by right the superior of all and every one of an entire half of the human race: including probably some whose real superiority to himself he has daily or hourly occasion to feel; but even if in his whole conduct he habitually follows a woman's guidance, still, if he is a fool, she thinks that of course she is not, and cannot be, equal in ability and judgement to himself; and if he is not a fool, he does worse—he sees that she is superior to him, and believes that, notwithstanding her superiority, he is entitled to command and she is bound to obey. What must be the effect on his character, of this lesson? And men of the cultivated classes are often not aware how deeply it sinks into the immense majority of male minds. For, among right-feeling and well-bred people, the inequality is kept as much as possible out of sight; above all, out of sight of the children. As much obedience is required from boys to their mother as to their father: they are not permitted to domineer over their sisters, nor are they accustomed to see these postponed to them, but the contrary; the compensations of the chivalrous feeling being made prominent, while the servitude which requires them is kept in the background. Well brought-up youths in the higher classes thus often escape the bad influences of the situation in their early years, and only experience them when, arrived at manhood, they fall under the dominion of facts as they really exist. Such people are little aware, when a boy is differently brought up, how early the notion of his inherent superiority to a girl arises in his mind; how it grows with his growth and strengthens with his strength; how it is inoculated by one schoolboy upon another; how early the youth thinks himself superior to his mother, owing her perhaps forbearance, but no real respect; and how sublime and sultan-like a sense of superiority he feels, above all, over the woman whom he honours by admitting her to a partnership of his life. Is it imagined that all this does not pervert the whole manner of existence of the man, both as an individual and as a social being? It is an exact parallel to the feeling of a heredi-

tary king that he is excellent above others by being
born a king, or a noble by being born a noble. The
relation between husband and wife is very like that
between lord and vassal, except that the wife is held
to more unlimited obedience than the vassal was. However the vassal's character may have been affected, for
better and for worse, by his subordination, who can
help seeing that the lord's was affected greatly for the
worse ? whether he was led to believe that his vassals
were really superior to himself, or to feel that he was
placed in command over people as good as himself,
for no merits or labours of his own, but merely for
having, as Figaro says, taken the trouble to be born.
The self-worship of the monarch, or of the feudal
superior, is matched by the self-worship of the male.
Human beings do not grow up from childhood in the
possession of unearned distinctions, without pluming
themselves upon them. Those whom privileges not
acquired by their merit, and which they feel to be
disproportioned to it, inspire with additional humility,
are always the few, and the best few. The rest are
only inspired with pride, and the worst sort of pride,
that which values itself upon accidental advantages,
not of its own achieving. Above all, when the feeling
of being raised above the whole of the other sex is
combined with personal authority over one individual
among them ; the situation, if a school of conscientious
and affectionate forbearance to those whose strongest
points of character are conscience and affection, is to
men of another quality a regularly constituted Academy
or Gymnasium for training them in arrogance and overbearingness ; which vices, if curbed by the certainty
of resistance in their intercourse with other men, their
equals, break out towards all who are in a position to
be obliged to tolerate them, and often revenge themselves upon the unfortunate wife for the involuntary
restraint which they are obliged to submit to elsewhere.
    The example afforded, and the education given to
the sentiments, by laying the foundation of domestic
existence upon a relation contradictory to the first

principles of social justice, must, from the very nature of man, have a perverting influence of such magnitude, that it is hardly possible with our present experience to raise our imaginations to the conception of so great a change for the better as would be made by its removal. All that education and civilization are doing to efface the influences on character of the law of force, and replace them by those of justice, remains merely on the surface, as long as the citadel of the enemy is not attacked. The principle of the modern movement in morals and politics, is that conduct, and conduct alone, entitles to respect : that not what men are, but what they do, constitutes their claim to deference ; that, above all, merit, and not birth, is the only rightful claim to power and authority. If no authority, not in its nature temporary, were allowed to one human being over another, society would not be employed in building up propensities with one hand which it has to curb with the other. The child would really, for the first time in man's existence on earth, be trained in the way he should go, and when he was old there would be a chance that he would not depart from it. But so long as the right of the strong to power over the weak rules in the very heart of society, the attempt to make the equal right of the weak the principle of its outward actions will always be an uphill struggle ; for the law of justice, which is also that of Christianity, will never get possession of men's inmost sentiments ; they will be working against it, even when bending to it.

The second benefit to be expected from giving to women the free use of their faculties, by leaving them the free choice of their employments, and opening to them the same field of occupation and the same prizes and encouragements as to other human beings, would be that of doubling the mass of mental faculties available for the higher service of humanity. Where there is now one person qualified to benefit mankind and promote the general improvement, as a public teacher, or an administrator of some branch of public or social affairs, there would then be a chance of two. Mental superiority of any kind is at present everywhere so much below the demand; there is such a deficiency of persons competent to do excellently anything which it requires any considerable amount of ability to do; that the loss to the world, by refusing to make use of one-half of the whole quantity of talent it possesses, is extremely serious. It is true that this amount of mental power is not totally lost. Much of it is employed, and would in any case be employed, in domestic management, and in the few other occupations open to women; and from the remainder indirect benefit is in many individual cases obtained, through the personal influence of individual women over individual men. But these benefits are partial; their range is extremely circumscribed; and if they must be admitted, on the one hand, as a deduction from the amount of fresh social power that would be acquired by giving freedom to one-half of the whole sum of human intellect, there must be added, on the other, the benefit of the stimulus that would be given to the intellect of men by the competition; or (to use a more true expression) by the necessity that would be imposed on them of deserving precedency before they could expect to obtain it.

This great accession to the intellectual power of the species, and to the amount of intellect available for the good management of its affairs, would be obtained, partly, through the better and more complete intellectual education of women, which would then improve *pari passu* with that of men. Women in general would be brought up equally capable of understanding business, public affairs, and the higher matters of speculation, with men in the same class of society; and the select few of the one as well as of the other sex, who were qualified not only to comprehend what is done or thought by others, but to think or do something considerable themselves, would meet with the same facilities for improving and training their capacities in the one sex as in the other. In this way, the widening of the sphere of action for women would operate for good, by raising their education to the level of that of men, and making the one participate in all improvements made in the other. But independently of this, the mere breaking down of the barrier would of itself have an educational virtue of the highest worth. The mere getting rid of the idea that all the wider subjects of thought and action, all the things which are of general and not solely of private interest, are men's business, from which women are to be warned off—positively interdicted from most of it, coldly tolerated in the little which is allowed them—the mere consciousness a woman would then have of being a human being like any other, entitled to choose her pursuits, urged or invited by the same inducements as any one else to interest herself in whatever is interesting to human beings, entitled to exert the share of influence on all human concerns which belongs to an individual opinion, whether she attempted actual participation in them or not—this alone would effect an immense expansion of the faculties of women, as well as enlargement of the range of their moral sentiments.

Besides the addition to the amount of individual talent available for the conduct of human affairs, which certainly are not at present so abundantly provided in that respect that they can afford to dispense with one-half of what nature proffers ; the opinion of women would then possess a more beneficial, rather than a greater, influence upon the general mass of human belief and sentiment. I say a more beneficial, rather than a greater influence ; for the influence of women over the general tone of opinion has always, or at least from the earliest known period, been very considerable. The influence of mothers on the early character of their sons, and the desire of young men to recommend themselves to young women, have in all recorded times been important agencies in the formation of character, and have determined some of the chief steps in the progress of civilization. Even in the Homeric age, αἰδώς towards the Τρωάδας ἑλκεσιπέπλους is an acknowledged and powerful motive of action in the great Hector. The moral influence of women has had two modes of operation. First, it has been a softening influence. Those who were most liable to be the victims of violence, have naturally tended as much as they could towards limiting its sphere and mitigating its excesses. Those who were not taught to fight, have naturally inclined in favour of any other mode of settling differences rather than that of fighting. In general, those who have been the greatest sufferers by the indulgence of selfish passion, have been the most earnest supporters of any moral law which offered a means of bridling passion. Women were powerfully instrumental in inducing the northern conquerors to adopt the creed of Christianity, a creed so much more favourable to women than any that preceded it. The conversion of the Anglo-Saxons and of the Franks may be said to have been begun by the wives of Ethelbert and Clovis. The other mode in which the effect of women's opinion has been conspicuous, is by giving a powerful stimulus to those qualities in men, which, not being themselves trained in, it was necessary for them that they should find in their protectors. Courage, and the military virtues generally, have at all times been greatly indebted to the desire which men felt of being admired by women: and the stimulus reaches far beyond this one class of eminent qualities, since, by a very natural effect of their position, the best passport to the admiration and favour of women has always been to be thought highly of by men. From the combination of the two kinds of moral influence thus exercised by women, arose the spirit of chivalry: the peculiarity of which is, to aim at combining the highest standard of the warlike qualities with the cultivation of a totally different class of virtues— those of gentleness, generosity, and self-abnegation, towards the non-military and defenceless classes generally, and a special submission and worship directed towards women; who were distinguished from the other defenceless classes by the high rewards which they had it in their power voluntarily to bestow on those who endeavoured to earn their favour, instead of extorting their subjection. Though the practice of chivalry fell even more sadly short of its theoretic standard than practice generally falls below theory, it remains one of the most precious monuments of the moral history of our race; as a remarkable instance of a concerted and organized attempt by a most disorganized and distracted society, to raise up and carry into practice a moral ideal greatly in advance of its social condition and institutions; so much so as to have been completely frustrated in the main object, yet never entirely inefficacious, and which has left a most sensible, and for the most part a highly valuable impress on the ideas and feelings of all subsequent times.

The chivalrous ideal is the acme of the influence of women's sentiments on the moral cultivation of mankind: and if women are to remain in their subordinate situation, it were greatly to be lamented that the chivalrous standard should have passed away, for it is the only one at all capable of mitigating the demoralizing influences of that position. But the changes in the general state of the species rendered inevitable the substitution of a totally different ideal of morality for the chivalrous one. Chivalry was the attempt to infuse moral elements into a state of society in which everything depended for good or evil on individual prowess, under the softening influences of individual delicacy and generosity. In modern societies, all things, even in the military department of affairs, are decided, not by individual effort, but by the combined operations of numbers; while the main occupation of society has changed from fighting to business, from military to industrial life. The exigencies of the new life are no more exclusive of the virtues of generosity than those of the old, but it no longer entirely depends on them. The main foundations of the moral life of modern times must be justice and prudence; the respect of each for the rights of every other, and the ability of each to take care of himself. Chivalry left without legal check all forms of wrong which reigned unpunished throughout society; it only encouraged a few to do right in preference to wrong, by the direction it gave to the instruments of praise and admiration. But the real dependence of morality must always be upon its penal sanctions—its power to deter from evil. The security of society cannot rest on merely rendering honour to right, a motive so comparatively weak in all but a few, and which on very many does not operate at all. Modern society is able to repress wrong through all departments of life, by a fit exertion of the superior strength which civilization has given it, and thus to render the existence of the weaker members of society (no longer defenceless but protected by law) tolerable to them, without reliance on the chivalrous feelings of those who are in a position to tyrannize. The beauties and graces of the chivalrous character are still what they were, but the rights of the weak, and the general comfort of human life, now rest on a far surer and steadier support; or rather, they do so in every relation of life except the conjugal.

At present the moral influence of women is no less real, but it is no longer of so marked and definite a character: it has more nearly merged in the general influence of public opinion. Both through the contagion of sympathy, and through the desire of men to shine in the eyes of women, their feelings have great effect in keeping alive what remains of the chivalrous ideal—in fostering the sentiments and continuing the traditions of spirit and generosity. In these points of character, their standard is higher than that of men; in the quality of justice, somewhat lower. As regards the relations of private life it may be said generally, that their influence is, on the whole, encouraging to the softer virtues, discouraging to the sterner: though the statement must be taken with all the modifications dependent on individual character. In the chief of the greater trials to which virtue is subject in the concerns of life—the conflict between interest and principle—the tendency of women's influence is of a very mixed character. When the principle involved happens to be one of the very few which the course of their religious or moral education has strongly impressed upon themselves, they are potent auxiliaries to virtue: and their husbands and sons are often prompted by them to acts of abnegation which they never would have been capable of without that stimulus. But, with the present education and position of women, the moral principles which have been impressed on them cover but a comparatively small part of the field of virtue, and are, moreover, principally negative; forbidding particular acts, but having little to do with the general direction of the thoughts and purposes. I am afraid it must be said, that disinterestedness in the general conduct of life—the devotion of the energies to purposes which hold out no promise of private advantages to the family—is very seldom encouraged or supported by women's influence. It is small blame to them that they discourage objects of which they have not learnt to see the advantage, and which withdraw their men from them, and from the interests of the family. But the consequence is that women's influence is often anything but favourable to public virtue.

Women have, however, some share of influence in giving the tone to public moralities since their sphere of action has been a little widened, and since a considerable number of them have occupied themselves practically in the promotion of objects reaching beyond their own family and household. The influence of women counts for a great deal in two of the most marked features of modern European life—its aversion to war, and its addiction to philanthropy. Excellent characteristics both; but unhappily, if the influence of women is valuable in the encouragement it gives to these feelings in general, in the particular applications the direction it gives to them is at least as often mischievous as useful. In the philanthropic department more particularly, the two provinces chiefly cultivated by women are religious proselytism and charity. Religious proselytism at home, is but another word for embittering of religious animosities : abroad, it is usually a blind running at an object, without either knowing or heeding the fatal mischiefs—fatal to the religious object itself as well as to all other desirable objects—which may be produced by the means employed. As for charity, it is a matter in which the immediate effect on the persons directly concerned, and the ultimate consequence to the general good, are apt to be at complete war with one another : while the education given to women—an education of the sentiments rather than of the understanding—and the habit inculcated by their whole life, of looking to immediate effects on persons, and not to remote effects on classes of persons—make them both unable to see, and unwilling to admit, the ultimate evil tendency of any form of charity or philanthropy which commends itself to their sympathetic feelings. The great and continually increasing mass of unenlightened and short-sighted benevolence, which, taking the care of people's lives out of their own hands, and relieving them from the disagreeable consequences of their own acts, saps the very foundations of the self-respect, self-help, and self-control which are the essential conditions both of individual prosperity and of social virtue—this waste of resources and of benevolent feelings in doing harm instead of good, is immensely swelled by women's contributions, and stimulated by their influence. Not that this is a mistake likely to be made by women, where they have actually the practical management of schemes of beneficence. It sometimes happens that women who administer public charities—with that insight into present fact, and especially into the minds and feelings of those with whom they are in immediate contact, in which women generally excel men—recognize in the clearest manner the demoralizing influence of the alms given or the help afforded, and could give lessons on the subject to many a male political economist. But women who only give their money, and are not brought face to face with the effects it produces, how can they be expected to foresee them? A woman born to the present lot of women, and content with it, how should she appreciate the value of self-dependence? She is not self-dependent; she is not taught self-dependence; her destiny is to receive everything from others, and why should what is good enough for her be bad for the poor? Her familiar notions of good are of blessings descending from a superior. She forgets that she is not free, and that the poor are; that if what they need is given to them unearned, they cannot be compelled to earn it: that everybody cannot be taken care of by everybody, but there must be some motive to induce people to take care of themselves; and that to be helped to help themselves, if they are physically capable of it, is the only charity which proves to be charity in the end.

These considerations show how usefully the part which women take in the formation of general opinion, would be modified for the better by that more enlarged instruction, and practical conversancy with the things which their opinions influence, that would necessarily arise from their social and political emancipation. But the improvement it would work through the influence they exercise, each in her own family, would be still more remarkable.

It is often said that in the classes most exposed to temptation, a man's wife and children tend to keep him honest and respectable, both by the wife's direct influence, and by the concern he feels for their future welfare. This may be so, and no doubt often is so, with those who are more weak than wicked; and this beneficial influence would be preserved and strengthened under equal laws; it does not depend on the woman's servitude, but is, on the contrary, diminished by the disrespect which the inferior class of men always at heart feel towards those who are subject to their power. But when we ascend higher in the scale, we come among a totally different set of moving forces. The wife's influence tends, as far as it goes, to prevent the husband from falling below the common standard of approbation of the country. It tends quite as strongly to hinder him from rising above it. The wife is the auxiliary of the common public opinion. A man who is married to a woman his inferior in intelligence, finds her a perpetual dead weight, or, worse than a dead weight, a drag, upon every aspiration of his to be better than public opinion requires him to be. It is hardly possible for one who is in these bonds, to attain exalted virtue. If he differs in his opinion from the mass—if he sees truths which have not yet dawned upon them, or if, feeling in his heart truths which they nominally recognize, he would like to act up to those truths more conscientiously than the generality of mankind—to all such thoughts and desires, marriage is the heaviest of drawbacks, unless he be so fortunate as to have a wife as much above the common level as he himself is.

For, in the first place, there is always some sacrifice of personal interest required; either of social consequence, or of pecuniary means; perhaps the risk of even the means of subsistence. These sacrifices and risks he may be willing to encounter for himself; but he will pause before he imposes them on his family. And his family in this case means his wife and daughters; for he always hopes that his sons will feel as he feels himself, and that what he can do without, they will do without, willingly, in the same cause. But his daughters—their marriage may depend upon it: and his wife, who is unable to enter into or understand the objects for which these sacrifices are made—who, if she thought them worth any sacrifice, would think so on trust, and solely for his sake—who can participate in none of the enthusiasm or the self-approbation he himself may feel, while the things which he is disposed to sacrifice are all in all to her; will not the best and most unselfish man hesitate the longest before bringing on her this consequence? If it be not the comforts of life, but only social consideration, that is at stake, the burthen upon his conscience and feelings is still very severe. Whoever has a wife and children has given hostages to Mrs. Grundy. The approbation of that potentate may be a matter of indifference to him, but it is of great importance to his wife. The man himself may be above opinion, or may find sufficient compensation in the opinion of those of his own way of thinking. But to the women connected with him, he can offer no compensation. The almost invariable tendency of the wife to place her influence in the same scale with social consideration, is sometimes made a reproach to women, and represented as a peculiar trait of feebleness and childishness of character in them: surely with great injustice. Society makes the whole life of a woman, in the easy classes, a continued self-sacrifice; it exacts from her an unremitting restraint of the whole of her natural inclinations, and the sole return it makes to her for what often deserves the name of a martyrdom, is consideration. Her consideration is inseparably connected with that of her husband, and after paying the full price for it, she finds that she is to lose it, for no reason of which she can feel the cogency. She has sacrificed her whole life to it, and her husband will not sacrifice to it a whim, a freak, an eccentricity; something not recognized or allowed for by the world, and which the world will agree with her in thinking a folly, if it thinks no worse! The dilemma is hardest upon that very meritorious class of men, who, without possessing talents which qualify them to make a figure among those with whom they agree in opinion, hold their opinion from conviction, and feel bound in honour and conscience to serve it, by making profession of their belief, and giving their time, labour, and means, to anything undertaken in its behalf. The worst case of all is when such men happen to be of a rank and position which of itself neither gives them, nor excludes them from, what is considered the best society; when their admission to it depends mainly on what is thought of them personally—and however unexceptionable their breeding and habits, their being identified with opinions and public conduct unacceptable to those who give the tone to society would operate as an effectual exclusion. Many a woman flatters herself (nine times out of ten quite erroneously) that nothing prevents her and her husband from moving in the highest society of her neighbourhood—society in which others well known to her, and in the same class of life, mix freely—except that her husband is unfortunately a Dissenter, or has the reputation of mingling in low radical politics. That it is, she thinks, which hinders George from getting a commission or a place, Caroline from making an advantageous match, and prevents her and her husband from obtaining invitations, perhaps honours, which, for aught she sees, they are as well entitled to as some folks. With such an influence in every house, either exerted actively, or operating all the more powerfully for not being asserted, is it any wonder that people in general are kept down in that mediocrity of respectability which is becoming a marked characteristic of modern times ?

There is another very injurious aspect in which the effect, not of women's disabilities directly, but of the broad line of difference which those disabilities create between the education and character of a woman and that of a man, requires to be considered. Nothing can be more unfavourable to that union of thoughts and inclinations which is the ideal of married life. Intimate society between people radically dissimilar to one another, is an idle dream. Unlikeness may attract, but it is likeness which retains; and in proportion to the likeness is the suitability of the individuals to give each other a happy life. While women are so unlike men, it is not wonderful that selfish men should feel the need of arbitrary power in their own hands, to arrest *in limine* the lifelong conflict of inclinations, by deciding every question on the side of their own preference. When people are extremely unlike, there can be no real identity of interest. Very often there is conscientious difference of opinion between married people, on the highest points of duty. Is there any reality in the marriage union where this takes place ? Yet it is not uncommon anywhere, when the woman has any earnestness of character ; and it is a very general case indeed in Catholic countries, when she is supported in her dissent by the only other authority to which she is taught to bow, the priest. With the usual barefacedness of power not accustomed to find itself disputed, the influence of priests over women is attacked by Protestant and Liberal writers, less for being bad in itself, than because it is a rival authority to the husband, and raises up a revolt against his infallibility. In England, similar differences occasionally exist when an Evangelical wife has allied herself with a husband of a different quality ; but in general this source at least of dissension is got rid of, by reducing the minds of women to such a nullity, that they have no opinions but those of Mrs. Grundy, or those which the husband tells them to have. When there is no difference of opinion, differences merely of taste may be sufficient to detract greatly from the happiness of married life. And though it may stimulate the amatory propensities of men, it does not conduce to married happiness, to exaggerate by differences of education whatever may be the native differences of the sexes. If the married pair are well-bred and well-behaved people, they tolerate each other's tastes ; but is mutual toleration what people look forward to, when they enter into marriage ? These differences of inclination will naturally make their wishes different, if not restrained by affection or duty, as to almost all domestic questions which arise. What a difference there must be in the society which the two persons will wish to frequent, or be frequented by ! Each will desire associates who share their own tastes : the persons agreeable to one, will be indifferent or positively disagreeable to the other ; yet there can be none who are not common to both, for married people do not now live in different parts of the house and have totally different visiting lists, as in the reign of Louis XV. They cannot help having different wishes as to the bringing up of the children: each will wish to see reproduced in them their own tastes and sentiments: and there is either a compromise, and only a half-satisfaction to either, or the wife has to yield—often with bitter suffering; and, with or without intention, her occult influence continues to counterwork the husband's purposes.

It would of course be extreme folly to suppose that these differences of feeling and inclination only exist because women are brought up differently from men, and that there would not be differences of taste under any imaginable circumstances. But there is nothing beyond the mark in saying that the distinction in bringing-up immensely aggravates those differences, and renders them wholly inevitable. While women are brought up as they are, a man and a woman will but rarely find in one another real agreement of tastes and wishes as to daily life. They will generally have to give it up as hopeless, and renounce the attempt to have, in the intimate associate of their daily life, that *idem velle, idem nolle*, which is the recognized bond of any society that is really such: or if the man succeeds in obtaining it, he does so by choosing a woman who is so complete a nullity that she has no *velle* or *nolle* at all, and is as ready to comply with one thing as another if anybody tells her to do so. Even this calculation is apt to fail; dullness and want of spirit are not always a guarantee of the submission which is so confidently expected from them. But if they were, is this the ideal of marriage? What, in this case, does the man obtain by it, except an upper servant, a nurse, or a mistress? On the contrary, when each of two persons, instead of being a nothing, is a something; when they are attached to one another, and are not too much unlike to begin with; the constant partaking in the same things, assisted by their sympathy, draws out the latent capacities of each for being interested in the things which were at first interesting only to the other; and works a gradual assimilation of the tastes and characters to one another, partly by the insensible modification of each, but more by a real enriching of the two natures, each acquiring the tastes and capacities of the other in addition to its own. This often happens between two friends of the same sex, who are much associated in their daily life : and it would be a common, if not the commonest, case in marriage, did not the totally different bringing-up of the two sexes make it next to an impossibility to form a really well-assorted union. Were this remedied, whatever differences there might still be in individual tastes, there would at least be, as a general rule, complete unity and unanimity as to the great objects of life. When the two persons both care for great objects, and are a help and encouragement to each other in whatever regards these, the minor matters on which their tastes may differ are not all-important to them ; and there is a foundation for solid friendship, of an enduring character, more likely than anything else to make it, through the whole of life, a greater pleasure to each to give pleasure to the other, than to receive it.

I have considered, thus far, the effects on the pleasures and benefits of the marriage union which depend on the mere unlikeness between the wife and the husband : but the evil tendency is prodigiously aggravated when the unlikeness is inferiority. Mere unlikeness, when it only means difference of good qualities, may be more a benefit in the way of mutual improvement, than a drawback from comfort. When each emulates, and desires and endeavours to acquire, the other's peculiar qualities, the difference does not produce diversity of interest, but increased identity of it, and makes each still more valuable to the other. But when one is much the inferior of the two in mental ability and cultivation, and is not actively attempting by the other's aid to rise to the other's level, the whole influence of the connexion upon the development of the superior of the two is deteriorating : and still more so in a tolerably happy marriage than in an unhappy one. It is not with impunity that the superior in intellect shuts himself up with an inferior, and elects that inferior for his chosen, and sole completely intimate, associate. Any society which is not improving, is deteriorating: and the more so, the closer and more familiar it is. Even a really superior man almost always begins to deteriorate when he is habitually (as the phrase is) king of his company: and in his most habitual company the husband who has a wife inferior to him is always so. While his self-satisfaction is incessantly ministered to on the one hand, on the other he insensibly imbibes the modes of feeling, and of looking at things, which belong to a more vulgar or a more limited mind than his own. This evil differs from many of those which have hitherto been dwelt on, by being an increasing one. The association of men with women in daily life is much closer and more complete than it ever was before. Men's life is more domestic. Formerly, their pleasures and chosen occupations were among men, and in men's company: their wives had but a fragment of their lives. At the present time, the progress of civilization, and the turn of opinion against the rough amusements and convivial excesses which formerly occupied most men in their hours of relaxation—together with (it must be said) the improved tone of modern feeling as to the reciprocity of duty which binds the husband towards the wife—have thrown the man very much more upon home and its inmates, for his personal and social pleasures: while the kind and degree of improvement which has been made in women's education, has made them in some degree capable of being his companions in ideas and mental tastes, while leaving them, in most cases, still hopelessly inferior to him. His desire of mental communion is thus in general satisfied by a communion from which he learns nothing. An unimproving and unstimulating companionship is substituted for (what he might otherwise have been obliged to seek) the society of his equals in powers and his fellows in the higher pursuits. We see, accordingly, that young men of the greatest promise generally cease to improve as soon as they marry, and, not improving, inevitably degenerate. If the wife does not push the husband forward, she always holds him back. He ceases to care for what she does not care for; he no longer desires, and ends by disliking and shunning, society congenial to his former aspirations, and which would now shame his falling-off from them; his higher faculties both of mind and heart cease to be called into activity. And this change coinciding with the new and selfish interests which are created by the family, after a few years he differs in no material respect from those who have never had wishes for anything but the common vanities and the common pecuniary objects.

What marriage may be in the case of two persons of cultivated faculties, identical in opinions and purposes, between whom there exists that best kind of equality, similarity of powers and capacities with reciprocal superiority in them—so that each can enjoy the luxury of looking up to the other, and can have alternately the pleasure of leading and of being led in the path of development—I will not attempt to describe. To those who can conceive it, there is no need; to those who cannot, it would appear the dream of an enthusiast. But I maintain, with the profoundest conviction, that this, and this only, is the ideal of marriage; and that all opinions, customs, and institutions which favour any other notion of it, or turn the conceptions and aspirations connected with it into any other direction, by whatever pretences they may be coloured, are relics of primitive barbarism. The moral regeneration of mankind will only really commence, when the most fundamental of the social relations is placed under the rule of equal justice, and when human beings learn to cultivate their strongest sympathy with an equal in rights and in cultivation.

Thus far, the benefits which it has appeared that the world would gain by ceasing to make sex a disqualification for privileges and a badge of subjection, are social rather than individual; consisting in an increase of the general fund of thinking and acting power, and an improvement in the general conditions of the association of men with women. But it would be a grievous understatement of the case to omit the most direct benefit of all, the unspeakable gain in private happiness to the liberated half of the species ; the difference to them between a life of subjection to the will of others, and a life of rational freedom. After the primary necessities of food and raiment, freedom is the first and strongest want of human nature. While mankind are lawless, their desire is for lawless freedom. When they have learnt to understand the meaning of duty and the value of reason, they incline more and more to be guided and restrained by these in the exercise of their freedom ; but they do not therefore desire freedom less ; they do not become disposed to accept the will of other people as the representative and interpreter of those guiding principles. On the contrary, the communities in which the reason has been most cultivated, and in which the idea of social duty has been most powerful, are those which have most strongly asserted the freedom of action of the individual—the liberty of each to govern his conduct by his own feelings of duty, and by such laws and social restraints as his own conscience can subscribe to.

He who would rightly appreciate the worth of personal independence as an element of happiness, should consider the value he himself puts upon it as an ingredient of his own. There is no subject on which there is a greater habitual difference of judgement between a man judging for himself, and the same man judging for other people. When he hears others complaining that they are not allowed freedom of action— that their own will has not sufficient influence in the regulation of their affairs—his inclination is, to ask, what are their grievances ? what positive damage they sustain ? and in what respect they consider their affairs to be mismanaged ? and if they fail to make out, in answer to these questions, what appears to him a sufficient case, he turns a deaf ear, and regards their complaint as the fanciful querulousness of people whom nothing reasonable will satisfy. But he has a quite

different standard of judgement when he is deciding
for himself. Then, the most unexceptionable administration of his interests by a tutor set over him, does
not satisfy his feelings : his personal exclusion from
the deciding authority appears itself the greatest grievance of all, rendering it superfluous even to enter into
the question of mismanagement. It is the same with
nations. What citizen of a free country would listen
to any offers of good and skilful administration, in
return for the abdication of freedom ? Even if he
could believe that good and skilful administration can
exist among a people ruled by a will not their own,
would not the consciousness of working out their own
destiny under their own moral responsibility be a compensation to his feelings for great rudeness and imperfection in the details of public affairs ? Let him rest
assured that whatever he feels on this point, women
feel in a fully equal degree. Whatever has been said
or written, from the time of Herodotus to the present,
of the ennobling influence of free government—the
nerve and spring which it gives to all the faculties,
the larger and higher objects which it presents to the
intellect and feelings, the more unselfish public spirit,
and calmer and broader views of duty, that it en-
genders, and the generally loftier platform on which
it elevates the individual as a moral, spiritual, and
social being—is every particle as true of women as of
men. Are these things no important part of individual
happiness ? Let any man call to mind what he himself felt on emerging from boyhood—from the tutelage
and control of even loved and affectionate elders—and
entering upon the responsibilities of manhood. Was
it not like the physical effect of taking off a heavy
weight, or releasing him from obstructive, even if not
otherwise painful, bonds ? Did he not feel twice as
much alive, twice as much a human being, as before ?
And does he imagine that women have none of these
feelings ? But it is a striking fact, that the satisfac-
tions and mortifications of personal pride, though all
in all to most men when the case is their own, have

less allowance made for them in the case of other people, and are less listened to as a ground or a justification of conduct, than any other natural human feelings; perhaps because men compliment them in their own case with the names of so many other qualities, that they are seldom conscious how mighty an influence these feelings exercise in their own lives. No less large and powerful is their part, we may assure ourselves, in the lives and feelings of women. Women are schooled into suppressing them in their most natural and most healthy direction, but the internal principle remains, in a different outward form. An active and energetic mind, if denied liberty, will seek for power: refused the command of itself, it will assert its personality by attempting to control others. To allow to any human beings no existence of their own but what depends on others, is giving far too high a premium on bending others to their purposes. Where liberty cannot be hoped for, and power can, power becomes the grand object of human desire; those to whom others will not leave the undisturbed management of their own affairs, will compensate themselves, if they can, by meddling for their own purposes with the affairs of others. Hence also women's passion for personal beauty, and dress and display; and all the evils that flow from it, in the way of mischievous luxury and social immorality. The love of power and the love of liberty are in eternal antagonism. Where there is least liberty, the passion for power is the most ardent and unscrupulous. The desire of power over others can only cease to be a depraving agency among mankind, when each of them individually is able to do without it: which can only be where respect for liberty in the personal concerns of each is an established principle.

But it is not only through the sentiment of personal dignity, that the free direction and disposal of their own faculties is a source of individual happiness, and to be fettered and restricted in it, a source of unhappiness, to human beings, and not least to women. There is nothing, after disease, indigence, and guilt, so fatal to the pleasurable enjoyment of life as the want of a worthy outlet for the active faculties. Women who have the cares of a family, and while they have the cares of a family, have this outlet, and it generally suffices for them : but what of the greatly increasing number of women, who have had no opportunity of exercising the vocation which they are mocked by telling them is their proper one ? What of the women whose children have been lost to them by death or distance, or have grown up, married, and formed homes of their own ? There are abundant examples of men who, after a life engrossed by business, retire with a competency to the enjoyment, as they hope, of rest, but to whom, as they are unable to acquire new interests and excitements that can replace the old, the change to a life of inactivity brings ennui, melancholy, and premature death. Yet no one thinks of the parallel case of so many worthy and devoted women, who, having paid what they are told is their debt to society —having brought up a family blamelessly to manhood and womanhood—having kept a house as long as they had a house needing to be kept—are deserted by the sole occupation for which they have fitted themselves ; and remain with undiminished activity but with no employment for it, unless perhaps a daughter or daughter-in-law is willing to abdicate in their favour the discharge of the same functions in her younger household. Surely a hard lot for the old age of those who have worthily discharged, as long as it was given to them to discharge, what the world accounts their only social duty. Of such women, and of those others to whom this duty has not been committed at all— many of whom pine through life with the consciousness of thwarted vocations, and activities which are not suffered to expand—the only resources, speaking generally, are religion and charity. But their religion, though it may be one of feeling, and of ceremonial observance, cannot be a religion of action, unless in the form of charity. For charity many of them are by nature admirably fitted ; but to practise it use-

fully, or even without doing mischief, requires the
education, the manifold preparation, the knowledge
and the thinking powers, of a skilful administrator.
There are few of the administrative functions of government for which a person would not be fit, who is fit
to bestow charity usefully.   In this as in other cases
(pre-eminently in that of the education of children),
the duties permitted to women cannot be performed
properly, without their being trained for duties which,
to the great loss of society, are not permitted to them.
And here let me notice the singular way in which the
question of women's disabilities is frequently presented
to view, by those who find it easier to draw a ludicrous
picture of what they do not like, than to answer the
arguments for it.   When it is suggested that women's
executive capacities and prudent counsels might sometimes be found valuable in affairs of state, these lovers
of fun hold up to the ridicule of the world, as sitting
in parliament or in the cabinet, girls in their teens, or
young wives of two or three and twenty, transported
bodily, exactly as they are, from the drawing-room to
the House of Commons.   They forget that males are
not usually selected at this early age for a seat in
Parliament, or for responsible political functions.
Common sense would tell them that if such trusts
were confided to women, it would be to such as having
no special vocation for married life, or preferring
another employment of their faculties (as many women
even now prefer to marriage some of the few honourable
occupations within their reach), have spent the best
years of their youth in attempting to qualify themselves for the pursuits in which they desire to engage ;
or still more frequently perhaps, widows or wives of
forty or fifty, by whom the knowledge of life and
faculty of government which they have acquired in
their families, could by the aid of appropriate studies
be made available on a less contracted scale.   There
is no country of Europe in which the ablest men have
not frequently experienced, and keenly appreciated,
the value of the advice and help of clever and ex-

perienced women of the world, in the attainment both
of private and of public objects; and there are important matters of public administration to which few
men are equally competent with such women; among
others, the detailed control of expenditure. But what
we are now discussing is not the need which society
has of the services of women in public business, but
the dull and hopeless life to which it so often condemns
them, by forbidding them to exercise the practical
abilities which many of them are conscious of, in any
wider field than one which to some of them never was,
and to others is no longer, open. If there is anything
vitally important to the happiness of human beings,
it is that they should relish their habitual pursuit.
This requisite of an enjoyable life is very imperfectly
granted, or altogether denied, to a large part of mankind; and by its absence many a life is a failure,
which is provided, in appearance, with every requisite
of success. But if circumstances which society is not
yet skilful enough to overcome, render such failures
often for the present inevitable, society need not itself
inflict them. The injudiciousness of parents, a youth's
own inexperience, or the absence of external opportunities for the congenial vocation, and their presence
for an uncongenial, condemn numbers of men to pass
their lives in doing one thing reluctantly and ill, when
there are other things which they could have done
well and happily. But on women this sentence is
imposed by actual law, and by customs equivalent to
law. What, in unenlightened societies, colour, race,
religion, or in the case of a conquered country, nationality, are to some men, sex is to all women; a peremptory exclusion from almost all honourable occupations,
but either such as cannot be fulfilled by others, or such
as those others do not think worthy of their acceptance.
Sufferings arising from causes of this nature usually
meet with so little sympathy, that few persons are
aware of the great amount of unhappiness even now
produced by the feeling of a wasted life. The case
will be even more frequent, as increased cultivation

creates a greater and greater disproportion between the ideas and faculties of women, and the scope which society allows to their activity.

When we consider the positive evil caused to the disqualified half of the human race by their disqualification—first in the loss of the most inspiriting and elevating kind of personal enjoyment, and next in the weariness, disappointment, and profound dissatisfaction with life, which are so often the substitute for it; one feels that among all the lessons which men require for carrying on the struggle against the inevitable imperfections of their lot on earth, there is no lesson which they more need, than not to add to the evils which nature inflicts, by their jealous and prejudiced restrictions on one another. Their vain fears only substitute other and worse evils for those which they are idly apprehensive of: while every restraint on the freedom of conduct of any of their human fellow creatures (otherwise than by making them responsible for any evil actually caused by it), dries up *pro tanto* the principal fountain of human happiness, and leaves the species less rich, to an inappreciable degree, in all that makes life valuable to the individual human being.

THE END

BIBLIOGRAPHY

A.   JOHN STUART MILL, *Utilitarianism* (London 1863).
     Autobiography (London 1873).
     Dissertations and Discussions 4 vols (London
        1875).
     On Liberty ed. Gertrude Himmelfarb (London
        1974).
     Essays on Politics and Culture by John Stuart Mill
        ed. Gertrude Himmelfarb (New York 1962).

     The Later Letters of John Stuart Mill 1849–1873 ed.
        Francis Mineka and Dwight N. Lindley
        (Toronto and London 1972).

B.   J. F. STEPHEN, *Liberty, Equality, Fraternity* (London 1874).

     BERNARD BOSANQUET, *The Philosophical Theory of
        the State* (London 1899).

     A. D. LINDSAY, *The Modern Democratic State*, Vol. I
        (London 1943).

     MICHAEL ST JOHN PACKE, *The Life of John Stuart
        Mill* (London 1954).

     BERTRAND RUSSELL, *John Stuart Mill* (London
        1955).

     J. C. REES, *Mill and his Early Critics* (Leicester
        1956).

     MAURICE CRANSTON, *John Stuart Mill* (London
        1958).

     J. C. REES, 'A Re-Reading of Mill on Liberty ',
        Political Studies, 8, 1960.

SHELDON S. WOLIN, *Politics and Vision* (London 1961).

ISAIAH BERLIN, *John Stuart Mill and the Ends of Life* (London 1962).

H. L. A. HART, *Law, Liberty, and Morality* (Stanford, Calif. and London 1963).

H. J. McCLOSKEY, 'Mill's Liberalism', *Philosophical Quarterly*, 13, 1963.

SHIRLEY ROBIN LETWIN, *The Pursuit of Certainty* (Cambridge 1965).

Mill: A Collection of Critical Essays ed. J. B. Schneewind (New York and London 1965).

ALAN RYAN, *The Philosophy of John Stuart Mill* (London 1970).

MARTIN HOLLIS, 'J. S. Mill's Political Philosophy of Mind', *Philosophy*, 47, 1972.

RICHARD WOLLHEIM, 'John Stuart Mill and the Limits of State Action', *Social Research*, 40, 1973.

GERTRUDE HIMMELFARB, *On Liberty and Liberalism: The Case of John Stuart Mill* (New York 1974).